Hands-On
Novell® NetWare® 5.0/5.1 with Projects
Enhanced Edition

Ted Simpson

Return to
Tom Romey
(503) 492-6330

COURSE TECHNOLOGY
TM
THOMSON LEARNING

Australia • Canada • Mexico • Singapore • Spain • United Kingdom • United States

COURSE TECHNOLOGY

THOMSON LEARNING

Hands-On Novell NetWare 5.0/5.1 with Projects *Enhanced Edition*
by Ted Simpson

Associate Publisher:
Kristen Duerr

Managing Editor:
Stephen Solomon

Product Manager:
Laura Hildebrand

Associate Product Manager:
Elizabeth Wessen

Editorial Assistant:
Janet Aras

Development Editor:
Jim Markham

Production Editor:
Anne Valsangiacomo

Quality Assurance Manager:
John Bosco

Cover Designer:
Efrat Reis

Composition House:
GEX Publishing Services

Marketing Manager:
Toby Shelton

Disclaimer
Course Technology reserves the right to revise this publication and make changes from time to time in its content without notice.

ISBN 0-619-03482-3

BRIEF

Contents

TABLE OF
Contents

CHAPTER NINE
Managing User Environments with Z.E.N.works

CHAPTER TEN
Operating the Server Console

1

NETWORKING BASICS

After reading this chapter and completing the exercises, you will be able to:
- Describe a network, including its basic function and physical components
- List the network services a CNA needs to administer
- Explain and perform the login procedure
- Access common network resources from Windows
- Identify common network systems and protocols
- Define NetWare command-line utilities, describe how they are used, and activate help

To become a **Certified Novell Administrator (CNA)** and successfully implement and manage computers attached to a local area network, you need to understand what a local area network is and how it differs from traditional mini- or mainframe computers. Essentially, a **local area network (LAN)** is a high-speed communication system consisting of cables and cards (hardware) along with software that provides a means for different types of computers to communicate and share resources over short distances such as within a building or room. One of the major differences between a LAN and a minicomputer system is that, with a minicomputer, all the processing is done by the minicomputer running the programs. The terminals or workstations attached to the minicomputer are simply used as input and output devices for entering data and displaying results. This type of processing is called **centralized processing** because all the processing is done by the "central" minicomputer.

The main purpose of a LAN is to provide a high-speed communication system among computers. The processing is normally performed by programs running on desktop computers or workstations rather than on a central host computer. This type of processing is referred to as **distributed processing** because the processing is distributed among each of the attached computers. The LAN gives the attached computers access to shared resources such as files, software, printers, and modems that are necessary to perform the processing requests.

As a CNA, you will need to be familiar with the hardware and software components that make up a LAN so that you can select, implement, and maintain a network system that will meet the communication and processing needs of your organization. This chapter also introduces you to the Universal Aerospace Corporation. Throughout this book, you will gain hands-on experience in network administration by designing and implementing a network system for Universal Aerospace. In this chapter, you will learn how you can apply the components that make up a LAN toward implementing a network system for this fictitious company.

NETWORK COMPONENTS

All networks, including human networks, consist of three basic types of components: entities that need to communicate, a common pathway for communication, and rules that control the communication process. In a local area network, **entities** typically consist of client and server computers and shared resources such as printers and volumes. The **pathway** is usually some type of cable system used to transmit bits of data, arranged in a particular physical layout or topology. Entities usually connect to the pathway via a network interface card (NIC). **Rules** are protocols that control the format of the data transmissions.

To set up a local area network, you first must define the required network entities and identify how they will be connected. As shown in Figure 1-1, LANs generally consist of a combination of client computers, servers, printers, network cards, and a network cable system to tie all the entities together. In this section, you will learn about each of these components, along with how Universal Aerospace plans to implement them using Novell NetWare 5.

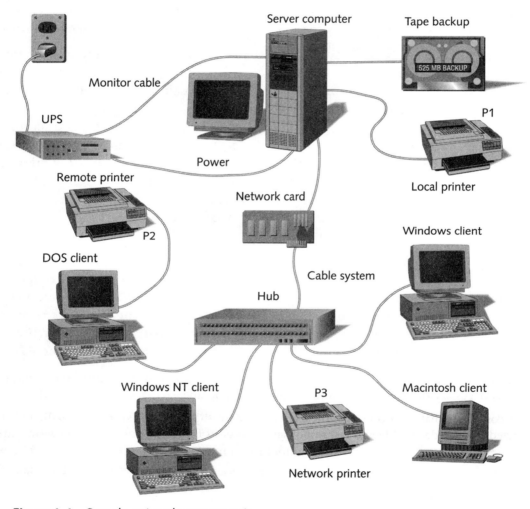

Figure 1-1   Sample network components

Client Computers

As described previously, computer information processing systems can be classified as either centralized or distributed. A centralized processing system utilizes terminals to run programs on central mini- and mainframe

1

The redirection area allows the data to be saved to disk without issuing an error message to the user. Redirection areas are established during installation of a disk drive, as described in Chapter 2. One of your responsibilities as network administrator for the Universal Aerospace Corporation will be to monitor the status of the redirection area periodically, as described in Chapter 10.

Disk Mirroring and Duplexing

You can further improve the reliability of the server computer by implementing one of two NetWare features: disk mirroring and disk duplexing. **Disk mirroring** involves duplicating the data on two disk drives attached to the same disk controller card, whereas **disk duplexing** improves on disk mirroring by using a separate controller card for each disk drive. Figure 1-8 compares disk mirroring and disk duplexing.

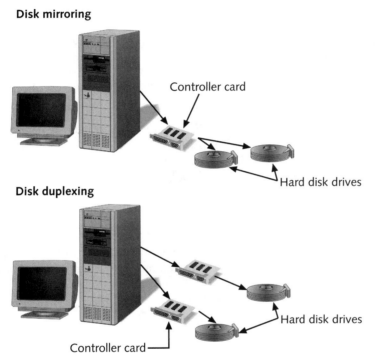

Figure 1-8   Disk mirroring and disk duplexing

For either disk mirroring or duplexing to succeed, the NetWare storage partitions on both drives must be the same size. Any data stored on the disk system is then written to both disk drives. Mirroring provides fault tolerance in the event of a disk drive failure by allowing NetWare to continue to access and store data using the alternate disk drive. The damaged disk drive can then be replaced when the server is not being used. After replacing the damaged disk drive with another of equal capacity, NetWare automatically synchronizes the disks by replicating all the data from the good drive to the new one. The disadvantage of disk mirroring is that it takes slightly longer to write the data to both drives and does not provide fault tolerance if a disk controller card fails.

Disk duplexing allows NetWare to access and store data on the disk system in spite of a failure occurring in either the disk or controller card. In addition, duplexing provides better performance when writing data to the disk by enabling data to be written to both disks simultaneously. For better performance and reliability, the consultant for Universal Aerospace has recommended that you implement disk duplexing on your NetWare server.

Server Mirroring

The best server fault-tolerance protection is to provide a second server computer that is kept synchronized with the primary computer and can instantly be available if the primary server crashes. This is called **server mirroring**. NetWare 5 provides the capability to synchronize servers by using specially designed hardware. Because this can be quite expensive and is necessary only if your organization depends on 100% server up time, your consultant has recommended making daily server backups in addition to keeping spare parts and implementing a preventive maintenance program. The preventive maintenance will reduce the probability of server failure, and if a failure occurs, having spare parts will help ensure that the server can be brought back online in the shortest possible time period.

Volumes

One of the primary uses of a network is to provide shared access to information and software. In a NetWare network, each server's disk storage is divided into one or more volumes. A **volume** is a physical amount of storage space contained on one or more hard disk drives or other storage media such as a CD-ROM or optical disk. Volumes are the major division of file storage in a NetWare network because all files are accessed through volumes and each volume is associated with a specific NetWare server. As a result, volume names usually consist of a combination of the server name along with the volume name.

Each server is required to have at least one volume named SYS that is created during installation to contain operating system files and programs. The network administrator often creates additional volumes to store company data and software. In Chapter 3, you will learn how to design a file storage system consisting of multiple volumes for the Universal Aerospace Corporation.

Printers

Providing shared access to sophisticated, high-speed printers is an important capability of a local area network. Among the advantages of placing printers on a network are cost savings, increased workspace, flexible printer selection based on application needs, and printer fault tolerance. Printers can be connected to a NetWare network in one of three ways:

- Attached to the NetWare server
- Attached to client computers
- Attached directly to the network cable

In most organizations, printers are not attached to the NetWare server since the server computer is usually secured in a locked room. Attaching network printers to client computers provides easy access but also results in slower performance when printing high-resolution graphics output from desktop publishing or presentation graphics applications. Attaching a printer directly to the network provides the best performance and reliability, but is more expensive because of the need for a dedicated network card inside the printer or an external control box for printer attachments.

Each network printer is associated with a **print queue** that is used to store output from a client computer until the printer is available. Print queues allow multiple clients to send output to a network printer at the same time. When a client has completed a print job, the network tags the printer as ready for printing. Generally, print queue jobs are printed in a first-in, first-out basis, maximizing the use of the network printer. If desired, a message can be sent to users' computers, notifying them when their jobs have been printed.

Network Cables

Data is represented in a computer using the binary system of ones and zeros. To send data between computers, you need a method of connecting computers and other network entities that allows the binary coded information to be sent across relatively long distances. The pathway of a local area network is based on the cable system used to connect network entities. A network cable system consists of the cable media and the topology. The **cable media** are the physical wires that are used to transfer data between network

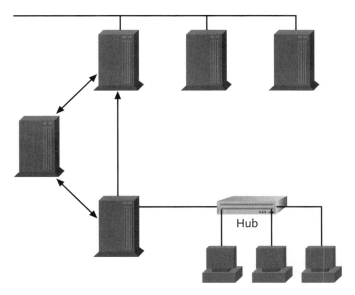

Figure 1-16   Internet mesh topology (hybrid)

Network Interface Cards

Once a plan for the cabling infrastructure has been established, the next component that needs to be selected is the type of network interface card that will be used to connect each computer to the cable system. **Network interface cards (NICs)** are responsible for transmitting data in packets consisting of 500 to 4,000 bytes. In addition to the data, each packet contains the address of the receiving computer's network card much like a letter contains the delivery box number. Although there are many manufacturers of NICs, there are four major standards commonly used today: token ring, Ethernet, 10BaseT, and 100BaseT. Each network card standard has its own method of transmitting data, thereby preventing the use of more than one type of card on a given network cable. Table 1-5 contains a comparison of the token ring, Ethernet, 10BaseT, and 100BaseT network systems in terms of topology, speed, access method, and distance. In this section, you will learn about each of the network card standards shown in Table 1-5 along with their advantages and disadvantages to an organization such as Universal Aerospace Corporation.

Table 1-5   Network Card Comparison

Network System	Cable Types	Topology	Max Nodes	IEEE Standard	Speed	Access Methods	Distance
Token Ring	UTP, STP Fiber	Star	96	802.5	4–16 Mbps	Token	150 ft per cable run
10BaseT	UTP Fiber	Star	512	802.3	10 Mbps	CSMA/CD	328 ft per cable run
Ethernet (10Base2)	Coaxial	Linear Bus	30 per segment with maximum of 3 populated segments	802.3	10 Mbps	CSMA/CD	607 ft per segment
100BaseT	UTP Fiber	Star	512	802.3	100 Mbps	CSMA/CD	328 ft per cable run

Token Ring

IBM originally designed the token ring system for use in industrial environments requiring reliable high-speed communications. Originally the standard, token ring cards transmitted at 4 Mbps; today, most token ring cards use 16 Mbps transmission speeds. (It is important to note that you cannot mix cards running at 4 Mbps with cards running at 16 Mbps on the same token ring network.) Today the token ring system is considered by many to be the best of network systems in terms of performance and reliability. As shown in Figure 1-17, a **token ring** system consists of a star topology in which each station is connected by a twisted-pair cable to a central hub called a **Multiple Station Access Unit (MSAU)**.

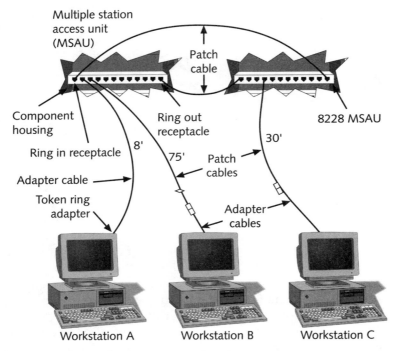

Figure 1-17   Token ring network system

Although each station on the token ring is connected to the central MSAU-forming star, the signals actually travel in a ring. The signal from Workstation A is transmitted to the MSAU, which relays the signal to the cable running to Workstation B. Workstation B retransmits the signal and sends it back to the MSAU. The MSAU relays the signal to the cable running to Workstation C, which transmits the signal back to the MSAU, where it is relayed to the originating Workstation A. If the cable running from the MSAU to Workstation B is broken, or if Workstation B is shut down, a relay in the MSAU passes the signal on to the connection leading to Workstation C. In this manner, the token ring system is very "fault tolerant" and resistant to breakdowns.

The advantages of token ring systems are speed, expandability, and fault tolerance. In addition, token ring systems are usually easier to troubleshoot because bad connections or cable runs can be isolated. The star topology requires extra wiring, which is a disadvantage, as is the generally higher cost of token ring cards as compared to other types of network cards. When you add the cost of purchasing an MSAU for every eight computers, token ring networks can be quite expensive to implement.

Ethernet

The **Ethernet** system shown in Figure 1-18 is based on the linear bus topology and uses the same Carrier Sense Multiple Access/Collison Detection (CSMA/CD) system standardized by the IEEE (Institute of Electrical and Electronic Engineers) 802.3 committee as 10Base2. The CSMA/CD system allows multiple

NETWORK APPLICATIONS

As described at the beginning of this chapter, the main reasons for implementing a local area network are to support communication between computers and provide access to shared files and printers. In this section, you will use what you have learned previously to log in to the network and then use file and print services to work with network files and printers. In addition, you will learn how to use some valuable DOS command-line utilities that can help you when performing certain network tasks.

Accessing Network Services from Windows

Starting with Microsoft Windows 95, the Windows operating system has provided a network-aware client environment that can perform many network operations for you. Novell's Client software for Windows provides additional NetWare functions that simplify many network tasks. In this section, you will learn how to customize the Novell Client software for use with your network as well as how to use Novell Client and Windows 98 features to access network resources and services.

Customizing the NetWare Client

As the network administrator for Universal Aerospace, you do not want your users to have to enter a tree name and context each time they log in. You can use Network Neighborhood to customize the login process to default to a particular tree name and context for each workstation.

 In this activity, you will customize your workstation login to default to the tree name UAS_TREE and the context ##UAS (where ## is your student number) whenever you log in.

1. If necessary, log in to the network using your assigned ##Admin username as described previously.

2. Right-click **Network Neighborhood** to display the shortcut menu shown in Figure 1-20.

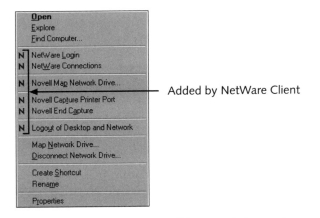

Added by NetWare Client

Figure 1-20   Network Neighborhood shortcut menu

3. Click the **Properties** option to display the Network Configuration dialog box shown in Figure 1-21.

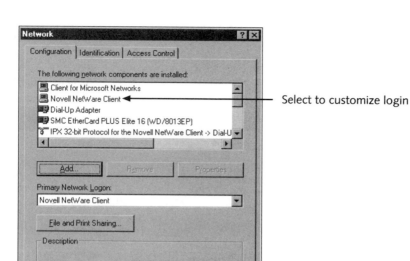

Figure 1-21   Network Configuration tab

4. On the **Configuration** tab, click **Novell NetWare Client** and click **Properties** to display the Novell NetWare Client Properties dialog box shown in Figure 1-22.

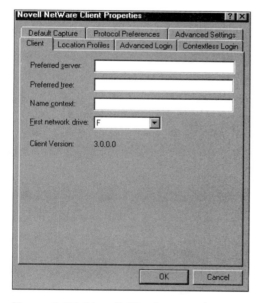

Figure 1-23 Novell Client properties

5. Click in the **Preferred Tree** field and enter **UAS_TREE**.

6. Click in the **Name** context field and enter **##UAS**, where ## represents your assigned student number.

7. Click **OK** to return to the Configuration tab.

COMMAND SUMMARY

Command	Syntax	Definition
CX	CX .container_name	Used to change the client computer's current context within the NDS tree.
LOGIN	LOGIN username	Allows access to the NetWare 5.0 network.
LOGOUT	LOGOUT	Ends the user's network session.
SETPASS	SETPASS	Changes the currently logged-in user's password.
NLIST	NLIST	Displays a variety of information about objects in the NDS tree.

KEY TERMS

10Base2 — An Ethernet system that uses coaxial cable on a linear bus to connect network entities.

10BaseT — A network system that uses CSMA/CD along with a star topology consisting of twisted-pair cables running from a central hub to each network device.

100BaseT — A 100 Mbps version of the 10BaseT network system.

acknowledgment window size — The number of packets to be sent before thesender stops and waits for the receiver to return an acknowledgment.

analog signals — Signals that use energy waves of continuously varying voltage and frequency to carry information across the network media.

application service — A network service that enables an application to run on a server computer to share its functions with other network entities.

bandwidth — A measurement used to determine the capacity and speed of a cable system.

baseband — A network that carries digital signals consisting of ones and zeros.

broadband — A network that carries analog signals such as those used with radio and cable television.

cable media — Wire used to transfer data between network components.

Carrier Sense Multiple Access with Collision Detection (CSMA/CD) — A method used to control access to Ethernet and 10BaseT networks by having a computer wait for an open carrier before transmitting a message. A collision occurs when two or more computers attempt to transmit at the same time, causing the computers to wait a random time instant before attempting to retransmit their messages.

centralized processing — A system in which all processing is done on a centralized mainframe using dumb terminals for input/output devices.

Certified Novell Administrator (CNA) — A NetWare certification that requires passing a single certification test. This book covers the test's objectives.

Certified Novell Engineer (CNE) — A NetWare certification that requires passing a battery of seven tests including material on such subjects as networking technologies, hardware support, software installation, and advanced network administration.

client — A computer that accesses network services such as shared files, printers, or communication systems.

client/server database — A database system where an application server is used to search for data records based on client requests, and then to send any found requested data back to the client.

coaxial cable — A type of cable commonly used for television networks that consists of a single copper wire surrounded by a wire mesh shield.

concentrator — A device used by the 10BaseT network as a hub to connect all machines to the star topology network.

digital signals — Signals that consist of voltages represented by either a one or zero.

disk duplexing — A fault-tolerance technique that involves synchronizing data on two disk drives attached to different controller cards to prevent loss of data in the event of a controller card or disk drive failure.

disk mirroring — A fault-tolerance technique that synchronizes two disk drives attached to a single controller. Should a disk drive fail, the system can continue to operate using the synchronized drive.

distributed processing system — A system where each user's computer runs its own software.

duplicate directories — A fault-tolerance feature of NetWare in which two copies of the disk directory and file allocation table are stored in different areas of the server's disk drives. Should one of the directories or file allocation tables become corrupted by a disk error or computer failure, NetWare can repair it using the backup copy.

entity — A device that can communicate on a network to provide or use network services.

Ethernet — A network system that uses CSMA/CD along with a linear bus consisting of computers attached by T-connectors to a coaxial cable segment.

fault tolerance — The ability of a computer to continue operating in spite of a device failure.

fiber-optic cable — A cable that consists of glass fibers designed to carry light generated by pulsing lasers or light-emitting diodes. Fiber-optic cable is resistant to electronic interference and can be used for very high-speed computer networks that cover long distances.

file allocation table (FAT) — A table stored on each disk drive that is used by NetWare to connect files that are stored in multiple disk blocks.

file cache buffer — A memory area in the server reserved for storing blocks of data from the disk driver.

file caching — The process of storing the most commonly accessed data blocks in a file server's memory to increase performance.

file service — A network service that allows files to be accessed by remote client computers.

graphical user interface (GUI) — An interface, such as the one used in Windows, that features a desktop environment of graphical icons representing programs and data files.

hot fix — A fault-tolerance technique that causes a NetWare server to move data from a bad disk block to a reserved area called the redirection area.

Intelligent Drive Electronics (IDE) — A high-speed controller card technology that can control up to four devices, including disk drives and CD-ROM devices.

Internetwork Packet eXchange (IPX) — A protocol stack commonly used to transfer packets between NetWare servers and clients.

linear bus topology — A layout where a single cable segment runs from one computer to the next.

local area network (LAN) — A high-speed communication system consisting of cables and cards (hardware) along with software that provides a means for different types of computers to communicate and share resources over short distances, such as within a building or room.

logging in — Supplying a username and official password, if already defined, to the NOS.

login security — A security system that identifies a valid user by requiring the user to enter the correct username and password if required.

mesh topology — A network topology that provides multiple paths for signals. The mesh topology is normally implemented between major computers to provide alternative paths if one line is down or overloaded. The mesh topology is found on the Internet, providing multiple paths to any location.

message service — A network service that can deliver messages from one network entity to another.

modem — A device that converts computer signals into analog frequencies.

Multiple Station Access Unit (MSAU) — A central hub used to connect cables in a token ring network.

NetBEUI — A Microsoft nonrouting protocol stack commonly used on Windows.

NetWare Core Protocol (NCP) — The protocol used by NetWare to access services on a NetWare server.

network interface card (NIC) — A component used to connect each computer or networking device to the cable system.

network operating system (NOS) — The software that is run on server computers to provide services to the network.

network service — A combination of computer hardware and software that provides network resources that client computers can access.

Novell Client for Windows 95/98 — A NetWare client designed to take advantage of the 32-bit capability of the latest Windows operating systems.

Novell Directory Services (NDS) — A global database, available to all servers, containing information on all network objects, including users, groups, printers, and volumes.

patch panel — A centralized wiring panel that contains connections to each computer on a network segment.

pathway — A type of cable or wireless system capable of reliably carrying data from one network entity to another.

peer-to-peer — A network operating system in which a computer can be both client and server.

print queue — A queue that stores output from a client computer, or from multiple clients at the same time, until the printer is available.\

print service — A network service that allows network entities to access one or more shared printers attached to the network.

protocol stack — Software that is responsible for formatting and routing packets of data between network devices.

redirection area — A reserved area on a NetWare disk partition used by the NetWare hot fix feature to provide fault tolerance in the event of a bad disk recording block.

ring topology — A network topology where the signals are passed in one direction from one computer to another until they return to the original sending computer.

Sequential Packet eXchange (SPX) — The protocol used by NetWare clients to provide additional reliability by requiring an acknowledgment of each packet sent from the client to the server.

server — A computer that provides one or more network services.

server mirroring — Providing a second server computer that is kept synchronized with the primary computer and can instantly be available if the primary server crashes.

server-centric — A network operating system, such as NetWare 5, in which the server functions run on a designated computer.

shielded twisted-pair (STP) — A cable that consists of pairs of insulated wires twisted together and encased in a wire mesh shield. The use of the grounded wire mesh shield reduces the effect of outside interference from other electrical sources.

Small Computer System Interface (SCSI-2) — A very high-speed controller card technology that can control up to seven devices, including disk drives, CD-ROMs, and tape backup units, from one controller card.

star topology — A layout where a cable runs from each network device to a central hub.

switching hubs — Intelligent concentrators used to reduce collisions in 10BaseT and 100BaseT network systems.

Thinnet — Another name for an Ethernet network using RG-58 coaxial cable.

token ring — A network system that uses a star topology with twisted-pair cable running from the central MSAU hub to each computer. A token-passing scheme is used to control access to the network by causing computers to wait for the token before transmitting their message, thereby eliminating collisions that might occur on CSMA/CD networks such as Ethernet and 10BaseT.

topology — The physical layout of the cable system.

Transport Control Protocol/Internet Protocol (TCP/IP) — The standard Internet protocol commonly used to format and route packets among computers running different operating systems on the Internet.

uninterruptible power supply (UPS) — A backup power system that uses batteries to provide continuous power to a computer in the event of a power outage.

unshielded twisted-pair (UTP) — Cable that consists of pairs of insulated wires twisted together to reduce electrical crosstalk. Twisted-pair cable is commonly used for telephone systems as well as many local area networks.

Virtual Loadable Module (VLM) — DOS-based software that establishes and maintains network sessions, and directs information and requests from the client to the NetWare server.

volume — The major division of NetWare storage. All files are stored in volumes associated with a specific NetWare server.

wire mesh shield — A shield surrounding the central conductor of the coaxial cable and used as a ground.

REVIEW QUESTIONS

1. List five components of a local area network.

   _____

   _____

   _____

   _____

   _____

2. _____ is used to describe a system where each user's computer runs its own software.

3. A(n) _____ computer accesses network services such as shared files and printers.

4. A(n) _____ allows multiple computers to access its disk system to retrieve and save data.

5. A(n) _____ assists client computers in running application software.

6. Operating system software that provides network services is referred to as the _____.

7. _____ network systems allow client computers to perform server functions.

8. Dedicated servers are used with _____ operating systems.

9. When a network uses NetWare 5, the _____ provides a network-wide database of user and other network objects.

10. _____ increases the performance of a NetWare server by keeping the most recently accessed disk blocks in RAM.

11. Allowing a computer to operate in spite of an equipment failure is referred to as _____.

12. A NetWare technique called _____ helps to prevent disk errors when writing data to a network disk drive.

13. _____ involves duplicating the data on two disk drives attached to the same disk controller card.

14. _____ signals consist of energy waves that travel through the cable media.

15. _____ signals are most compatible with computers because they consist of sending discrete voltages representing either a one or zero.

16. _____ may be used for both television and computer networks.

17. Of the cable types discussed in this chapter, _____ has the least resistance to outside interference.

2

DEFINING NETWORK OBJECTS

After reading this chapter and completing the exercises, you will be able to:

♦ Describe how a workstation communicates with the network, and list the software components required to connect a workstation to the network

♦ Install and configure Novell NetWare client software

♦ Describe the function and purpose of NDS, including leaf and container objects

♦ Use NetWare Administrator to browse the Directory tree, view object information, and create new objects

♦ Describe replicas and partitions

♦ Use NDS Manager to view and create partitions and replicas

In Chapter 1, you learned the major components of a network include clients, servers, printers, network cards, and cable topology. The NetWare operating system allows these components to work together by providing a communication protocol that consists of software installed on each client computer along with the NetWare operating system installed on the server computer(s). In addition to allowing communication among the physical components and services, the NetWare operating system also provides a secure way for users to access only the resources and services they are authorized to use. To set up a secure network system that is easy to use, a CNA (Certified Novell Administrator) must be able to install client software as well as define network users and the objects they will be authorized to access or control.

In this chapter, you will learn what a CNA needs to know about defining network users and components using Novell Directory Services (NDS) along with how to apply these concepts to designing and maintaining an NDS structure for the Universal Aerospace Corporation. In addition, you will learn how to install the client software and then to use NetWare utilities to navigate the NDS database and view information about network objects.

IMPLEMENTING THE CLIENT

As a CNA, you will need to install and configure client computers on your network. To communicate and access network services, a client computer requires a network card and certain software components, as shown in Figure 2-1. Before setting up the client computers for Universal Aerospace, it is important to first understand the role that each of these software components plays in the network communication process.

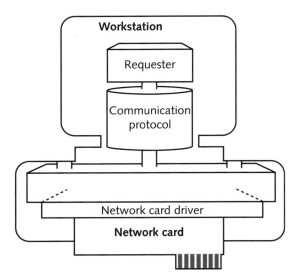

Figure 2-1   Client components

The network **card driver** software performs the process of controlling the network interface card (NIC) so it can send and receive packets over the network cable system. The manual that comes with your network card should include information on the correct driver program for use with NetWare. The client installation software from Novell includes drivers for the most commonly used network cards.

The **communication protocol** or **protocol stack** is responsible for formatting the data within a network packet as well as routing packets between different networks. A major difference between NetWare 5 and previous versions of NetWare is that by default NetWare 5 servers and clients use the TCP/IP protocol stack rather than Novell's proprietary SPX/IPX protocol. To communicate with other NetWare servers using SPX/IPX, NetWare 5 provides a compatibility mode option that allows a network to support both protocols. Because Universal Aerospace currently has a NetWare 3.12 server, the new NetWare 5 server has been installed to use both protocols as described in Appendix A. In the future, Universal Aerospace wants to upgrade the NetWare 3.12 server to NetWare 5 and then convert the network completely to TCP/IP, removing need for SPX/IPX. In Chapter 10, you will learn how to plan and configure a TCP/IP network for Universal Aerospace clients.

In addition to TCP/IP and SPX/IPX, other client computers may need additional protocol stacks, such as Microsoft NetBIOS or Macintosh AppleTalk, to share resources. For example, in addition to TCP/IP and SPX/IPX, Universal Aerospace will need to implement NetBIOS to share the CD-ROM located on a computer in the Desktop Publishing department.

The **requester** carries out the function of providing access to the NetWare server from the local operating system. The requester program works very closely with Windows to provide access to network services from the client computer. Operating systems such as Windows 95, Windows 98, and Windows NT have a NetWare requester already included in the operating system software. Other operating systems such as DOS or Windows for Workgroups require that the NetWare requester software be installed on the client computer before they can access NetWare services.

Client Versions

As new computers and software have become available, Novell has provided software solutions that allow these clients to access network services. NetWare 5 offers Novell Client software for all major desktop operating systems, including Windows 95/98, Windows NT, DOS, Windows 3.x, OS/2, Macintosh, and UNIX. Previously, Universal Aerospace used earlier versions of NetWare to provide file and print services to office staff. Currently, some workstations are still running DOS/Windows and other have Windows 95. The president of Universal Aerospace wants to standardize the environment by upgrading all workstations to Windows 98 and installing the latest Novell Client software. To upgrade all the Universal Aerospace computers and better understand the significance and capability of the new Novell NetWare client software, it is helpful to review some of these client software solutions and understand their capabilities and limitations. In this section, you will learn about some of the earlier Novell clients such as NETX and ODI, as well as current client options such as the Microsoft NDS Client and Novell Client for Windows 95/98.

NETX Client

Early versions of NetWare client software, referred to as **NETX clients**, combined the IPX protocol and network card driver into one program named IPX.COM. To install this client, the network administrator ran an installation program that linked the selected network card driver software to IPX, creating the IPX.COM program. If any changes needed to be made to the network card configuration, or a newer version of the network card driver became available, the network administrator would need to run the installation program again to link the revised network card driver into the IPX.COM program. Because the DOS operating system is not NetWare-aware, a requester program named NETX.EXE was used to manage the connection between DOS and NetWare. To load the client software, you needed to run both IPX.COM and NETX.EXE after starting your DOS computer. After NETX was loaded, a user could change to drive F (where F is configured as the first network drive) and log in to the network using the LOGIN command. In addition to being difficult to configure, the NETX client could not work directly with the NDS Directory tree or support additional protocols such as TCP/IP.

VLM Client

Several DOS/Windows workstations in the Universal Aerospace Business department use a client referred to as the VLM client. The VLM (Virtual Loadable Module) client, which shipped with NetWare 4.1, provides support for multiple protocols as well as the ability to access objects in the NDS Directory tree. In addition, the VLM client is modular, making it much easier to configure. Because the VLM client fits on a disk, it is still used at Universal Aerospace on boot disks to initially attach a workstation to the network to install Windows. As a result, you should become familiar with the VLM client components and how they are loaded.

To provide the VLM client with support for multiple protocol stacks, as well as make it easier for network administrators to update configurations and driver software, Novell developed the Open Data Interface software and driver specifications. The **Open Data Interface (ODI)** standard provides a standard link support layer along with driver specifications for network card companies to use in developing card drivers that are compatible with Novell Client software. Network card drivers developed for use with ODI specifications are called Multiple Link Protocol Drivers, or MLID. The **link support layer (LSL)** included with the ODI software allows a client to run multiple protocol stacks simultaneously using the same MLID network card driver. For example, at Universal Aerospace, the Engineering department wants to be able to copy files directly from the Internet into a shared directory on the NetWare server where all users can have access to them. To do this, the department's clients must be able to support both TCP/IP and IPX.

As illustrated in Figure 2-2, the ODI driver software is composed of four components: the ODI-compatible card driver, the LSL program, the IPXODI protocol, and the VLM requester.

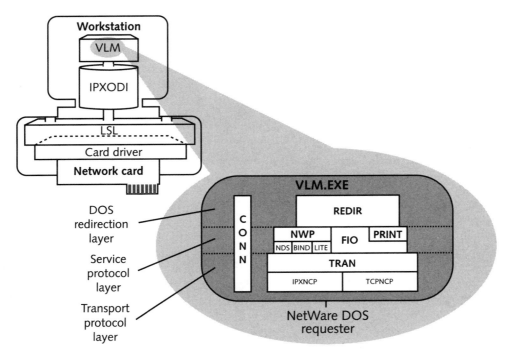

Figure 2-2 VLM client components

When you load the ODI software, the LSL.COM program is loaded first and provides the link support layer between the protocol stack and the card driver so that more than one protocol stack can share the same network card. Next the MLID software is loaded to initialize the network card and connect to the LSL. The protocol stack(s) are loaded next. The IPXODI.COM program provides the SPX/IPX protocol stack normally used to communicate with earlier NetWare servers, while the TCP/IP protocol provides communication to NetWare 5 servers and the Internet. The VLM is the requester software that communicates directly with DOS or Windows 3.1 to transfer network requests to the NetWare server. The VLM requester consists of a manager, VLM.EXE, along with several other virtual modules having a .VLM file-name extension. You load the VLM client by running the STARTNET.BAT file shown in Figure 2-3. As software modules are loaded, they obtain their configuration information from a file named NET.CFG. The NET.CFG file contains section headers for the network card driver, link support, and DOS requester as illustrated in Figure 2-3.

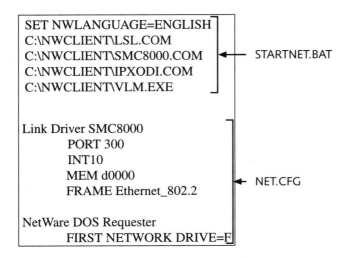

Figure 2-3 VLM client configuration files

In this hands-on activity, you will use Network Neighborhood to remove the Novell Client and then add the client for Microsoft networks.

1. If necessary, start your computer but click **Cancel** when asked to log in to NetWare. If you are already logged in, log out by selecting the Log Off option from the Start button.

2. Click **Cancel** when asked to enter a Windows password.

3. Right-click **Network Neighborhood** and click **Properties** to display the Configuration dialog box. Record the name of your network adapter card on the worksheet provided by your instructor.

4. Click the entry for your network adapter card and click the **Properties** button.

5. Click the **Resources** tag if available and record any values shown there or on the worksheet provided by your instructor.

6. Click **Cancel** to return to the Network Neighborhood Properties dialog box.

7. Click **Novell NetWare Client** and click the **Remove** button. The Novell Client should now be removed from the Components dialog box.

8. If your computer does not have the Client for Microsoft Networks, you should add it at this time, as follows:

   a) Click **Add** and then click **Client**.

   b) Click the **Add** button again to display the Select Network Client dialog box.

   c) Click **Microsoft** in the Manufacturers pane and then double-click **Client for Microsoft Networks**. The Microsoft client should now appear in your Components area.

9. Click **OK** to close the Network Configuration window.

10. At this time Windows will update the client files. If the necessary *. CAB files are not located on your workstation, you will be asked to enter the path to the files. Enter the path specified by your instructor.

Although you can use the Control Panel to remove the Novell Client, this procedure does not remove all client software components. To restore the Windows 95/98 workstation to the state it was in prior to installing the Novell Client, you must use the UNC32 uninstall program provided by Novell. For example, the CNE consultant recently used the following procedure to remove the current Novell Client from your workstation and return it to the state it was in before the Novell Client was installed.

1. After starting the computer, the consultant logged in using his assigned username.

2. Next the consultant clicked the **Start** button to select the **Run** command.

3. He then browsed to the Public\Client\Win95\ibm_env\Admin folder on the F drive and ran the UNC32 program.

4. He then clicked **OK** to display the Novell Client Uninstall window and clicked **Continue** to remove the existing client files.

5. After the uninstall process was completed, the consultant clicked the **ReBoot** button to restart the workstation.

6. Because the Novell Client was removed, when restarting, the workstation displayed only the Microsoft Windows 98 login window. Rather than logging in to the network, the CNE consultant clicked the **Cancel** button to return to the desktop. The workstation was now ready to completely reinstall the Novell Client software.

Installing the Microsoft Client

Rather than recommending installing clients off the Novell Client CD-ROM, Universal Aerospace's CNE consultant has suggested that you install the Novell Client from the NetWare server. To assist you in this task, the Novell Client software has already been loaded into a directory on the server. To access these files, you will first need to configure the workstation to use the Microsoft NetWare client.

 In this hands-on activity, you will use Network Neighborhood and the Control Panel to set up the Microsoft NetWare client.

1. If necessary, restart your computer.

2. Right-click **Network Neighborhood** and click **Properties**. Network Neighborhood does not display when there are no clients installed. Follow the steps below to configure the network components when there is no Network Neighborhood icon:

   a) Click the **Start** button, then point to **Settings**.

   b) Click the **Control Panel** icon to display the Control Panel dialog box.

   c) Double-click the **Network** icon to display the configuration tab of the "Network" dialog box. If you receive the message telling you that the network is not complete, click **Yes** to continue.

3. If necessary, add a network adapter as follows:

   a) Click **Add**.

   b) Click **Adapter** and click **Add**.

   c) Select the network adapter you recorded in a previous activity.

   d) Click **OK** to add the adapter.

   e) Click the adapter and then click the **Properties** button.

   f) Click the **Resources** tab (if present) and select the values that you recorded in a previous activity. After making your entries, click **OK** to return to the Network Configuration window.

4. Add the Microsoft NetWare client:

   a) Click **Add**.

   b) Click **Client** and click **Add**.

   c) Click **Microsoft**, click **Client for NetWare Networks**, and click **OK**. The Client for NetWare Networks should now appear in the components list.

5. Add the Microsoft service for NDS as follows:

 In some cases after removing the Novell NetWare Client, the Microsoft service for NDS does not properly load. If your Microsoft Service for NDS does not load, you can still continue to do the installation; however, you will not be able to log in to other containers.

   a) Click **Add**.

   b) Click **Service** and click **Add**.

   c) Click **Microsoft** and click **Service for NetWare Directory Services**.

   d) Click **OK** to return to the Select Network Component Type dialog box. If necessary, click **Cancel** to return to the Network Configuration dialog box. If the Service for NetWare Directory Services does not appear, the problem may be due to the previous installation of the Novell NetWare Client.

5. Double-click the **Moon** Organizational Unit and list any printer objects on the following lines:

Houston

Houston_P

2

6. Right-click a printer object and click **Properties** to display print queue information. Record the NetWare Queue Type: *Novell directory Services queue*

7. Click **Cancel** to close the Properties window.

8. Close all Network Neighborhood windows.

Another way to identify an object in the NDS tree is to type in its context. Just as you sometimes need to type a path to specify the location of a file on a disk drive, you will also find times when you are configuring systems or working with login scripts, as described in Chapter 8, that you need to type the context to specify the location of an object within an NDS tree. One difference between typing a disk path to a filename and using the NDS context is that the NDS context is specified starting with the object and working up the tree, whereas a disk path is specified from the top of the directory down to the filename. For example, to identify the disk path to the MEMO file located in the DOCUMENT directory, you would type \DOCUMENT\MEMO, whereas to identify the context of the printer named Houston in the Moon container shown in Figure 2-6, you would use .CN=Houston.OU=Moon.O=Frontier. Notice that another difference between NDS and the disk path is that you specify the NDS context by using periods to separate each level rather than a slash or backslash, such as is used on disk paths. The period at the beginning of the context is very important because it is used to specify that the context leads from the object all the way to the root of the tree. The two-letter abbreviation preceding the name of an object identifies the object's type. The CN= identifies Houston as a leaf object, the OU= identifies Moon as an Organizational Unit container, and the O= identifies Frontier as an Organization container object. (To see the abbreviation for each NDS object type along with its NDS definition, see Table 2-1.)

You can uniquely specify each object in the NDS database by typing its **distinguished name**, which consists of the object's name along with its complete context starting from the root of the NDS tree. A context specification that includes the object abbreviations is referred to as **typeful**. For example, the printer object Houston could be identified using the typeful distinguished name .CN=Houston.OU=Moon.O=Frontier.

Using typeful distinguished names that include the object type abbreviation along with the context requires extra time and introduces the possibility for errors. As a result, Novell enables NDS to assume object types as long as the rightmost object is an Organization or Organizational Unit. A distinguished name that does not contain the object type abbreviations is referred to as **typeless**. For example, the typeless distinguished name for the printer object Houston would be specified as .Houston.Moon.Frontier.

The location of your client computer within the NDS tree is referred to as its **current context**. You can access any object located in the current context of your client simply by specifying its common name. If you want to access an object outside the current context of your client, you can specify its distinguished or relative name.

For example, if the current context of your client is already within one of the containers specified in a distinguished name, you can save keystrokes by using a relative name. A **relative name** starts with the current context of the client. You specify a relative name by omitting the leading period. For example, assume you are writing a login script command that will send output to the Houston printer object located in the Moon organizational unit of the Frontier organization. If the client's current context is the Frontier Organization container, you can write your login script command using a relative name as follows:

```
CAPTURE P=Houston.Moon
```

Note that a period is *not* used at the beginning of the relative name. If the current context of the client is set to the Moon organizational unit, you can map the drive by simply using the common name as shown here:

```
CAPTURE P=Houston
```

Working with NDS Context and Naming

As you learned in Chapter 1, the CX command allows you to view and change your current context from the DOS prompt. In addition to enabling you to view and change your current context, the CX command may also be used to view the entire NDS tree structure or just the leaf objects in your current context. Although you no longer need to know how to use the DOS command-line utilities to pass the CNA test, it is important that you learn how to use NDS names and navigate the Directory tree. The activities in this section will teach you how to use NDS distinguished and relative names as well as how to navigate the Directory tree using the CX command-line utility. In today's Windows-based environment, you can now perform most networking tasks without accessing the DOS prompt; however, the concepts you learn by doing the hands-on activities will help you to apply the NDS naming techniques necessary when configuring workstations or developing login scripts.

The syntax of the CX command-line utility is as follows:

```
CX [context]
```

You can use the *context* option to specify the NDS container you want to make the current context. Entering the CX command without any options will display your current context. You can also use the following switches:

```
CX [/R /T /CONT /A]
```

- The /R option changes the current context to the root of the tree.
- The /T option displays the tree structure starting with the current context.
- The /CONT option lists all container objects in the current context.
- The /A option lists all objects, including leaf objects, in each of the containers and is normally used along with the /CONT or /T options.

Using CX to View the NDS Tree

One of the most common problems encountered when working with the NDS hierarchical tree is knowing where resources are located. The CX command can be very helpful in finding network resources such as users, printers, and volumes by allowing you to list part or all of the NDS tree structure. To give yourself easy access to resources, you need to be able to configure a workstation's current context.

 In this hands-on activity, you learn how to use the CX command to display the current context of your workstation, view the tree structure, and list objects within a container.

1. If necessary, start your computer and press [Esc] when you see the Novell Login dialog box. If you are already logged in, click **Start** and then click the **Log Off** option. (If you do not have a Log Off option, click **Shut Down** and then choose the option to close all programs and Log in as another user.)

2. Open a DOS window by clicking **Start**, point to **Programs**, and click **MS-DOS Prompt**.

3. Enter **F:** and press **[Enter]** to change to the network drive (F).

4. Type **CX /R /T** and press **[Enter]** to view the entire NDS tree structure starting at the root of the tree. Alternatively, you could first change the context to the root of the tree and then display the structure by entering **CX /R [Enter]** and then **CX /T [Enter]**. Your screen should appear similar to the one shown in Figure 2-7.

Creating a NetWare Administrator Shortcut

As network administrator, you will be using NetWare Administrator often to implement and maintain the Universal Aerospace network system. As a result, it will be important to be able to start NetWare Administrator easily by creating a Windows desktop shortcut as well as adding the utility to the Start button. Adding the NetWare Administrator to the Start menu will provide an additional method of launching the utility if the desktop icon is deleted.

 In this hands-on activity, you will add a NetWare Administrator shortcut to your desktop as well as to your Start menu.

1. If necessary, start your client computer and log in to the network using your assigned ##Admin username.

2. Open the F:\Public\win32 directory as follows:

   a) Double-click **My Computer.**

   b) Double-click the **F** drive.

   c) Double-click the **Public** folder, and then double-click the **win32** folder.

3. Drag and drop the **Nwadmn32** program onto the desktop.

4. Next, to add the NetWare Administrator to your Start menu options, drag and drop the **NwAdmn32** shortcut on the Start button.

5. Click the **Start** button. The Shortcut to Nwadmn32 option should now appear in the upper half of the Start menu.

6. Click anywhere on the desktop outside of the Start menu to close the window.

Customizing NetWare Administrator Buttons

Instead of accessing commonly used functions by going through multiple menus, the new NetWare Administrator allows you to save time with toolbar buttons for commonly used functions, as illustrated in Figure 2-11.

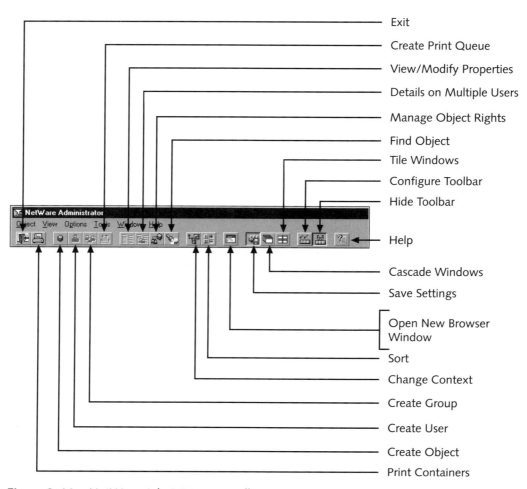

Figure 2-11   NetWare Administrator toolbar

As you can see from looking at the NetWare Administrator window, Novell has provided NetWare Administrator with many default function buttons. In fact, there are almost too many buttons to keep track of. To make the buttons easier to use, you may wish to simplify the options by removing unnecessary buttons or adding new buttons that better meet your needs.

 In this hands-on activity, you will learn how to customize NetWare Administrator by adding and removing buttons from the toolbar.

1. If necessary, start your client computer and log in to the network using your assigned ##Admin username.

2. Double-click the **Shortcut to Nwadmn32** to start NetWare Administrator. If the NDS tree name has changed since the last time NetWare Administrator was used, you will receive an error message indicating the previous browser settings could not be restored. Select **No** if asked to restore the previous connection.

   Notice that the NetWare Administrator contains a toolbar at the top of the screen and a status bar at the bottom of the screen, as illustrated in Figure 2-12. By default, the status bar contains such information as the name of your current Directory tree, current context, and number of objects selected. The toolbar contains buttons used to activate various NetWare Administrator options.

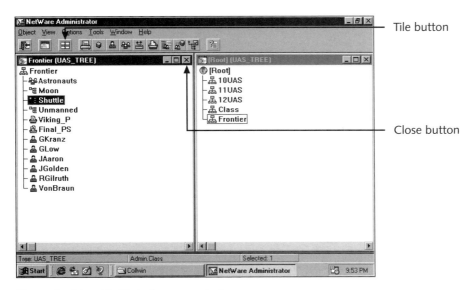

Tile button

Close button

Figure 2-17   Multiple browse windows

13. Close the Frontier browse window by clicking its **Close** button.

14. Click the **Tile** toolbar icon to resize the [Root] browse window.

Viewing Object Properties

In addition to browsing the tree structure, you can use NetWare Administrator to view the properties of both container and leaf objects. Since information about network objects is stored in properties, learning how to use NetWare Administrator to view object properties is very important if you are to manage the NDS environment effectively.

In this hands-on activity, you learn how to view property information on container objects, printers, users, and groups.

1. If you have not already done so, log in to the network using your ##Admin username and start NetWare Administrator as instructed in the previous activity.

2. If necessary, open a browse window for the Class container as instructed in the previous hands-on activity.

3. To view information on the **Class** container, first highlight the Class container by single-clicking it and then press **[Enter]** to display the Identification window for the Class container as shown in Figure 2-18. You can now click the buttons located on the right side of the window to view information on the container's properties.

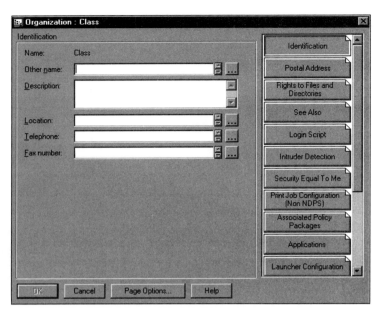

Figure 2-18   Container detail information

4. Click **Cancel** to return to the browse window.

5. Highlight the **Students** group name and press **[Enter]** to display the Identification window for the Students group.

6. Click the **Members** button to view members of the Student group.

7. Click **Cancel** to return to the browse window.

8. To view information about the classroom printer, highlight the **Class_P** printer object and press **[Enter]**.

9. Click the **Assignments** button to view the name of the print queue associated with the Classroom printer. Record the name here or on the answer sheet provided by your instructor:
   _____

10. Click the **Configuration** button to view the printer type. Record the type here or on the answer sheet provided by your instructor: _____

11. Click **Cancel** to return to the browse window.

12. Open a browse window for the Frontier organization.

13. Tile your browse windows.

14. View information on the user JLovell. What Apollo mission was he on? Record your answer here or on the answer sheet provided by your instructor:
   _____

15. Click the various property buttons to view login, password, and time restrictions. If requested, record this information on the answer sheet provided by your instructor.

16. View group memberships. If requested, record this information on the answer sheet provided by your instructor.

17. Click **Cancel** to return to the browse window.

18. Close the Frontier browse window and retile the screen.

Creating NDS Objects

Now that you have tested your system and are becoming more comfortable using the new NetWare Administrator utility, it's time to begin creating NDS components for the Universal Aerospace Directory tree. To begin implementing the Directory tree design for Universal Aerospace, you will need to create Organizational Unit objects named Engineering and Business within your ##UAS organization. In addition, to provide easier access to data and applications, you will need to create volume leaf objects in the containers that reference the SYS and CORP volumes on your classroom server. In the hands-on activities in this section, you will create Organizational Units along with Alias and Volume objects that reference the classroom server and its file system.

Creating Alias and Volume Objects

The classroom Directory tree has been set up to allow you to create your own version of the Universal Aerospace structure within your assigned ##UAS Organization. Currently your ##UAS Organization contains only your ##Admin username. The actual NetWare server and volume objects are located in the Class Organization. The server and volume objects are important in that they provide a connection from NDS to the physical data stored on the server. You will learn more about NetWare volumes and volume objects in Chapter 3. To simulate the network environment that would exist after the NetWare server has been installed as shown previously in Figure 2-10, you will need to create objects to represent the NetWare server and volumes. An **Alias object** is a pointer to the real object located in another container. Alias objects are important when users need to access resources located in other containers. Using Alias objects allows you to create a single object that contains information about a physical resource and then allows users in multiple containers to access the object. For example, you can create a printer object in your ##UAS container and then create Alias objects in the Engineering and Mfg containers so those users can send output to the printer.

In this hands-on activity, you will create in your ##UAS container an Alias object that points to the actual server object located in the Class container. You will then be able to access information about the server without having to change context to the Class container. In addition, you will use the Alias server object to create two volume objects that you can use to access data on the server's data volumes.

1. If necessary, start your client computer and log in to the network using your assigned ##Admin username.

2. Start NetWare Administrator by double-clicking its desktop shortcut.

3. If necessary, open a browse window showing the contents of your ##UAS container.

4. Click your ##UAS container and press **[Insert]** to display the New Object window.

5. Double-click **Alias** to display the Create Alias window.

6. Type **UAS_HOST** in the Alias name field.

7. Click the **browse** button to the right of the Aliased object field to display the Select Object window. Use the Browse context pane to navigate to the Class container.

8. Double-click the **UAS_HOST** server object from the Available objects pane.

9. Click the **Create** button to create the server Alias object.

10. Double-click your new Alias object to display the NetWare server identification window.

11. Click **Cancel** to return to NetWare Administrator.

12. Follow these steps to create a Volume object named UAS_HOST_SYS that points to the SYS volume of the UAS_HOST server:

    a) Click your ##UAS container to highlight it.

b) Click the **Create a new object** button on your toolbar to display the New Object window.

c) Scroll down until you see the **Volume** object, and double-click it to display the Create Volume dialog box shown in Figure 2-19

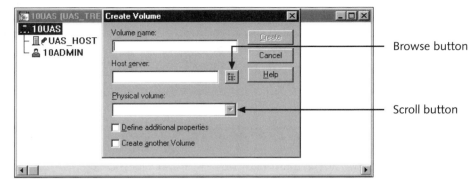

Figure 2-19   Create Volume dialog box

d) Enter **UAS_HOST_SYS** in the Volume name field.

e) Click the **browse** button to the right of the Host server field to display the Select Object dialog box.

f) Double-click your **UAS_HOST** alias from the Available Objects window.

g) Click the **scroll** button to the right of the Physical volume window to display a list of all volumes on the UAS_HOST server.

h) Click the **SYS** volume and then click **Create**. A UAS_HOST_SYS volume should now be displayed in your ##UAS container.

13. Repeat Steps 12a through 12h, substituting **UAS_HOST_CORP** for UAS HOST_SYS in Step 12d, and volume **CORP** for SYS in Step 12h, to create a volume named UAS_HOST_CORP. When you've finished, your NetWare Administrator screen should look like the one shown in Figure 2-20.

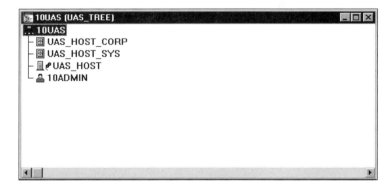

Figure 2-20   Netware Administrator with volumes and a server alias

Creating Organizational Units

The president of Universal Aerospace would like some of the users in the Engineering and Manufacturing departments to begin taking advantage of the new network as soon as possible. Therefore, now that you have installed and tested the clients, your next task is to create containers for the Engineering and Manufacturing departments. Because the Engineering department monitors many of the manufacturing processes, the consultant from Computer Technology Services has recommended that you initially place the container for Manufacturing within the Engineering Organizational Unit.

 In this hands-on activity, you use NetWare Administrator to create Engineering and Manufacturing containers and then make accessing data easier by placing SYS and CORP volume objects in the Engineering container.

1. If necessary, start your client computer, log in to the network using your assigned ##Admin username, and start NetWare Administrator by double-clicking its desktop shortcut.

2. If necessary, open a browse window showing your ##UAS container objects.

3. Highlight your ##UAS container name and create an Organizational Unit named Engineering as follows:

   a) Press **[Insert]** or click the **Create a New Object** icon on the toolbar to display the New Object window.

   b) Scroll down and double-click the **Organizational Unit** object class to display the Create Organizational Unit window.

   c) Enter the name **Engineering** in the Organizational Unit name field.

   d) Click the **Create** button to create your Engineering container.

4. Create volume objects named UAS_HOST_CORP and UAS_HOST_SYS within your Engineering container:

   a) Highlight your **Engineering** container and press **[Insert]** to display the New Object window.

   b) Scroll down and double-click the **Volume** object class.

   c) Follow the procedure in the previous activity to create a Volume object named UAS_HOST_SYS in the Engineering container that points to the SYS volume of your UAS_HOST server.

   d) Repeat Steps 4a through 4c to create a Volume object named UAS_HOST_CORP in the Engineering container that points to the CORP volume of your server.

5. Create an Organizational Unit named Mfg within the Engineering container as follows:

   a) Click your **Engineering** container to highlight it.

   b) Press **[Insert]** or click the **Create New Object** button to display the New Object window.

   c) Scroll down and double-click the **Organizational Unit** object class to display the Create Organizational Unit window.

   d) Enter the name **Mfg** in the Organizational Unit name field.

   e) Click the **Create** button to create your Mfg container.

6. Double-click your **Engineering** container to view your newly created Mfg container.

Creating Initial Users

Now that you have established a basic network system, you will next need to create some user accounts to test the network further. When you are piloting a new system, one of the best places to start is the Information System (IS) department. Currently there are two people in the IS department, you and Kellie Thiele. Kellie is a programmer in charge of developing and modifying application software for use by Universal Aerospace. In addition to using software development tools, Kellie will use network applications such as word processing and email. You will also be a user of the network when you access software packages to perform such tasks as word processing or electronic mail. Whenever you log in with the Admin username, you take a risk of accidentally changing the system configuration or erasing or corrupting server files. In addition, if the workstation you are logging in from has a computer virus in memory, the virus could infect program files on the server, causing the virus to spread quickly throughout the network. To reduce the chance for these problems to occur, you should also create a username for yourself and log in only as Admin when you need the capability to maintain or configure the network.

 In this hands-on activity, you will use NetWare Administrator to create a user account for yourself and Kellie Thiele in the ##UAS organization.

1. If necessary, start your client computer, log in to the network using your assigned ##Admin username, and start NetWare Administrator by double-clicking its desktop shortcut.

2. If necessary, open a browse window showing your ##UAS container objects.

3. Create a username, KThiele, for Kellie Thiele, and create a home directory for Kellie in your ##CORP directory as follows:.

   a) Highlight your **##UAS** container.

   b) Press **[Insert]** or click the **Create a New Object** toolbar button to display the New Object window.

   c) Scroll down and double-click the **User** object class to display the Create User dialog box.

   d) Enter **KThiele** in the Login name field.

   e) Enter **Thiele** in the Last name field.

   f) Click the **Create Home Directory** check box.

   g) Click the **Browse** icon to the right of the Path field to display the Select Object dialog box.

   h) Double-click the **UAS_HOST_CORP** Volume object in the right-hand Browse context pane window to display your ##CORP directory in the Available objects pane.

   i) Select the ##CORP directory as the location for Kellie's home directory by double-clicking your **##CORP** directory name from the Available objects windows. Your Create User dialog box should now appear similar to the one shown in Figure 2-21.

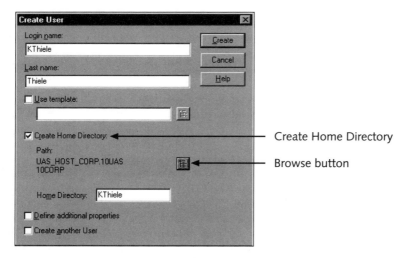

Figure 2-21   Create User window

   j) Click the **Create** button to create Kellie's username.

4. The consultant for Universal Aerospace has recommended that you not log in with your ##Admin username unless you need to perform administrative functions. As a result, you will need to create a username that you can use to access network resources and applications. Using the following steps, create a username for yourself. Use the first letter of your first name and up to the first seven letters of your last name. Create a home directory for your username in your assigned ##CORP directory.

   a) Highlight your ##UAS container.

   b) Click the **Create User object** toolbar button to display the Create User dialog box.

   c) Enter your username in the Login name field.

   d) Enter your last name in the Last name field.

   e) Click the **Create Home Directory** check box.

   f) Click the **Browse** icon to the right of the Path field to display the Select Object dialog box.

   g) Double-click the **UAS_HOST_CORP** Volume object in the right-hand Browse context pane browse window to display your ##CORP directory in the Available objects pane.

   h) Select the ##CORP directory as the location for your home directory by double-clicking your ##CORP directory name from the Available objects window.

   i) Click the **Create** button to create your username.

   After creating the user accounts, your ##UAS organization windows should appear similar to Figure 2-22.

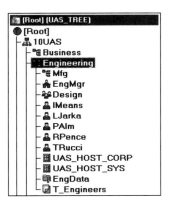

Figure 2-22   NetWare Administrator with new users

5. Exit NetWare Administrator.

6. Test Kellie's account by logging in with the username KThiele as follows:

   a) Click the **Start** button and then click the **Log Off** option. (If you do not have a Log Off option, click **Shut Down** and then select the option to close all programs and Log in as a different user.) Click **Yes** to confirm that you want to log off. A new Novell NetWare Login dialog box will be displayed.

   b) Enter **KThiele** in the Name field. No password should be required.

   c) Click OK to log in as Kellie Thiele.

7. Start Wordpad and create a document describing the steps necessary to log in.

8. Save the document in Kellie's home directory (located on the G drive), using the name **LOGIN**.

9. Exit Wordpad.

10. Double-click **Network Neighborhood** and browse to Kellie's home directory to confirm that the document has been saved.

NDS PARTITIONING AND REPLICATING

As described earlier, the NDS tree is a global database containing information on network objects. Each record in the database represents a single network object. The database itself is a hidden file that is stored somewhere on the NetWare server when the first server is installed on the network. NDS is a global database because the records it contains are shared among all servers in the Directory tree.

NDS Replicas

To start with, the Universal Aerospace Corporation will have only one NetWare server. This means that initially the global NDS database resides on the UAS_HOST NetWare server, and that the server must be up and running for users to be able to access the network. Future expansion plans for Universal Aerospace include adding a dedicated NetWare 5 server for Engineering and Manufacturing use. When the new server is added, NetWare 5 will automatically place a copy of the entire NDS database on the new server, as shown in Figure 2-23.

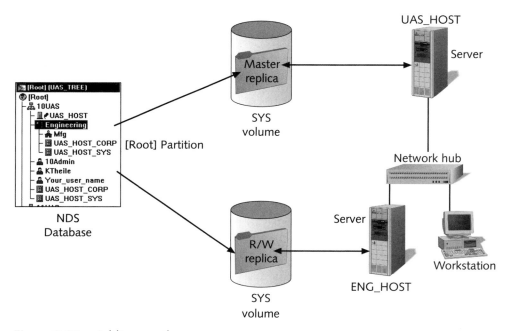

Figure 2-23   Adding another server

The copy of the NDS database placed on the new server is called a **replica**. There are four types of replicas: Master replicas, Read/Write replicas, Read/Only replicas, and Subordinate replicas. Read/Only and Subordinate replicas are created by the system and are not a concern for small to medium-sized networks. A **Master replica** is the original main copy of the NDS data. As network administrator, you may want to create additional **Read/Write replicas** for two major reasons: They improve performance by reducing the time required to authenticate or access a network object, and they provide additional reliability and fault tolerance. Placing a Read/Write replica on the Engineering server, ENG_HOST, would increase performance for the users in the Engineering department, because ENG_HOST could authenticate access to network objects immediately without having to communicate with the primary UAS_HOST server. In addition to improving performance, you can also improve reliability and fault tolerance by maintaining a separate replica of the NDS database on the Engineering server. For example, if the Business server, UAS_HOST, were down, users in the Engineering department could still log in and access the resources available on the Engineering department's ENG_HOST server. In addition, the replica of the NDS database stored on the ENG_HOST server would allow Business department users also to log in and access certain resources such as network printers or electronic mail, or use information stored on the ENG_HOST server. The data files stored on the primary UAS_HOST server's file system would not be accessible until that server was brought back online.

NDS Partitions

Although keeping a complete copy of the NDS database on each server improves reliability and performance when authenticating objects, it can also create extra communication overhead time, especially when servers are connected over wide area networks. The extra communication time is caused by the need to synchronize any changes to NDS objects across all servers containing replicas of the NDS database. Novell has provided a way to reduce this overhead by partitioning the NDS database. An NDS **partition** is a division of the NDS database that allows a network administrator to replicate only a part of the entire NDS tree. Initially the Directory tree contains only one partition that starts at the root of the tree and is referred to as the **[Root] partition**. Additional partitions must start with a container and include all objects and subcontainers from that point down the tree. The start of an NDS partition is referred to as the **partition root**.

For example, in addition to installing the new server in Engineering, Universal Aerospace is planning to install another server in the Desktop Publishing department. Creating replicas of the entire Directory tree on all three servers would create extra communication overhead to maintain partition synchronization. As a result, the CNE has recommended making the Engineering container a separate partition from the [Root] partition. This would allow the Engineering partition objects to be replicated only on the Engineering and UAS_HOST servers. The Desktop Publishing server PUB_HOST could then contain only a Read/Write replica of the [Root] partition, as illustrated in Figure 2-24.

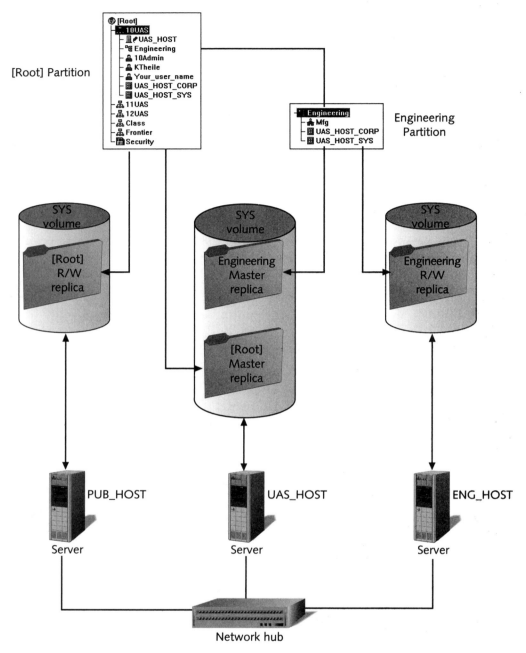

Figure 2-24   Partitioning NDS

Another use of partitioning is to move a container to another location in the Directory services tree. For example, if you wanted to move the Engineering container to place it under the Business container, you would first need to create a partition starting with the Engineering container. You would then be able to move the Engineering partition's container into the Business container by using the partition manager utility. After completing the move, you could merge the Engineering partition back with the Business division. In Chapter 4, you will learn how to use the NDS Manager utility to partition and move container objects.

 Generally, on smaller networks such as Universal Aerospace, which consist of less than five servers within the same local area network, partitioning of the NDS database is not necessary.

Working with Partitions and Replicas

The initial network system is looking good and Universal Aerospace's president, Dave Heise, is happy that you have started to set up workstations and users. At a recent meeting with Dave, you learned that rapid expansion of the Universal Aerospace company is likely, and you have been told to plan for additional servers in the Engineering and Desktop Publishing departments in the near future. Although the current size of the Universal Aerospace Directory tree does not require partitions, Novell recommends that it is best to create partitions prior to installing multiple servers into different containers of the Directory tree. To provide for the expected growth, you have decided create a separate partition for the Engineering container. To do this, you will have to use a special NetWare 5 utility called NDS Manager. You can use NDS Manager to view, create, move, or merge partitions. In this section, you will learn how to start NDS Manager, view current partitions, as well as create a new partition for the Engineering container.

Starting NDS Manager

As with NetWare Administrator, for your convenience you should create a shortcut that you can use to start the NDS Manager utility easily.

 In this hands-on activity, you create a shortcut in your Novell Program group that you can use to start NDS Manager.

1. If necessary, start your computer and log in using your assigned ##Admin username.

2. Open **My Computer** and browse to the Public\win32 folder on your **F** drive.

3. Right-click the **Start** button and click **Open**.

4. Double-click the **Programs** icon.

5. In the Public\Win32 window, scroll down until you find the Ndsmgr32 program.

6. Click the **Ndsmgr32** program and drag and drop it onto the Novell folder in the Program window. The NDS Manager program will now be available in the Novell Program group.

7. Close all open windows.

Viewing Partitions and Replicas

As mentioned earlier, the NDS Manager utility allows you to identify what partitions exist in the Directory tree as well as what servers the replicas of the partitions are stored on.

 In this hands-on activity, you use NDS Manager to identify partitions and what servers contain replicas of the partitions.

1. Click the **Start** button and trace to open the **Programs** menu.

2. Trace to the **Novell** option. The Ndsmgr32 option should now appear in the shortcut menu.

3. Launch NDS Manager by clicking the shortcut to **Ndsmgr32**. A window similar to the one shown in Figure 2-25 should be displayed

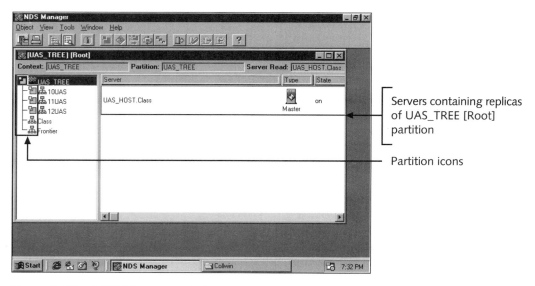

Figure 2-25   NDS Manager window

Notice the icons that appear as a square with a corner cut out to the left of the UAS_TREE and ##UAS containers in Figure 2-25. These icons indicate that the containers they are associated with are separate partitions. The first partition next to the UAS_TREE is the Directory tree [Root] partition. The [Root] partition is the first and the only required partition in the tree. Additional partitions have been created for each student's UAS Organization container. Notice that the [Root] partition contains the Class and Frontier Organizations.

The right-hand half of the NDS Manager window shows what servers contain replicas of the selected partition as well as the replica type and state. In Figure 2-25, the server UAS_HOST contains a Master replica of the highlighted UAS_TREE [Root] partition. If your classroom network contains multiple servers, you may find that the [Root] partition is also stored on other servers. The State column indicates the status of the replica on that server. You should not create or merge partitions if the State is not "on."

4. To view all replicas contained on the UAS_HOST server, double-click the **Class** container to expand it.

5. Click the **UAS_HOST** server to view all replicas in the right-hand Server window as shown in Figure 2-26. Notice that Master replicas of all ##UAS student partitions are stored on the UAS_HOST server.

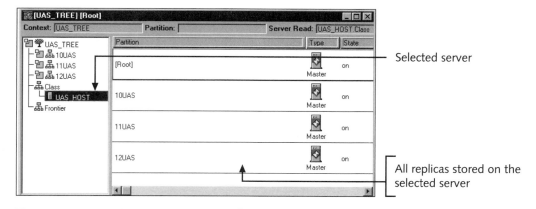

Figure 2-26   NDS Manager server replicas

Creating a Partition

As described earlier, Universal Aerospace is expecting rapid expansion in the Engineering department and is planning to add additional servers dedicated to Engineering and Desktop Publishing. To prepare the Directory tree for this expansion, you will make an additional partition for the Engineering Organizational Unit prior to installing additional servers in the tree.

 In this hands-on activity, you use NDS Manager to create a new partition for the Engineering department.

1. If necessary, log in to the network using your assigned ##Admin username and start NDS Manager.

2. Double-click your **##UAS** partition to display the Engineering Organizational Unit.

3. Right-click your **Engineering** Organizational Unit to display the shortcut menu.

4. Click the **Create Partition** option to display the Create Partition dialog box.

5. Click **Yes** to create a partition from your Engineering container. The system will now check system availability and rights to perform the operation.

6. When preconditions have been met, click **Yes** to continue with the operation of creating a new partition.

7. After a short time, the partition will be created and a partition icon will appear to the left of the Engineering container. Notice that the Master replica of the new Engineering partition has initially been placed on the UAS_HOST server.

8. Right-click your new **Engineering** partition to display the shortcut menu. Notice the Add Replica option. This option can be used in the future to place a Read/Write replica of this partition on another server.

9. Click the **Add Replica** option to display the Add Replica dialog box shown in Figure 2-27. You can use the Browse icon to the right of the Server name field to select a server on which to place the replica.

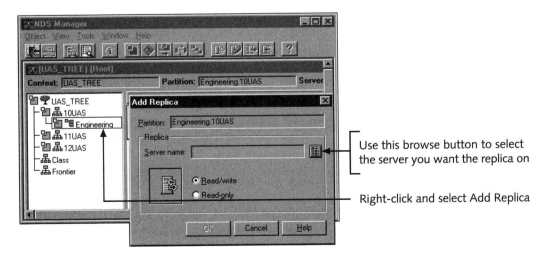

Figure 2-27   Add Replica dialog box

10. Click **Cancel** to return to the NDS Manager main window.

11. Exit NDS Manager and log off the network.

Dave is impressed with your progress on the network and that you have implemented a plan that allows for scalability. In Chapter 3, your next step will be to set up a file system that will allow users access to network data and applications.

CHAPTER SUMMARY

❑ Once the server has been installed, one of the next steps in implementing the network system is to install NetWare on client computers. To communicate on a NetWare network, a client computer must have a card driver program, a protocol stack, and a requester. Earlier clients such as NETX were limited to using only the IPX protocol; with NetWare 3, Novell introduced ODI drivers that allow clients to work with multiple protocols such as TCP/IP and IPX at the same time. Windows 95 brought a true 32-bit operating system with built-in network capability to desktop computers. Although the Microsoft NetWare client that ships with Windows 95/98 allows access to NetWare 5 networks, it does not take full advantage of NetWare capabilities. As a result, the new Novell Client for Windows 95/98 is important to take advantage of the 32-bit Windows environment along with NetWare features that enable you to add more capabilities to and improve the performance of NetWare clients. In this chapter, you learned about the basic components of the Novell Client along with how to install it from a NetWare server.

❑ One of the major capabilities of NetWare 5 is the implementation of the global Novell Directory Services (NDS) database, which allows NetWare 4 and NetWare 5 servers to share access to a common set of network objects that can be organized into a hierarchical tree structure. Allowing all NetWare servers to use the same global database of objects reduces the redundancy of objects that had to be maintained on NetWare 3.x networks, where each server maintained its own list of objects in a set of files called the bindery. NDS objects can be classified as either container objects or leaf objects. Container objects are used to organize other objects, and include the [Root], Country, Organization, and Organizational Unit. The [Root] object identifies the beginning of the entire tree and may contain either Country or Organization objects. Country objects are optional, but every NDS tree must have at least one Organization container. Organizational Unit containers are used to subdivide objects within an organization into divisions and departments. Organizational Unit objects can exist within other Organizational Unit objects, allowing complex tree structures. Leaf objects represent actual network entities, such as users, printers, groups, servers, and volumes. Each leaf object has several property fields that contain additional required as well as optional information or values about the object. Each type of leaf object has different properties based on its function. An important responsibility of a CNA is designing a workable NDS tree structure that provides secure and convenient access to network resources. Small networks can have a simple NDS tree structure consisting of all leaf objects within a single Organization container. Larger organizations will require more complex trees broken into multiple Organizational Units.

❑ The location of an object within the NDS tree is called its context. You can always uniquely identify an object by specifying its name along with its complete context path, called its distinguished name. A distinguished name can be either typeful or typeless. A typeful distinguished name includes the object type along with the name of the object. Object types include CN= for leaf objects, OU= for Organizational Unit containers, O= for Organization containers, and C= for Country containers. An example of a typeful distinguished name is CN=LJarka.OU=Engineering.O=UAS. A typeless name, such as .LJarka.Engineering.UAS, does not include the object type specification. Although not as specific as a typeful name, a typeless name is much easier to enter. The location of the client within the NDS tree is called the current context. You can use the current context to make access to objects easier by simply entering the objects' common name.

❑ NetWare 5 provides a graphical Windows-based utility called NetWare Administrator. NetWare Administrator plays an important role in implementing and maintaining a NetWare network and is a tool you will need to know how to use to pass the CNA exam. In this chapter, you learned how to use NetWare Administrator to browse an NDS tree structure and view information about specific objects as well as how to create leaf and Organizational Unit objects. You will continue to use NetWare Administrator throughout this book to implement the Universal Aerospace network system.

❑ Replicas are copies of the NDS database that are placed on NetWare servers. Replicas provide fault tolerance when a server is down as well as allow faster access to network resources by placing replicas on local servers. When a NDS database becomes large or is spread over several servers, a network administrator can increase performance by breaking the database into smaller segments called partitions. Replicas of partitions can be kept only on servers that need that data, thereby decreasing the amount of network traffic required to keep all servers synchronized.

COMMAND SUMMARY

Command	Syntax	Definition
CX	CX [*/T /A /CONT*]	Displays a view of the NDS tree structure.
	CX [**Context**]	Changes the client computer's context to the specified context.
LOGIN	LOGIN server/username	Allows access to a NetWare network.

KEY TERMS

Admin — A very important user object with supervisor rights to the entire NDS tree.

Alias object — An NDS object that is used to reference another object usually located in a different container.

Bindery — A separate set of files managed by each NetWare 3.x server to store information on network objects such as users and printers.

card driver — Software that controls the process of controlling the network adapter card.

communication protocol — Software responsible for formatting data within a network packet.

container object — An NDS object used to group other objects together.

context — location of an object in the NDS tree.

Country container object — A special type of container object that is used to group Organization container objects by country. Country containers must be assigned a valid two-digit country code and can exist only at the root of an NDS tree.

current context — The default location of the client computer within the NDS tree.

distinguished name — A name that uniquely identifies an object in the NDS database.

leaf object — An object that represents network entities such as users, groups, printers, and servers. Leaf objects must exist within Organization or Organizational Unit containers.

Lightweight Director Access Services (LDAP) — An industry standard method for applications to locate objects in an x.500-based directory system.

link support layer (LSL) — A network client software component that redirects an incoming packet to the proper protocol stack for processing.

Master replica — The controlling copy of an NDS partition stored on a NetWare server.

NETX client — An older DOS-based client that provided a shell through which earlier versions of DOS could access NetWare services.

Novell DirectoryServices (NDS) — A hierarchical global database of network objects and resources that is shared across a network by multiple servers and allows secure access to resources with a single login.

object — A network component composing the NDS database.

Open Data Interface (ODI) — A Novell specification that provides a standard LSL along with driver specifications.

Organization container object — An object that groups objects that belong to an organization. Organization objects may exist either at the root of an NDS tree or within a Country container.

Organizational Unit container object — An object that groups leaf objects that belong to a subdivision of an organization. Organizational Unit container objects may exist either within an Organization container or within another Organizational Unit.

partition — A division of the NDS structure that starts with a single container and includes any subcontainers.

property — A field containing information about an object. Not all object types have the same properties.

protocol stack — Same as communication protocol.

Read/Write replica — A copy of the Master replica partition that is stored on another NetWare server to provide better performance and fault tolerance if the server with the Master replica is unavailable.

relative name — An object name that starts with the current context of the client, omitting the leading period.

replica — A copy of the NDS database stored on a NetWare server.

requester — Software providing access to the network from the local operating system.

[Root] object — An NDS object representing the beginning of the network directory service tree.

typeful name — A distinguished name that includes object type abbreviations such as O=, OU=, and CN=.

typeless name — A distinguished name that assumes object type based on position rather than including the object type abbreviations.

VLM (Virtua lLoadable Module) client — Software shipped with NetWare 4.1 to provide support for multiple protocols as well as the ability to access objects in the NDS Directory tree.

volume object — An NDS leaf object that provides a connection to the physical data partitions located on a server's disk drives.

REVIEW QUESTIONS

1. NDS is based on an industry naming standard called ——————————
——————————————————————.

2. List two advantages of NDS as compared to NetWare 3.1x.

3. NDS objects consist of ———————————————————— and
————————————————.

4. List three types of container objects.

5. Identify each of the following objects as either Country, Organization, Organizational Unit, or leaf. For all leaf objects, include the type of leaf object (User, Group, Printer, Server, and so on).

   Accounting ————————————   ————————————

   NASA ————————————   ————————————

   Neil Armstrong ————————————   ————————————

   Spain ————————————   ————————————

   CTS_Host ————————————   ————————————

6. A(n) ———————————————————— is a field that can contain information about an object.

2

7. Which object types can be placed in the root of an NDS tree?

_____

_____

8. In which types of containers can leaf objects be placed?

_____

_____

9. List two advantages of replicas.

_____

_____

10. A(n) _____ is a division of the NDS database that starts at a container.

11. The location of an object within the NDS tree is referred to as its _____ .

12. Write a typeful distinguished name for the user JMeek who is located in the Sales Organizational Unit of the AstorFurs organization.

_____

13. Write a typeless relative name for the SAL_HP3 laser printer located in the MKTG department's Organizational Unit within the Western division of the Newfrontier organization. Assume your client's current context is the Western Organizational Unit.

_____

14. Using the structure described in Question 13, write a command to move the current context of the Western organizational unit of the Newfrontier organization up one level.

_____

15. Using the structure described in Question 13, write a command that would change the current context to the MKTG department container independently of your current context.

_____

16. Using the structure described in Question 13, write a command to log in as user JBridger located in the Sales department of the Western division without changing your current context from the [Root].

_____

17. Write the commands necessary to list all objects in the Newfrontier organization.

_____

18. List the four types of replicas.

_____

_____

_____

_____

19. You can right-click _____ and select Properties to view client configuration information.

20. Match each of the following ODI software programs to its function:

LSL.COM	a. The NetWare protocol stack.
SMC8000.COM	b. The DOS requester.
IPXODI.COM	c. The card driver.
VLM.EXE	d. Provides support for multiple protocol stacks on the same card.

The Universal Aerospace Project

Step 1: Create the Business Organizational Unit

Now that the structure for the Engineering department has been completed, your next task is to set up the Business Organizational Unit. Begin by creating a Business container in your assigned ##UAS Organization and then create volume objects for UAS_HOST_SYS and UAS_HOST_CORP in the Business container.

Step 2: Create User Accounts

Dave Heise, the president of Universal Aerospace, is anxious to try the new network for himself. To allow him to experiment with the network, create a username for Dave and his secretary, Lynn Dai, within the Business Organizational Unit. Also create home directories for Dave and Lynn in your ##CORP folder.

Step 3: Create a Publishing Partition

Assume you wish to run some tests for the Desktop Publishing department using a separate partition. In this exercise, you are to follow the steps below to create a container for Desktop Publishing, place a server alias in the container, and then make the container a separate partition. After testing the partition, you will need to clean up the structure by deleting the Desktop Publishing container and all its objects.

1. Create a container named Publish within the Business container.

2. Within the Publish container, create an Alias object named Pub_Host and point it to the UAS_HOST server.

3. Create a SYS volume object in the Publish container that points to the SYS volume on the UAS_Host server. Record the name of the NetWare server used:
   UAS_Host.Class

4. Create user accounts for Diana Brady and Bradley Dahl within Publish. Do not create home directories for Diana or Bradley.

5. Click the Print button to print your new container contents.

6. Use NDS Manager to make Publish a separate partition.

7. Print the screen showing your Publish partition. Record the distinguished name of the server containing the Master replica of the Publish partition:

8. Record the steps necessary to place a Read/Write replica on your Pub_Host server. Note that the system will not allow you to actually place a replica on Pub_Host since it is only an Alias object.

9. Try to delete the Publish container with NetWare Administrator. Record your results:

10. Use NDS Manager to delete the Publish container. Record your results:

11. Use NDS Manager to merge Publish back into the [Root] partition.

12. Try to delete Publish using NetWare Administrator. Record your results:

13. Use NetWare Administrator to remove all objects from Publish and then delete the Publish container.

Additional Exercises

The following exercises are not necessary to complete future Universal Aerospace network projects. They are included to give you more practice working with NetWare and utilities, to help you pass your CNA exam and become a more competent network administrator.

Exercise 2-1: Designing an NDS Tree

While coming up with a design for the Universal Aerospace NDS tree structure, the consultant has asked you to experiment with a design that would place the Sales department users in a separate Organizational Unit. This Organizational Unit could be located either within the Business Organizational Unit or as a separate container under the organization ##UAS. Your management (that is, your instructor) will identify which structure you should design or whether you should design both structures. In addition to designing the structure, include any benefits that you see in the new structure as compared to the one presented in this chapter.

Exercise 2-2: Exploring an NDS Tree Structure

In this project, you gain hands-on experience with NDS naming by using the CX command to view and change your context in an existing NDS tree structure.

1. Start your computer but do not log in. If you are already logged in, click the **Start** button and log out.

2. Open a DOS window and change to drive F.

3. Use the appropriate CX command to print out a copy of the complete NDS tree structure. Highlight your ##Admin username and your ##UAS container (replace ## with your assigned student number). On the following line, record the command you use:

   _____

4. Change the current context of your workstation to the organization ##UAS (replace ## with your assigned student number). Record the command you use on the following line:

   _____

5. Log in using your assigned ##Admin username (replace ## with your assigned student number).

6. Use the appropriate commands to change to the root of the NDS tree and then enter the **NLIST USERS /S /A** command to list all active users throughout the tree. Record the commands you use on the following lines:

   _____

   _____

7. Use the appropriate commands to change to the Frontier container and then use the **NLIST PRINTERS /S** command to list all printers in the entire Frontier organization and its Organizational Units. On the following spaces, record the commands you use along with the printer names:

   Commands used:

   _____

   _____

   Printer names:

   _____

   _____

   _____

8. Use a CX command with a typeless distinguished name to change your current context to your ##UAS container. Record the command you use on the following line:

   _____

9. Use a CX command with a typeful distinguished name to change to the Moon division of the Frontier organization and then use the **NLIST /S** command to list all users in the division. In the following space, record the command you use:

_____

_____

10. Use a relative context along with the CX command to change to the Shuttle division. Record the command you use on the following line:

_____

11. Use the appropriate options of the CX command to list all objects in only the current container. Record the command you use on the following line:

_____

12. Use a typeful distinguished context to change to the Satellites department of the Unmanned division. Record the command you use in the following space:

_____

13. Use a typeless relative context to change your current context to the Planets department of the Unmanned division. Record the command you use on the following line:

_____

14. Without changing your current context, use the appropriate CX command to display all objects in the Moon container of the Frontier Organization. Record the command you use along with the usernames in the following space:

_____

15. Log out of the network.

Exercise 2-3: Working with NetWare Administrator

In this exercise, you need to run the NetWare Administrator program to perform the operations described.

1. If you have not already done so, start your client computer, and log in to the network using your assigned ##Admin username.

2. Start NetWare Administrator.

3. Open a browse window for the Frontier organization.

4. Use NetWare Administrator to determine the flight for each astronaut in the Moon.Frontier division. Record each astronaut's distinguished name and his or her flight description on the following lines:

_____   _____

_____   _____

_____   _____

_____   _____

_____   _____

_____   _____

5. Determine the type of printer used in the Moon division. Record the printer type on the following line:

_____

6. Use NetWare Administrator to determine which users in the Frontier organization are scientists. Record the distinguished names on the following lines:

   _____

   _____

   _____

7. On the following line, write the description for the user NArmstrong:

   _____

8. On the following line, record the description of the Moon Organizational Unit:

   _____

9. On the following lines, record the name of the Frontier print server along with the distinguished name of each printer it controls:

   Print server name: _____

   Printers: _____

                        _____

                        _____

10. Exit NetWare Administrator.

11. Exit Windows and log out.

3

DESIGNING THE FILE SYSTEM

After reading this chapter and completing the exercises, you will be able to:

♦ Describe the components of the NetWare file system

♦ Describe the purpose of each NetWare-created directory and Novell-suggested directories

♦ Apply directory design concepts to developing and documenting a directory structure for Universal Aerospace

♦ Use NetWare Administrator to work with files and directories in the NetWare file system

♦ Describe drive pointer types and their purpose

♦ Use Windows along with the MAP command to establish network drive pointers

---

Now that the server and clients are installed and tested, the engineers at Universal Aerospace are anxious to begin using the network to store their data. However, prior to creating additional user accounts, you will need to organize the network file system to designate areas for user home directories, applications, and shared data. Designing a network file system that will meet the special needs of an organization such as Universal Aerospace is an important step that a CNA needs to perform in setting up a network system. In this chapter, you will learn the components of the NetWare file system as well as how to design a network file system that will facilitate the workflow of the people who use the network.

The NetWare file system provides many benefits for making information available on a network. These benefits can be classified into the following five categories:

- *Centralized management of data and backups.* When data is stored on a server, many users can have access to centralized database files that contain current and accurate information. In addition, centralizing data allows important files to be backed up at regular intervals and provides a recovery process in the event of lost data or a downed file server.

- *Improved security.* This benefit prevents users from modifying or accessing data that they are not responsible for maintaining.

- *Improved reliability and fault tolerance.* NetWare's disk mirroring and duplexing features can be used to ensure that duplicate copies of data are automatically available for users in the event of hardware failure.

- *Shared and private storage areas.* This feature facilitates the creation of workgroups by allowing users to share files or transfer a file to another user without having to carry disks between machines. Private storage areas allow individuals to save their own work in a secure area of the file server.

- *Access to data by many different operating system platforms.* NetWare supports Apple, UNIX, Windows 95, and OS/2 file structures, in addition to DOS. This support for multiple file formats saves money by avoiding the need for different servers to support each operating system. Additionally, there are situations where it is necessary to pass files between different operating system environments. The NetWare file system can allow compatible applications running on DOS and Apple Macintosh—for example, Microsoft Word—to share data files. As networks grow, it becomes ever more important for a CNA to know how to integrate different operating systems' file formats in the file system efficiently.

FILE SYSTEM COMPONENTS

Because the file system is used to organize and secure the information stored on the network, a good design is necessary to facilitate the setup, use, and growth of your network. On a NetWare network, the main components of the file system are volumes, directories or subdirectories, and files, as shown in Figure 3-1.

3

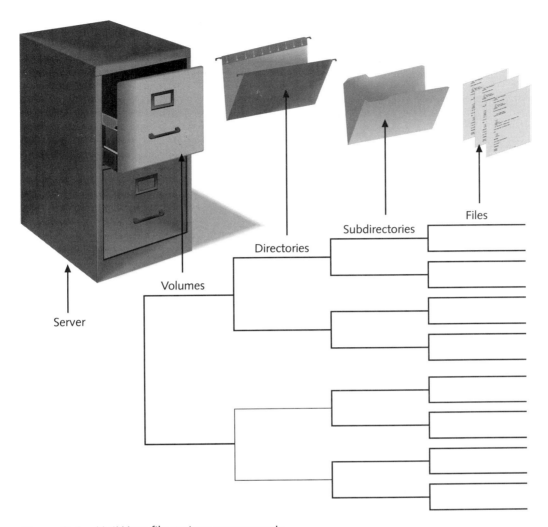

Figure 3-1   NetWare file system components

Volumes

In Chapter 1, you learned that **volumes** are used to organize the NetWare server disk space to store programs and files for access by network users. With NetWare 5, Novell has improved the network file system by developing Novell Storage Services (NSS). NSS improves on the previous file system by providing additional capacity and high-speed mounting of data volumes. The previous file system supported up to 64 volumes per server and 16 million files per volume. By contrast, NSS supports a virtually unlimited number of volumes per server and files per volume. One of the most important improvements that network administrators will notice is how fast NSS volumes can be mounted on the server. In the past, mounting a volume involved loading the File Allocation Table (FAT) into the server's memory. On large volumes, this could take several minutes and require megabytes of RAM. For example, using the previous file system, a 10 GB volume would take 160 MB of RAM to mount. Instead of using a large FAT, NSS uses a more memory-efficient system called **balanced trees** or **B-trees**. Using B-trees, NSS can mount large volumes consisting of over 400 million files in just three seconds and require a maximum of 32 MB of RAM. In addition, using the B-tree system, NetWare can retrieve any file blocks that are not in memory in just four processor cycles, making NSS much faster than the previous file system versions. In Chapter 10, you will learn more about NSS, including its ability to recover from volume errors. Figure 3-2 illustrates how a server's disk space may be allocated to volumes in the following three ways:

- One volume per disk drive
- Multiple volumes per disk drive
- One volume spanning multiple drives

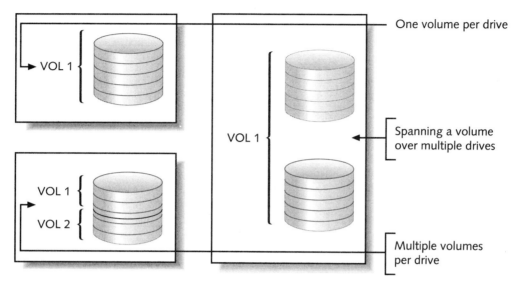

Figure 3-2   Volume disk space options

Data is stored on NetWare volumes in units called blocks. A **block** is the amount of data that is written to or read from the volume at one time. Block size is determined when a volume is created, and can range from 4 KB to 64 KB. Larger block sizes can speed up disk access by being able to read or write large files with fewer disk requests. As a result, larger block sizes are important for volumes that contain large files such as those used in desktop publishing or other graphical presentation applications.

In versions of NetWare before 4.1, each block in a volume could be assigned to only one file. This resulted in small files wasting disk space on volumes with large block sizes. For example, if you stored a 1 KB file on a volume with 16 KB block size, 15 KB of disk space would be wasted. The problem of small files wasting disk space was solved in NetWare 4 and NetWare 5 by a process called suballocation. **Suballocation** allows data from multiple files to be stored in the same block by dividing the block into 512-byte suballocation units. When using suballocation, a file must always start at the beginning of a block; other files can then use the space remaining in the block as necessary. Figure 3-3 illustrates using suballocation to store three files on the CORP volume. File1 requires 2.5 KB and occupies the first five suballocation units in block 1. File2 is 1.5 KB in size and occupies the first three suballocation units in block 2. File3 requires 7 KB and uses all of block 3 along with three suballocation units in block 1 and three suballocation units in block 2.

 Currently NSS cannot be used for the server's SYS volume. In addition, NSS does not support file compression or suballocation.

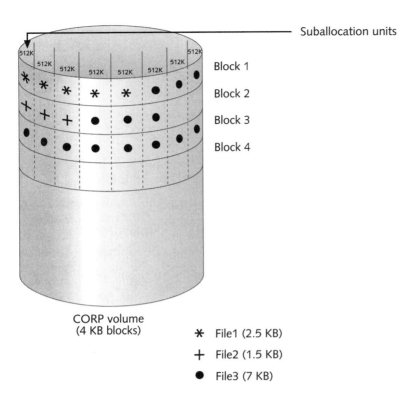

Figure 3-3   Block suballocation

In addition to suballocation, another feature introduced in NetWare 4.1 volumes is **file compression**. When file compression is enabled on a volume, the server automatically compresses all files that have not been used for a specified time period. By default, the system compresses files that have not been used for seven days provided there is at least a 5% savings in disk space. In Chapter 5, you will learn how you can selectively enable or disable compression on individual files and directories.

Each NetWare server is required to have at least one volume named SYS. During installation, NetWare creates and stores its operating system files and utility programs in directories it creates on the SYS volume. In addition to the NetWare operating system files and documentation, print queues are major users of disk space on the SYS volume. Unless you specify otherwise, by default NetWare stores print queues on the SYS volume when they are created. Therefore, when planning space for the SYS volume, it is important to include adequate space for print queue usage. To avoid filling up the SYS volume and causing system problems, you should generally plan to reserve at least 10 MB of disk space for each print queue on a volume. More space may be necessary for a print queue if it is used by multiple computers for large graphics printouts.

 Sometimes you'll see volume names such as SYS followed by a colon (SYS:). Technically, a colon after the volume name is necessary only when it is entered in a DOS path. On the server, the volume name is entered without the colon. When using the Microsoft Universal Naming Convention (UNC), you specify a network path using the server name and volume name separated by a backslash. For example, you would specify the Public directory on the SYS volume as \\UAS_HOST\SYS\Public.

If you do run low on space on a volume, you can increase the volume's size by adding another disk drive to the system and then using space available on the new drive to expand the existing volume; this process is called **spanning** a volume. When a volume spans more than one disk drive, you should be sure to mirror the disk drives, since a disk error on either drive would make the entire volume unavailable. As described in Chapter 1, mirroring synchronizes the data on two disk drives so that an error on one drive will not prevent access to the volume's data.

Including the SYS volume, you can define up to 64 volumes on one NetWare server. The rules for naming volumes are:

- The name must be two to fifteen characters long.

- Spaces, commas, backslashes, and periods are not legal characters.

- Each physical volume on a server must have a unique name.

- The volume name is followed by a colon when specified as part of a path.

- When specifying the physical name of a volume on a server, you must use a backslash or forward slash to separate the NetWare server name from the volume name.

Many network administrators prefer to use at least two volumes in the file structure of their network. When using multiple volumes, a network administrator will usually reserve the SYS volume on each server for operating system files and possibly certain general-purpose application software, such as spreadsheets and word processors. In addition to the SYS volume, one or more volumes are defined to store the organization's data files, print queues, and applications. Placing the organization's data files and special applications on separate volumes allows the administrator to ensure that free space is always available on the SYS volume for NetWare's use. As a network administrator, you may wish to use the following guidelines suggested by Novell for planning NetWare volume usage:

- Reserve the SYS volume for NetWare operating system files.

- Create one or more additional volumes for application and data files.

- Consider placing files from workstations that support long filenames, such as Macintosh, OS/2, or Windows 95/98, on a separate volume.

- If fault tolerance is more important than performance, create one volume per disk drive.

- If performance is more important than fault tolerance, span NetWare volumes over multiple disk drives.

- If both performance and fault tolerance are required, span volumes over duplexed disk drives.

Viewing Volume Information

Each physical NetWare volume is represented by a volume object in the NDS (Novell Directory Services) system. Volume objects play an important role in NDS by providing a link between NDS and the network file system. As a result, before you can use NetWare Administrator to access the network file system, you need to have an NDS object for each physical network volume. During NetWare 5.0 installation, NDS volume objects are created and placed in the same NDS container as the NetWare server. By default, the volume object is given an object name consisting of the server's name, an underscore character, and the volume's name. For example, the default volume object name for the SYS volume on server UAS_HOST would be UAS_HOST_SYS.

As a network administrator, it is often important to know how much space on a volume has been used so that you can make decisions regarding the location of new network directories, or to plan for system expansion. You can view information about NetWare volumes by using server console commands (as described in Chapter 10), DOS command-line utilities, or the Windows-based NetWare Administrator. In the following sections, you will learn how to view information about volumes on your network by using both DOS command-line utilities and NetWare Administrator.

Using NLIST to View NDS Volume Information

As described earlier, each NetWare volume is represented by a volume object in the NDS database. In Chapter 1, you learned how to use the NLIST command to view information on NDS objects, such as users, printers, and servers.

stored in directories off a NetWare volume or on the local client hard drives. Special purpose packages, such as Payroll, are restricted to just certain users or departments, and many times contain their own data directories and files that may become very large. As a result, these special-purpose packages are often stored on a separate data volume.

Another type of application software directory is used to hold installation files. For example, in Chapter 2, you learned that Windows 98 and the Novell client may be installed from a network drive rather than from CD-ROM. In addition, other software packages such as Microsoft Office or Lotus Notes also provide the option of installing the software from a network drive. Using the network installation option requires the network administrator to establish a directory on the network file system to contain the original software. Installing software from a network drive can save time and provide the administrator with automatic setup scripts that help to standardize the software environment.

User Home Directories   Each user will need a **home directory** for storing his or her own files and documents. When planning your disk storage needs, you should allow space for each user to store personal projects and files with which they work. Generally, other users are not given access to files in a home directory; instead, files that are needed by multiple users should be stored in separate, shared directory areas.

Shared Directories   One of the benefits of using a network is access to shared files. As a CNA, you will need to establish **shared directories**, where multiple users can work with common files and documents. Files stored in the shared directory areas are generally available to only one user at a time. Having one file accessed by multiple users at the same time requires special software to prevent one user's changes from overwriting the changes made by another.

DOS Directories   If you have a network that supports DOS-based clients, you may want to store the DOS command files for these clients on the server rather than on the local computers. Storing DOS command files on the server ensures that all workstations have access to the DOS commands and protects the commands from erasure or corruption by viruses Because your network may have workstations that are running different versions of DOS, it might be necessary to create a separate subdirectory for each DOS version. DOS commands for Windows 95/98 are stored in the WINDOWS\COMMAND directory of the C drive. Although it is possible to place these files on the server, the benefit is not worth the extra complexity. The DOS structure, shown in Figure 3-7, provides for different machine types and DOS environments prior to Windows 95/98.

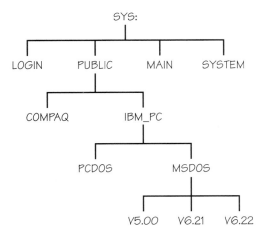

Figure 3-7   Recommended DOS directory structure

For example, you may have Compaq machines on your network along with other IBM machines and compatibles. The Compaq machines use a special version of DOS from the Compaq company, the IBM machines use PC DOS, and the compatibles use MS-DOS version 6.2. When a user logs in to the network, you can use a login script command to map the workstation to the correct version of DOS it is using.

 Although Windows 95 and Windows 98 use version 7.0 of DOS to manage DOS applications and provide the DOS prompt window, you gain little by placing a version 7.0 directory on the server, as most Windows 95/98 workstations have the operating system files on their local disk drives.

ESTABLISHING THE UNIVERSAL AEROSPACE DIRECTORY STRUCTURE

Now that you know the components used in a network file system, the next step is to design and implement a directory structure that will meet the file processing needs of the Universal Aerospace Corporation. Designing the directory structure involves identifying the directories and subdirectories you will need, along with deciding where to place these directories in the structure. Implementing the directory structure will involve using such utilities such as NetWare Administrator to create and manage the directories and files. Before you can begin this process, you need to analyze the processing needs of the users in the organization to determine what directories will be needed. Once you have defined the directories, you can design a directory structure in a logical and organized fashion.

When designing a directory structure, you should be aware that there is not one best method with which all network administrators agree; instead, each network administrator develops an individual style and preferences for arranging and defining directories. In this section, you learn how the consultant applied the concepts of file system design to UAS, as well as how to implement the design by using NetWare Administrator.

Defining Processing Needs

In many ways, designing a directory structure is similar to creating a blueprint for a building. Just as the blueprint allows the builder to determine the construction details and materials needed, the directory structure design allows the network administrator to allocate storage space and implement the file system on a network.

The first step in designing a directory structure is to determine the storage requirements for the file services that the server will provide to your users. To do this, the consultant, Jennifer Almquest, has summarized the processing needs for Universal Aerospace, as described in Figure 3-8.

Generally, storage areas or directories may be divided into five different types: system, software package, application, shared data, and private data. Table 3-1 contains the Storage Requirements Form used by Jennifer to document the storage areas needed to support processing for the Engineering and Manufacturing departments at Universal Aerospace.

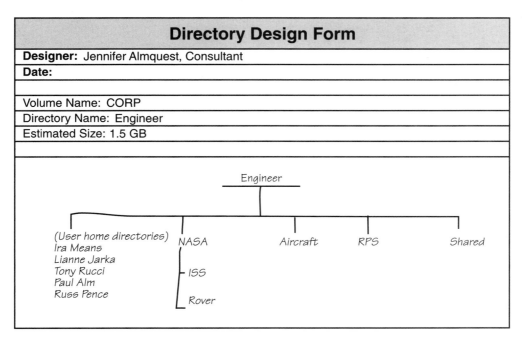

Figure 3-11   Engineer Directory Design form

The directory structure recommended by Jennifer is referred to as a departmental structure because the user home directories, shared work directories, and applications are located within the workgroups of the departments that control them. Directories that contain files available to all users, such as the Forms and Inventry directories, are located at the root of the volume. Shared directories are located within each department's directory to provide separate shared file access for all users in the department. The Shared directory located off the root of the CORP volume is available so that users in all departments can exchange files or work on common projects. For example, the Engineering department can use the CORP:Shared directory to save drawing files that will be needed by the Desktop Publishing and Sales people in preparing documentation and presentations.

Directory names have been limited to eight or fewer characters, in order to comply with DOS/Windows 3.x naming conventions. Thus the directory for inventory is named Inventry.

An alternative way to organize directories on a volume is by application rather than department. Figure 3-12 shows an example of how the directories for Universal Aerospace might be organized in an application-oriented structure.

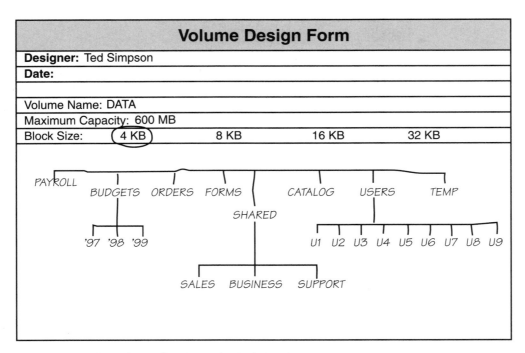

Figure 3-12   Sample application-oriented structure

Notice that in an application-oriented structure, all user home directories are placed under a common directory called USERS. The shared directories can then be grouped according to their use, and applications can be placed in separate directories located on the root of the volume. The advantage of an application-oriented structure is that it is fairly shallow, making it easier to locate files without going through multiple layers of directories. In larger directory structures, the shallow nature of the application-oriented structure can actually be a disadvantage, making it difficult to know which directories are used by which departments. When using an application-oriented structure, the network administrator will need to make more trustee assignments because a user's rights will not automatically flow into the other directories.

The organization method selected by a network administrator depends upon personal preference, as well as the size and type of processing performed by the organization. Generally, smaller network file systems are easier to organize using an application-oriented structure, as it keeps the design simple and the system easy to use. With larger file systems, where there are multiple workgroups and many data directories, it is often easier to maintain security and locate data when you use a departmental structure. In some cases, you may find that a combination of both methods will work the best for your situation. No matter what design method you use, a good rule of thumb is not to exceed six subdirectory layers with no more than 20 subdirectories in any one directory (this makes it easier for you to view all directories on the screen at the same time).

Implementing the Directory Structure

Once the directory structure has been defined, the next step in establishing the network file system involves creating the necessary directories and subdirectories on their associated volumes. NetWare volumes may be created either during or after the process of installing NetWare on the server computer. When the NetWare server for the Universal Aerospace company was installed (as described in Appendix A), two 9 GB SCSI drives were duplexed on separate controllers, and then two separate volumes were created: a 500 MB SYS volume and an 8 GB CORP volume. After creating the CORP volume, about 500 MB of disk space were left unassigned. Having free disk space allows the flexibility of assigning more space to either the CORP or SYS volume as necessary in the future.

Since running out of free space on the SYS volume can affect the operation of the NetWare 5 server, possibly resulting in loss of data and services, you should always leave approximately 100 MB of disk space unassigned. NetWare provides a warning feature that will display a "SYS volume low" message on the server console, as well as broadcast the message to all clients, should the capacity of the SYS volume fall below a predefined value. By leaving some open space on the NetWare partition, you can quickly add capacity to the SYS volume while the server is still operating, thereby averting possible server problems.

You can create the network directory structure from Windows using either My Computer or Windows Explorer, or from the DOS prompt using the MD (Make Directory) command, just as on a local hard drive. In addition to using Windows or DOS commands, you can also use Novell's NetWare Administrator utility to create or work with the network directory structure. When working with NetWare Administrator, it is often more convenient to use it to perform network file system activities rather than flipping to another screen or utility. As a result, Novell requires CNAs to know how to perform file system functions from NetWare Administrator. In this section, you learn how to use the NetWare Administrator utility to create the Universal Aerospace directory structure shown in Figures 3-10 and 3-11, and then limit the amount of disk space a directory should occupy as specified on the Directory Design form.

Creating Directories with NetWare Administrator

As you learned previously in this chapter, after an NDS volume object has been created, you can access the physical volume's directories and files from NetWare Administrator by selecting the volume object from the NDS database. Once you select the NDS volume object, you can use NetWare Administrator to manage the network file system, performing any necessary file operations without leaving the NetWare Administrator utility.

Although you can create directories from the DOS prompt or by using My Computer or Explorer in Windows, it is often convenient to work with the directory structure directly from NetWare Administrator.

 In this hands-on activity, you use NetWare Administrator to build and work with the Engineering directory structure shown previously in Figures 3-10 and 3-11.

1. If necessary, start your computer and log in using your assigned ##Admin username.

2. Start NetWare Administrator by double-clicking its desktop shortcut.

3. Open a browser window for your ##UAS Organization container.

4. Open your **UAS_HOST_CORP** volume by double-clicking its object name.

5. Open your **##CORP** directory by double-clicking its folder. Your browser window should now appear similar to the one shown in Figure 3-13.

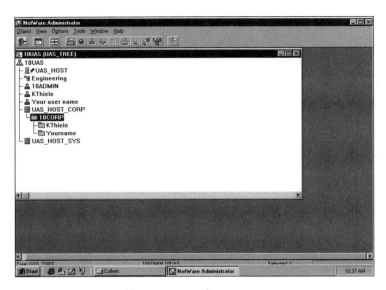

Figure 3-13   Initial browser window

6. To open another browser window for your ##CORP directory and tile the windows, follow these steps:

   a) Highlight your **##CORP** directory.

   b) Click **Tools, NDS Browser**.

   c) Click **OK** to open the new window.

   d) Click **Window, Tile**.

7. To create the main directories shown in Figure 3-10, follow these steps:

   a) Click your **##CORP** directory to highlight it.

   b) Press **[Ins]** and enter the name **IS** in the Directory name field.

   c) Click the **Create** button. The IS directory should now appear in the browser window.

   d) Repeat Steps 7a and 7b to create the remaining main directories shown in Figure 3-10. (Hint: Click the **Create another Directory** option to speed up the process.)

8. To create the Win98, CAD, Office, and Utility subdirectories of the Apps directory, and the Web subdirectory of the IS directory, follow these steps:

   a) Click the **Apps** directory to highlight it.

   b) Press **[Ins]** and enter **Win98** in the Directory name field.

   c) Click the **Create** button.

   d) Double-click **Apps** to display the Win98 subdirectory.

   e) Repeat Steps 8a through 8c to create the CAD, Office, and Utility subdirectories.

   f) Click the **IS** directory to highlight it.

   g) Press **[Ins]** and enter **Web** in the Directory name field.

   h) Click the **Create** button.

3

9. To create the subdirectory structure for the Engineer directory as shown in Figure 3-11, follow these steps:

 a) Click the **Engineer** directory to highlight it.

 b) Press **[Ins]** and enter the directory name **NASA** in the Directory name field.

 c) Click the **Create** button.

 d) Double-click the **Engineer** directory to display the NASA subdirectory.

 e) Repeat the preceding steps to create the Aircraft, RPS, and Shared subdirectories.

10. To create the NASA project subdirectories, follow these steps:

 a) Click the **NASA** subdirectory to highlight it.

 b) Press **[Ins]** and enter **ISS** in the Directory name field.

 c) Click the **Create** button.

 d) Press **[Ins]** and enter **Rover** in the Directory name field.

 e) Click the **Create** button.

 f) Double-click your **NASA** directory to display the new subdirectories.

11. Your browser window should now appear similar to the one shown in Figure 3-14.

Figure 3-14 Completed UAS window

Setting Directory Space Limitations

During her analysis, Jennifer determined a starting directory size for each of the directories as shown on the Directory Design form. To be sure no one directory structure grows at the expense of other directory needs, it will be important to utilize NetWare's capability to limit directory sizes. With NetWare, you can place limitations on the amount of volume space a directory and all its files can occupy. You can set directory space limitations using NetWare Administrator.

In this hands-on activity, you learn how to use NetWare Administrator to place the recommended size limits on each of the main directories you have created.

1. If necessary, start your computer and log in using your assigned ##Admin username.

2. Start NetWare Administrator and open a browser window for your ##CORP directory as described in the previous activity.

3. Right-click the **Forms** directory to display the shortcut menu.

4. Click the **Details** option to display information about the Forms directory.

5. Click the **Facts** button to display the window shown in Figure 3-15.

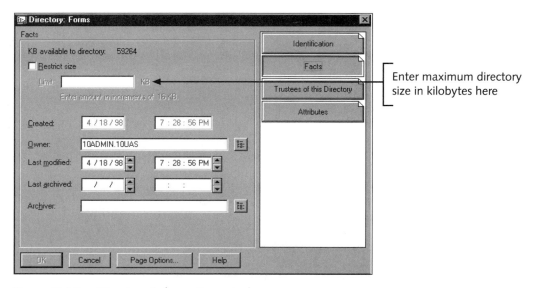

Figure 3-15   Directory information window

6. Click the **Restrict size** box and enter **50000** in the Limit _____KB field.

7. Click **OK** to save your directory restriction.

8. Repeat the preceding steps to set directory size restrictions, using the values in the capacity column, for each of the directories included in Table 3-1.

9. Close your ##CORP browser window.

10. Exit NetWare Administrator.

WORKING WITH NETWORK FILES

Now that you have established a directory structure for the Universal Aerospace CORP volume, your next job is to place some data in the structure so users can begin to use the system. In addition to using NetWare Administrator when working with volumes and directories, you can also use it to view and manage file information. Files are used to store data in the network file system in much the same way as they are used to store data and software on your local disk drives. Properly planning the location of files on network volumes is an important part of organizing the file system. Although it is possible for files to exist on the root of a volume, storing files within directories and subdirectories provides for better organization, as well as increased file system security, as described in Chapter 5.

NetWare stores information about each file in the directory entry table (DET) located at the beginning of each volume. In addition to the file's name and storage location, NetWare includes such information as owner, size, creation dates, access dates, and attributes in the DET. As a CNA, you will need to know the importance of this information, as well as how to display file information using the NDIR command.

3

By default, the file owner is the user who creates the file. By keeping track of file owner and size information, NetWare enables the network administrator to limit disk space usage by the user. Creation and access date information is important in that it allows a network administrator to perform such functions as listing files that have not been accessed for a specified time period. File attributes allow the administrator to control what actions the user can perform on a file. For example, placing the read-only attribute on a file prevents users from modifying its contents. (You will learn about file attributes along with file system security in Chapter 5.)

As a CNA, you should know how to use the NDIR command along with NetWare Administrator to access information about files, as well as how to salvage files if they are accidentally deleted. The following hands-on activities give you practice copying files and viewing file information as well as salvaging deleted files.

Copying Files

In the hands-on activities in this section, you will get practice copying files using NetWare Administrator, Windows 98, and the Novell NCOPY command.

Copying Files with NetWare Administrator

Ira Means, the Engineering department secretary, has requested that you make the standard company forms available on the new network as soon as possible.

 In this hands-on activity, you will use NetWare Administrator to copy the company forms from the SYS volume to the new Forms directory you created.   .

1. If necessary, start your computer and log in using your assigned ##Admin username.

2. Start NetWare Administrator and open your ##UAS Organization.

3. To open a browser window for the SYS volume, follow these steps:

    a) Click your **UAS_HOST_SYS** volume object to highlight it.

    b) Click **Tools, NDS browser**.

    c) Click **OK** to open the SYS volume browser window.

    d) Click **Window, Tile** to tile the windows.

4. Open the WP subdirectory of the SOFTWARE.CTI directory as follows:

    a) Double-click the **SOFTWARE.CTI** directory.

    b) Double-click the **WP** subdirectory to display all the .FRM files.

5. Right-click the **BID.FRM** file and then click the **Details** option.

6. Click the **Facts** button to display file size, owner, and access date information. Notice that the information fields on your screen are grayed out, indicating that you cannot change them. This is because you do not have Supervisory rights to the files in the SYS volume. You will learn more about file system access rights in Chapter 5.

7. Click the **Cancel** button to return to the browser window.

8. Hold down **[Ctrl]** while you click each file that has the .FRM extension.

9. Double-click your **UAS_HOST_CORP** volume and double-click your **##CORP** directory to open it. Your screen should now look similar to the one shown in Figure 3-16.

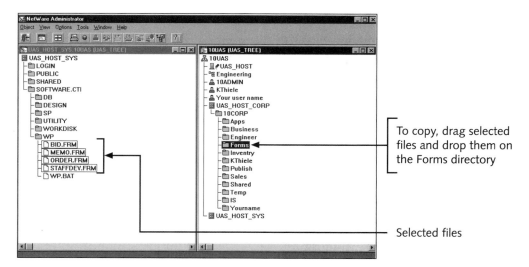

Figure 3-16   Selected files window

10. Click and drag the files from the WP directory on the left side of the screen and drop them on your Forms directory located on the right side of the screen. A Move/Copy window that shows the files you have selected will be displayed.

11. Click **OK** to copy the files to the destination shown at the bottom of the window.

12. Double-click your **Forms** directory to display the copied files.

13. Right-click the **BID.FRM** file in your **Forms** directory and click the **Details** option.

14. Click the **Facts** button to display file information. Notice that because you are now the administrator of the file, you can change file information, such as owner and access date.

 Being able to change owner information can be important if a user creates a large shared file and you do not want the space used by the file to be accumulated against that user's total disk space.

15. Click the **Cancel** button to return to the browser window.

16. Minimize NetWare Administrator.

Copying Network Files Using Windows 95/98

Recently, the Engineering department received a new workstation, and you have been asked to install the CAD software on it as soon as possible. In addition, management is anxious to see how the CAD software will run off the server.

 In this hands-on activity, you will simulate the process of using Windows to place the CAD software on the server.

1. If necessary, start your computer and log in using your assigned ##Admin username.

2. Double-click **My Computer** to show all your drives.

3. Double-click **C:** drive and open the **Program Files** folder.

3

4. Double-click the **Accessories** folder to open it and then verify that all files and extensions are shown as follows:

   a) Click **Options** from the View menu.

   b) Click the **View** tab.

   c) Remove the check from the **Hide MS-DOS file extensions for file types that are registered** check box.

   d) Under Hidden files, click **Show all files**.

   e) Click **OK** to save the changes.

5. Hold down **[Ctrl]** while you click each of the following files:

   Mspaint.exe, mspcx32.dll, pcximp32.flt

6. Click **Edit**, **Copy**.

7. Close all windows.

8. Double-click **Network Neighborhood**, and browse to your Apps\CAD folder (double-click the **UAS_HOST** server, double-click the **CORP** volume, then double-click your **##CORP** directory, double-click your **Apps** directory, then double-click your **CAD** subdirectory). (If you have a drive mapped to the CORP volume, you could also use My Computer to browse to your Apps\CAD folder.)

9. Click **Edit**, **Paste** to copy the selected files to your CAD directory.

10. Close all browser windows.

Copying Network Files Using the NCOPY Command

Being an effective network administrator often requires using some magic wands we call network utilities. As network administrator for Universal Aerospace, you will want to have your tools easily available by copying them to the network. Although copying files with Windows and Windows utilities is often easier and more intuitive, the NCOPY command-line utility can be faster to use and is available from computers running DOS. One of the advantages of the NCOPY command over the DOS COPY or XCOPY commands is that it can work with server and volume names. The COPY and XCOPY commands require that you assign drive letters to each volume.

In this hands-on activity, you learn how to use the NCOPY command to copy some programs from the SYS volume to your Utility directory.

1. If necessary, start your computer and log in using your assigned ##Admin username.

2. Open a DOS window (click **Start**, point to **Programs**, click **MS-DOS Prompt**).

3. Enter the following commands to copy all utility files from the SYS volume to your Utility directory. Replace the ## with your assigned student number.

   a) Type **F: [Enter]** to change to the network drive.

   b) To copy the files, type
      NCOPY SYS:SOFTWARE.CTI\UTILITY*.* CORP:##CORP\APPS\UTILITY /S/E/V [Enter]

   c) Type **EXIT [Enter]** to return to Windows.

4. Use **My Computer** or **Network Neighborhood** to verify that the files have been copied to your Utility directory.

5. Close all browser windows.

Moving a Directory Structure

When implementing a directory structure, it is often useful to be able to move a directory along with all its files and subdirectories to another location in the volume. For example, when you created user accounts for Kellie Thiele and yourself in Chapter 2, you placed the user home directories in the root of your ##CORP directory. To correspond to the directory structure plan, you will need to move these directories to the IS directory structure. By moving the directories, you also move the data and any subdirectories to the new location. When you move Kellie's home directory, you must be careful to select the option to move the rights to the new location along with the directory structure. If you do not select to move the rights, you will need to restore Kellie's rights to her home directory before she will be able to access it.

In this hands-on activity, you will use NetWare Administrator to move your home directory and Kellie Thiele's home directory to the IS directory structure.

1. If necessary, start your computer and log in using your assigned ##Admin username.

2. Start NetWare Administrator and open a browser window for the ##CORP volume.

3. To check access rights to the user home directories, follow these steps:

   a) Right-click the **KThiele** directory to display a shortcut menu.

   b) Click the **Details** option.

   c) Click the **Trustees of this Directory** button to display a window showing trustees of the directory.

   d) Click **KThiele** to display her rights. Notice that the user KThiele has all access rights to the directory. You will learn more about trustees and access rights in Chapter 5.

   e) Click **Cancel** to return to the browser window.

4. Hold down **[Ctrl]** and click your own user directory. Both directories should now be highlighted.

5. Click **Object, Move** to display the Move/Copy window.

6. Click the **Browse** button to the right of the Destination field to display the Select Object window.

7. Double-click the **IS** directory in the left-hand Available Objects pane.

★8. Click the **Copy trustee assignments** box to copy the access rights along with the directories.

9. Click **OK** to move both directories.

10. Double-click the **IS** directory to display the revised directory structure.

11. Check the trustees of the user home directories as described in Step 3.

12. Close all windows and exit NetWare Administrator.

Copying and Removing Directories

In addition to moving a directory, you can also use NetWare Administrator to delete a directory if all subdirectories and files have been removed. For example, in addition to moving the user home directories, Kellie thinks it would be a good idea to move the Utility directory from Apps to the IS department.

In this hands-on activity, you will use NetWare Administrator to copy the Utility subdirectory from the Apps directory into the IS department directory and then delete the original Utility directory.

1. If necessary, start your computer and log in using your assigned ##Admin username.

2. Start NetWare Administrator and open a browser window for the ##CORP volume.

3. Double-click your **Apps** directory to open it.

3

4. To copy your Utility subdirectory from Apps into IS, follow these steps:

   a) Click your **Utility** directory to highlight it.

   b) Click **Object**, **Copy** to display the Move/Copy window.

   c) Click the **Browse** button located to the right of the Destination field.

   d) Double-click the **up arrow** in the Browse context window to display the IS directory in the Available objects window.

   e) Double-click the **IS** directory in the Available objects window.

   f) Click **OK** in the Move/Copy window to make a copy of the Utility subdirectory in your IS directory.

5. Double-click your **IS** directory to open it. Notice that it now includes the Utility subdirectory.

6. Double-click the **Utility** directory to verify that all files have been copied.

7. Use the following steps to try to delete the old Utility subdirectory from the Apps directory using NetWare Administrator:

   a) Click the **Apps\Utility** directory and press **[Del]**. Click **Yes** when asked whether you really want to delete the object.

   b) Notice the error message informing you that the Utility directory contains subordinate objects and could not be deleted. Before removing the old Utility directory, you will need to delete all files and any subdirectories. Click **OK** to close the window.

8. To delete all files and subdirectories in the Utility directory, follow these steps:

   a) Double-click the **Apps\Utility** directory to display its contents.

   b) Highlight all files in the directory. (Click the first file and then hold **[Shift]** while you click the last file.)

   c) Press **[Del]** to delete the files in the Utility directory. Click **Yes** at the prompt.

9. Double-click the **Apps** directory to close the window.

Renaming a Directory

After reviewing the directory structure you have created, it has been suggested that the Aircraft directory be renamed to Boeing since that is the only company with which Universal Aerospace currently has contracts. If additional contracts with other companies are added in the future, management at Aerospace would like to see them placed in separate directories for better security.

 In this hands-on activity, you use NetWare Administrator to rename the Aircraft directory to Boeing.

1. If necessary, start your computer and log in using your assigned ##Admin username.

2. Start NetWare Administrator and open a browser window for the ##CORP volume.

3. Double-click the **Engineer** directory to open it.

4. Click the **Aircraft** subdirectory to highlight it.

5. Click **Object**, **Rename**.

6. Press **[Del]** to erase the existing directory name. Enter the name **Boeing** and click **OK**. The new directory name will appear in the browser window.

7. Minimize NetWare Administrator.

VIEWING FILE SYSTEM INFORMATION

As you have learned from working with NetWare Administrator, the NetWare file system stores information about directories and files, including owner, creation date, attributes, and the directory inherited rights filter. The president of Aerospace, Dave Heise, would like to know how he can view this network file information from Windows. In addition, he would like some printouts showing information about the network file system you have created. Although he can view information about a single directory or file from NetWare Administrator or Windows, he would like some reports he can use when discussing the file system with other managers in the company. In addition, Dave would like all users to be able to access files in the Forms directory as well as use the Shared directory to exchange certain engineering drawings and files. In this section, you will learn how to use Windows 95/98 to view and change file system information as well as how to use the NDIR command to print directory and file system information.

Accessing NetWare File System Information from Windows

The Novell Client for Windows 95/98 enables users of the Windows 95/98 workstation to view and modify NetWare file system information that previously required using NetWare utilities such as NetWare Administrator. As a network administrator, you will often find it faster to use Windows Explorer or Network Neighborhood to view and even configure the NetWare file system.

 In this hands-on activity, you will use Windows to view statistics about the NetWare file system as well as change certain network settings.

1. If necessary, start your computer and log in using your assigned ##Admin username.

2. Use Network Neighborhood to browse to your ##CORP directory as follows:

    a) Double-click **Network Neighborhood**.

    b) Double-click your **##UAS** Organization.

    c) Double-click your **UAS_HOST_CORP** volume object.

    d) Double-click your **##CORP** folder.

3. To view information on the Forms directory, right-click the **Forms** directory and choose **Properties** from the shortcut menu. The General tab is displayed as shown in Figure 3-17. The General tab displays Windows directory information. On the following lines, record the size of the directory, number of files and folders, and the date the directory was created:

    1.59 KB _____   4 files & folders   Wed 4/22/2003

3

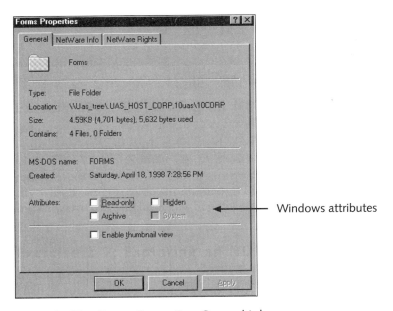

Windows attributes

Figure 3-17   Forms Properties, General tab

4. Click the **NetWare Info** tab to display the Novell window shown in Figure 3-18. Notice the additional information showing the owner along with the last update and last archive dates. NetWare also provides several additional directory attributes.

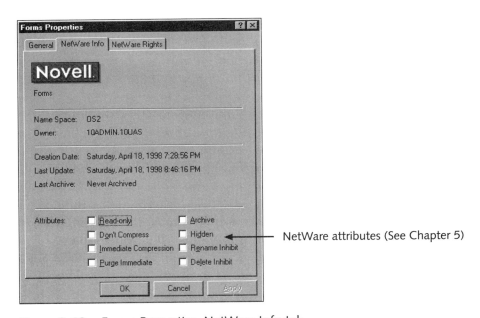

NetWare attributes (See Chapter 5)

Figure 3-18   Forms Properties, NetWare Info tab

5. To protect the Forms directory from being accidentally deleted or renamed, click the **Rename Inhibit** and **Delete Inhibit** attribute check boxes. You will learn more about file and directory attributes in Chapter 5.

6. Click the **NetWare Rights** tab to display the dialog box shown in Figure 3-19. From this dialog box, you can view what rights you have in this directory by looking at the Effective Rights information at the bottom of the dialog box. You can also use this dialog box to assign rights to other users. In Chapter 5, you will learn about these access rights and how you assign them.

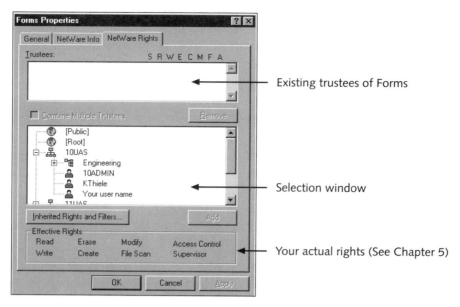

Figure 3-19 Forms Properties, NetWare Rights tab

7. To give all users in your ##UAS Organization rights to access the company forms, follow these steps:

a) Click your **##UAS** Organization to highlight it.

b) Click the **Add** button. Notice that your ##UAS Organization is added to the Trustees window with R and F rights.

c) Click **OK** to close the Forms Properties dialog box and return to your ##CORP window.

8. To allow all users the rights necessary to access and save files in the Shared directory, follow these steps:

a) Right-click the **Shared** directory and click **Properties.**

b) Click **NetWare Rights** tab.

c) Click your **##UAS** Organization and click **Add**.

d) In the Trustees window, click all rights except A.

e) Click **OK** to save the trustee assignment.

9. Next, to remove Kellie's Access Control right from her home directory, follow these steps:

a) Double-click your **IS** directory to open it.

b) Right-click **KThiele** and click **Properties**.

c) Click the **NetWare Rights** tab.

d) Remove the check from the **A** right by clicking it.

e) Click **OK** to save your changes.

10. Repeat the preceding process to remove the A right from your username.

11. Log out.

12. Log in as KThiele.

13. Use Network Neighborhood to browse to your ##CORP folder as described in Step 2.

5. To show all files in the SYS:Shared directory sorted by owner, enter the following command:

   NDIR SYS:SHARED /SORT OW > PRN[Enter]

6. To sort all .EXE files in the PUBLIC directory by last access date, enter the following command:

   NDIR SYS:PUBLIC*.EXE /SORT AC > PRN [Enter]

Listing Selected Files

The NDIR command contains options that allow you to include only files that match the criteria you specify. For example, when a network volume is getting low on free disk space, you can use the NDIR command to help determine what files to remove by listing all files that have not been accessed for several months. In addition, you can sort this list by owner to determine which users should be reviewed and whether they should be deleted or archived on backup media.

 In this hands-on activity, you will practice using the NDIR file selection options to display only specific file information.

1. If necessary, start your computer and log in using your assigned ##Admin username.

2. Open a DOS window and change to drive F (or your network drive).

3. Change your default path to the PUBLIC directory by typing the following command:

   CD SYS:PUBLIC [Enter]

4. To list all files in the SYS:PUBLIC directory that are over 500,000 bytes, enter the following command:

   NDIR *.* /SI GR 500000 [Enter]

5. To list all files in the SYS:PUBLIC directory that have not been accessed this month, enter the following command, replacing month with the number of last month, and year with the correct year for the specified month:

   NDIR *.* /AC BEF month/01/year [Enter]

6. To list all files you own on the SYS volume, enter the following command, replacing ## with your assigned student number. The files you created in Chapter 1 should be displayed.

   NDIR SYS:*.* /OWNER=##ADMIN /S [Enter]

7. You can combine multiple NDIR options to create more complex commands. For example, to list all files on the SYS volume that are greater than 500,000 bytes and that have not been accessed this month, in sequence from largest to smallest, enter the following command:

   NDIR SYS:*.* /SI GR 500000 AC BEF month/01/year SORT SI S [Enter]

Salvaging Deleted Files

Sometimes files are accidentally deleted and need to be restored. For example, at Universal Aerospace, Ira Means recently logged in using the Admin username and, thinking he was working on his local drive, accidentally deleted all files in the Forms directory. In the following two hands-on activities, you will first play the role of Ira Means and delete all files in the Forms directory, and then, as network administrator, you will recover the deleted files.

 In this hands-on activity, you will delete all files in the Forms directory.

1. If necessary, start your computer and log in using your assigned ##Admin username.

2. Open a DOS window and change to drive F (or your network drive).

3. Enter the following commands to change your default drive to the Forms directory and obtain a listing of all files in that directory:

CD CORP:##CORP\Forms [Enter]

NDIR [Enter]

4. Use the following command to simulate Ira Means's deletion of all the .FRM files.

DEL *.FRM [Enter]

NDIR [Enter]

5. Enter **Exit** to return to Windows.

One of the strengths of NetWare's file system is its ability to recover files reliably even after they have been deleted for a long time. When a file is deleted, NetWare does not overwrite its space until the space from all previously deleted files has been reused. As a result, you can often restore deleted files many months after they have been deleted. The Novell Client software enables Windows to salvage files if a drive letter is assigned to the physical volume containing the files to be salvaged.

In this hands-on activity, you learn how to use NetWare Administrator's Salvage Files option to recover deleted files.

1. If necessary, start your computer and log in using your assigned ##Admin username.

2. Use Network Neighborhood to browse to the physical volume containing your ##CORP folder as follows:

a) Double-click **Network Neighborhood** to display a list of Network Objects.

b) Double-click your **##UAS** Organization.

c) Double-click the **UAS_HOST_CORP** volume object.

d) Double-click your **##CORP** folder to open it.

3. Right-click the **Forms** directory and click the **Salvage Files** option to display all deleted files.

4. Click the **Salvage All** button.

5. Click **Close** to return to your ##CORP window.

6. Double-click the **Forms** directory to confirm that the files have been salvaged.

7. Close all windows.

Purging Files

As you have learned in the previous section, deleting files does not necessarily destroy their contents; instead, deleted files are reused on a last-deleted, last-reused basis. It is sometimes convenient, either for security or for operating system efficiency, to give space from deleted files directly back to the operating system for reuse. The process of removing files from salvage and giving their space directly back to the operating system is called **purging** files. When files are purged, NetWare reclaims their space and you can no longer recover them. As a result, purging deleted files can be important for security purposes because it prevents the deleted files from being salvaged.

Another advantage of purging files is to make space immediately available to the NetWare server to reuse. This not only increases the efficiency of NetWare, but it also prevents other possibly valuable files from being reused as quickly. For example, assume Kellie recently informed you that she installed a software package in the Apps directory and then later decided to delete the software directory and place it on her local computer. Purging files in the Apps directory will make any disk space used by the files available for other purposes.

 In this hands-on activity, you learn how to use the Purge Files option of NetWare Administrator to purge deleted files from the Utility directory.

1. If necessary, start your computer and log in using your assigned ##Admin username.

2. Use Network Neighborhood to browse to the physical volume containing your ##CORP folder as follows:

   a) Double-click **Network Neighborhood** to display a list of Network Objects.

   b) Double-click your **##UAS** Organization.

   c) Double-click the **UAS_HOST_CORP** volume object.

   d) Double-click your **##CORP** folder to open it.

3. Open your **##CORP** folder by double-clicking it.

4. Double-click your **Apps** directory.

5. Right-click the **Utility** directory and click the **Purge Files** option to display all deleted files.

6. Click **Purge All** and click **Yes** to return the file space to NetWare for immediate reuse.

7. Click **Close** to return to the Apps directory window.

8. Click the **Utility** directory and press **[Del]**. Click **Yes** to confirm the directory deletion.

9. Close all windows.

10. Log out.

DRIVE POINTERS

In both NetWare and DOS environments, drive pointers play an important role in the accessing of files located on different volumes and directories. A **drive pointer** is a letter of the alphabet used to reference storage areas in the file system. By default, DOS reserves the first five drive pointers (A through E) to reference storage devices on the local workstation, so these letters are often referred to as the **local drive pointers**. For example, letters A and B are reserved for floppy disk drives, C and D are normally used for hard disks, and E is often reserved for a CD-ROM or other external storage device. References to drive pointers generally include a following colon.

Network drive pointers are letters of the alphabet (usually F through Z) that represent directory paths and volumes in the network file system. Establishing network drive pointers is important for two major reasons:

■ Network drive pointers make it easier to access data files without needing to specify a complete path. (A **complete path** includes the volume name followed by all necessary directories and subdirectories; network paths are discussed later in this chapter.) For example, if the G drive pointer is assigned to your ##CORP directory on the CORP volume, you can specify a path to your Apps directory by typing G:Apps rather than UAS_HOST_CORP:##CORP\Apps.

- Network drive pointers allow applications and DOS commands that do not recognize volume names to access data and programs on multiple volumes and servers.

Network drive pointers can be one of three types: regular, root, or search. Regular and root drive pointers are usually assigned to directories containing data files, whereas search drive pointers are assigned to network software directories. A **regular drive pointer** is assigned to a directory path and shows all directories and subdirectories leading to the storage area. In addition to assigning regular drive pointers to commonly used directories, you should assign a regular drive pointer to each volume because this allows application software packages that cannot use NetWare volume names in their paths to access the data on any volume.

A **root drive pointer** appears to the user or application as if the directory path were at the root of the drive or volume. Figure 3-20 shows an example of using two drive pointers, G and H, to access the same directory area.

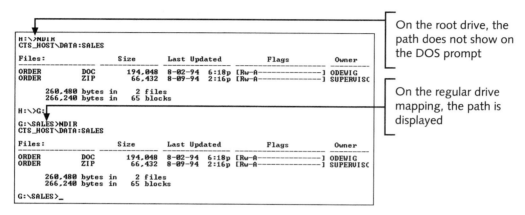

On the root drive, the path does not show on the DOS prompt

On the regular drive mapping, the path is displayed

Figure 3-20 Regular and root drive pointers

Notice that the G drive pointer is a regular pointer because it shows the entire path leading to the directory, whereas H is a root drive pointer that appears as if it were the first level in the directory structure.

Both drive pointers are assigned or mapped to the directory and, as you can see in the figure, have access to the same files. The advantage of using the root drive pointer is that it helps to prevent an application or DOS command from changing the driver pointer's mapping to some other location in the directory structure. Root drive pointers are normally used to access user home directories along with shared data directories.

A **search drive pointer** is a regular or root drive pointer that has been added to the DOS path. The **DOS path** specifies a sequence of locations in which DOS and the NetWare shell will look for program files that are not in the current directory. Search drive pointers play an important role in accessing the file system from DOS because they allow a network administrator to place data files in separate directories from the application software. Search drive pointers act like a Windows shortcut, enabling a user or application located in one directory path to access software and data located elsewhere in the directory structure.

For example, as illustrated in Figure 3-21, when you enter a command, DOS first determines that the command is not one of DOS's internal commands and looks in the current directory for a program or batch file with the name you specified. If no program or batch file exists in the current directory, each search drive specified in the path will be searched starting with S1 until either the program is found or the message "Bad command or filename" is displayed. By assigning a search drive to the SYS:PUBLIC directory, NetWare enables you to run utilities such as NDIR and LOGOUT from any directory in the file system.

3

assigned paths. When mapping drives from Network Neighborhood, you can use the Reconnect at logon option, as you did for the G drive in Chapter 1, to reconnect a drive letter to the specified network path the next time a user logs in from that workstation. The problem with using the Reconnect at logon option is that when other users log in from the workstation, Windows will attempt to make the same drive assignments for them. This can cause problems if a user does not have access rights to the specified network directory or if a user wants a drive letter to point to a different path.

One solution to this problem is to use NetWare user login scripts to assign drive pointers. Login scripts can map drive letters to network directory paths by using MAP commands that are processed by the workstation when a user logs in. The MAP command can be used in login scripts or from the DOS prompt to assign drive letters to network paths. In Chapter 8, you will learn how to create and manage more complex login script files that are necessary to automate user access to the network system.

Because of the importance of drive pointers, as a CNA you will be required to be able to work with drive mappings from both Windows and the MAP command. In this section, you will continue to work with Network Neighborhood to establish the drive pointers for one of the users in the Engineering department as well as learn how to use MAP commands to establish drive pointers from the DOS prompt or within login scripts.

Mapping from Windows

Kellie, your coworker in the IS department, is starting to use the network quite frequently to store files for her software development work. To help her navigate the network more easily, she would like you to set up her workstation with the standard drive mappings.

 In this hands-on activity, you will apply the drive pointer usage chart shown in Table 3-2 to Kellie's workstation.

1. If necessary, start your workstation and log in using your ##Admin username.

2. Double-click **My Computer** to display all drive mappings.

3. To disconnect all existing network drive pointers except drive F and drive Z, follow these steps:

 You should not disconnect the F and Z pointers, as your client may need to use these drives to access system files.

    a) Right-click the **G** drive pointer and click the **Disconnect** option.

    b) Repeat Step 3a for any remaining drive pointers except F and Z.

4. Close the My Computer window.

5. Double-click **Network Neighborhood** and browse to your ##CORP folder.

6. To create a root drive pointer G to the ##CORP folder, follow these steps:

    a) Right-click your **##CORP** folder.

    b) Click the **Novell Map Network Drive** option.

    c) Click the **Map Root** and **Reconnect At Logon** options.

    d) Select drive letter **G:** in the Device field.

    e) Click the **Map** button.

    f) Close the G: drive window.

7. To create a root drive pointer H to Kellie's home directory, follow these steps:

   a) Double-click the **IS** directory to open it.

   b) Right-click the **KThiele** directory.

   c) Click the **Novell Map Network Drive** option.

   d) Click the **Map Root** and **Reconnect At Logon** options.

   e) Select drive letter **H:** in the Device field.

   f) Click the **Map** button.

   g) Close the H: drive window.

8. To create a root drive pointer L to the IS department directory, follow these steps:

   a) Right-click the **IS** directory.

   b) Click the **Novell Map Network Drive** option.

   c) Click the **Map Root** and **Reconnect At Logon** options.

   d) Select drive letter **L:** in the Device field.

   e) Click the **Map** button.

   f) Close the L: drive window.

9. To create a search drive mapping to the SYS:PUBLIC\WIN95 directory, follow these steps:

   a) Click the **Back** button in Windows 98, or the **Close** button in Windows 95, until you return to the UAS_HOST window showing the UAS_HOST_CORP and UAS_HOST_SYS volumes.

   b) Double-click the **UAS_HOST_SYS** volume.

   c) Double-click the **Public** directory.

   d) Right-click the **Win95** directory.

   e) Click the **Novell Map Network Drive** option.

   f) Click the **Map Root** and **Reconnect At Logon** options.

   g) Click the **Map Search Drive** option.

   h) Click the **Map Insert End of Path** option.

   i) Select drive letter **Y:** in the Device field.

   j) Click the **Map** button.

   k) Close all windows.

10. Double-click **My Computer** and notice that you now have drive pointers to the IS and Win95 directories.

11. Close the My Computer window.

12. Log out.

13. Log in as KThiele.

14. Double-click **My Computer** and verify that the preceding drive mappings are reconnected.

15. Log out.

Because G is mapped as a "root" drive, you can use a slash between the drive letter (G:) and the path. If G were not a root drive, placing a slash in the command would cause the system to search in the root of the CORP volume for the Engineer directory. Since the Engineer directory is not on the root of the CORP volume, a message indicating an invalid path would be displayed.

9. The MAP NEXT [*path*] command can be used to assign the specified path to the first available drive letter proceeding from F through Z. This command is useful when you want to map an unused drive letter to a directory path and you do not care what letter is used. To map the next available drive letter to the Shared directory on the SYS volume using a physical volume name, enter the following command:

    MAP NEXT SYS:SHARED [Enter]

10. To delete drive mappings, use the MAP DEL *drive*: command, replacing *drive* with the drive letter you want to delete. To delete the drive letters created in Step 5, enter the following commands:

    MAP DEL I: [Enter]

    MAP DEL J: [Enter]

    MAP DEL K: [Enter]

 If you use a local drive pointer (A through E), the MAP command will ask whether you want to override the local pointer with a network path. If you answer Yes, the local drive pointer will access the network path rather than the local drive. This can be useful in certain situations where a software package will not use drive letters after E.

11. Enter the following commands to map your A drive to the Forms directory, display a directory of drive A, and then delete the drive mapping:

    MAP A:=G:FORMS [Enter]

    [Enter]

    (You can press [Enter] again to accept the option to override the local drive mapping.)

    A: [Enter]

    DIR [Enter]

    F: [Enter]

    MAP DEL A: [Enter]

12. Use the **Exit** command to return to Windows and log out.

Creating and Deleting Search Drive Pointers

As you learned earlier in the chapter, search drives are drive pointers that are added to a workstation's DOS path to allow the workstation to access software that is stored in other directories. A maximum of 16 search drives can be assigned, starting with S1 and ending with S16. You can add new search drives to the list by using the MAP command either to assign the next available search drive number or insert the search drive between two existing search drives. The syntax of the MAP command used when adding new search drives is MAP [INS] S#:=[*path*].

The INS option inserts the new search drive at the number specified and then pushes the current search drives down. When adding a search drive to the end of the list, omit the INS option and replace # with the next available search drive number from 1 through 16. If you skip search drive numbers, the MAP command will automatically assign the next available number. When adding a new search drive, NetWare automatically assigns the next available drive letter starting with Z for S1 and ending with K for S16.

In this hands-on activity, you will delete all existing search drives except the one mapped to the SYS:PUBLIC directory for Kellie, and then use various MAP commands to establish a set of search drive pointers to software directories on your network.

1. If necessary, start your computer and log in using your assigned ##Admin username.

2. Open a DOS window and change to your F drive.

3. Use the following command to change the current context of your workstation to your ##UAS container, then log in using your assigned username:

   CX .##UAS [Enter]

4. View your current search drive mappings by typing **MAP** and pressing **[Enter]**.

5. Use the **MAP DEL S#:** command to delete each of the search drives (but not the one mapped to the SYS:Public directory) by replacing the # with the search drive number.

 When you delete search drive S2, the remaining search drives are renumbered, causing search drive S3 to become search drive S2. When you have completed this step, the only search drive remaining should be S1 mapped to the SYS:Public directory. If you accidentally delete the search drive mapping to the SYS:Public directory, you will not be able to run commands, such as MAP or LOGOUT. To restore S1 to the Public directory, enter the following commands:

CD SYS:PUBLIC [Enter]

MAP S1:=SYS:PUBLIC [Enter]

6. Try running the DB program without a search drive by typing the command **DB [Enter]**. When you enter the command, you should receive a "Bad command or filename" message, because NetWare cannot find a program file named DB.

7. To use the DB program, you first need to use the following command to map search drive S2 to the DB software directory.

MAP S2:=SYS:SOFTWARE.CTI\DB [Enter]

Notice the use of a physical volume for SYS in the MAP command. A server name is not necessary, since your current path is to the UAS_HOST server.

8. Test your search drive by entering the following command:

DB [Enter]

If your new search drive works, the program will display the database test screen.

9. When inserting a search drive between two existing drives, include the INS option and replace the search drive number with the number of the existing search drive you want the new drive to be placed before. When setting up search drives, you should give the most commonly used paths lower search drive numbers. This makes the system more efficient by reducing the number of directories NetWare has to search through when looking for a program file. To insert a search drive mapping between the existing S1 and S2 search drives and then view your drive mappings, enter the following commands:

MAP INS S2:=SYS:SOFTWARE.CTI\SP [Enter]

MAP [Enter]

10. It is sometimes convenient to add a new search drive to the beginning of the list and then delete it when it is no longer needed. To add a search drive to the WP directory before the existing S1 search drive, enter the following commands:

MAP INS S1:=SYS:SOFTWARE.CTI\WP [Enter]

MAP [Enter]

Notice that the next available drive letter (for example U:) has now been assigned to the S1: search drive. You should also notice that while the other search drivers were renumbered, they have retained their original drive letter assignments. This helps to illustrate that the search drive numbers (S1, S2, S3, …, S16) simply specify the sequence of the drive letters. The drive letters, not the S# search drive numbers, are actually assigned to a directory path.

11. To verify the sequence of search drive letters in your DOS path, type **PATH** and press **[Enter]**.

12. To remove the search drive to the WP directory and resequence the search drives, enter the following commands:

MAP DEL S1: [Enter]

PATH [Enter]

13. Because search drives are really the sequence of the drive letter in the DOS path, NetWare will not skip search drive numbers. As a result, you can use the command MAP S16:=[*path*] if you want to add a search drive to the end of the search list but do not know the number of the last search drive. For example, enter the following commands to add a search drive to the end of your list and then verify your results:

MAP S16:=SYS:SOFTWARE.CTI\ [Enter]

MAP [Enter]

Notice that while you specified S16: in the MAP command, the next available search drive number has been assigned to the SYS:SOFTWARE.CTI directory path.

14. Enter the **Exit** command to return to Windows and log out.

Using Directory Map Objects

As you have learned in this chapter, drive pointers play an important role in providing access to the network file system. Setting up drive pointers requires that a user or network administrator know the physical location of the directory being mapped to the drive letter. Maintaining drive pointers for many users can become a problem if certain files or directories are moved from one volume to another. Although not an essential part of the network system, the Directory Map object is useful in simplifying the maintenance of drive pointers. A Directory Map object contains a path to a volume and directory in the network file system. You can simplify the maintenance of drive pointers by creating Directory Map objects that contain the path to the desired data. Multiple user and container login scripts can then establish drive pointers relative to the Directory Map object rather than needing to specify the complete path to the data. Because Directory Map objects allow drive pointers to be relative to the value specified in the Directory Map object's Path property, when the location of a directory is moved in the future, only the path in the Directory Map object needs to be changed. MAP statements contained in login scripts and menu files that use the Directory Map object will not need to be modified. To use a Directory Map object, users need to be given rights to read the Path property of each Directory Map object they will access. In Chapter 6, you will learn how to give users the necessary property rights to access directories using Directory Map objects.

The consultant, Jennifer, has recommended establishing Directory Map objects for each department's directory. For example, as defined previously in Table 3-2, drive letter L is to point to each department's work directory. Currently the Engineer directory is planned for storage on the CORP volume. However, in the future, Universal Aerospace is planning to add an additional server to the network for use by the

Engineering department. Using a Directory Map object when mapping drive letters for the Engineer directory will make it easier to expand the system in the future by simply changing the path in the Directory Map object.

In this hands-on activity, you will create a Directory Map object named EngData for the Engineer directory and another Directory Map object named ISData that points to the IS directory. You will then use the Directory Map objects to map drive letters.

1. If necessary, start your workstation, log in using your ##Admin username, and start NetWare Administrator.

2. Open a browse window in ##UAS.

3. Create a Directory Map object named EngData in the Engineering container, as follows:

   a) Highlight the **Engineering** container and press **[Ins]** to display the New Object window.

   b) Double-click the **Directory Map** object to display the Create Directory Map window.

   c) Enter **EngData** in the Directory Map Name field and press **[Tab]**.

   d) To enter the volume name, click the **browse** icon located to the right of the Volume entry box. The familiar Select Object window will be displayed.

   e) Double-click the **UAS_HOST_CORP** volume object located in the left-hand Available Objects window to display the full distinguished name of the CORP volume in the Volume field.

   f) Click the **Path** field and then click the **browse** icon (the same button you clicked in Step d) located to the right of the Path entry box to redisplay the Select Object window.

   g) Double-click the **UAS_HOST_CORP** volume object located in the right-hand Browse Context window to view all directories in the CORP volume that you have access rights to see.

   h) Double-click your **##CORP** directory in the right-hand window to display the Engineer directory in the left-hand Available Objects window.

   i) Double-click the **Engineer** directory object displayed in the left-hand Available Objects window. The path to the Engineer directory should now be displayed in the Path field of the Create Directory Map window.

   j) Click the **Create** button to make the new Directory Map object in the Engineering container.

4. Create a Directory Map object named ISData in your ##UAS Organization:

   a) Highlight your **##UAS** Organization and press **[Ins]** to display the New Object window.

   b) Double-click the **Directory Map** object to display the Create Directory Map window.

   c) Enter **ISData** in the Directory Map Name field and press **[Tab]**.

   d) To enter the volume name, click the **browse** icon located to the right of the Volume entry box. The familiar Select Object window will be displayed.

   e) Double-click the **UAS_HOST_CORP** volume object located in the left-hand Available Objects window to display the full distinguished name of the CORP volume in the Volume field.

   f) Click the **Path** field and then click the **browse** icon located to the right of the Path entry box to redisplay the Select Object window.

   g) Double-click the **UAS_HOST_CORP** volume object located in the right-hand Browse Context window to view all directories in the CORP volume that you have access rights to see.

3

h) Double-click your **##CORP** directory in the right-hand window to display the IS directory in the left-hand Available Objects window.

i) Double-click the **IS** directory object displayed in the left-hand Available Objects window. The path to the IS directory should now be displayed in the Path field of the Create Directory Map window.

j) Click the **Create** button to make the new Directory Map object.

k) Minimize the NetWare Administrator application.

5. To test the newly created Directory Map object, open the MS-DOS Prompt window by clicking **Start**, pointing to **Programs**, clicking **MS-DOS Prompt**, then completing the following steps:

a) Map drive letter L to the IS directory by using the following MAP command:

F: [Enter]

MAP ROOT L:=ISData [Enter]

b) Change your context to the Engineering container and then map drive letter N to the Engineer directory by entering the following commands:

CX .Engineering.##UAS [Enter]

MAP root N:=EngData [Enter]

c) Type **MAP [Enter]** to confirm that the drive letters now point to your Engineer and IS directories.

d) Type **Exit** and press **[Enter]** to exit the MS-DOS Prompt window and return to Windows.

6. Double-click **My Computer** and confirm that the drive letter assignments for L and N exist in Windows.

7. At this time, you may exit NetWare Administrator and end your Windows session, or continue with the hands-on exercises in the next section.

Using Login Scripts

When multiple users share a workstation or a mobile user moves between different workstations, it is necessary to map drives based on the user's needs. Novell provides a way to do this using login scripts. As network administrator, you will occasionally need to log in from other user workstations and still maintain your normal drive mappings. By creating a user login script with MAP commands, you can have the drive assignments made for you wherever you log in.

 In this hands-on activity, you will use NetWare Administrator to establish a login script for your user name that will assign the standard drive pointers defined in Table 3-2 for you when you log in.

1. If necessary, start your workstation and log in using your ##Admin username.

2. Start NetWare Administrator.

3. If necessary, open a browser window for your ##UAS Organization.

4. If necessary, expand your ##UAS Organization by double-clicking **##UAS**.

5. Right-click your username and click the **Details** option.

6. Click the **Login Script** button.

7. Enter the following MAP commands in the Login Script window:

MAP F:=UAS_HOST_SYS:

MAP ROOT G:=UAS_HOST_CORP:##CORP

MAP ROOT L:=G:IS

MAP INS S1:=SYS:PUBLIC

MAP INS S2:=L:UTILITY

MAP INS S3:=SYS:PUBLIC\WIN95

8. Click **OK** to save the login script.

9. Exit NetWare Administrator.

10. Double-click **My Computer**.

11. Right-click all network drive pointers and click **Disconnect**.

12. Log out.

13. Log in using your username. Use Windows Explorer or My Computer to verify that you have drive letter G mapped to your ##CORP directory and drive letter L mapped to the IS directory.

14. Log out.

Congratulations! You have now started to set up a basic file system for the Universal Aerospace Corporation. In the following chapters, you will learn more efficient ways to create and secure user accounts as well as provide users with access to the data and applications with which they need to work.

CHAPTER SUMMARY

❏ A network administrator must master the NetWare commands and utilities necessary to set up and manage the network file system. In this chapter, you learned about the basic components of the network file system, including volumes, directories, subdirectories, and files. The volume is the physical storage medium on the network and is comparable to a file cabinet in that it holds folders and files. Each server is required to have a minimum of one volume named SYS consisting of at least 300 MB. During installation, NetWare creates the Login, Public, and System directories on the SYS volume. The Login directory contains programs and files necessary to log a user into the network. The Public directory contains program commands and utilities that may be run by a user after logging in to the network. The SYS volume may also contain print queues used to hold printer output until network printers are available. However, as you will learn in Chapter 7, whenever possible you should located your print queues on volumes other than SYS in order to prevent the SYS volume from running out of space due to a large amount of printed output.

❏ Files are used to store network data and software. In addition to storing the filename and size, NetWare stores additional information about each file including owner, access dates, and attributes in the directory entry table located at the beginning of each volume. In addition to NetWare Administrator and Windows Explorer, the DOS-based NDIR command provides a variety of options to list file information, as well as select and sort files by size, access date, and owner.

❏ One of the jobs of a network administrator is to plan a directory structure for the network file system that will support the organization's processing needs. When you are planning the directory structure, Novell suggests that you set aside private home directories for each user, shared directories to store files that are needed by multiple users, application software directories, and a directory for each version of DOS used by the client computers. To provide space for these directories, many network administrators use multiple volumes. The SYS volume is reserved for operating system files, whereas one or more data volumes are usually designated to store print queues, user files, and applications.

local drive pointer — A letter, usually A through E, used to represent a storage device, such as a disk drive or CD-ROM attached to the local computer.

Login directory — A NetWare operating system directory that contains files and programs needed by DOS clients to log in to the network.

login script — A list of commands performed when you first log in to the network. An important use of the login script is establishing the initial drive pointer mappings.

network drive pointer — A letter, usually F through Z, used to represent a storage location on a network volume.

path — The location of a file or directory in the network file system.

physical volume name — The name of the volume given when it was created. The physical volume name is often preceded by the server name. A backslash (\) is used to separate the server name and physical volume name.

Public directory — A NetWare operating system directory that contains NetWare utility programs and commands available to all users.

purging — Removing deleted files from the salvage area and making their space available for reuse by the server. After files are purged, they cannot be undeleted or salvaged.

regular drive pointer — A drive pointer that is assigned to a data directory on each volume.

relative path — A path that starts from your current directory and leads to the desired file or subdirectory.

root drive pointer — A regular drive pointer that acts as if it were the root of the volume.

search drive pointer — A drive pointer that is used to access software through a DOS path.

shared directory — A directory where multiple users have access rights, so they can share files.

spanning — A technique that places a volume on more than one disk drive.

suballocation — A technique used in NetWare 4.1 and later that divides blocks into smaller, 512-byte increments to save disk space by allowing multiple files to share the same block.

system directory — A NetWare-created operating system directory that contains system software and commands available only to the server and ADMIN user, not accessible to the users.

volume — The major division of NetWare file storage used to organize network data and program files.

REVIEW QUESTIONS

1. _____ are the main components of the NetWare file system.

2. List three required NetWare directories that are created when NetWare is installed on a server.

   _____

   _____

   _____

3. The _____ directory contains files and programs that the user can access and run prior to logging in to the network.

4. The _____ directory contains NetWare utility programs that are available to all users.

5. The _____ directory contains operating system files that are not available to users.

6. List four types of directories that Novell suggests you create in the file system.

   _Pg 104_

   _____

   _____

   _____

   _____

7. Describe a benefit of placing user files and programs on a separate volume.

   _Pg 100_

8. Describe an advantage of implementing an application-oriented directory structure.

   _Pg 104_   _Pg 112_

9. Larger file systems are easier to manage when using a(n)
   _Pg 112_   _____ directory structure design.

   _Pg 110_

10. What is the advantage of not assigning all NetWare disk space to volumes?

    _Pg 112_

11. Write a path using a physical volume name to the Business directory on the root of the DATA volume located on the server named CTS_HOST.

    _137_   _____ CTS_HOST\DATA:Business

12. Write a path to the Business directory on the DATA volume using the NDS volume object name, CTS_DATA, located in your current context.

    _____ CTS_DATA.DATA:Business

13. List two ways you can use Windows to manage the network file system.

    _____

    _____

14. How would you quickly delete a complex directory structure, including all its subdirectories?

    _Pg 107_

15. The _____ NDS object acts as a link between NDS and the file system.

16. A(n) _____ Root _____ drive pointer appears to the user or applica-
    _Pg 130_   tions as if the default path were at the beginning of the volume.

    _130_

17. A(n) _____ Regular _____ drive pointer is added to the DOS path.

18. Write a command to assign drive letter M to the Menus directory on the UAS_HOST_CORP volume object.

    _____

19. Write a command to insert the first search drive to the SOFTWARE.CTI\DB directory located on the SYS volume of the UAS_HOST file server. (Write the command using the volume object name UAS_HOST_SYS located in your current context.)

    _____

20. Write a command to delete the first search drive.

_____

21. Write a command to insert the first search drive to the SOFTWARE.CTI\SP directory located on the SYS volume of the UAS_HOST file server. (Write the command using the physical server and volume name.)

_____

22. Write a command to insert the first search drive to the SOFTWARE.CTI\WP directory located on the SYS volume of the UAS_HOST file server. (Write the command using the volume object name UAS_HOST_SYS located in the context .O=CLASS, assuming your current context is .O=UAS.)

_____

23. Directory Map objects may be used to help simplify the maintenance of drive pointers. True or False?

24. Write a MAP command that maps drive L to the path contained in the Directory Map object named NASA_DATA.

_____

25. Briefly explain what changes you would need to make to move the data specified in the NASA_DATA Directory Map object to another volume.

_____

26. When creating a Directory Map object, what security assignment will users need to use the Directory Map object in a MAP command?

The Universal Aerospace Project

Management is pleased that you have already been able to create the proposed Engineering directory structure and set up directories for application software and company forms. Your next step in implementing the file system is to design and create a directory structure for the Universal Aerospace Business and Sales departments. In these projects, you will implement the remaining directory structure for the Business users.

Step 1: Identify Storage Requirements

Given the Business and Sales department processing needs as shown in Figure 3-23, fill out a Storage Requirements Form Design that includes the following information for each directory: description, users, name, and estimated size.

You can copy blank forms from Appendix B.

Step 2: Design the Directory Structure

Using the existing UAS directory structure along with the Directory Design form you have completed, design a directory structure for each of the following departments and record them on separate Directory Design forms.

Business department

Sales department

Publishing department

Business and Sales Users

The Business department uses an accounting package that includes general ledger and payroll applications. Currently, this DOS-based software is installed on the NetWare 3.12 server and is used by Terry Blackwell, George, and Amy. However, to provide improved performance, security, and reliability, a new Windows-based accounting package has been purchased and will be installed on the NetWare 5 server in a single directory structure named AcctApp, within the Business directory. The storage requirements for the accounting packages and data should not exceed 100 MB. In addition to requiring the accounting applications, all Business staff will need the Excel spreadsheet program to create and update budget data. Because Terry, George, and Amy all need access to the budget and accounting data, it should be stored in a shared budget subdirectory within the Business directory. Currently, the projected storage needs for the budget directory are not to exceed 150 MB.

In addition to having access to the new inventory system, the Sales users currently use Microsoft Access to keep a database of the customers and vendors they work with on their notebook computer. Since the Sales staff often works with the same customers and vendors, duplicate and sometimes conflicting information is being maintained on each notebook computer. To solve this problem, separate directories for both the customer and vendor databases are to be stored within the Sales directory structure on the NetWare 5 server. These directories should not exceed 50 MB each. The department secretary, Laurie Hiller, will maintain the customer and vendor database files by entering new customer and vendor data obtained from the Sales staff. When in the office, the database files will be accessed directly off the network. Initially, the Sales users will need to be able to copy the database files to their notebook computers prior to going "on the road." In the future, these users would like to have direct access to the server database from a dial-up phone connection. In addition, the Sales staff uses the word processing software for correspondence as well as work on promotional material. A 50 MB shared document directory will be necessary to allow Sales staff to interchange promotional material within the department as well as with Desktop Publishing users.

The Desktop Publishing department is responsible for working with the Engineering and Marketing departments to create operation and installation manuals for NASA Space Station and Mars Rover projects. As a result, shared directories for up to 500 MB will need to be created for these projects within the Publish directory structure.

Figure 3-23   Business and Sales processing needs

Step 3: Create the Remaining UAS Directory Structure

In this phase of the project, you will create the remainder of the Universal Aerospace directory structure in your ##CORP directory using the Directory Design forms from Step 2. You may use either NetWare Administrator or Network Neighborhood to create the directory structure.

Step 4: Document the Structure

Create a printout showing your newly created directory structure.

Step 5: Set Directory Space Limitations

Use NetWare Administrator to enter the directory space limitations you defined on the Directory Design form.

Step 6: Set Attributes

Use Network Neighborhood to set the Delete Inhibit attribute to "on" for each of the main directories off the root of your UAS directory structure.

Step 7: Map Drives

Using the Universal Aerospace Drive Pointer Usage form in Table 3-2, record the following drive mappings for users in the Business department:

Drive Letter	Path
S1:	
S2:	

Step 8: Create Directory Map Objects

To make it easier to maintain drive mappings if the location of data directories changes as additional servers and volumes are added to the network, create the Directory Map objects and paths shown in Table 3-3 for the Business Organizational Unit.

Table 3-3   Business Unit Directory Map Objects

Object Name	Path
SalesData	UAS_HOST_CORP:##CORP\Sales
AcctData	UAS_HOST_CORP:##CORP\Business
PubData	UAS_HOST_CORP:##CORP\Publish

Step 9: Enter a Business Login Script

In addition to the user login scripts described in this chapter, each container can also have a login script. When a container has a login script, the login script commands are executed for each user of that container when he or she logs in. This saves you from the redundancy of entering and maintaining so many individual login script files. However, for all users to share one login script file, a variable is needed to represent their home directory name. The %LOGIN_NAME variable may be used in the MAP command to represent the user's login name. For example, you can map the H drive to a Business users home directory using the following command:

```
MAP ROOT H:=CORP:##CORP\BUSINESS\%LOGIN_NAME
```

In this assignment, you will need to follow these steps to enter a login script that will be used by all users in the Business department:

1. Start NetWare Administrator.

2. Open a browser window for your ##UAS Organization.

3. Right-click your **Business** Organizational Unit and click the **Details** option.

4. Click the **Login Script** button.

5. Enter the login script MAP commands necessary to implement the drive pointers identified in Step 7.

6. Click **OK** to save your Business container login script.

7. Exit NetWare Administrator.

8. To print the Business container login script, open the MS-DOS Prompt window by clicking **Start**, **Programs**, **MS-DOS Prompt**, then completing the following NLIST command:

NLIST "Organizational Unit" = Business SHOW "Login Script" > PRN

You will get a chance to test the login script when you create users in the next chapter.

Additional Exercises

The following exercises are not necessary to implement your Universal Aerospace file system, but are included to give you more practice working with NetWare file system utilities to help you pass your CNA exam. To perform these exercises, you should have completed the Universal Aerospace case projects.

Exercise 3-1: Design a Directory Structure for the Portsmith Private School

The Portsmith Private School has recently installed NetWare 5.0 on its server computer. While you were visiting with the administrator at a school activity, he asked you to help the school set up the file system on its network. He explained that initially the school wants to use the network to share documents being worked on by the three secretaries, as well as be able to run attendance and scheduling applications off the network. The staff feels it is important to be able to store and access standard school forms when typing letters, memos, and other reports. In addition, the business teachers would like to connect the 12 computers in their lab to the network to allow the students to run the word processing and spreadsheet software from the server, as well as retrieve and store assignments. After talking with the teachers, you discover that they would like to have a storage area for each teacher's assignments. Students could then retrieve an assignment, perform the work, and store the results in their home directory. Initially, approximately 25 students will be using the network for file storage purposes. The administrator stressed that it is important that the students not be able to access the administrative documents or software. Using volume and directory design forms, your job is to design a network file system that you feel will best meet the needs of the Portsmith Private School. Include the SYS volume along with any required NetWare directories.

Exercise 3-2: Use MAP to Establish Drive Mappings

In this exercise, you will gain experience in using MAP commands to implement a set of drive pointers by following these steps:

1. Use MAP commands to establish the drive pointers you defined in Step 7 of the UAS project.

2. After implementing the MAP commands, enter the following command to obtain a printout of your drive mappings:

MAP > PRN

3. Log out and then log back in to the network to observe the effect that logging out has on your drive mappings. Record your observations on the following line:

_____

CHAPTER

4

MANAGING USER ACCESS

After reading this chapter and completing the exercises, you will be able to:

- ◆ Use NetWare Administrator to establish user login account restrictions
- ◆ Use NetWare Administrator to create user accounts from templates
- ◆ Use NetWare Administrator to create and manage Group and Organizational Role objects
- ◆ Use UIMPORT to help create groups of users
- ◆ Use NDS Manager to move container objects

Now that you have established a file system with locations for user home directories, you have the structure needed to create and secure the Universal Aerospace user accounts. In Chapter 2, you learned that Novell Directory Services (NDS) uses a global database consisting of container and leaf objects to store information on network objects such as users, groups, printers, and volumes so they are accessible to all NetWare servers. In addition, you have learned how to use NetWare Administrator to create containers, volumes, and user accounts. In this chapter, you will learn how to secure user accounts against intruders as well as how to make creating user accounts more efficient through the use of templates and the UIMPORT utility. In previous versions of NetWare, it was necessary to perform administrative tasks such as creating NDS objects from a client computer. With NetWare 5, Novell has introduced a new administrative utility named ConsoleOne that runs from the server console. In Chapter 10, you will learn how the ConsoleOne utility can be used to create and manage user accounts from the NetWare server console.

In the future, look for Novell to enhance the ConsoleOne utility to enable you to manage the server and NDS tree over the Internet using your browser software.

ESTABLISHING LOGIN SECURITY

In addition to establishing a network file system and NDS structure, a network administrator must properly secure the network so that users will be limited to accessing only the network resources and services they have been authorized to use. NetWare provides a network administrator with the following five security systems that are used in setting up a secure network environment:

- Login security
- NDS security
- File system security
- Printing security
- Server console security

In this section, you will learn how to use NetWare login security to protect user accounts from unauthorized access. Later chapters will cover file system security, NDS security, printing security, and server console security. The purpose of login security is to ensure that only authorized users have access to network resources. Creating user objects and assigning passwords is only one part of implementing login security, which also consists of user account restrictions, intruder detection, and user authentication. In this section, you will learn what a CNA needs to know about each of these security measures as well as how they can be applied to the Universal Aerospace Corporation.

User Account Restrictions

User account restrictions help to ensure that the user logging in is actually the authorized person by allowing the network administrator to establish password restrictions, time restrictions, and station restrictions. In this section, you will learn about each of these account restrictions and how they can be used to increase network security.

Passwords that are known only to the user are a necessary part of login security to authenticate the person logging in as a valid user. However, after time, passwords have a way of becoming common knowledge among other users and lose their ability to authenticate a specific user properly. To help keep passwords secret, you need to change them periodically. Since users often neglect this task, NetWare password restrictions enable network administrators to require users to change passwords within a given time period. In addition to requiring users to change passwords periodically, NetWare password restrictions also include a unique password option that you can use to ensure that users come up with a different password each time they change it rather than rotating between a few favorite passwords.

Despite all your efforts, you cannot prevent users from revealing their passwords to other persons or keep them from leaving their passwords on desks or in wastebaskets. To provide security in the event a user's password is known, NetWare provides administrators with the ability to set time and station restrictions. By using time and station restrictions, you can further restrict certain high-security users by allowing them to log in only during certain time periods or from specific workstations. If you place time and station restrictions on users' accounts, potential intruders who know users' passwords would have to enter users' offices during normal business hours and access their computers to log in. Others would likely notice this suspicious behavior even if the users were not in their offices. Another way to increase user account security is by limiting the number of stations from which a user can log in. By default, a user can be logged in concurrently from multiple stations. This can be a security problem for mobile users if they forget to log out before moving to another station. As a result, you should normally restrict user accounts to being logged in from only one station at a time.

As a network administrator, you will use NetWare Administrator to set password restrictions along with time and station restrictions on existing users, or place these restrictions on a container's user template (you'll learn to create user templates later in this chapter). Placing account restrictions on the user template saves time by automatically applying these restrictions to all new users that are created in that container. By doing the hands-on activities in this section, you learn how to establish account restrictions on existing user accounts in the Universal Aerospace organization.

Setting User Account Restrictions

The user account with the most security needs on your network is the Admin user. Because Admin has all rights to the network, management at Universal Aerospace is concerned about other users or intruders gaining access to the network by logging in using the Admin username.

In this hands-on activity, you will satisfy concerns about the security of the Admin username by using NetWare Administrator to set up the following account and password restrictions on your ##Admin account:

- Require a unique password of at least six characters every 30 days
- Limit accounts to only one concurrent connection
- Restrict users to logging in from only certain workstations

1. If necessary, start your computer, log in using your assigned ##Admin username, and start NetWare Administrator.

2. If necessary, open a browse window for your ##UAS container.

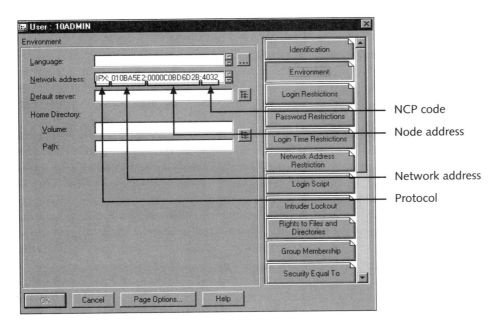

Figure 4-1   Environment window

3. Determine your workstation's network address by doing the following:

a) Double-click your **##Admin** username.

b) Click the **Environment** button to display a screen similar to the one shown in Figure 4-1. For a workstation using IPX, the first entry in the Network address field designates the IPX protocol followed by a colon, the network address followed by a colon, and the node address assigned to your network card. The NCP code specifies the task to be performed by the NetWare server. Record your IPX network and node address on the following line:

Network address: _O O O O O O O I B_

Node address: _O O O O 2 B 3 2 A 6 5 7 7_

_I P X : O O O O O O O I B : O O O O 2 B 3 2 A 6 5 7 7 : 4 0 8 2_

For a workstation using TCP/IP, the first entry in the Network address field designates the IP protocol followed by a four-byte TCP/IP address separated by periods. TCP/IP addresses contain both network and node components as described in Chapter 10.

4. Click the **Network Address Restriction** button and verify that the IPX/SPX button is selected.

5. Click the **Add** button to display the window shown in Figure 4-2.

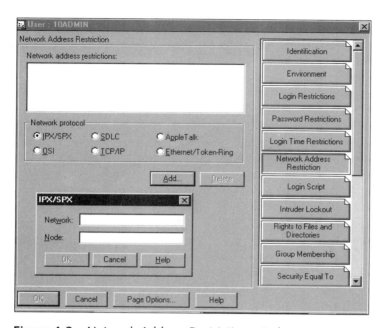

Figure 4-2   Network Address Restriction window

6. In the IPX/SPX dialog box, enter the network and node address values you recorded in Step 3. *Be careful to enter the correct values* or you may accidentally lock out your ##Admin user account. Leaving the node address blank will allow your account to log in from any workstation on the network address specified.

7. Click **OK** to enter the address.

8. Verify that the address is the same as displayed in the Environment window. You may want to enter a second workstation address to provide an additional station from which you can log in if your computer is down.

9. Click the **Login Restrictions** button to display the Login Restrictions window.

10. Click the **Limit Concurrent Connections** box to limit your ##Admin account to being logged in from only one computer at a time.

11. Click the **Password Restrictions** button to display the Password Restrictions window shown in Figure 4-3.

12. Click the **Require a password** check box and change the minimum password length from 5 to **6** characters.

13. Click the **Force Periodic password changes** check box and enter **30** in the Days between forced changes field.

14. Click the **Require unique passwords** check box to require a different password each time.

15. Click the **Limit grace logins** check box to allow a maximum of six logins after the password expires.

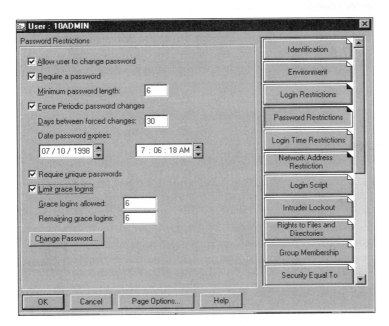

4

Figure 4-3   Password Restrictions window

16. Verify that your Password Restrictions window appears similar to the one shown in Figure 4-3.

17. Click **OK** to save the account restrictions.

18. Exit NetWare Administrator and log off.

19. Attempt to log in using your ##Admin username from another station. On the following line, record the error message you receive:

_____

Kellie Thiele would like to provide additional security for her account. She sometimes forgets to change her password for a long time and therefore would like the system to require her to enter a new password every 60 days. Since she has certain favorite passwords, she does not want to come up with a unique password every time. In addition, she would like you to secure her account so that it is active only from 6:30 a.m. until 11:00 p.m.

In this hands-on activity, you will secure Kellie's account by requiring a password change every 60 days as well as allowing use only from 6:30 a.m. through 11:30 p.m. on her assigned workstation.

1. Log in using your ##Admin username and start NetWare Administrator.

2. If necessary, open a browse window for your ##UAS container.

3. Double-click **KThiele**.

4. Click **Password Restrictions**.

5. Require a password of at least five characters to be changed every 60 days. Do not require unique passwords.

6. Click the **Login Time Restrictions** button to display the Login Time Restrictions window.

7. To restrict Kellie's account to access the network only during normal business hours, move the mouse pointer to the upper-left position in the time chart. Notice that the current location of the cursor including day and time is displayed beneath the time chart. After you have pointed to **Sunday, 12:00 a.m.**, hold down the mouse button and drag the cursor to the right until you reach the right-most column, then release the mouse button to shade in all of Sunday.

8. Next, point to **12:00 a.m. Monday**, then click and drag the pointer right and down to block in the hours 12:00 a.m. to 6:30 a.m. Monday through Saturday. Repeat this process to shade the hours from 11:00 p.m. through 11:30 p.m. on Monday through Friday. Finally, click and drag the mouse pointer on **Saturday** to shade 6:00 p.m. through 11:30 p.m. When you finish your time restrictions, the screen should be similar to Figure 4-4.

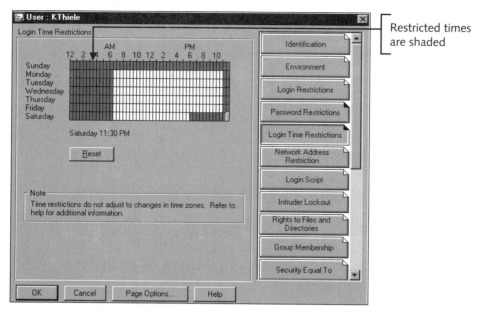

Figure 4-4   Login Time Restrictions window

9. Finally, to save the new login security restrictions, click the **OK** button located at the bottom of the window.

10. Exit NetWare Administrator and log out.

11. Log in as **KThiele**.

12. If the Windows Password dialog box opens, click **Cancel**.

13. Double-click **Network Neighborhood**.

14. Right-click the **Uas_host** server object.

15. Point to **User Administration** to display the Novell Password Administration option.

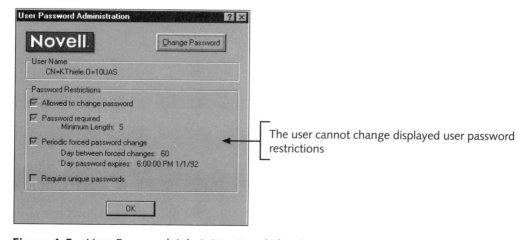

Figure 4-5   User Password Administration dialog box

16. Click the **Novell Password Administration** button to display the User Password Administration dialog box shown in Figure 4-5.

17. Click **Change Password** and enter **uashost** as the new password for Kellie.

18. Click **OK** to display the NetWare Password Synchronization window.

19. Click **OK** to synchronize the password with the UAS_Tree, click **OK** to confirm the NetWare password, and then click **OK** to confirm the password change.

20. Click **OK** to return to the Network Neighborhood dialog box.

21. Close the Network Neighborhood dialog box and log out.

Setting Intruder Detection Limits

Another potential login security problem is an intruder who can successfully guess another user's password. Forcing user passwords to be longer than four characters and training users to create nonobvious passwords that contain numbers as well as characters can go a long way toward preventing password guessing. This is critical because an intruder could get lucky, or, even more frightening, he or she might possess a password-guessing program that can send hundreds of password combinations into a computer in just a few seconds. An effective way to deter password guessing by intruders or software is to implement NetWare intruder detection in the container. **Intruder detection** works at the container level by setting a limit on the number of incorrect login attempts that can be made on a user account within that container during the specified time period. When a potential intruder makes the maximum number of incorrect login attempts in the established time period, the user's account may be locked up for the time period specified and a message indicating the time and station address of the login attempt appears. The user account will become available again at the end of the lockout time period, or the Admin user may free the account at any time.

 In this hands-on activity, you enable intruder detection in the Engineering and UAS containers to lock out a user's account for 15 minutes when more than five incorrect login attempts have been made in a 10-minute period.

1. If necessary, start your computer, log in using your assigned ##Admin username, and start NetWare Administrator.

2. Right-click your **##UAS** container.

3. Click the **Details** option to display the Organization information window.

4. Click the **Intruder Detection** button to display the Intruder Detection window.

5. Click the **Detect intruders** check box.

6. Change the 7 in the Incorrect login attempts field to **5**.

7. Change the Minutes field to **10**.

8. Click the **Lock account after detection** check box and verify a lockout time of 15 minutes as shown in Figure 4-6.

9. Click the **OK** button to save the intruder detection settings for your ##UAS container.

10. Repeat Steps 2 through 9 to set intruder detection on the Engineering container.

11. To test intruder detection, exit NetWare Administrator and log out.

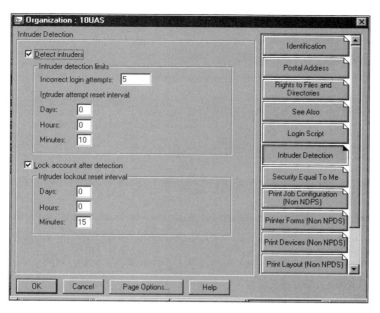

Figure 4-6 Intruder Detection window

12. Repeatedly attempt to log in as **KThiele** with an incorrect password. After five unsuccessful attempts, you will receive a message indicating the user account has been locked, or that you have encountered an unexpected login failure.

13. Now try logging in using the correct password. Record the error message you receive on the following line:

_____

14. Log in using your assigned ##Admin username.

15. Start NetWare Administrator.

16. Right-click the user **KThiele**.

17. Select the **Details** option and click the **Intruder Lockout** button located to the right of the window.

18. Note the time and location of the lockout.

19. Click the **Account Locked** check box to clear the lockout status.

20. Click **OK** to return to the browse window.

21. Exit NetWare Administrator and log out.

22. Log in as **KThiele**. Your login should be successful.

23. Log out of the network.

Understanding Authentication

NetWare security consists of two major parts, authorization and authentication. **Authorization** involves validating a user login request by verifying correct username, password, and any account restrictions. Once a user logs in successfully, NetWare **authentication** security validates each network request to guarantee the following:

- The authorized user sent the message.

- The message was sent from the client where the authorized user logged in.

- The message pertains to the user's current login session.

- The message has not been corrupted or modified.

Because the authentication security process occurs in the background, it is not visible to the user or network administrator. The authentication process starts when the user logs in by sending the client an encrypted private key specific for that user. The client then creates a **signature** using the private key, along with information identifying the user, workstation, and session. The signature is used along with the packet message to create **proof** that the NetWare 5.0 authentication security system uses to validate the packet as coming from the authorized user's workstation.

Authentication is an ongoing process that prevents an intruder from building message packets that appear to the network to have come from an authorized user. For example, suppose an intruder were able to capture packets from your client. Without authentication, it would be possible for the intruder to use software that would build a message in a packet that would seem to come from your client. This would allow an intruder to access any information or services to which the user has rights as long as the user is logged in. Authentication prevents this from happening because each packet has a unique proof field that is created by applying the user's signature to the information in the message. Without the user's password and signature, the intruder cannot fool the system into accepting falsified packets.

CREATING USERS AND GROUPS

In previous chapters, you learned how to use Novell's NetWare Administrator utility to create and manage objects in the NDS database. This section will enhance your ability to use NetWare Administrator by explaining what a CNA needs to know to create user accounts with templates. Securing access to the network is a very important responsibility of the network administrator. Novell has provided NetWare with a lot of features you can use to implement secure network access. As a CNA, you will need to know how to set up the various NetWare security options that will meet the security needs of your user accounts. The hands-on activities in this section will walk you through using templates to create and secure the users defined in Chapter 2 for the Engineering and Manufacturing divisions. The Universal Aerospace project at the end of the chapter will allow you to apply what you have learned to create and secure the remainder of the Universal Aerospace user objects.

Creating Groups

It is often convenient to establish groups to provide two or more users with access to shared resources and services. Instead of assigning rights directly to user accounts, many network administrators would rather assign rights to groups and then make a user a member of the group or groups that have the necessary rights. For example, within the Engineering department, only design engineers will be given access to certain software and files they need for their work. Rather than repetitively giving access rights to each of the design engineer user accounts, it is better to create a Design group and then add the design engineers as members. This group can then be given the rights and privileges necessary to access the restricted resources and services.

In addition to reducing the redundancy of assigning the same rights to multiple users, groups can also provide a convenient way to change user job responsibilities. For example, currently Kellie Thiele and Julie DamRau have responsibility for the Universal Aerospace Web site. Rather than giving both Julie and Kellie rights to maintain the Web site files, you could create a group called WebMgr and make both Julie and Kellie members. Should Kellie get too busy programming to carry out her Web management tasks, and if another person were assigned the responsibility of Web management, your NetWare administrative task would be simply to remove Kellie and then add the new user to the WebMgr group. Table 4-1 is a Group Planning form that lists the groups and members the consultant has recommended for the Universal Aerospace Engineering division.

Table 4-1   Group Name

Group Planning Form			
Designer: Jennifer Almquest, Consultant			
Date:			
Group Name	Members	Context	Description
ISMgrs	Kellie Thiele Your_user_name	.##UAS	Information systems staff that have rights to install, configure, and manage software and workstation environments.
WebMgr	Julie DamRau Kellie Thiele	.##UAS	Responsible for the design and maintenance of home page.
Design	Ira Means Lianne Jarka Tony Rucci Kellie Thiele Paul Alm	Engineering.##UAS	Design engineers who will be working with CAD software to create and maintain engineering design files.
Production	Russ Pence Receive terminals Ship terminals	Mfg.Engineering.##UAS	Access to Inventory system to record shipments and receipts. Access to read information from RPS system.

In this hands-on activity, you will create all the groups shown on the Group Planning form in Table 4-1 and then make your username and KThiele members of their associated groups.

1. If necessary, start your workstation, log in using your ##Admin username, and start NetWare Administrator.

2. If necessary, open a browse window for your ##UAS Organization.

3. Create the ISMgrs group and make your username and Kellie's members by following these steps:

   a) Highlight your **##UAS** Organization and press **[Ins]** to display the New Object window.

   b) Double-click the **Group** object to display the Create Group window.

   c) Enter the group name **ISMgrs** and click the **Define additional properties** box.

   d) Click the **Create** button to create the group and display the ISMgrs group details window.

   e) Click the **Members** button and click **Add** to display the Select Object window.

   f) Hold down **[Ctrl]** while you click your username and **KThiele**.

   g) Click **OK** to add yourself and KThiele to the ISMgrs group.

The group members window should now include the full distinguished names for Kellie and your username as shown in Figure 4-7.

   h) Click **OK** to save your changes and return to the browse window.

4. Create the WebMgr group and make Kellie and your username members, as follows:

   a) Highlight your **##UAS** Organization and press **[Ins]** to display the New Object window.

   b) Double-click the **Group** object to display the Create Group window.

   c) Enter the group name **WebMgr** and click the **Define additional properties** dialog box.

   d) Click the **Create** button to create the group and display the WebMgr group details window.

e) Click the **Members** button and click **Add** to display the Select Object window.

f) Hold down **[Ctrl]** while you click your username and **KThiele**.

g) Click **OK** to add your username and KThiele to the WebMgr group.

h) Click **OK** to save your changes and return to the browse window.

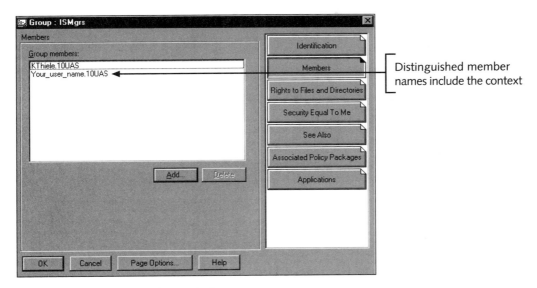

Figure 4-7   Group members window

5. Highlight the **Engineering** container and create the Design group. Do not add any users at this time.

6. Users from other contexts can also be made members of a group, allowing the group object to be used to assign rights to users in multiple containers. Follow these steps to make KThiele a member of the Design group:

   a) Right-click the **Design** group to highlight it and display the options menu.

   b) Click the **Details** option to display the Group window.

   c) Click the **Members** button to display the Members window.

   d) Next click **Add** to display the Select Object window.

   e) Double-click the **up arrow** in the right-hand Browse context window to move up one level.

   f) Double-click the user **KThiele** to add her to the existing group. Notice that Kellie's distinguished name includes the context of her object.

   g) Click **OK** to return to the NetWare Administrator browse window.

7. Create the Production group within the Mfg Organizational Unit. Do not add any users at this time.

Creating User Templates

Now that the necessary containers and file structure have been created, you will next want to create accounts for all the users. Although you could create each user individually as you did in Chapter 2, this method is time consuming and could also result in missing a step that would affect the user account usage or at least result in a nonstandard setup. As a result, an important step in the user creation process is to establish templates that can be used to simplify and standardize creating user accounts. A **user template** defines certain standard settings you want to establish for each user created with that template. For example, users in most organizations are like Universal Aerospace in that they will have certain account restrictions, as described in the previous section, along with a home directory where the users can create and manage their own files. User template properties allow a network administrator to define certain desired restrictions, as well as the location of the user's home directory, for all users created within that container. Table 4-2 contains the template requirements recommended by the consultant for use in creating users in the Engineering and IS departments.

 Using the T_ prefix prior to each template name helps to identify the object as a template and also distinguishes the name from corresponding group names.

Table 4-2   User Template

User Template Planning Form	
Designer: Jennifer Almquest, Consultant	
Date:	
Template Name	T_ISMgrs
Context	O=##UAS
Home Directory Path	UAS_HOST_CORP:##CORP\IS
Minimum Password Length	6
Require Unique Passwords	No
Days Between Password Changes	90
Grace Logins	6
Valid Login Times	All day
Maximum Connections	1
Groups	ISMgrs, WebMgr
Users	Kellie Thiele, your username
Template Name	T_Engineers
Context	OU=Engineering.O=##UAS
Home Directory Path	UAS_HOST_CORP:##CORP\ENGINEER
Minimum Password Length	6
Require Unique Passwords	Yes
Days Between Password Changes	90
Grace Logins	6
Valid Login Times	All day
Maximum Connections	1
Groups	Design
Users	Ira Means, Tony Rucci, Lianne Jarka, Paul Alm
Template Name	T_Station
Context	OU=Mfg.OUEngineering.O=##UAS
Home Directory Path	No home directory
Minimum Password Length	4
Require Unique Passwords	User cannot change the password
Days Between Password Changes	Password does not expire
Grace Logins	Not applicable
Valid Login Times	8:00 a.m. until 5:00 p.m.
Maximum Connections	2
Groups	Production
Users	Receiver, Shipper

Universal Aerospace has several computers in the manufacturing area that will be used mostly for entering shipment and receipt data. Rather than creating user accounts for each user who may enter data on these stations, Russ Pence has recommended having a generic account for each station based on its function. The T_Station template has been defined for setting up station accounts for the shipping and receiving stations.

In this hands-on activity, you will use NetWare Administrator to create user templates for engineers and IS users as defined on the Template Planning Form shown in Table 4-2.

1. If necessary, start your computer, log in using your ##Admin username, and start NetWare Administrator.

2. Open the Engineering container.

3. Press **[Ins]** to display the New Object window.

4. Double-click the **Template** object to display the Create Template window.

5. Enter **T_Engineers** in the Name field.

6. Click the **Define additional properties** field.

7. Click the **Create** button to create the template and display the Engineers detail window.

8. Click the **Environment** button and enter the path to the user home directory as shown in the following steps:

   a) Click in the **Volume** field and then click the **browse** button to display the Select Object window.

   b) Double-click the **UAS_HOST_CORP** volume object from the Available objects window.

   c) Click in the **Path** field and click the **browse** button to display the Select Object window.

   d) Use the Browse context window to open the **UAS_HOST_CORP** volume.

   e) Use the Browse context window to open your **##CORP** directory.

   f) Double-click the **Engineer** directory from the Available objects window. Your screen should look similar to Figure 4-8.

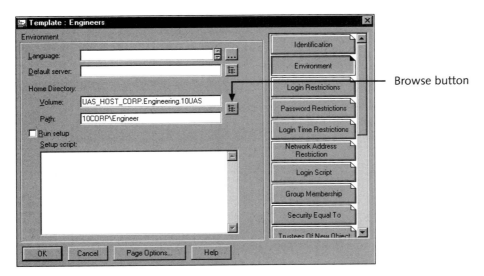

Figure 4-8   Environment window

9. Click the **Login Restrictions** button to display the Login Restrictions window.

10. Click the **Limit Concurrent Connections** box to limit new user accounts to being logged in from only one computer at a time.

11. Click the **Password Restrictions** button to display the Password Restrictions window.

12. Click the **Require a password** check box and change the minimum password length as defined on the Template Planning Form in Table 4-2.

13. Click the **Force periodic password changes** check box and enter the number of days between forced changes as defined on the Template Planning Form in Table 4-2.

14. Click the **Require unique passwords** check box if the User Template Planning form requires new users to use a different password each time they change.

15. Click the **Limit grace logins** check box to allow new users a maximum number of logins after their password expires as specified on the User Template Planning form.

16. Click the **Group Membership** button and add the group or groups defined on the User Template Planning form.

17. Click **OK** to save the changes and return to the browse window.

18. Click your **##UAS** container and create the **T_ISMgrs** user template as defined in Table 4-2.

19. Click on the **Mfg** container and create the **T_Station** template as defined in Table 4-2.

20. Create UAS_HOST_CORP and UAS_HOST_SYS volume objects in the Mfg container. Your ##UAS browse window should now appear similar to the one shown in Figure 4-9.

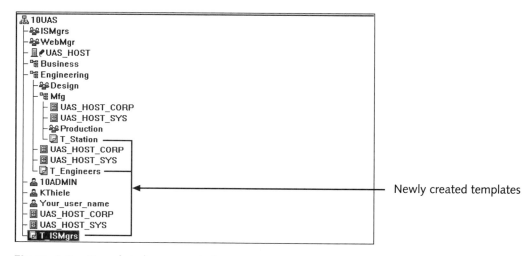

Figure 4-9 Template browse window

Creating User Objects from Templates

Controlling access to the network requires a login name to be created for each user. In NetWare, you provide users with login names by creating a User object within an NDS container for every network user. In addition to creating login names, you can also use NDS to keep track of many other fields of information, called properties, for each user. As you learned in Chapter 2, User objects must be assigned a login name and last name; other properties such as title, address, home directories, passwords, and time restrictions are optional. Because certain properties—for example, the location of the user's home directory or password requirements—are often common for many users, using templates, as described in the previous section, can make creating User objects easier and more standardized. By working with management and the consultant, you can identify all users in the Engineering and Manufacturing divisions on a User Planning form. The User Planning Form shown in Table 4-3 contains a list of the users along with their context and template requirements.

Organizational Role objects allow you to assign rights to an object rather than a specific user. You can then make any user an occupant of the Organizational Role to gain the associated rights and privileges given to the Organizational Role object.

 In this hands-on activity, you will create an engineering manager Organizational Role object and then make Ira Means the occupant of that object.

4

1. If necessary, log in using your assigned ##Admin username and start NetWare Administrator.

2. Create an Organizational Role object named EngMgr:

   a) Highlight your **Engineering** container.

   b) Press **[Ins]** and double-click the **Organizational Role** object from the New Object window.

   c) Enter the name **EngMgr** in the Organizational Role name field and click the **Define additional properties** box.

   d) Click the **Create** button to display the Organizational Role dialog box shown in Figure 4-11.

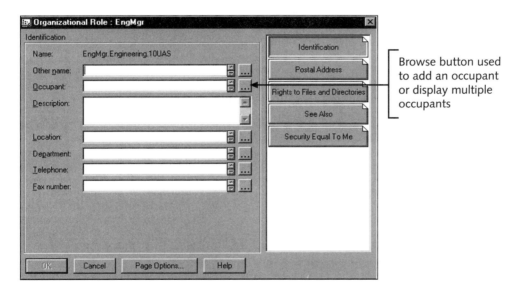

Figure 4-11   EngMgr identification window

3. Make Ira Means an occupant of the EngMgr Organizational Role object as follows:

   a) Click the **browse** button to the right of the Occupant field to display the Occupant window.

   b) Click the **Add** button in the Occupant window to display the Select Object window.

   c) Double-click **IMeans** from the Available objects window. IMeans should now appear in the Occupant window.

   d) Click **OK** to return to the Identification window.

   e) Click **OK** to close the Organizational Role Identification window.

Another good use for an Organizational Role object is to create a backup administrator account that can be used in case your Admin username is disabled. To give another user or Organizational Role object administrative status, you need to provide the NDS Supervisor object right to the organization. In Chapter 6, you will learn how to assign NDS rights to objects in the Directory tree.

In this hands-on activity, you will create a Sysop Organizational Role object and then make a new username (CKent) an occupant of the Sysop Organizational Role. In Chapter 6, you will learn how to give the Sysop object Supervisor rights to your ##UAS Organization.

1. If necessary, log in using your assigned ##Admin username and start NetWare Administrator.

2. Create a new user named CKent without a home directory in your ##UAS container using your ISMgr user template by completing the following steps:

   a) Click your **##UAS** container to highlight it.

   b) Click the **Create User object** icon from the toolbar.

   c) Enter **CKent** as the Login name and **Kent** as the Last name.

   d) Click the **Use template** box.

   e) Click the **browse** button to the right of the Use Template field to display a Select Object window.

   f) Double-click the **T_ISMgrs** template.

   g) Remove the check from the **Create Home Directory** box by clicking it.

   h) Click **Create** to create the new user.

3. Create an Organizational Role object named Sysop as follows:

   a) Highlight your **##UAS** container.

   b) Press **[Ins]** and double-click the **Organizational Role** object from the New Object window.

   c) Enter the name **Sysop** in the Organizational Role name field and click the **Define additional properties** box.

   d) Click the **Create** button to display the Organizational Role Identification window as shown previously in Figure 4-11.

4. Make Clark Kent an occupant of the Sysop Organizational Role object as follows:

   a) Click the **browse** button to the right of the Occupant field.

   b) Click the **Add** button to display the Select Object window.

   c) Double-click **CKent** from the Available objects window. The user CKent should now appear in the Occupant window.

   d) Click **OK** to return to the Identification window.

   e) Click **OK** to close the Organizational Role Identification window.

Automating User Creation with UIMPORT

In the near future, Universal Aerospace would like to implement a company intranet that would allow all employees to have an email address as well as use a browser program to access company information, such as benefits, policy information, announcements, and products. To implement a secure intranet, the company will need to assign each employee a network username and password. Currently the 25 employees in the Manufacturing division will need to have usernames created to allow them to access the network and have an email account. Although you could create accounts for Manufacturing division users with NetWare Administrator, Novell has provided a more automatic way of creating user accounts from a data file using a utility called UIMPORT.

As illustrated in Figure 4-12, the UIMPORT utility uses an ASCII data file containing user information along with a control file to create user accounts in the NDS database.

4

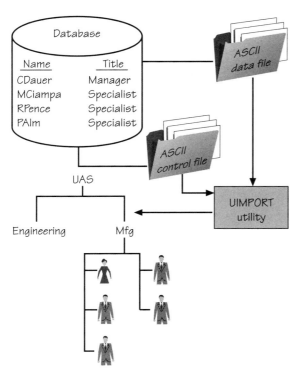

Figure 4-12   UIMPORT utility

The ASCII data file contains fields of information such as user login name, full name, address, and department separated by a delimiter such as a comma. Because it is an ASCII file, a data file can be produced using a text processor, spreadsheet, or database program such as Microsoft Access. The control file allows you to specify the format and field sequence of the user information in the ASCII data file as well as the delimiter used to separate the fields. In addition, the control file describes how the data will be imported into NDS by allowing you to set the context where the user accounts will be located and whether you want to create new objects or update existing objects. For example, Figure 4-13 shows a data file and a control file that can be used to create several of the users in the Manufacturing division.

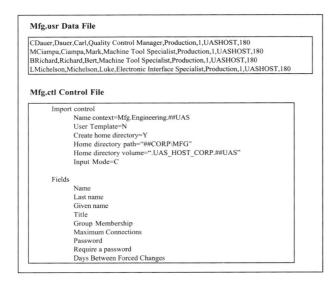

Figure 4-13   UIMPORT control files

Notice that the control file is divided into two sections: the Import control section and the Fields section. The Import control section has keywords to define the context where the user accounts will be created along with options such as whether to use a template or to create home directories automatically. The Fields section contains a list of each NDS field name included in the data file along with the sequence of fields. Table 4-4 contains a list of common NDS field names that may be used in the Fields section of a UIMPORT control file. The SKIP keyword indicates that a field of information in the data file is not to be included in the NDS database.

Table 4-4   UNIMPORT Field and Control File Definitions

Control Parameter	Description
Name context=	Specify the context of the container where the user accounts will be created.
User template=	Specify whether or not to use a template when creating user accounts by entering a Y or N.
Create home directory=	Specify whether or not to create a user home directory by entering either a Y or N.
Home directory path=	Specify the directory path that will contain the user home directories.
Home directory volume=	Specify the name of the volume where home directories will be created.
Import mode=	Enter one of the following codes to control UIMPORT actions: C=Create new objects only U=Update existing objects only B=Both C and U options R=Remove objects
Separator=	Specify the character used to delineate data fields in the data file. If no separator is specified, a comma is used as the default separator.

Field Name	Description
Name	User's login name. An entry for this field is required.
Last name	User's last name. An entry for this field is required.
Given name	User's first name.
Full name	User's full name.
Title	Title(s) that are associated with the user.
Description	A description of the user.
Location	User's work location.
Department	Department(s) with which the user works.
Telephone	User's telephone number(s).
Fax number	User's fax telephone number(s).
Home directory	User's home directory location specified as *VolumeName:Path*
Account has expiration date	Date the user's account will expire. Use the MM/DD/YY format.
Maximum connections	Number of simultaneous logins for the user. Enter 0 for unlimited.
Allow user to change password	Y or N. Default is Y.
Require a password	Y = a password is required. N = a password is optional.

Table 4-4   UIMPORT Field and Control File Definitions *(continued)*

Field Name	Description
Minimum password length	The minimum number of characters in the user's password.
Days between forced changes	The maximum number of days the user can use the same password.
Require unique passwords	Y = the user must specify a different password each time he or she changes it. N = the user can reuse previous passwords.
Grace logins allowed	The number of grace logins after the password has expired. Enter 0 for unlimited.
Password	User's initial password.
Street address	User's street address.
Post office box	User's post office box designation.
Login script	Path (in DOS format) and filename of an ASCII text file containing the user's login script commands.
Profile	Profile object name to be associated with the user account.
Group membership	NDS Group object name of each group to which the user is to belong.
City	User's city name.
State or province	User's state or province abbreviation.
Postal (zip) code	User's zip code.
Mailing label information	Use this field once for each line (up to six) of information in the mailing label.
SKIP	Special field name that causes UIMPORT to ignore a data field in the ASCII data file.

Once you have created the data and control files, you can use the UIMPORT utility to create the user accounts contained in the data file.

 In this hands-on activity, you will create the data and control files described in this section and then use the UIMPORT utility to create the new Manufacturing users. You will then use NetWare Administrator to verify the creation of the new user accounts.

1. If necessary, start your workstation and log in using your assigned ##Admin username.

2. If necessary, start NetWare Administrator and open a browse window for your ##UAS directory.

3. If necessary, create a subdirectory named Mfg under your ##CORP directory as shown in Figure 4-14.

4. Minimize NetWare Administrator.

5. Start the Notepad application (click **Start**, **Programs**, **Accessories**, **Notepad**).

6. Type in and save the data file shown previously in Figure 4-13. Name the data file **Mfg.usr** and save it in the Mfg directory.

7. Use Notepad to create and save the control file shown previously in Figure 4-13. Name the control file **Mfg.ctl** and save in the Mfg directory.

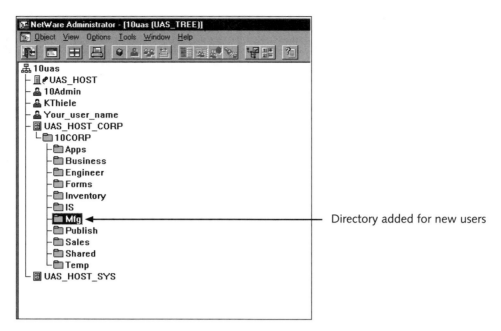

Figure 4-14   Mfg directory structure

8. Open a DOS window (click **Start**, **Programs**, **MS-DOS Prompt**).

9. Enter the following commands to change to your Mfg directory and run the UIMPORT utility:

   G: [Enter] (where G is your networked drive)

   CD Mfg [Enter]

   UIMPORT   Mfg.ctl   Mfg.usr [Enter]

   Check for any errors. If you receive error messages, use Notepad to fix the incorrect statement in either the data or control file and then rerun the UIMPORT program. Prior to rerunning the UIMPORT program, you will need to use NetWare Administrator to remove any user accounts and home directories created from your previous UIMPORT attempt. An alternative to using NetWare Administrator to remove the user accounts is to change the Import Mode flag to "R" in your Mfg.Ctl file and then run UIMPORT again to delete the users specified in the Mfg.usr file. However, since UIMPORT does not remove home directories, you will still need to use NetWare Administrator or Windows Explorer to delete the user home directories.

10. If you receive a "Bad command or file name" message, your search drive is not pointing to the SYS:PUBLIC directory. Enter the following commands to change the mapping:

    CD Z:\PUBLIC [Enter]

11. Type **Exit** and press **[Enter]** to return to Windows.

12. Restore NetWare Administrator.

13. Open your Mfg directory and verify that the user home directories have been created as shown in Figure 4-15.

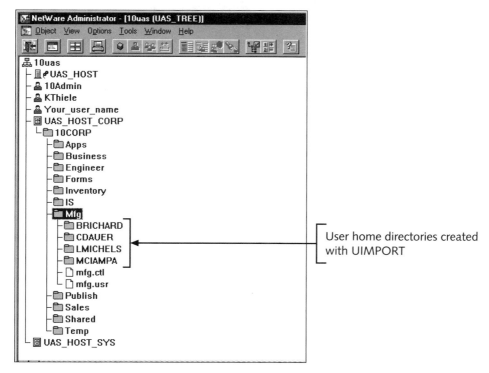

User home directories created
with UIMPORT

Figure 4-15   UIMPORT users

Notice that the directory names shown on the leftmost window are capitalized and truncated to eight characters. This is because UIMPORT defaults to using capitalized directory names that have a maximum length of eight characters to conform to DOS naming conventions.

14. Double-click on your Mfg organizational unit to verify that the new user accounts have been created. Double-click on one of the users and verify that maximum connections has been set to "1" with a password expiration of 180 days. Click **Cancel** to return to the NetWare Administrator browse window.

15. Exit NetWare Administrator.

16. Log out.

MOVING OBJECTS AND CONTAINERS

When working with the NDS system, you may sometimes want to move an object or container from one location to another to better organize the structure. To move a leaf object, such as a user or volume, you simply need to highlight the object and select the Move option from the Object menu. Moving container objects is more difficult because you must first create a partition from the container to move it, using the NDS Manager utility described in Chapter 2. In this section, you will learn how to use NetWare Administrator to copy a volume object, as well as how to use NDS Manager to move container objects.

Moving a User Object

When reorganizing an NDS structure, it is sometimes necessary to move a User object from one container to another. For example, as production manager, Russ Pence should have his user account in the Mfg container.

In this hands-on activity, you use NetWare Administrator to move the User object RPence from the Engineering Organizational Unit to the Mfg Organizational Unit.

1. If necessary, start your workstation, log in using your ##Admin username, and start NetWare Administrator.

2. If necessary, open a browse window for your ##UAS container.

3. Open your **Engineering** container.

4. Highlight the User object **RPence** by clicking it.

5. Click **Object**, **Move** to display the Move dialog box.

6. Click the **browse** button to the right of the Destination field to display the Select Object window.

7. Double-click **Mfg** in the Available objects window to insert the destination as shown in Figure 4-16.

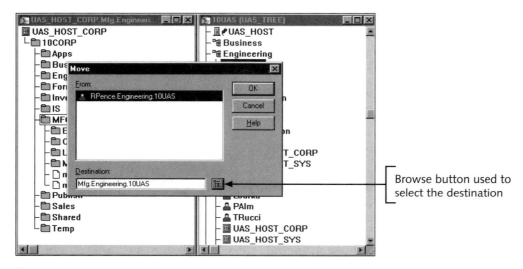

Figure 4-16   Moving a User object

8. Click **OK** to move the User object.

9. Double-click the **Mfg** container to verify that you have moved the User object RPence.

10. Move the home directory for Russ Pence to the Mfg directory structure as follows:

  a) Double-click the **UAS_HOST_CORP** volume.

  b) Double-click your **##Corp** directory.

  c) Double-click your **Mfg** directory.

  d) Open your **Engineer** directory and click the **RPence** directory to highlight it.

  e) Click the **Move** option from the **Object** menu to display the Move/Copy window.

  f) Click the **browse** button to the right of the Destination field to display the Select Object window.

  g) Double- click the **up-arrow** in the right-hand Browse context pane to move up one level in the directory structure.

  h) Double-click the **Mfg** directory in the left-hand Available object pane.

  i) Click the **Copy Trustee Assignments** check box.

signature — A component of authentication security that is created from the user's password, identification, and workstation address.

user template — An NDS object that contains user property information that can be applied when creating new user accounts.

REVIEW QUESTIONS

4

1. List five security systems used in setting up a secure NetWare 5.0 network:

    _____

    _____

    _____

    _____

    _____

2. A(n) _____ object can be used to simplify the maintenance of drive mappings.

3. The _____ allows the network administrator to define certain standard settings, such as the location of home directories for all new users.

4. The _____ utility can be used from the DOS prompt to create users automatically from information contained in control and data files.

5. List three steps you would need to perform to move the Mfg container from the Engineering container to the Business container:

    _____

    _____

    _____

6. The _____ utility can be used to create users from the NetWare server console.

7. List the three components of login security.

    _____

    _____

    _____

8. List three types of account restrictions.

    _____

    _____

    _____

9. The _____ system allows you to set a maximum number of times a user can enter an incorrect password.

10. _____ involves validating a user's login request.

11. _____ involves validating network requests to ensure they are from authorized users at appropriate workstations.

12. Write a UIMPORT command to create the user accounts in the TEMP.USR data file using control commands contained in the TEMP.CTL file.

    _____

13. The _____ utility is used to move a container to another location in the NDS tree.

14. A good use for a(n) _____ object is to provide a backup administrator account.

15. A(n) _____ defines certain standard settings you want to establish for multiple users.

The Universal Aerospace Project

The management of Universal Aerospace is pleased with the progress made in setting up the server and establishing user accounts for the Engineering and Manufacturing departments. Now there is an increasing need to start using the network and provide Business and Sales users with secure access to shared data and resources. Once the NDS setup is complete, you will be able to give users access to the file system by proceeding to the material in Chapter 5.

Step 1: Create the Groups

Create the Business group accounts shown in Table 4-5.

Table 4-5   Business Group Planning Form Account Information

Group Name	Members	Context	Description
Marketing	Michael Horowitz Darrell Minick Laura Hiller	Business.##UAS	Marketing and Sales staff who maintain customer data, access inventory, and work with orders.
Publishing	Diana Brady Bradley Dahl Julie DamRau	Business.##UAS	Responsible for the design of marketing literature, home page design, and development of operation instruction manuals.
Accounting	Terry Blackwell George Perez Amy Pan	Business.##UAS	Access to accounting software and data. Maintain inventory.
Mgmt	David Heise Lynn Dai	Business.##UAS	Access to certain company policies and contracts.
AdmAsst	Ira Means, Laura Hiller, Maria Frias, Lynn Dai	Business.##UAS	Maintain company forms and other documents.

Step 2: Create User Templates for Business and Sales

To make creating users easier and more standardized, the first step in setting up the Business division is to create the user templates defined for the Business department users. In this step, you are to use NetWare Administrator to create the remaining templates shown in Table 4-6.

Table 4-6   Business User Template Planning Form Information

Template Name	T_Account
Home Directory Path	UAS_HOST_CORP:##CORP\BUSINESS
Minimum Password Length	6
Require Unique Passwords	Yes
Days Between Password Changes	90
Grace Logins	6
Valid Login Times	7:00 a.m. until 10:00 p.m.
Maximum Connections	1
Groups	Accounting
Users	Terry Blackwell, George Perez, Amy Pan

Template Name	T_Marketing
Home Directory Path	UAS_HOST_CORP:##CORP\SALES
Minimum Password Length	6
Require Unique Passwords	No
Days Between Password Changes	90
Grace Logins	6
Valid Login Times	All day
Maximum Connections	1
Groups	Marketing
Users	Michael Horowitz, Darrell Minick, Laura Hiller

Template Name	T_Publish
Home Directory Path	UAS_HOST_CORP:##CORP\PUBLISH
Minimum Password Length	6
Require Unique Passwords	No
Days Between Password Changes	90
Grace Logins	6
Valid Login Times	All day
Maximum Connections	1
Groups	Publishing
Users	Diana Brady, Bradley Dahl, Julie DamRau

Step 3: Create the Users

Now you will create the Business user accounts.

a) With the exception of Lynn Dai, Maria Frias, and David Heise, use the appropriate templates to create the Business department user accounts shown in Table 4-7. Use NetWare Administrator to modify Lynn's, Maria's, and David's user account to provide the group membership and login restrictions included in Table 4-7.

b) After creating the users, open an MS–DOS Prompt window and enter the following commands to change to your F: drive and print a copy of all users in the Business container:

F:[Enter]

NLIST USERS/CO Business/S

c) Make Julie DamRau a member of the WebMgr group.

Table 4-7   Business User Planning Form Information

User Name	Login Name	Context	Template Name	Home Directory	Groups	Additional Properties
Dave Heise	DHeise	.##UAS		Yes	Mgmt	
Lynn Dai	LDai	.##UAS		Yes	Mgmt AdmAsst	
Michael Horowitz	MHorowitz	Business .##UAS	T_Marketing	Yes	Marketing	
Darrell Minick	DMinick	Business .##UAS	T_Marketing	Yes	Marketing	
Laura Hiller	LHiller	Business .##UAS	T_Marketing	Yes	Marketing	
Diana Brady	DBrady	Business .##UAS	T_Publish	Yes	Publishing	
Julie DamRau	JDamRau	Business .##UAS	T_Publish	Yes	Publishing WebMgr	
Bradley Dahl	BDahl	Business .##UAS	T_Publish	Yes	Publishing	
Terry Blackwell	TBlackwell	Business .##UAS	T_Account	Yes	Accounting	
George Perez	GPerez	Business .##UAS	T_Account	Yes	Accounting	
Amy Pan	APan	Business .##UAS	T_Account	Yes	Accounting	
Maria Frias	MFrias	Business .##UAS		Yes	AdmAsst	

Step 4: Enable Intruder Detection

Enable intruder detection on the Business Organizational Unit so that a user account will be locked up for 15 minutes after five invalid login attempts made within a 10-minute period. If requested by your instructor, print the screen showing your Business container intruder detection settings.

Step 5: Move User Accounts and Directories

Currently the users Dave Heise and Lynn Dai are located in the Business container and their home directories are located off the root of your CORP volume. Since Dave is the company president, the consultant has recommended moving his user name up one level to be in the ##UAS organization. To help standardize the directory structure, you should move user Dave Heise up to your ##UAS organization and then move Lynn Dai's home directory to the Business folder.

a) In the following spaces, briefly describe the steps you used to perform this move along with the name of the utility you used.

Utility used: _____

Steps: _____

4

_____

_____

_____

_____

b) Using the techniques you learned in Chapter 3, move Lynn's home directory to the Business folder and verify that she has all rights to the relocated directory.

c) Restrict Dave's account to logging in only from your workstation.

d) Restrict Lynn's account to prevent use during daylight hours.

Step 6: Create an Organizational Role Object

As described in this chapter, Organizational Role objects can simplify network administration. For example, currently the head of the Accounting department needs to have rights to access information in the Sales and Publishing departments. Rather than giving these rights to Terry Blackwell, Dave would like you to create an Organizational Role object and then make Terry an occupant. In this way, when Terry is gone, another user can assume the role by simply making himself or herself a temporary occupant of the Accounting manager object. In this step, you are to create an Organizational Role object named AccMgr and make Terry an occupant. Record the steps you use to do this in the following space:

Step 7: Test User Accounts

After all users and security have been established, the final step in implementing NDS is to test the user accounts and restrictions to be sure they work correctly. To make this test, perform the following steps and record the results for users Terry Blackwell and Lynn Dai:

a) Log out of the network.

b) Change the current context to the Business container.

c) Log in as Terry Blackwell.

d) Change your password to uashost. Record the steps you used to change the password in the following space:

e) Map drive H to Terry's home directory.

f) Open a DOS window.

g) Use the MAP > PRN command to print a copy of the user's drive mappings.

h) Log out of the network.

i) Test intruder detection by attempting to log in to Terry's user account with an incorrect password. How many login attempts did it take before the account was locked out?

_____

j) Attempt to log in as Dave Heise from another workstation. Record the error message on the following line:

_____

k) Attempt to log in as Lynn Dai. Record the error message you receive on the following line:

_____

l) Log in using your ##Admin username and start NetWare Administrator.

m) Free up the locked account. Record the station number and time that the lockup occurred.

Station number: _____

Time: _____

n) Change Lynn Dai's time restriction to allow access between 7:00 a.m. and 5:00 p.m.

ADDITIONAL EXERCISES

These exercises are included to give you more practice working with NetWare Administrator and the NDS system and to help you pass the CNA exam. It is assumed that you have already completed the previous required Universal Aerospace project steps.

Exercise 4-1: Modify Multiple User Accounts

Dave would like all users in each department to have their department's phone and fax numbers included in their user accounts. In this exercise, you are to use the appropriate groups along with the Details on Multiple Users function to add the following phone and fax numbers to department users:

Department	Phone	Fax
Accounting	(715) 555-7363	(715) 555-7364
Marketing	(715) 555-4323	(715) 555-4324
Publishing	(715) 555-7120	(715) 555-7121
Engineering	(715) 555-7115	(715) 555-7116

Exercise 4-2: Create an Organizational Role Object

Create an Organizational Role object named BusMgr to manage the Business Organizational Unit. Make Lynn Dai the occupant of the BusMgr role object. In Chapters 5 and 6, you will give this object rights to the Business container and directory structure.

Exercise 4-3: Use UIMPORT to Set Up Training Accounts

Dave would like you to hold a special training session to show all Business users how to access and use the new network system. Rather than having users use their own accounts, you want to have them log in using special usernames that have been set up to perform the special training activities. Since you are planning to train a maximum of five users at a time, you plan to create five of these temporary accounts. In this activity, you will use UIMPORT to create the users by setting the appropriate data and control files from the following specifications:

As its name implies, the **Access Control (A) right** allows users to control what other users can access in the directory or file by granting access rights to other users. Since allowing users to grant rights to other users can make it difficult for the network administrator to keep track of file system security, the Access Control right should not normally be given to other users.

Having the **Supervisor (S) right** is different from having all rights because the Supervisor right cannot be changed or blocked at a lower directory or file. The Supervisor right is also different from other rights because it can be assigned only by another user who has Supervisor rights to the directory. Having the Access Control right does not allow a user to assign the Supervisor right to himself or herself or another user. The Supervisor right is often granted to workgroup managers to allow them to control some section of the file system's directory structure. For example, if IMeans is the workgroup manager for the Engineering department, he could be granted the Supervisor right to the Corp:Engineer directory structure.

 If users have the Access Control right in a directory but do not have the Supervisor right, they could restrict themselves from working in the directory by accidentally assigning their username less rights than they need to the directory or a subdirectory. For that reason, in most cases, the Access Control right should not be granted to a user unless it is absolutely necessary for the user to assign rights to others.

To help you better understand which access rights are necessary for performing functions in the network file system, Table 5-2 contains a list of typical operations that users need to perform on files and directories, along with the access rights required to perform those operations.

Table 5-2   Rights Required for Common Functions

Task	Right(s) Required
Read a file	Read
Obtain a directory listing	File Scan
Change the contents of data in a file	Write
Write to a closed file using a text editor that creates a backup file	Write, Create, Erase, Modify (not always required)
Execute a program file	Read
Create and write to a new file	Create
Copy a file from a directory	Read, File Scan
Copy a file into a directory	Create
Copy multiple files to a directory with existing files	Create, File Scan
Create a subdirectory	Create
Delete a file	Erase
Salvage deleted files	Read and File Scan on the file, and Create in the directory or on the filename
Change attributes	Modify
Rename a file or subdirectory	Modify
Change the Inherited Rights Filter	Access Control
Make or change a trustee assignment	Access Control

Trustee Assignments

A **Directory trustee** is a user, group, or container object that has been granted access rights to a directory. As stated earlier, directory trustees are kept track of in the directory entry table (DET) of each volume. A DET entry can hold up to six trustee assignments. If more than six trustees are assigned to a directory, an additional entry in the DET is made for that directory's name. For this reason, it is good to keep trustee assignments to six or fewer for each directory. This is usually done by making a group a trustee of a directory and then adding users to the group if they need access to that directory.

A **File trustee** is a user or group that has been granted access rights to a file. As with Directory trustees, File trustees are kept track of in the DET. If more than six trustees are assigned to a file, an additional entry in the DET is needed for that filename.

Effective rights consist of a subset of the access rights and control what functions users can perform in a specific directory or file. In many cases, users' effective rights are the same as their trustee assignments. However, other assignments may also affect effective rights. There are basically five types of assignments that affect what effective rights a user will have to a directory or file. A user's effective rights are the result of one or more of following five factors:

- A trustee assignment made directly to the username
- A trustee assignment made to a group of which the user is a member
- A trustee assignment made to a container in which the user or a group to which the user is a member resides
- Container, group, and user rights inherited by a file or directory from a higher-level directory
- Inherited rights being blocked by an Inherited Rights Filter applied to a directory or file

In this chapter, you will learn each of the five ways in which a user can acquire effective rights and how to apply this knowledge to establish a file security system on your Universal Aerospace network.

User Trustee Assignment

The simplest and most straightforward way for a user to obtain effective rights in a directory or file is by being granted a direct trustee assignment consisting of a specific set of access rights to the directory or file. This is called a **trustee assignment** because it makes the user a trustee of the directory or file with certain access privileges. If no trustee assignments have been made to any groups or containers of which the user is a member, users' effective rights will always be equal to their trustee assignments. When making trustee assignments, you usually specify access rights by using the first letter of each access right enclosed in brackets. For example, you would use [R F C] to specify that a user has Read, File Scan, and Create rights. The word [All] enclosed within the brackets is often used to represent all access rights except Supervisor and is more convenient than specifying each right individually.

The most common application of user trustee assignments is providing users with all rights to their home directory. When you created home directories for the users in Chapter 4, you gave each user a trustee assignment of all rights to their home directory.

 Providing users with the Access Control right to their home directory creates possible security problems. First, having the Access Control right allows a user to make other objects trustees of their directory. In addition to making it harder for you to manage file system security, providing this right increases the probability of intruders accessing or destroying data. Second, having the Access Control right without Supervisor rights allows users to reassign their own rights to a file or subdirectory accidentally, possibly locking themselves out of a portion of their directory and eventually requiring your assistance to bail them out.

In Chapter 3, you learned how you could use My Computer from Windows to make and change trustee assignments. In addition to using My Computer, you can also use Windows Explorer and Network Neighborhood to make and maintain user trustee assignments. Although it is often convenient to make trustee assignments in Windows, NetWare Administrator provides additional capability when making and maintaining trustee assignments. For example, you will need to use NetWare Administrator to assign the Supervisor right, make multiple trustee assignments to a user, or view a user's effective rights. In this chapter, you will use the Windows utilities along with NetWare Administrator to implement file system security. Although file system security is usually maintained using NetWare Administrator, the new Novell NetWare Client for Windows 95/98 can assign and modify access rights, making it sometimes more convenient to use Windows Explorer when modifying user access rights.

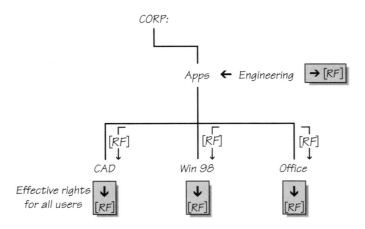

→ Indicates trustee assignment

↓ Indicates inherited rights

Figure 5-4   Inherited rights

In this hands-on activity, you will use My Computer or Windows Explorer to assign your ##UAS container Read and File Scan rights to the Apps directory and then verify that the rights are inherited by each of the application subdirectories.

1. If necessary, start your computer and log in using your assigned ##Admin username.

2. Double-click **My Computer** or start Windows Explorer.

3. Open your ##Corp directory.

4. To make your ##UAS container a trustee of Apps with Read and File Scan rights:

   a) Right-click your **Apps** directory and click the **Properties** option.

   b) Click the **NetWare Rights** tab.

   c) Click your **##UAS** container and click **Add**. Your ##UAS container should now appear in the Trustees window with Read and File Scan rights checked.

   d) Click **OK** to close the window and save your changes.

5. Double-click the **Apps** directory to open it.

6. Check inherited rights to each of the subdirectories as follows:

   a) Right-click the **CAD** subdirectory and click **Properties**.

   b) Click the **NetWare Rights** tab. Click the **Inherited Rights and Filters** button to display the dialog box shown in Figure 5-5. Notice that your ##UAS container appears with inherited rights of Read and File Scan.

   c) Click **Cancel** to return to the Properties window.

   d) Click **Cancel** to return to the Apps directory window.

   e) Repeat Steps 6a through 6d to check inherited rights in the Office and Win98 directories.

7. Close the Apps window.

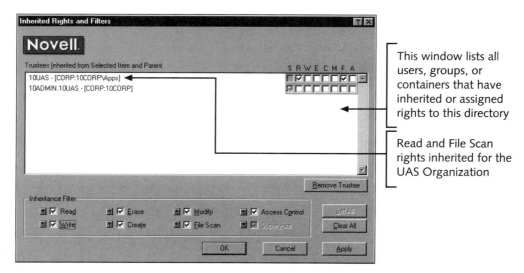

This window lists all users, groups, or containers that have inherited or assigned rights to this directory

Read and File Scan rights inherited for the UAS Organization

Figure 5-5   Inherited Rights and Filters dialog box

The Inherited Rights Filter

In some cases, you do not want user and group rights to be inherited by a lower directory. NetWare allows you to stop a lower subdirectory from inheriting rights by providing each directory with what is called an Inherited Rights Filter. An **Inherited Rights Filter (IRF)** acts as a block to keep selected rights from passing into the lower subdirectory structure or files. Each directory or file has an Inherited Rights Filter field stored in the directory entry table (DET).

The IRF works by applying a logical AND between the user's effective rights and the Inherited Rights Filter. When you use the logical AND operator, a right must be present in both the user's effective rights as well as the Inherited Rights Filter to pass through to the subdirectory. Within this system, any rights specified in the IRF of a directory or file may be inherited by that directory or file. By default, when you create a directory or file, all rights are included in the IRF for that file or directory. You can then block a directory or file from inheriting rights by removing the rights you do not want inherited from the IRF.

The exception to the use of IRF to block rights is the Supervisor right. To prevent you from restricting the Supervisor right, the IRF does not enable you to remove the Supervisor access right from it, whereas in the file system you cannot use an IRF to block the Supervisor right.

Because the IRF filters only inherited rights from the parent directory, it has no effect on the direct trustee assignments made to the directory or file. For example, Ira Means has only enough CAD software licenses for the design engineers. However, since CAD is located in the Apps directory, currently all users could run the CAD software and thereby violate the license agreement.

In this hands-on activity, you will use My Computer or Windows Explorer to remove all rights from the IRF of the CAD directory and then assign only the Design group rights to run the software. You will then use NetWare Administrator to verify user effective rights to the CAD software.

1. If necessary, start your computer and log in using your assigned ##Admin username.

2. Double-click **My Computer** or start Windows Explorer.

3. Browse to the **Apps** directory.

4. Remove all rights from the IRF of the CAD directory as follows:

   a) Right-click **CAD** and click the **Properties** option.

   b) Click the **NetWare Rights** tab and then click the **Inherited Rights and Filters** button.

c) Remove the check marks from all rights in the Inheritance Filter by clicking each of the check boxes. As you click each check box, the green light will change to red and the check mark will be removed. Notice that you cannot remove the check from the Supervisor rights filter box. Because the Supervisor right cannot be removed from an IRF, a user who has been granted the Supervisor rights to a higher directory is not affected by the IRF.

d) Click the **OK** button to save your changes.

5. Add the Design group as a trustee of CAD with Read and File Scan rights:

a) Double-click your **Engineering** container to display users and groups.

b) Click the **Design** group and click the **Add** button. The Design group should now appear in the Trustees window with Read and File Scan rights.

c) Click **OK** to save your changes and return to the Apps window.

d) Close the Apps window.

6. Start NetWare Administrator.

7. If necessary, open a browse window for your ##Corp directory. Double-click **Apps**.

8. Right-click your **CAD** directory and click the **Details** option.

9. Check effective rights for your username and the design engineers by following these steps:

a) Click the **Trustees of this Directory** button.

b) Click the **Effective Rights** button to display the Effective Rights window.

c) Click the **browse** button and double-click your username. Your username should have no effective rights in the CAD directory.

d) Click the **browse** button and double-click the **Engineering** container in the right-hand Browse context window.

e) Double-click the user **LJarka**. Lianne should have Read and File Scan rights because she is a member of the Design group.

f) Verify effective rights for other users. Notice that the user KThiele will have Read and File Scan rights as a result of being a member of the Design group. Click **Cancel**.

10. Exit NetWare Administrator.

Combining Trustee Assignments and Inherited Rights

When combining inherited rights and trustee assignments, it is important to remember that whenever a user, group, or container object is granted a new trustee assignment, that new assignment overrides the inherited rights for that object and becomes that object's effective rights, with one exception. That exception is when a user, group, or container has been granted the Supervisor right ([S]) to a directory. When this is the case, new trustee assignments made to subdirectories or files will not override the inherited Supervisor right. For example, the consultant has recommended limiting your use of the Admin user whenever possible. To help do this, you could provide your username rights to manage certain directory structures such as the Apps and IS directories. You could do this in one of two ways: Either grant your username all rights ([R F C W E M A]) to the Apps and IS directories, or grant the Supervisor right, [S]. If you grant your username all rights ([R F C E M A]), the rights can be redefined in a subdirectory. However, if you grant your username the Supervisor right, [S], to a directory, your rights cannot be reduced by another trustee assignment or IRF, as illustrated in Figure 5-6.

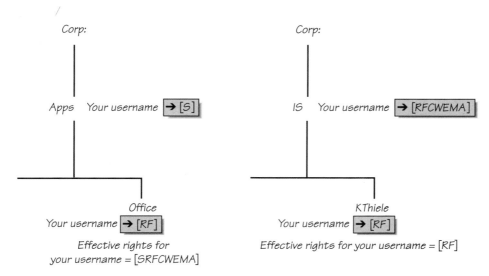

Figure 5-6   Granting Supervisor rights

 In this hands-on activity, you will use NetWare Administrator to grant your username Supervisor rights to the Apps and IS directories and then verify your effective rights in each location.

1. If necessary, start your computer and log in using your assigned ##Admin username.

2. If necessary, start NetWare Administrator and open a browse window for your ##Corp directory.

3. Add your username as a trustee of Apps with Supervisor rights:

   a) Right-click the **Apps** directory and click the **Details** option.

   b) Click the **Trustees of this Directory** button.

   c) Click the **Add Trustee** button to display the Select Object dialog box.

   d) Double-click your username in the left-hand Available objects window to add it to the Trustees window.

   e) Click the **Supervisor** right and click **OK** to save the assignment.

4. Provide your username with Supervisor rights to the IS directory:

   a) Right-click the **IS** directory and click the **Details** option.

   b) Click the **Trustees of this Directory** button.

   c) If your username is not currently a trustee, click the **Add Trustee** button to display the Select Object dialog box. Double-click your username in the left-hand Available objects window to add it to the Trustees window.

   d) Highlight your username and then click the **Supervisor** right.

   e) Click **OK** to save the assignment.

5. Check your effective rights in the Web and Utility subdirectories of your IS directory:

   a) If necessary, open your **IS** directory by double-clicking it.

   b) Right-click the **Web** subdirectory and then click the **Details** option.

   c) Click the **Trustees of this Directory** button and then click the **Effective Rights** button to display the Effective Rights dialog box.

5

d) Click the **browse** button and then double-click your username to display your effective rights in the Web subdirectory. Notice that your username now has all effective rights in the Web subdirectory. This is the result of the Supervisor right assignment to your username in the IS directory.

e) Click the **Close** button and click **Cancel** to return to the NetWare Administrator browse window.

f) Repeat steps 5b through 5e to check your effective rights in the Utility and KThiele subdirectories.

6. Check your effective rights in the CAD and Office subdirectories of the Apps directory:

a) If necessary, open your **Apps** directory by double-clicking it.

b) Right-click the **CAD** directory and click the **Details** option.

c) Click the **Trustees of this Directory** button and then click the **Effective Rights** button to display the Effective Rights dialog box.

d) Click the **browse** button and then double-click your username to display your effective rights in the CAD directory. Notice that your username now has all effective rights in the CAD subdirectory. This is the result of the Supervisor right assignment to your username in the Apps directory.

e) Click the **Close** button and click **Cancel** to return to the NetWare Administrator browse window.

f) Repeat Steps 6b through 6e to check your effective rights in the Office and Win98 subdirectories.

Kellie does not seem very happy with the idea of your username having Supervisor rights to her home directory. She would rather you had only Read and File Scan rights.

 In this hands-on activity, you will reassign your rights to Kellie's home directory by making a new trustee assignment for your username, and then check your username's effective rights.

1. If necessary, start your computer, log in using your assigned ##Admin username, and start NetWare Administrator.

2. If necessary, open a browse window for your ##Corp directory. Double-click **IS** to open it.

3. Add your username as a trustee of Kellie's home directory with only Read and File Scan rights:

a) Right-click the **KThiele** subdirectory and click the **Details** option.

b) Click the **Trustees of this Directory** button and then click the **Add Trustee** button to display the Select Object dialog box.

c) Double-click your username to add it into the Trustees window with Read and File Scan rights.

d) Click **OK** to save the assignment.

4. Check your username's effective rights in Kellie's home directory by doing the following:

a) Right-click the **KThiele** subdirectory and click the **Details** option.

b) Click the **Trustees of this Directory** button and then click the **Effective Rights** button to display the Effective Rights dialog box.

c) Click the **browse** button to display the Select Object dialog box.

d) Double-click your username in the left-hand Available objects window to display your effective rights.

5. Notice that despite the assignment of Read and File Scan rights, your username still has all rights to Kellie's directory. This is because your username is a Supervisor of the IS directory structure and therefore cannot be reassigned fewer rights in a subdirectory. For your username's trustee assignment in Kellie's directory to work, you will need to remove the Supervisor right from your trustee assignment in the IS directory and replace it with all rights.

6. Remove the Supervisor right from your trustee assignment in the IS directory and replace it with all rights:

   a) Click the **Close** and **Cancel** buttons to return to the NetWare Administrator browse window.

   b) Right-click your **IS** directory and click the **Details** option.

   c) Click the **Trustees of this Directory** button to display your trustee assignment.

   d) Click your username's trustee assignment and then change the access rights to remove Supervisor and then select all other rights as shown in Figure 5-7.

   e) Click **OK** to save the trustee assignment changes.

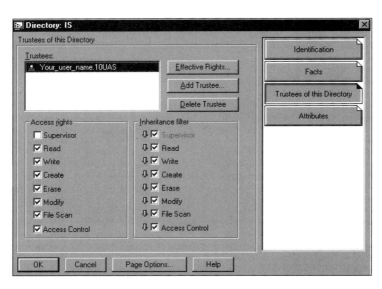

Figure 5-7   Trustees of the IS directory

7. Check your username's effective rights in Kellie's home directory by doing the following:

   a) Right-click the **KThiele** subdirectory and click the **Details** option.

   b) Click the **Trustees of this Directory** button and then click the **Effective Rights** button to display the Effective Rights dialog box.

   c) Click the **browse** button to display the Select Object dialog box.

   d) Double-click your username in the left-hand Available objects window to display your effective rights.

8. Notice that you now have only Read and File Scan rights to Kellie's directory.

9. Click the **Close** and **Cancel** buttons to return to the NetWare Administrator browse window. Exit NetWare Administrator.

As described earlier, a user's effective rights in any given directory are a combination of the user object's trustee assignment or inherited rights along with the effective rights the user receives from any container or group memberships. As a network administrator, you can sometimes reduce the rights granted to a specific user by taking group or container rights into consideration. For example, Kellie has recently written a software package for the Manufacturing department to maintain quality standards in the manufacturing process. To test this package, you have agreed to create a subdirectory named Quality in the Apps directory and give Kellie all rights except Supervisor to this directory.

In this hands-on activity, you will create a Quality subdirectory and then provide Kellie with all rights to the subdirectory as illustrated in Figure 5-8.

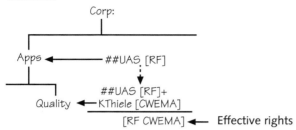

Figure 5-8   Creating the Quality directory

Since your ##UAS Organization will inherit Read and File Scan rights as a result of the trustee assignment you made previously, you would need only to assign Kellie the [CWEMA] rights to have all effective rights in the Quality subdirectory.

1. If necessary, start your computer and log in using your assigned ##Admin username.

2. Double-click **My Computer** and browse to your Apps directory.

3. Create a Quality subdirectory by doing the following:

    a) Click **File**, point to **New**.

    b) Click the **Folder** option.

    c) Enter the name **Quality** and press **[Enter]**.

4. Assign Kellie [CWEMA] rights to the Quality subdirectory:

    a) Right-click the **Quality** directory and click the **Properties** option.

    b) Click the **NetWare Rights** tab.

    c) Click the **KThiele** username and click the **Add** button.

    d) Click the boxes for **W**, **E**, **C**, **M**, and **A** to give Kellie the corresponding rights.

    e) Click **OK** to save your changes and then close the Apps window.

5. Start NetWare Administrator.

6. Check Kellie's effective rights in the Quality subdirectory by doing the following:

    a) If necessary, open a browse window to your ##Corp directory. Double-click the **Apps** directory.

    b) Right-click the **Quality** subdirectory and click the **Details** option.

    c) Click the **Trustees of this Directory** button and then click the **Effective Rights** button to display the Effective Rights dialog box.

    d) Click the **browse** button to display the Select Object dialog box.

    e) Double-click Kellie's username to display her effective rights of Read, Write, Create, Erase, Modify, File Scan, and Access Control. In the following space, describe how Kellie obtained Read and File Scan rights.

7. Close the Effective Rights dialog box and click the **Cancel** button to return to the NetWare Administrator browse window. Exit NetWare Administrator.

When calculating effective rights for a user, it is important to remember that NetWare tracks inherited rights separately for each type of object. This means that a user object's inherited rights in a directory are separate from the inherited rights for a container or group. Users' effective rights are therefore a combination of their individual rights plus the effective rights of any groups or containers to which the users belong. For example, Kellie has completed the first step in the testing process by installing and running the software in the Quality subdirectory structure you established. Her next step is to provide the user Carl Dauer in the Manufacturing department with the rights he will need to run the package. Kellie has determined that Carl should need only Read, File Scan, and Write rights to run the programs, but before assigning these rights she wants to reduce the rights assigned to her username to only those rights and test the package. However, to reestablish her full rights, she will also need to retain the Access Control right to the Quality subdirectory.

In this hands-on activity, you will simulate the process of Kellie testing the software package by logging in as KThiele and reducing your rights to only Write and Access Control. You will then exercise the Access Control right to give Kellie back her full rights.

1. If necessary, log out and then log back in as KThiele.

2. Double-click **My Computer** and browse to your **Apps** directory.

3. Assign Kellie Write and Access Control rights to the Quality subdirectory:

   a) Right-click the **Quality** directory and click the **Properties** option.

   b) Click the **NetWare Rights** tab.

   c) Remove the checks from the [**E C M**] rights check boxes.

   d) Click **OK** to save your changes and then close the Apps window.

4. Start NetWare Administrator.

5. Check Kellie's effective rights in the Quality subdirectory:

   a) If necessary, open a browse window to your ##Corp directory. Double-click the **Apps** directory.

   b) Right-click the **Quality** subdirectory and click the **Details** option.

   c) Click the **Trustees of this Directory** button and then click the **Effective Rights** button to display the Effective Rights dialog box. Notice that because you are logged in as KThiele, her effective rights in the Quality directory are automatically displayed.

6. Notice that in addition to having Write and Access Control rights Kellie also has Read and File Scan rights. The Read and File Scan rights are the result of the ##UAS container's inherited rights from the Apps directory. Because Kellie's username is part of the ##UAS container, she also receives the Read and File Scan rights.

7. Close the Effective Rights dialog box and click the **Cancel** button to return to the NetWare Administrator browse window.

8. Exit NetWare Administrator.

PLANNING FILE SYSTEM SECURITY

As you have learned, NetWare file system security is a sophisticated and complex system that has many options you can use to provide necessary access to network data. Providing users with the effective rights necessary to perform their work while still protecting data from unauthorized access requires careful thought and planning on the part of a network administrator. To make file system security less complex when multiple group and user trustee assignments are involved, it is important to plan the security system to use as few trustee assignments as possible and keep the use of IRFs to a minimum.

This section provides several guidelines and suggestions that will help you to design a secure network file system. You will also learn how to apply these guidelines to define the trustee assignments for the Engineering department.

File System Security Guidelines

To help keep file system security as simple and effective as possible, Novell suggests that CNAs follow certain guidelines when planning file system security. In this section, you will learn about each of the guidelines recommended by Novell and how you can use them to improve your file system security plan.

Identify Rights Needed for Each User

The first guideline in successfully establishing file system security is to analyze each user's processing needs and then determine and document the access rights that will be required for each directory to meet the processing requirements. An advantage of the analysis process is that you can identify processing needs that are common to multiple users. This is an important part of being able to use proper directory structures and groups or containers to reduce and simplify the number of trustee assignments you need to make. When several users need the same rights to a set of files, it is much easier to keep track of and maintain a single trustee assignment to a group or container as compared to making redundant trustee assignments to multiple users.

Use Appropriate Directory Design

A proper directory design takes advantage of the principle that lower subdirectories and files inherit rights from higher directories to implement a top-down inherited rights strategy. The key is planning a directory structure to take advantage of this top-down principle while preventing users from inheriting rights into directories where the users do not belong. Some suggestions to help you implement a top-down strategy are:

- Design a directory structure with the directories requiring the most security near the top of the structure and separated from the directories that allow general user access. The proper design of the directory structure can help to reduce the number of trustee assignments by using the inherited rights principle to allow a common set of rights to flow down to subdirectories. A good example of this is the Universal Aerospace Apps directory structure that contains subdirectories for all application software packages that are available to the users.

- Directories that limit user access to only specific users or access rights should not be included in a directory structure that has a trustee assignment for other users.

- Use IRFs to protect high-security directories against accidentally inheriting unwanted trustees. The IRF is a good way to protect effective rights from accidentally flowing into a directory from a parent directory.

The need for an IRF as part of your security plan may indicate that you have placed a directory that requires more security within a general-purpose directory and that you need to rethink your directory structure design. For example, assume the file system on one of the servers in your company has a directory structure as shown in Figure 5-9. Notice that the spreadsheet budget files are stored in a subdirectory of the Apps/SP directory and that the [Root] container has been made a trustee of Apps with Read and File Scan rights. Because [Root] is a trustee of Apps with [RF] rights, all users inherit the [RF] rights to the Budgets subdirectory, creating a potential license problem where all users have rights to read the budget data. To prevent this, you could block inherited rights by removing all rights from the IRF of the Budgets subdirectory, providing rights to only the Accting group, which is a trustee of the Budgets subdirectory. Although this solution works, it does not address the real problem of placing a subdirectory that has higher security needs within a general-purpose directory. A better solution in this case would be to move the Budgets subdirectory to another location in the file system and then make the appropriate trustee assignments as shown in Figure 5-10.

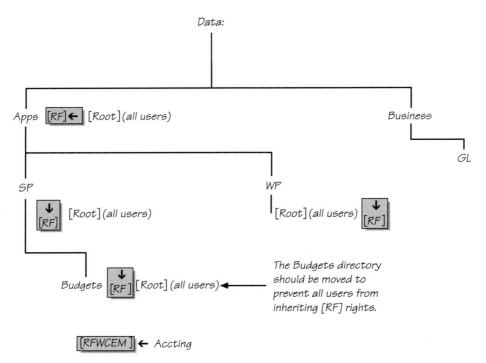

Figure 5-9   Poor directory design

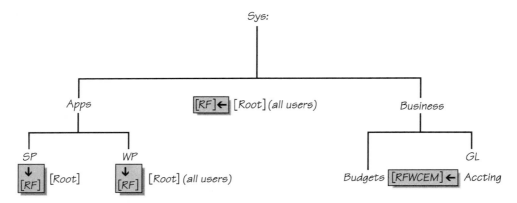

Figure 5-10   Proper directory location

Minimize Trustee Assignments

When planning trustee assignments, you can often keep user trustee assignments to a minimum by start-ing with assigning rights to the containers or groups that have the most users and then proceeding to user trustee assignments. Some network administrators go to the extreme of never making trustee assignments to users; instead they make the trustee assignment to a group name and then make the users who need access rights members of the appropriate group. Although it may mean having to create and maintain addi-tional group names, this approach has the advantage of making it easier for the network administrator to deal with large numbers of users changing job functions, as may happen during a company reorganization.

A similar technique that you can employ with NetWare 5 is to create Organizational Role objects and then make the Organizational Role object, rather than a User object, a trustee of a directory or file. You can then assign the Organizational Role object to users who need access to the directory or file information. If your company does a lot of reorganizing, you may wish to consider using groups or Organizational Role objects rather than assigning rights to individual users.

An effective way to minimize the number of trustee assignments you will need is to make trustee assignments in the following order:

1. Assign rights to the containers first.
2. Assign rights to departmental groups.
3. Assign rights to Organizational Role objects.
4. Assign rights to individual users.

Avoid Complex Combinations

The last guideline in planning file system security is to avoid combinations of assignments to groups, containers, and individual users within the same directory structure. To keep things as simple as possible, when you need to make an individual user a trustee of a directory, assign all rights needed rather than relying on certain rights to be inherited from membership in groups or containers.

Universal Aerospace File System Security

As described in the previous section, the first step in planning file system security for an organization is to define the processing functions each user needs to perform in the file system. Table 5-3 contains file system usage information for each user in the Engineering and Administrative departments. File system usage information for the other departments is given in the Universal Aerospace project found at the end of the chapter.

Table 5-3   Universal Aerospace File System Usage

User	File System Usage
All users	Read files from the Forms directory. Run all Apps except the UTILITY and CAD software. Read files in the Web directory. Create and update files in the ##Corp\Shared and Temp directories.
Lynn Dai	Read files from all department shared directories. Update and maintain the files in your ##Corp\Forms directory. Maintain your ##Corp:Business directory structure.
Dave Heise	Keep track of progress and call up files from any directory in the system. Dave does not want rights to make any changes to the file system (Lynn Dai will do most of the file system work for Dave and, as a result, at this time Dave wants only rights to modify files in his home directory).
Engineering department	Create and update files in the Engineer\Shared directory. Read files in the NASA and Boeing directories. Run the CAD software.
Ira Means	Maintain the Engineer directory structure, but provide only Read access to the user home directory files. Update Engineering files in the Web directory (in the near future).
Lianne Jarka	Currently Lianne and Paul Alm are the engineers responsible for the International Space Station project (ISS). However, this may change in the future as additional engineers are moved on and off the project.

Table 5-3   Universal Aerospace File System Usage (continued)

User	File System Usage
Tony Rucci	Currently Tony is the only engineer assigned to the Mars Rover project. However, as the needs for this project change, additional engineers may be moved on or off the project.
Paul Alm	Paul's primary responsibility is Boeing projects; however, at this time, he will also be assisting Lianne with the International Space Station (ISS) project.
Manufacturing department	**Work with files in the Engineer\Shared directory.** **Should have Read and File Scan rights to the RPS software.** **Should have Read, File Scan, and Write rights to inventory.**
Russ Pence	As head of the Manufacturing department, Russ will be given rights to maintain the Requirements Planning System (RPS) files.

After identifying the processing needs for each user, the next step in implementing file system security is to review the directory structure to determine whether it meets the proper directory structure guidelines described previously. In the Universal Aerospace directory structure, the CAD software is currently located in a subdirectory of the Apps directory. Because your ##UAS Organization is a trustee of Apps with [RF] rights, all users inherit the [RF] rights to the CAD subdirectory, creating a potential license problem since the company currently has licenses for only the Engineering users. In a previous activity, you prevented other users from accessing the CAD software by removing all rights from the IRF of the CAD subdirectory, providing rights to only the DESIGN group. Although this solution works, it does not address the real problem of placing a subdirectory that has higher security needs within a general-purpose directory. A better solution in this case is to move the CAD subdirectory to the Engineer directory and then make the appropriate trustee assignments. Another change to the directory structure needed to facilitate file system security is the creation of a subdirectory in the Web directory for engineering files. This will allow Ira Means to update Engineering Web-based files without affecting other Web documents maintained by Julie and Kellie.

 In this hands-on activity, you will make the following changes to the file system structure to facilitate file system security: (1) Use My Computer to move the CAD software along with its trustee assignments to the Engineer directory; (2) create an Engineer subdirectory within the Web directory.

1. If necessary, start your computer and log in using your assigned ##Admin username.

2. Double-click **My Computer** and browse into your Apps directory as shown in Figure 5-11.

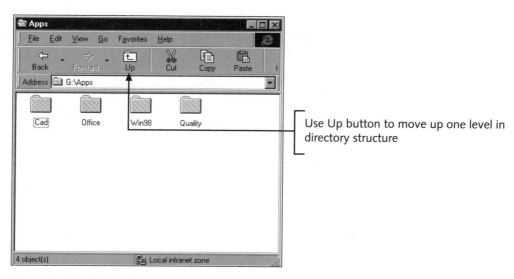

Figure 5-11   Apps directory

3. View and record the current trustees and IRF of the CAD directory:

   a) Right-click your **CAD** subdirectory and click the **Properties** option.

   b) Click the **NetWare Rights** tab and record the trustee assignments and inherited rights filter on the following lines:

   Trustees: _Design-Engineering RF_____

   IRF: _12UAS TRomey RF_____

4. Click **Cancel**.

5. Use My Computer to move the CAD directory from Apps to your Engineer directory as follows:

   a) Click your **CAD** directory to highlight it, and then click **Edit**, **Cut**.

   b) Click the **Up** button in Windows 98, or close the Apps window in Windows 95, to display all directories at the beginning of your ##Corp directory.

   c) Double-click your **Engineer** directory.

   d) Click **Edit**, **Paste**. The CAD subdirectory should now appear in your Engineer directory window.

6. Check to see that the trustee assignments were moved along with the directory:

   a) Right-click your **CAD** subdirectory and click the **Properties** option.

   b) Click the **NetWare Rights** tab and compare the trustee assignments and inherited rights filter to the ones you recorded in Step 3. Click **Cancel**.

It is important to be aware that when you move a directory using My Computer or Windows Explorer, the directory's trustee assignments and IRF are also moved to the new location. This does not happen when you move a directory with NetWare Administrator.

7. Click the **Up** button to return to your ##Corp directory.

8. Create an Engineer subdirectory within the Web directory as follows:

   a) Double-click the **IS** directory.

   b) Double-click the **Web** directory.

   c) Click **File**, point to **New**.

   d) Click the **Folder** option and then type **Engineer** and press **[Enter]**.

9. Exit My Computer by closing the Engineer directory window and any other open windows.

Once you feel that the directory structure meets the file system security guidelines, the next step in implementing file system security is to plan your trustee assignments. When planning trustee assignments, you will want to minimize the number of trustee assignments you will need by following the guidelines described in the previous section. To help perform this task, the UAS consultant has designed a Directory Trustee Worksheet as shown in Table 5-4. Using the previously described guidelines, the consultant has filled in a Directory Trustee Worksheet that shows trustee assignments made to each directory as well as any changes made to the directory's IRF. Notice that to reduce rights assigned to individual users, three additional Organizational Role objects have been defined. The AdmAsst object will be used to give the Business user Lynn Dai all rights to the Forms and Business directories. The ISS Engineer and Rover Engineer objects are given all rights to their corresponding project directories.

Table 5-4   Directory Trustee Worksheet

Directory Trustee Worksheet

DIRECTORY TRUSTEE WORKSHEET for: Universal Aerospace Corporation

Page 1 | **of** 2

Directory Path	IRF	##UAS Container	Engineer Container	Mfg Container	Design Group	WebMgr Group
#Corp directory	All					
Apps	All	RF				
Forms	All	RF				
Shared	All	RWCEMF				
Inventry	All			RWF		
IS\Web	All	RF				RWCEMF
IS\Web\Engineer	All					
Business	All					
Engineer	All					
Engineer\CAD	All				RF	
Engineer\RPS	All			RF		
Engineer\Shared	All		RWCEMF	RWCEMF		
Engineer\Boeing	All		RF			
Engineer\NASA	All		RF			
Engineer\NASA\ISS	All					
Engineer\NASA\Rover	All					
Engineer\username	RF					
Apps\Quality	All			RWF		

Table 5-4   Directory Trustee Worksheet (continued)

Directory Trustee Worksheet

DIRECTORY TRUSTEE WORKSHEET for: Universal Aerospace Corporation

Page 2 | **of** 2

Directory Path	IRF	AdmAsst	ISS Engineer	Rover Engineer	Eng Manager	Mfg Manager	DHeise	IMeans
#Corp directory	All						RF	
Apps	All							
Forms	All	RWCEMF						
Shared	All							
Inventry	All							
IS\Web	All							
IS\Web\Engineer	All				RWCEMF			RWCEMF
Business	All	RWCEMF						
Engineer	All				RWCEMF			RWCEMF
Engineer\CAD	All					RWF		
Engineer\RPS	All					RWCEMF		
Engineer\Shared	All							
Engineer\Boeing	All							
Engineer\NASA	All							
Engineer\NASA\ISS	All		RWCEMF					
Engineer\NASA\Rover	All			RWCEMF				
Engineer\username	RF							
Temp	All	RWCEMF						
Mfg						Supervisor		

Notice that the left-hand column lists directories starting from the highest level down to the lower levels. Making higher-level directories' trustee assignments first helps to reduce the number of trustee assignments through inheritance. Also notice that the worksheet columns are arranged with containers and groups on the left followed by Organizational Role objects and finally any individual user assignments. The reason for making assignments to containers and groups first is that it helps to reduce the number of trustee assignments and makes maintaining file system security simpler. The access rights to be granted to each directory are then listed in the corresponding row under the Trustee's column. In this example, the top-level container, ##UAS, is listed in the first column and given a trustee assignment to the Apps, IS\Web, Forms, and Shared directory structures. Next the Engineer container is listed in the second column and given a trustee assignment to the Engineer\Shared, Engineer\NASA, and Engineer\Boeing directories.

After rights have been assigned to the containers and groups, Organizational Role objects along with individual users who need special rights are made trustees of the appropriate directories. In this case, Ira Means will maintain the Engineer directory structure and therefore is given all rights. In addition, Ira Means is given the rights necessary to work with files in the IS\Web\Engineer directory. Finally, the IRFs have been modified to allow only the Read and File Scan rights to pass into the user home directories.

Although the consultant has set most of the rights needed for the Engineering department in Table 5-4, in the end-of-chapter projects, you will be required to fill out the Trustee Directory Security Worksheets to include the Business users and provide appropriate access to their directories.

IMPLEMENTING TRUSTEE ASSIGNMENTS

After completing the work of defining the trustee assignments on a Trustee Directory Security Worksheet, you can begin the fun by using NetWare utilities to implement the trustee assignments. NetWare 5 provides three ways of making a trustee assignment or changing the IRF:

- Windows: Explorer, My Computer, or Network Neighborhood
- NetWare Administrator
- The RIGHTS command-line utility

In this chapter, you have used Windows along with NetWare Administrator to practice making trustee assignments and checking effective rights. In the hands-on activities in this section, you continue to use these utilities to implement the trustee assignments and IRFs defined previously in Table 5-4. You will first use Windows to make the trustee assignments for the containers and groups and set the directory IRFs. Next you will use NetWare Administrator to create the Organizational Role objects and make trustee assignments for them and individual users as well as check effective rights. Finally you will use the RIGHTS command to document trustee assignments and directory IRFs.

 Prior to performing the hands-on activities in this section, compare the directories in your structure to be sure you have created all the directories in the paths shown in Figure 5-12. If necessary, log in to the network using your ##Admin username and create the directories you need.

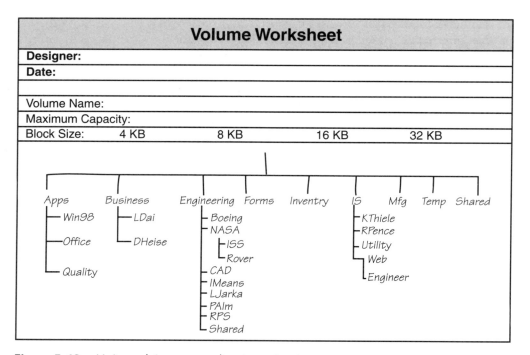

Figure 5-12   Universal Aerospace directory structure

Trustee Assignment Using Windows

As you have learned in this chapter, Windows Explorer, My Computer, and Network Neighborhood offer convenient ways to make trustee assignments when working in the Windows environment.

 In this hands-on activity, you will use these Windows utilities to make trustee assignments for the containers and groups identified on page 1 of the Directory Trustee Worksheet shown previously in Table 5-4.

1. If necessary, start your computer and log in using your assigned ##Admin username.

2. Double-click **My Computer** and browse to your ##Corp directory.

3. Verify that your ##UAS container is a trustee of the Forms directory with Read and File Scan rights.

4. If necessary, make your ##UAS container a trustee of the Shared and Temp directories with all rights.

5. Make the Mfg container a trustee of the Inventry, Engineer\RPS, Engineer\Shared, MfgShared, and Apps\Quality folders as shown in Table 5-4.

6. Make your ##UAS container and the WebMgr group trustees of the IS\Web directory.

7. Close the My Computer window(s).

8. Start Windows Explorer.

9. Browse to your Corp\Engineer directory.

10. Make your Mfg and Engineering containers trustees of the Engineer\Shared directory with all rights except Access Control.

11. Make your Engineering container a trustee of the Engineer\Boeing directory with Read and File Scan rights.

12. Make your Engineering container a trustee of the Engineer\NASA directory with Read and File Scan rights.

13. Use Windows Explorer to give the Design group the rights shown in Table 5-4.

14. Close Windows Explorer.

15. Double-click **Network Neighborhood**.

16. Browse to your ##Corp directory.

17. Open the **Engineer** directory by double-clicking it.

18. Remove all rights except Read and File Scan from the IRF of Ira Means's home directory as follows:

   a) Right-click the **IMeans** home directory and click the **Properties** option.

   b) Click the **NetWare Rights** tab and then click the **Inherited Rights and Filters** button.

   c) Remove the check marks from all rights except Read and File Scan in the Inheritance Filter group as shown in Figure 5-13.

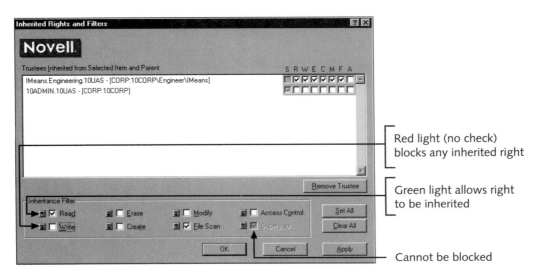

Figure 5-13   Removing inherited rights for IMeans

   d) Click **OK** to save your changes.

   e) Click **OK** again to return to the Engineer directory window.

19. Repeat the preceding process to remove all rights except Read and File Scan from the IRF of LJarka, TRucci, and PAlm home directories.

20. Close the Network Neighborhood window.

Trustee Assignment Using NetWare Administrator

As a CNA, you will be required to use NetWare Administrator to implement file system security by performing such functions as making directory trustee assignments, changing an IRF, and checking effective rights. As you learned earlier in this chapter, calculating effective rights by hand can sometimes be a complex task in which it is easy to make a mistake by overlooking certain factors. As you have learned, NetWare Administrator can help you with this task by allowing you to see a user's effective rights in any directory.

In this hands-on activity, you will get more practice using NetWare Administrator to make the trustee assignments identified on page 2 of the Directory Trustee Worksheet shown previously in Table 5-4. However, before making the trustee assignments, you will need to use NetWare Administrator to create any User, Group, or Organizational Role objects identified on the Directory Trustee Worksheet.

1. If necessary, start your computer and log in using your assigned ##Admin username.

2. Start NetWare Administrator.

4. Create the AdmAsst Organizational Role object in your ##UAS container and make the user Ira Means the occupant as follows:

a) Click your **##UAS** container to highlight it.

b) Press **[Ins]** to display the New Object window.

c) Double-click the **Organizational Role** object.

d) Enter the name **AdmAsst** and click the **Define additional properties** box.

e) Click the **Create** button to create the Organizational Role object and display the Identification window.

f) Click the **browse** button to the right of the Occupant field to display the Occupant window.

g) Click the **Add** button to display the Select Object dialog box.

h) Use the Browse context window to find the user Ira Means.

i) Double-click **IMeans** in the Available objects window.

j) Click **OK** to add Ira Means as an occupant of the Organizational Role object.

k) Click **OK** to save your changes and return to the NetWare Administrator browse window.

5. Follow the preceding procedure to create the ISS Engineer Organizational Role object in your Engineering container and make both LJarka and PAlm occupants.

6. Follow the preceding procedure to create the Rover Engineer Organizational Role object in your Engineering container and make TRucci the occupant.

7. Make Dave Heise a trustee of your ##Corp directory with Read and File Scan rights as follows:

a) If necessary, create a user named DHeise in your Business container.

b) Right-click your **##Corp** directory and click the **Details** option.

c) Click the **Trustees of this Directory** button and then click the **Add Trustee** button to display the Select Object dialog box.

d) Use the Browse context window to find Dave's username, DHeise, in the Business container.

e) Double-click **DHeise** in the Available objects window to add him as trustee to the ##Corp directory as shown in Figure 5-14.

f) Click **OK** to save the assignment and return to the NetWare Administrator browse window.

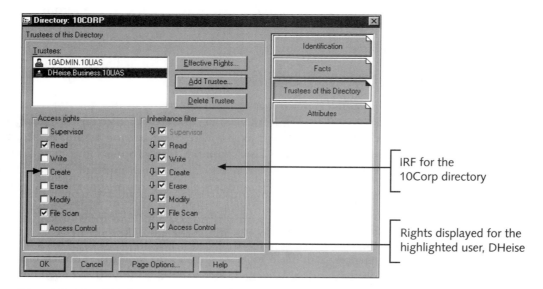

Figure 5-14 DHeise trustee assignment

8. Create the MfgMgr Organizational Role object in your Mfg container and make RPence the occupant.

9. When a user is being made a trustee of multiple directories, it is often more efficient to click on the user and then add each directory to the directories of which the user is a trustee. For example, follow these steps to make the AdmAsst Organizational Role object a trustee of the Forms and Business directories with all rights except Access Control:

a) Right-click the **AdmAsst** Organizational Role object and click the **Details** option.

b) Click the **Rights to Files and Directories** button.

c) Click the **Add** button to display the Select Object dialog box.

d) Double-click your **UAS_HOST_CORP** volume in the Browse context window.

e) Double-click your **##Corp** directory in the Browse context window.

f) Hold down **[Ctrl]** and click your **Forms** and **Business** directories to highlight both directories as shown in Figure 5-15.

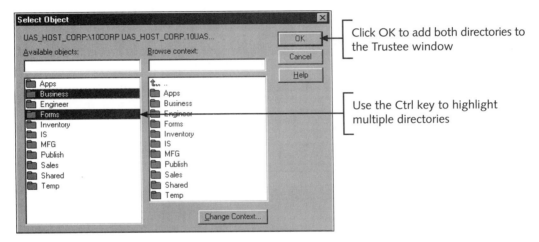

Figure 5-15   Selecting multiple trustee assignments

g) Click **OK** to add both directories to the Files and Directories area of the AdmAsst Organizational Role Rights window as shown in Figure 5-16.

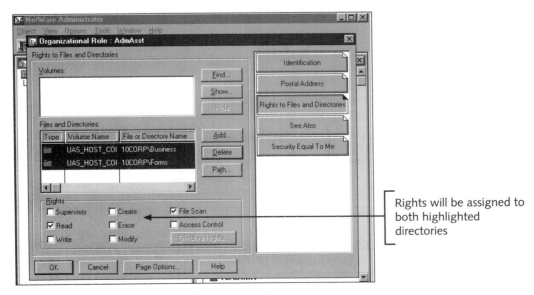

Figure 5-16   Changing multiple trustee rights

h) Click to check all rights except Supervisor and Access Control.

i) Click **OK** to save the trustee assignments.

10. Use the preceding procedure to make Ira Means a trustee of all of the IS\Web\Engineer and Engineer directories with all rights except Supervisor and Access Control.

11. Make your EngMgr a trustee of the Engineer and IS\Web\Engineer directories with all rights except Supervisor and Access Control.

12. Make the MfgMgr Organizational Role object a trustee of the Engineer\CAD directory with [RFW] rights, and Supervisor rights to the Mfg directory structure.

13. Make the ISS Engineer Organizational Role object a trustee of the Engineer\NASA\ISS directory with all rights except Supervisor and Access Control.

14. Make the Rover Engineer Organizational Role object a trustee of the Engineer\NASA\Rover directory with all rights except Supervisor and Access Control.

15. Create a Shared subdirectory within the Mfg directory as follows:

a) Click your **Mfg** directory to highlight it.

b) Press **[Ins]** and enter the directory name **Shared**.

c) Click the **Create** button to create the Shared directory.

16. Repeat Step 15 to create a Shared subdirectory in your IS directory.

17. Make the ISMgrs group a trustee of the IS\Shared, Engineer\Shared, and Mfg\Shared directories with all rights except Supervisor and Access Control as follows:

a) Double-click your **ISMgrs** group to display the Details window.

b) Click the **Rights to Files and Directories** button.

c) Click the **Add** button to display a Select Object window.

d) Use the right-hand browse window to navigate to the IS directory.

e) Double-click the **Shared** directory in the left-hand Available objects window to add the IS\Shared directory to the Files and Directories pane.

f) Click the **Add** button to display a Select Object window.

g) Use the right-hand browse window to navigate to the Engineer directory.

h) Double-click the **Shared** directory in the left-hand Available objects window to add the Engineer\Shared directory to the Files and Directories pane.

i) Click the **Add** button to display a Select Object window.

j) Use the right-hand browse window to navigate to the Mfg directory.

k) Double-click the **Shared** directory in the left-hand Available objects window to add the Mfg\Shared directory to the Files and Directories pane.

l) Use **[Ctrl]**-click to highlight each of the directories in the File and Directories pane.

m) Click all rights check boxes except Supervisor and Access Control.

n) Click **OK** to save the trustee assignment.

18. Exit NetWare Administrator.

Documenting Trustee Assignments

Dave Heise, president of Universal Aerospace, has requested that you document the trustee assignments for future reference and use. Although you could use NetWare Administrator to print each directory's trustee window, this would be a time-consuming process. A better solution is to use the NetWare RIGHTS command-line utility. In addition to printing lists of trustee assignments, the RIGHTS command can be convenient to use when working at the DOS prompt or if you are accessing the network from a station that does not have Windows 95 or 98 installed. Because the RIGHTS command has several different options, Novell provided it with a help function that you can use to review the syntax for a specific function. By doing the hands-on activities in this section, you will learn how to use the RIGHTS command to obtain help information, view or print trustee assignments, view or print directory IRFs, and make a simple trustee assignment.

In this hands-on activity, you will use the RIGHTS command to view help information and print a report for Dave Heise showing the current directory trustee assignments and IRFs.

1. If necessary, start your computer and log in using your assigned ##Admin username.

2. Open a DOS window (Click **Start**, point to **Programs**, click **MS-DOS Prompt**).

3. Change to your G drive.

4. To view help information, type **RIGHTS /?** and press **[Enter]**. If you receive the "Bad command or file name" message, enter the command **CD Z:\PUBLIC** and then repeat this step.

5. To view the trustees of all directories in your ##Corp directory, type **RIGHTS *.* /T** and press **[Enter]**. After each screen, the system will halt and wait for you to press [Enter]. Notice that trustee assignments are displayed for each directory as shown in Figure 5-17.

```
UAS_HOST\CORP:\10CORP\IS
User trustees:
       Your_user_name.10uas                           [ RWCEMFA]
----------
No group trustees have been assigned.

UAS_HOST\CORP:\10CORP\ENGINEER
User trustees:
       IMeans.Engineering.10uas                       [ RWCEMF ]
----------
No group trustees have been assigned.

UAS_HOST\CORP:\10CORP\FORMS
No group trustees have been assigned.
----------
Other trustees:
       10UAS                                           [ R    F ]
       AdmAsst.10uas                                   [ RWCEMF ]

UAS_HOST\CORP:\10CORP\SHARED
No group trustees have been assigned.
----------
Other trustees:
       10UAS                                           [ RWCEMF ]
>>> Enter = More    C = Continuous    Esc = Cancel
```

Figure 5-17   RIGHTS command output

6. To view trustee assignments for all directories and subdirectories, you need to include the /S option. Type **RIGHTS *.* /S /T** and press **[Enter]** to view all trustee assignments in all your directories and subdirectories.

7. You can print this information by including >PRN at the end of the command to redirect output to the printer assigned to your LPT1 printer port. To print your trustee assignments, enter the command **RIGHTS *.* /S /T > PRN** and press **[Enter]**.

8. Obtain your printout and close your DOS window. Compare the rights to Table 5-4 and use NetWare Administrator to make any necessary corrections and then obtain updated printouts.

9. Log out.

Kellie Thiele is currently setting up Carl Dauer's computer to run the quality control software she has designed and is receiving "Access denied" error messages. Although Carl has the necessary rights in the Quality directory, the software is programmed to store temporary files in the ##Corp\Temp directory. Kellie has asked you to come down to the Manufacturing department and help her resolve the problem.

Since Windows is not yet installed on Carl's computer, in this hands-on activity, you will use the RIGHTS command to check Carl's rights in the directories and then make any necessary trustee assignments.

1. If you are currently logged in, click the **Start** button and log out to display the Novell Client window.

2. Log in as Carl Dauer as follows:

   a) Enter **CDauer** in the Username field.

   b) Click the **Advanced** button on the Novell Client Login window.

   c) In the Context field, enter **Mfg.##UAS** (## represents your assigned student number).

   d) Click **OK** to log in. If you cannot log in, log in as your ##Admin and check Carl's password. Enter the password to log in.

3. Open a DOS window and change to the G drive. If necessary, map G: to ##Corp.

4. Enter the command **RIGHTS Apps\Quality** and press **[Enter]**. Notice that Carl has only Read and File Scan rights. On the following lines, document how Carl obtained the Read and File Scan rights to the Apps\Quality subdirectory. According to Kellie, in addition to the Read and File Scan rights Carl inherited to the Quality directory, he will also need Write rights to run the software.

   _____

   _____

   _____

5. Enter the command **LOGOUT** and press **[Enter]** to log out.

6. Enter the command **LOGIN .##Admin.##Uas** and press **[Enter]** to log in using your assigned ##Admin username.

7. Enter the command MAP to check your drive mappings. If necessary, map drive G to your ##Corp directory by entering the following command: **MAP ROOT G:=CORP:##CORP [Enter]**.

8. Enter **G: [Enter]** to change to drive G.

9. Use the RIGHTS command to add Carl as a trustee of Quality with Write rights as follows:

   a) Enter **RIGHTS /? T** and press **[Enter]** to display the help screen for adding a trustee.

   b) Enter the following command:

   RIGHTS G:Apps\Quality W /NAME=.CDAUER.Mfg.##UAS [Enter]

It is necessary to use Carl's distinguished username to identify his context.

10. Enter the command **LOGOUT [Enter]** to log out.

11. Enter the command **LOGIN .CDauer.Mfg.##UAS [Enter]** to log in as Carl Dauer.

12. Map drive G to your ##Corp directory as shown in Step 7.

13. Change to drive G and enter the command **RIGHTS Apps\Quality** and press **[Enter]** to check Carl's effective rights. He should now have Read, Write, and File Scan rights.

14. Enter **EXIT** and press **[Enter]** to close the DOS window and return to Windows.

15. Log out.

ATTRIBUTE SECURITY

As introduced previously, attributes are flags or codes that may be associated with files and directories to allow the NOS to determine what type of processing can be performed on the associated file and directory. The network administrator often places attributes on directories and files to provide additional protection to the directory or file against accidental change or deletion, or to specify special processing such as controlling file compression, making a file sharable, or purging files immediately after they are deleted.

As a CNA, you need to know the file and directory attributes, what they are used for, and how to use NetWare utilities to work with the attributes.

5

File and Directory Attributes

Attributes placed on files and directories override a user's effective rights in that file or directory. This means that if a file is flagged with the Read Only attribute, no matter what the effective rights are, the only operations you can perform on the file are Read and File Scan. For example, Ira Means has all rights to the Engineer directory and, therefore, would inherit all rights to the files and subdirectories in the Engineer directory structure. If a file named PARTLIST.DAT is stored in the NASA directory and is flagged with the Read Only attribute, even though Ira has all effective rights as a result of the trustee assignment, he will still have only read access to the PARTLIST.DAT file. However, since Ira has inherited the Modify right to the directory as a result of his trustee assignment to the Engineer directory, the Modify right would allow him to remove the Read Only attribute and then change or even delete the PARTLIST.DAT file.

File Attributes

Table 5-5 contains a list of all file attributes used by NetWare, along with their corresponding abbreviation. As a CNA, you will need to learn about each of these.

Table 5-5   File Attributes

Attribute	Abbreviation	Attribute	Abbreviation
Archive Needed	A	Migrated	M
Can't Compress	Cc	Purge	P
Copy Inhibit	Ci	Read Only	Ro
Delete Inhibit	Di	Read Write	Rw
Don't Compress	Dc	Rename Inhibit	Ri
Don't Suballocate	Ds	Sharable	Sh
Execute Only	X	System	Sy
Hidden	H	Transactional	T
Immediate Compress	Ic		

Archive Needed (A)   The **Archive Needed** attribute is assigned automatically to files when the contents of a file are modified. Copy or backup utilities may remove this attribute after copying the file to another storage location. This attribute is important for controlling what files are copied to a backup disk, making it possible to back up only the files that have been changed since the last backup. The use of this attribute along with backup utilities will be explained in detail in Chapter 10.

Can't Compress (Cc)   The **Can't Compress** attribute is set by the system on files that cannot be compressed. A user or network administrator is not allowed to change this attribute setting.

Copy Inhibit (Ci)   The **Copy Inhibit** attribute is used only to protect specified files from being copied by Macintosh users. Setting on this attribute prevents Macintosh computers running the Apple Filing Protocol v2.0 and above from copying the file.

Delete Inhibit (Di)   The **Delete Inhibit** attribute is used to prevent a file from being deleted while allowing changes to be made to the file's content or allowing the file to be renamed. To delete the file, a user must be granted the Modify right to remove the Delete Inhibit attribute first. The Delete Inhibit attribute is often useful to protect an important data file from accidentally being deleted, yet still allowing its contents to be changed. You should consider setting the Delete Inhibit attribute on many of your organization's permanent files, such as customer, payroll, inventory, and accounting.

Don't Compress (Dc)   Either a user or a network administrator might set the **Don't Compress** attribute to prevent a file from being compressed. Preventing file compression might improve performance slightly when that file is accessed since, as described in Chapter 3, the file will not need to be decompressed.

Don't Suballocate (Ds)   A user or network administrator sets the **Don't Suballocate** attribute to prevent a file from being suballocated to other files. Using this attribute provides a way to run certain applications and a database system that will not work with files that have been suballocated.

Execute Only (X)   The major use of the **Execute Only** attribute is to protect software files from being illegally copied. Execute Only can be set only on .EXE and .COM files by a Supervisor equivalent user; once set, not even the Supervisor can remove this attribute.

 Do *not* assign Execute Only to files unless backup copies of the files exist. Certain program files will not run when they are flagged Execute Only because these programs need to copy information from their program files into the workstation's memory, and the Execute Only attribute prevents them from applying the copy functions. Because the Execute Only attribute cannot be removed, to get rid of it you need to delete the file and reinstall it from another disk.

Hidden (H)   The **Hidden** attribute is used to hide files from DOS utilities and certain application software. NetWare utilities will display hidden files when the [H] attribute is turned on.

 One simple way to help protect software from illegal copying is to use the Hidden attribute to make software directories and files hidden from normal DOS utilities, and then move the NCOPY and NDIR commands from the SYS:Public directory to the SYS:System directory or some other location where standard users will not have access to them.

Immediate Compress (Ic)   The **Immediate Compress** attribute is usually assigned to large files that you want to be compressed immediately after they are closed, to save disk space. As described in Chapter 3, by default, files are compressed after seven days of no activity.

Migrated (M)   The system sets the **Migrated** attribute on files that have been migrated to a high-capacity storage medium such as an optical disk drive or tape backup system. Although Migrated files are accessible to users, a rather long delay time may be needed to restore the file before it can be accessed.

Purge (P)   As described in Chapter 3, NetWare allows deleted files to be salvaged using the NetWare Administrator Salvage feature until either the deleted file's space is reused by the file server or the directory is purged. Space from files that have been purged is no longer available to the operating system, preventing the file from being recovered using Salvage. You might assign the **Purge** attribute to a file if you want the NetWare server to reuse the space from that file immediately when it is deleted. You might also assign the Purge attribute for security reasons to files that contain sensitive data, thereby preventing an intruder from salvaging and then accessing information from these files after they have been deleted.

Read Write (Rw)   The **Read Write** attribute applies only to files, and is used to indicate that the contents of the file may be added to or changed. When files are created, the Read Write attribute is automatically set.

Read Only (Ro) The **Read Only** attribute applies only to files, and may be used to protect the contents of a file from being modified. It performs a function similar to opening the write protect tab on a disk. Files whose contents are not normally changed, such as a zip code file or a program file, are usually flagged Read Only. When you first set on the Read Only attribute, the Delete Inhibit and Rename Inhibit attributes are also set by default. If for some reason you want to allow the file to be renamed or deleted but do not want its contents changed, you can remove the Rename Inhibit and Delete Inhibit attributes.

Rename Inhibit (Ri) When assigned to a file, the **Rename Inhibit** attribute protects the file's name from being changed. During installation, many software packages create data and configuration files that may need to be updated or changed, but those filenames must remain constant for the software package to operate properly. After installing a software package that requests certain filenames, it is a good idea to use the Rename Inhibit attribute on these files to prevent future changing of the file or directory name, causing the program to signal an error or crash.

Sharable (Sh) Files are available to only one user at a time. For example, suppose that you created a file called BUDGET95.WK3 on the file server and a coworker opens up this file with his or her spreadsheet program. If any other users attempt to access the BUDGET95.WK3 file, those users will receive an error message informing them that the file is in use or is not accessible. With spreadsheet files and word processing documents, you would not want more than one user to have a copy of the file at one time, since any changes the person makes may be overwritten by another user. Program files and certain database files should be made available to multiple users at the same time. For example, you would want as many users as you have licenses for to be able to run the word processing software that you have just installed or perhaps to access a common database of customers. To allow a file to be opened by more than one user at a time, you must set the **Sharable** attribute for that file, as described in the next section. Usually you need to flag all program files sharable after performing an installation, as described in Chapter 3.

System (Sy) The **System** attribute is often assigned to files that are part of the NOS (NetWare operating system). As with the Hidden attribute, the System attribute hides files from DOS utilities and application software packages, but additionally marks the file as being for operating system use only.

Transactional (T) The **Transactional** attribute can be assigned only to files, and is used to indicate that the file will be protected by the **Transaction Tracking System (TTS)**. TTS ensures that when changes or transactions are applied to a file, either all transactions are completed or the file is left in its original state. This is particularly important when working with database files where a workstation may start updating a record and then crash before the update is complete. For example, assume a NetWare file server is used to maintain an online order-entry system containing customer and inventory files. When you enter an order, at least two transactions are necessary: one to update the customer's account balance, and the other to record the inventory item to be shipped. Suppose that while you are entering the order, the workstation crashes after it updates the customer balance and therefore fails to record the item on the shipping list. In this case, TTS would cancel the transaction and restore the customer's balance to its original amount, allowing you to reenter the complete order. Because TTS is a feature used by application software, using the Transactional attribute does not implement TTS protection. You also need to have the proper system design and application software.

Directory Attributes

With the exception of the Don't Migrate attribute, the directory attributes shown in Table 5-6 are actually a subset of the file attributes and have similar functions. Some directory attributes affect only the directory, whereas others apply to all files in the directory. As a network administrator, you should know the differences between directory attributes and file attributes, as well as how directory attributes affect the files stored in the directory.

Table 5-6   Directory Attributes

Attribute	Abbreviation
Delete Inhibit	Di
Don't Compress	Dc
Don't Migrate	Dm
Normal	N
Hidden	H
Immediate Compress	Ic
Purge	P
Rename Inhibit	Ri
System	Sy

In this section, you will learn about the role of each of the directory attributes and how it affects the directory's files.

Delete Inhibit (Di)   Setting the Delete Inhibit attribute on a directory will prevent the directory's name from being removed, but will not prevent the contents of the directory—its files and subdirectories—from being deleted. You may wish to protect the fixed parts of your organization's directory structure from being modified by flagging all main directories with the Delete Inhibit attribute.

Don't Compress (Dc)   Setting the Don't Compress attribute on a directory will prevent all files in the directory from being compressed. If disk space is not a problem, preventing file compression in a directory may provide slightly faster performance, since NetWare will not have to decompress the file when it is opened by a user.

Don't Migrate (Dm)   If you have data migration enabled on a volume, as described in Chapter 3, you can set the Don't Migrate attribute on a directory to prevent files in that directory from being migrated to a high-capacity storage device. This can be helpful if users need quick access to these archive files and cannot wait for the data migration system to load them from the high-capacity storage medium.

Hidden (H)   As with the file attribute, the Hidden directory attribute is used to hide directories from DOS utilities and certain application software. Although Hidden directories can still be viewed using NetWare utilities, DOS commands and Windows applications will not be able to see the directory structure. The Hidden directory attribute can be useful when you have workstations using the Microsoft Windows environment. With Windows, it is very easy for users to explore the directory structure using the File Manager. By hiding directories, you can make the file structure a lot less accessible.

Immediate Compress (Ic)   The Immediate Compress attribute is usually assigned to directories containing several large files that you want to be compressed immediately after they are closed, to save disk space.

Normal (N)   The **Normal** directory attribute removes all directory attributes.

Purge (P)   The Purge attribute may be assigned to a directory so that the NetWare file server will immediately reuse the space from any files deleted in that directory. When the Purge attribute is assigned to a directory, any file that is deleted from the directory will be automatically purged and its space reused. The Purge attribute is often assigned to directories that contain temporary files to reuse the temporary file space as soon as the file is deleted.

Rename Inhibit (Ri)   Using the Rename Inhibit attribute on a directory prevents that directory's name from being changed, while still allowing files and subdirectories contained within that directory to be renamed. Directories that are part of the system drive mappings and application software paths should be protected by the Rename Inhibit attribute, since changing the directory's name would affect the execution of software, and would also affect drive mappings made to data within that directory structure.

System (Sy)   The System attribute is often assigned to directories that are part of the NOS or certain client software. Print queues, to be described in Chapter 6, are actually subdirectories and are flagged with the System attribute. As with the Hidden attribute, the System attribute hides directories from the DOS utilities and application software packages, but additionally marks directories as being for operating system use only.

Planning Attribute Usage at Universal Aerospace

Users who have been granted Delete and Rename rights to a directory have the ability to remove or rename the directory, as well as the files it contains. Without proper planning, renaming directories in a structure could cause problems with directory map commands and could prevent certain applications from finding data within a predefined path. One of the important uses of directory attributes is protecting the directory structure from name changes as well as accidental deletion. In addition to using the Delete Inhibit and Rename Inhibit attributes, you can further protect certain directories by hiding them from DOS or Windows using the Hidden attribute. The Purge attribute is useful on directories that contain temporary files that are frequently deleted. Using the Purge attribute on directories containing temporary files results in deleted files from other directories being available for salvaging for a longer time.

Table 5-7 lists the directory attributes the consultant has suggested for each of the directories in the Universal Aerospace file system.

Table 5-7   Directory Attributes for Universal Aerospace

Directory	Attribute(s)	Directory	Attribute(s)
Shared	Di Ri	Apps	Ri
Inventry	Di Ri	Apps\Win98	Di Ri P Ic Hidden
Forms	Di Ri	Apps\Office	Di Ri P Ic Hidden
IS\Web	Di Ri P	Apps\Quality	Di Ri
Engineer	Di Ri	IS\Utility	Di Ri Hidden

The Delete Inhibit and Rename Inhibit attributes have been suggested for all major directories to prevent deletion or name changes. The Purge attribute was suggested on the Temp directory because of the number of temporary files created by the menu system. Placing the Purge attribute on the Win98 and Office application directories will allow the system to reuse space from old software files immediately when a new version of the software is copied to these directories.

The most commonly used file attributes are Read Only and Sharable. Most software programs and help files used by multiple users need to be flagged with the Sharable attribute to allow more than one user to access a program or help file at the same time. At this time, the consultant recommends setting the Delete and Rename Inhibit attributes on all files in the Forms directory to prevent accidental erasure or renaming.

The Read Only attribute is often used on program files to prevent the software from being accidentally changed or deleted as well as to protect it against virus infection. If users are granted only Read and File Scan rights to a software directory, protecting the program files with the Read Only attribute is not necessary. However, with some software packages, users need to maintain configuration or temporary files located in the same software directory as the program files. With these software packages, you will need to grant users Write, Create, and Delete rights in addition to the Read and File Scan rights to maintain their configuration files as well as create and delete temporary files. When users have more than Read and File Scan rights in a software directory, placing the Read Only attribute on the program files becomes very important to protect them from deletion or changes by either a user or computer virus.

In addition to the Sharable and Read Only attributes, the Execute Only attribute is important when software is placed in an environment where there is a possibility of illegal copying. In Chapter 9, you will get more practice setting attributes on program files.

Implementing Directory and File Attributes

As a network administrator, you need to be able to use NetWare utilities along with Windows to implement directory and file attributes in the network file system. Although knowing how to use the Windows-based NetWare Administrator is required for the CNA test, as a network administrator you will also find it convenient to know how to use Windows Explorer or My Computer to set directory and file attributes. In this section, you will learn how to use NetWare Administrator along with Windows Explorer or My Computer to set and view file and directory attributes.

 In this hands-on activity, you will use NetWare Administrator to set directory attributes on the directories specified in Table 5-7 except the Apps and Utility directory structures. In the next activity, you will practice using Windows along with the FLAG utility to set attributes on the Apps and Utility directory structures.

1. If necessary, start your computer and log in using your assigned ##Admin username.

2. Start NetWare Administrator.

3. If necessary, open a browse window for your ##Corp directory.

4. Set the Delete Inhibit and Rename Inhibit attributes on the Shared directory as follows:

    a) Right-click the **Shared** directory and click the **Details** option.

    b) Click the **Attributes** button.

    c) Click to check the **Delete Inhibit** and **Rename Inhibit** attributes.

    d) Click **OK** to save your attribute assignment.

5. Repeat the preceding process to set the attributes specified in Table 5-7 for all directories except the Apps and IS directories.

6. Exit NetWare Administrator.

 In this hands-on activity, you will use Windows to set the attributes defined by the consultant in Table 5-7 for the Apps directories.

1. If necessary, start your computer and log in using your assigned ##Admin username.

2. Double-click **My Computer** or start Windows Explorer.

3. Browse to your ##Corp directory.

4. Set Rename Inhibit attributes on the Apps directory as follows:

    a) Right-click your **Apps** directory and click the **Properties** option.

    b) Click the **NetWare Info** tab.

    c) Click the **Rename Inhibit** attribute.

    d) Click **OK** to save the attribute settings.

5. Open the Apps directory.

6. Set the attributes for the subdirectories of Apps as specified in Table 5-7.

7. Close and then open your Apps directory. The Win98 and Office directories should no longer be displayed because they have been flagged as "hidden."

8. Configure Windows to show hidden directories by completing these steps:

   a) Click **View**, and then click **Folder Options**.

   b) Click the **View** tab to display the window shown in Figure 5-18.

   c) Click the **Show all files** option.

   d) Click **OK** to save the settings.

   e) Your Office and Win98 folders should now appear in the Apps directory window. Notice that they are lighter and have a dotted border around them to indicate that they are hidden folders.

9. Close your directory window(s).

10. Log out.

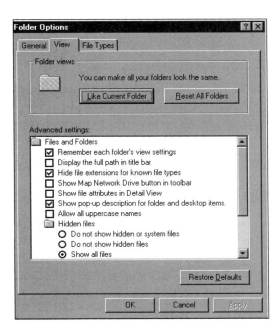

Figure 5-18   Folder Options, View tab

 Recently you showed Ira Means how to use Windows to access network files. In this hands-on activity, you will log in as Ira Means and then use Windows to copy files and set attributes.

1. Log in as ##Admin as follows:

   a) Click the **Advanced** option and enter **Engineering.10UAS** in the Context field.

   b) Enter **IMeans** in the Username field and click **OK** to log in.

   c) Click **No** when asked to change the Windows password.

2. Use My Computer or Windows Explorer to copy any files from the F:\SOFTWARE.CTI\DESIGN directory into the NASA\ISS directory.

3. Use My Computer to set the file attributes to Read Only.

4. Close your directory window.

Using the FLAG Command-Line Utility

Just as the RIGHTS command is useful for documenting or setting access rights from the DOS prompt, the NetWare FLAG command-line utility is useful for documenting and setting directory and file attributes. The FLAG command has two different options to work with either file or directory attributes. As a network administrator, it is important to know how to use the directory and file options of the FLAG command to work with attributes.

Setting and Viewing Directory Attributes

The FLAG command uses the /DO (Directory Only) parameter as follows to set and view directory attributes:

```
FLAG [path] [+ / -] [attribute_list] /DO
```

You can replace [attribute_list] with one or more of the directory attributes shown in Table 5-6. Use the [+] option if you wish to add the attribute to the directory, or the [-] attribute to remove the attribute from the directory. The [path] is optional, and if you enter only the FLAG /DO command, you will be given a list of the attribute settings for all subdirectories of the current directory.

In this hands-on activity, you will use the FLAG command to document your directory attributes as well as hide the Utility directory.

1. If necessary, start your computer and log in using your assigned ##Admin username.

2. Open a DOS window.

3. Change to drive G.

4. View help information on the FLAG command by entering the command **FLAG /? [Enter]**. If you receive the "Bad command or file name" message, enter the command **CD Z:\PUBLIC [Enter]** and repeat the FLAG command.

5. To view help information on setting directory attributes, enter the command **FLAG /? DO [Enter]**.

6. To view all your directory attribute settings, enter the command **FLAG *.* /DO [Enter]**.

7. To view the attribute settings for all subdirectories, enter the command **FLAG *.* /DO /S [Enter]**.

8. To set the Delete Inhibit, Rename Inhibit, and Hidden attributes on your Utility directory, enter the command **FLAG IS\UTILITY +Di +Ri +H /DO [Enter]**.

9. Exit the DOS window.

10. Use My Computer to verify your Utility directory attribute settings.

Setting and Viewing File Attributes

The FLAG command uses the /FO (Files Only) parameter as follows both to set and view file attributes:

```
FLAG [path] [+/-] [attribute_list] /FO
```

You can replace [attribute_list] with one or more of the file attributes shown in Table 5-5. Use the [+] option if you wish to add the attribute to the file(s), or the [-] attribute to remove the attribute from the file(s). The [path] is optional, and if you enter only the FLAG /FO command, you will be given a list of the attribute settings for all files of the current directory. You can also use global parameters in the [path] parameter to specify a group of filenames in the specified directory.

Sometimes you may need to run a utility program from a computer that may be infected with a virus. To prevent a virus from modifying any files in your Utility directory, you can make all the files in the Utility directory Read Only and then remove the Modify right from your username's trustee assignment.

In this hands-on activity, you will use the FLAG command to set on the Read Only attribute on all files in your Utility subdirectory and then use either the RIGHTS command or Windows to remove the Modify right from your username's trustee assignment.

5

1. If necessary, start your computer and log in using your assigned ##Admin username.

2. Open a DOS window.

3. Change to drive G.

4. To view help information on setting directory attributes, enter the command **FLAG /? FO [Enter]**. If you receive the "Bad command or file name" message, enter the command **CD Z:\PUBLIC [Enter]** and repeat the FLAG command.

5. View all file attribute settings in your Utility directory by entering the command **FLAG IS\Utility*.* /FO [Enter]**.

6. To set the Read Only attribute on all files in your Utility directory, enter the following FLAG command: **FLAG IS\UTILITY*.* +RO /FO [Enter]**.

7. Use the command from Step 5 to view the file attributes in your Utility directory. Notice that the Delete Inhibit and Rename Inhibit attributes are set on by default when you use the Read Only attribute.

8. To use the RIGHTS command to remove the Modify right from your username, enter the following command:

   RIGHTS IS\Utility –M /NAME=.your_user_name.##UAS [Enter]

9. Exit the DOS window.

10. Use My Computer to verify the attribute settings for the files in your Utility directory along with your modified trustee assignment. Close My Computer.

11. Start NetWare Administrator and verify your effective rights in the Utility directory.

12. Exit NetWare Administrator and log out.

In a recent department meeting with Dave and other department managers, you explained that you have now established file system security in the Engineering and Manufacturing departments allowing users to take advantage of the network's file sharing capabilities. Of course, the Business and Sales managers were anxious to know when their departments' file systems will be secure. You are going to implement their file system access rights in the projects at the end of this chapter.

CHAPTER SUMMARY

- Just as a physical building such as a warehouse needs to be secured by using locks and keys, the NetWare file system must be secured by using trustee assignments to provide access rights. Access rights are like keys in that they allow users to access the storage areas they need. NetWare provides eight access rights: Read, File Scan, Write, Create, Erase, Modify, Access Control, and Supervisor. The Modify right allows users to change attributes or rename a file or subdirectory. The Access Control right allows users to assign other rights, except Supervisor, to other users. The Supervisor right can be assigned only by a Supervisor-equivalent user, and provides users with all rights to the directory and all subdirectories, including the right to assign the Supervisor right to other users. In addition, because the Supervisor right cannot be revoked or blocked at any lower level, assigning the Supervisor right is a good way to enable a user to act as a Supervisor of a portion of the directory structure.

❑ Rights are granted to users or groups for a directory by trustee assignments. Effective rights for a user are a combination of rights given to the user's name combined with the rights given to any groups of which the user is a member. Trustee rights granted to a user or group for a directory are then inherited by all the subdirectories and files within the directory for which the trustee assignment was made. A user's effective rights often involve inherited rights that have flowed down to the directory or file from a trustee assignment made to a group or username in a higher-level directory.

❑ An Inherited Rights Filter (IRF) exists in each directory and file to control what rights the directory or file may inherit from higher-level directories. When a file or directory is first created, the IRF allows all rights to flow down into that directory or file. Later you can remove rights from the IRF to block that directory or file from inheriting those rights.

❑ As a network administrator, you need to know how to use NetWare Administrator as well as Windows Explorer to set and view trustee assignments and the IRFs. In addition to using Windows utilities, you can use the RIGHTS command from the DOS prompt to view and set trustee assignments. The RIGHTS /T command may be used to view, change, or remove trustee assignments made to users, groups, and containers for the specified directory or file. You can use the RIGHTS /F command to set and view the IRF for the specified directory or file.

❑ Attributes play an important role in file system security because they allow you to protect files and directories from certain operations such as deleting, renaming, and copying. You can also use attributes to make files sharable, hidden, or protected by the Transaction Tracking System (TTS). File attributes include Archive, Execute Only, Read Only, Read Write, Sharable, Hidden, System, Transactional, Purge, Copy Inhibit, Delete Inhibit, Rename Inhibit, Migrated, Immediate Compress, and Don't Compress. Directory attributes include Hidden, System, Purge, Delete Inhibit, Rename Inhibit, Don't Migrate, and Don't Compress. As this chapter explained, you should know how to use the Windows-based NetWare Administrator along with Windows Explorer to view and set directory and file attributes. In addition, the FLAG command-line utility can also be used from the DOS prompt to set attributes on both files and directories.

COMMAND SUMMARY

Command	Syntax	Definition
RIGHTS	RIGHTS *path* /T	Displays all trustee assignments made to the directory specified in *path*.
	RIGHTS *path* [+/-] *rights_list* /T /NAME=*object_name*	Makes the object specified in the /NAME= parameter a trustee of the directory specified in *path* with the access rights given in the *rights_list*. Use a minus sign preceding rights you want to remove from an existing trustee assignment.
	RIGHTS *path* [+/-] *rights_list* /I	Modifies the Inherited Rights Filter of the directory specified in the given *path* by adding or removing the rights specified in the *rights_list*.
	RIGHTS *path* /I	Displays the Inherited Rights Filter of the directory specified in the given *path*.

FLAG	FLAG *path* /DO	Displays the directory attributes for the directory specified in the *path* parameter.
	FLAG *path [+/-] [attribute_list]* /DO	Adds or removes the directory attributes specified in the *attribute_list* from the directory specified in the *path* parameter.
	FLAG *path* /FO	Displays the file attributes for the filenames specified in the *path* parameter.
	FLAG *path [+/-] [attribute_list]* /FO	Adds or removes the file attributes specified in the *attribute_list* to or from the file(s) specified in the *path* parameter.

5

KEY TERMS

Access Control right — An access right that allows the user to grant access rights to other users for this directory.

Access Rights — In the file system security, eight rights that control what operations a user may perform in a file or directory: File Scan, Read, Create, Write, Erase, Modify, Access Control, and Supervisor.

Archive Needed (A) — A file attribute that indicates that the file has been changed since it was last backed up.

attributes — Flags or codes associated with files and directories to control what type of processing can be performed on the file or directory.

Can't Compress (Cc) — A file attribute indicating that the operating system was unable to compress the file.

Copy Inhibit (Ci) — A file attribute that prevents Macintosh computers from copying the file.

Create right — An access right that allows the user to create files and subdirectories.

Delete Inhibit (Di) — An attribute that protects a file or directory from being deleted.

Directory trustee — A user, group, or container object that has been granted access rights to a directory.

Don't Compress (Dc) — A file attribute that tells the operating system not to compress the file. When you apply this attribute to a directory, none of the files in the directory will be compressed.

Don't Migrate (Dm) — An attribute that prevents files from being migrated to a high-capacity storage device.

Don't Suballocate (Ds) — A file attribute that tells the operating system not to use block suballocation on the file.

effective rights — A subset of the access rights that control what functions a user can perform in a directory or file.

Erase right — An access right that allows the user to delete files and remove subdirectories.

Execute Only (X) — A file attribute that may be applied to .COM and .EXE files to prevent them from being copied. Once applied, the Execute Only attribute cannot be removed.

File Scan right — An access right that allows the user to obtain a directory of file and subdirectory names.

File trustee — A user, group, or container object that has been granted access rights to a file.

Hidden (H) — A file or directory attribute that prevents standard DOS and Windows applications from seeing the associated file or directory.

Immediate Compress (Ic) — A file or directory attribute that tells the system to compress a large file immediately after it has been used.

inherited rights — A subset of a user or group's effective rights to a directory which are provided to the user or group in the files and subdirectories.

Inherited Rights Filter (IRF) — A field belonging to each file and subdirectory that contains a list of access rights that may be inherited by that file or subdirectory. Removing a right from the filter prevents that right from being inherited by the subdirectory or file.

Migrated (M) — A file attribute set by the system, indicating that a file has been moved to an archive data medium.

Modify right — An access right that allows the user to change file and subdirectory names—without changing the contents of the file—as well as use the FLAG and FLAGDIR commands to change the attribute settings on files or subdirectories.

Normal (N) — A directory attribute setting that removes all directory attributes.

Purge (P) — A file or directory attribute that prevents a file or all files in the directory from being salvaged after deletion.

Read right — An access right that allows the user to read files or run programs in the directory.

Read Only (Ro) — A file attribute that prevents the contents of the file from being modified.

Read Write (Rw) — A default file attribute that allows the contents of the file to be changed.

Rename Inhibit (Ri) — A file or directory attribute that prevents the name of the file or directory from being changed.

Sharable (Sh) — A file attribute that allows multiple users to use the file at the same time.

Supervisor right (S) — An access right that grants a user all rights to the directory and all subdirectories; this right cannot be blocked or reassigned at a lower subdirectory or file level.

System (Sy) — A file or directory attribute that flags the file or directory for operating system use.

Transactional (T) — A file attribute that is used on database files to enable the system to restore the file to its previous state if a transaction is not completed.

Transaction Tracking System (TTS) — A system that protects the transactional attribute, ensuring that all transactions are completed or left in the original state.

trustee — An object such as a group, user, or container that has been given certain access rights to a folder, directory, or file.

trustee assignment — An assignment that makes the user a trustee of the directory or file.

Write right — An access right that allows the user to change or add data to files in a particular directory.

REVIEW QUESTIONS

1. _____ define(s) functions that can be performed in the NetWare file system.

2. The _____ right allows a user to change data within an existing file.

3. The _____ right allows a user to assign rights to other users.

4. The _____ right cannot be revoked or blocked within the directory structure it defines.

5. _____ consists of a subset of the access rights and controls what functions a user can perform in a directory or file.

6. Given that you are a member of the Admin group that has been granted the [R F W] rights to a directory called Business, and have a trustee assignment of [R F C] to the Business directory, what are your effective rights in the Business directory?

   _____

7. Assume you have been given a trustee assignment of [R F C] to the Business directory and a trustee assignment of Erase and Write to the Business\SPData\Budgets subdirectory. What are your effective rights in the Business\SPData subdirectory?

   _____

For Questions 8 through 13, use the following rights assignment information: You have a trustee assignment of [C W E] to the Business directory along with a trustee assignment of [E W] to the Business\SPData\Budgets subdirectory. In addition, you belong to a group that was granted [R F] to the Business directory.

8. What are your effective rights in the Business\SPData\Budgets subdirectory?

   _____

9. Assume all rights except [R] and [F] are removed from the IRF of the Business\SPData subdirectory. What are your rights in the Business\SPData subdirectory?

   _____

10. What are your rights in the Business\SPData\Budgets subdirectory?

    _____

5

11. Write the commands to give the user JoeMan the [C W E M A] rights to the Data:Business\Budgets directory, and the Admin group the [R F W] rights to the Data:Business directory.

    _____

    _____

12. Assume the user JoeMan was given a trustee assignment of [R F C W E M] to the Business\SPData directory. What are JoeMan's effective rights in the Business\SPData\Budgets subdirectory after deleting his trustee assignment to Budgets?

    _____

13. Did the user JoeMan gain or lose rights in the Budgets directory, and why?

    Gain or lose: _____

    Why: _____

    _____

14. Write a command that will display trustee assignments in each of the subdirectories of the Engineer directory structure.

    _____

15. If you are using Windows, which utility would you select to make the user BillSim a trustee of the following three directories: Business\AR, Sales\Inventry, and Data:Projects?

    _____

16. Define the term *attributes*: _____

17. When you set the Read Only attribute, what other attributes are also set by default?

    _____

    _____

18. Which of the following attributes are used with directories?

    Purge   Sharable   Read Only   Delete Inhibit   Copy Inhibit   Hidden   System   Don't Migrate

19. The _____ attribute would prevent deleted files in the SYS:Software\Temp directory from being salvaged.

20. What is the advantage of preventing deleted files from being salvaged?

    _____

21. The _____ DOS-based utilities can be used to set attributes.

22. What right(s) do you need in a directory to change trustee assignments?

    _____

23. What right(s) do you need in a directory to allow you to flag all files Delete Inhibit?

_____

24. When a user is first added as a trustee of a directory, he or she is given the _____ rights by default.

The Universal Aerospace Project

From the department meeting, you were pleased to learn that Dave and the other managers are very happy with your progress. However, it was obvious that the Business and Sales managers were anxious to give their user accounts access to the network file system. Now that Jennifer, the consultant, has completed her analysis of the company's processing needs as shown in Table 5-8, you can complete this phase of the network setup so that users will be able to log in and access or store information in your network file system.

Table 5-8   Business and Sales File System Usage

User	Responsibilities
Sales department	**Creates and updates files in the Sales\Shared.** **Reads information from Inventry and enters new orders by writing to the database.**
Michael Horowitz	Reads the **Sales\customer** and **Sales\vendor** database files.
Darrell Minick	Reads the **Sales\customer** and **Sales\vendor** database files.
Laura Hiller	Updates the **Sales\customer** and **Sales\vendor** database files.
Desktop publishing department	**Creates and updates files in the Publish\Shared directory.** **Reads files from the Engineering department's Shared directory.**
Diana Brady	Works on all the promotional material in the **Publish\Promote** directory. Reads information from **Publish\Manuals** directory maintained by Bradley Dahl.
Bradley Dahl	Maintains the **Publish\Manuals** directory. Reads information from the promotional directory maintained by Diana Brady.
Julie DamRau	Works with Diana to maintain the promotional directory files. Designs and develops the Web site.
Accounting department	**Creates and updates files in the Business\Shared directory.**
Terry Blackwell	Maintains the files in the Inventry directory. Reads **Business\Payroll** information for reporting. Reads general ledger information from the **Business\GL** directory for reporting. Maintains the **Business\Budget** directory files.
Amy Pan	Performs the weekly payroll and updates the files in the **Business\Payroll** directory. Works with Terry Blackwell to maintain the **Business\Budget** files. Manages accounts payable and maintains files in the **Business\AP** directory.
George Perez	Performs the billing functions and updates the **Business\AR** directory. Performs monthly general ledger processing and maintains files in the **Business\GL** directory. Needs to read data from the **Business\AP**, **Business\Payroll**, **Business\AR**, and **Inventry** directories to update the general ledger and print reports.

In this chapter, you learned how the processing requirements of each user were used to define directory trustee assignments for the Engineering and Manufacturing departments. Prior to completing the implementation of the trustee assignments for Universal Aerospace, you need to apply the guidelines described in this chapter to complete the process of defining access rights required for users or groups to perform the processing functions defined on the Directory Trustee Worksheets. To do this, you will need to obtain Directory Trustee Worksheets from your instructor or copy them from Appendix B and then continue to plan trustee assignments for the Business, Sales, and Publishing departments. Before continuing to Step 1, have your instructor check the trustee assignments against the recommended trustee assignments provided on the answer sheet. Although there are many ways in which to write trustee assignments, it is important that you implement the trustee assignments provided in the answer sheet to make future assignments work correctly.

5

Step 1: Implementing Trustee Assignments

Log in to the network using your assigned ##Admin username and then use Windows or NetWare Administrator to implement the trustee assignments defined on your finalized Directory Trustee Worksheet. For this project you should already have completed the hands-on exercise in the section, "Trustee Assignment Using Netware Administrator."

Step 2: Documenting Trustee Assignments

In this step, you need to use the appropriate option of the RIGHTS command to print reports documenting trustee assignments, as well as the IRF made to each of the following directories:

Inventry

Forms

Publish

Business

Print the IRFs for each of the directories in the Business, Sales, and Publish structures.

Step 3: Defining Attributes

In this chapter, you learned about the importance of using directory attributes to enhance file system security. To implement attribute security, you first need to fill out a Directory Attribute form identifying the attributes you feel are necessary for the Business, Publish, and Sales directory structures. At a minimum, you should define attributes that will protect the directory structures from being renamed or deleted. Define additional attributes that you feel are important to the system security and operation.

Step 4: Setting Attributes

Use Windows or NetWare Administrator to set the attributes you identified in Step 4.
Use the FLAG command to flag all files in the Forms directory to be Delete Inhibit and Rename Inhibit. Record the command you use on the following line:

_____

Step 5: Copying Files

Terry Blackwell wants to copy all budget files to his new Budget directory and then protect them from being deleted. Log in as Terry Blackwell and then copy the files to this Budget directory and set the attributes.

Step 6: Documenting Directory and File Attributes

Use the appropriate parameters of the FLAG command-line utility to print reports documenting the directory attributes you set in Step 4.

ADDITIONAL EXERCISES

The following exercises are not needed for implementing file system security for the Universal Aerospace projects, but are included to give you more practice in working with the NetWare Administrator along with trustee assignments and the IRF. This will help you to pass your CNA exam. To perform these exercises, you should have already completed the required Universal Aerospace projects.

Exercise 5-1: Create Directory Structure and Users

In this exercise, you will create a directory structure along with two users and then use NetWare Administrator to grant trustee assignments and set up an IRF to observe how effective rights are inherited.

1. Log in using your assigned ##Admin student username.
2. Start NetWare Administrator.
3. Open your ##UAS container by double-clicking it.
4. Open the UAS_HOST_CORP volume and expand your directory structure.
5. In your ##Corp\Shared directory, create a subdirectory named Chap5.
6. Modify the IRF on the Chap5 directory to block all rights.
7. In the Chap5 directory, create two subdirectories, Orders and Users.
8. Create two users in your Business container named Clerk1 and Clerk2. Do not use the Business USER_TEMPLATE for these users, but instead create home directories for the new users in the Shared\Chap5\Users directory.
9. Create a group named CLERKS in your Business container and make Clerk1 and Clerk2 members of the CLERKS group.
10. Give the group CLERKS Read and File Scan rights to the Chap5 directory.
11. Make Clerk1 a manager of the Chap5 directory structure by granting Clerk1 all rights except the Supervisor right.
12. Make Clerk2 a trustee of the Chap5\Orders directory with [W C E M] rights.
13. Exit NetWare Administrator.
14. Log out.

Exercise 5-2: Check Effective Rights

In this exercise, you will log in as Clerk2 and use the RIGHTS command or Windows' My Computer to check your effective rights.

1. Change the context to Business.##UAS.
2. Log in as Clerk2.
3. Use the RIGHTS command or My Computer to record your effective rights in the directories listed in the following table:
4. Log out of the network.

Directory	Clerk2 Effective Rights	How Obtained
##Corp\Shared		
##Corp\Shared\Chap5		
##Corp\Shared\Chap5\Users		
##Corp\Shared\Chap5\Users\Clerk1		
##Corp\Shared\Chap5\Orders		

Exercise 5-3: Modify Trustee Assignments

In this exercise, you will observe how making a trustee assignment of no rights to the CLERKS group in the subdirectory Orders will change the effective rights that user Clerk2 has to this directory.

1. Log in using your ##Admin username.

2. Use Windows' My Computer to assign the CLERKS group no rights to the Chap5\Orders subdirectory.

3. Use NetWare Administrator to record Clerk2's effective rights in the directories listed in the following table:

Directory	Clerk2 Effective Rights	How Obtained
##Corp\Shared		
##Corp\Shared\Chap5		
##Corp\Shared\Chap5\Users		
##Corp\Shared\Chap5\Users\Clerk1		
##Corp\Shared\Chap5\Orders		

4. What rights are missing from the Chap5\Orders directory as compared to Exercise 5-2?

_____

5. Explain what happened to the rights.

_____

_____

6. How would you restore these rights to Clerk2?

_____

_____

Exercise 5-4: Use IRFs to Change Effective Rights

Because the group CLERKS has been given Read and File Scan rights to the Chap5 directory, all members of CLERKS have rights to user home directories. To block users from inheriting rights into home directories, you can either move the home directories to another part of the directory structure or use the Inherited Rights Filter. In this exercise, you will practice using Windows to implement an IRF to secure user home directories.

1. Double-click **My Computer**.

2. Browse to your Chap5 directory.

3. Remove all rights except Supervisor from the IRF of the Chap5\Users directory.

4. To allow Clerk2 to maintain the Orders directory, modify the trustee assignment for the user Clerk2 to include the Read and File Scan rights.

5. Use NetWare Administrator to record the effective rights for Clerk1 and Clerk2 in the Chap5\Orders directory.

    Clerk1:

    Clerk2:

6. Use NetWare Administrator to record the effective rights for Clerk1 and Clerk2 in the Chap5\Users directory.

    Clerk1:

    Clerk2:

7. Record Clerk1's effective rights in the subdirectories shown in the following table:

Directory	Clerk1 Effective Rights	How Obtained
##Corp\Shared\Chap5		
##Corp\Shared\Chap5\Orders		
##Corp\Shared\Chap5\Users		
##Corp\Shared\Chap5\Users\Clerk1		
##Corp\Shared\Chap5\Users\Clerk2		

8. Record Clerk2's effective rights in the subdirectories shown in the following table:

Directory	Clerk1 Effective Rights	How Obtained
##Corp\Shared\Chap5		
##Corp\Shared\Chap5\Orders		
##Corp\Shared\Chap5\Users		
##Corp\Shared\Chap5\Users\Clerk1		
##Corp\Shared\Chap5\Users\Clerk2		

6

WORKING WITH NDS SECURITY

After reading this chapter and completing the exercises, you will be able to:

♦ Describe NDS security and list the object and property rights

♦ Identify the NDS security needs for Universal Aerospace

♦ Use NetWare Administrator to set up NDS security

♦ Identify the default object and property rights for the NDS system

♦ Identify the similarities and differences between NDS security and file system security

At a recent management meeting, Dave Heise, president of Universal Aerospace, announced the acquisition of AeroDyn Industries. AeroDyn Industries specializes in manufacturing aircraft fuselages and has the equipment and tooling Universal Aerospace will need to build certain International Space Station components. Dave explained that currently AeroDyn has a 100BaseT network that uses a Windows NT server to run some of the manufacturing software, and that you will be working with Chuck Botsford, a Microsoft Certified Systems Engineer (MCSE) for AeroDyn. Dave is planning to install a NetWare 5 server at AeroDyn that will become part of the Universal Aerospace Novell Directory Services (NDS) tree as shown in Figure 6-1. The consultant has recommended making the AeroDyn container a separate partition and placing the master replica of the partition on the Universal Aerospace server. This plan will allow you to manage the tree structure easily from the home office, but allows the AeroDyn users to be logged in by their local server.

Dave has contracted with the phone company for a T1 line that will be used to connect the Universal Aerospace and AeroDyn networks. As network administrator, you will need to modify the network structure to facilitate the integration and management of the new AeroDyn container and its users. Because of Chuck's knowledge of Windows NT and familiarity with the AeroDyn users and their applications, he will work with you in administrating the AeroDyn server and users.

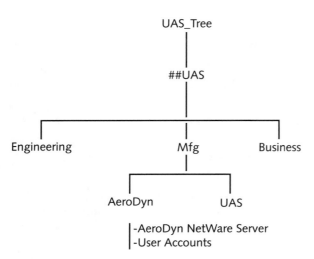

Figure 6-1   Proposed AeroDyn NDS merger

In this chapter, you will modify the Universal Aerospace NDS tree structure to accommodate AeroDyn users as well as learn how you can use the NDS security system to provide access to network resources. You will also learn how to provide certain users with the rights needed to manage other users. Later chapters will cover printing security (Chapter 7) and server console security (Chapter 10).

NDS SECURITY OVERVIEW

The NDS security system allows users to view, access, create, or modify objects and their properties in the NDS database. In many ways, NDS security is very similar to file system security. In Chapter 5, you learned that to work with the file system, users, groups, and containers are made trustees of directories or files and then granted certain access rights. In a similar way, you can use NDS security to make users, groups, or containers trustees of other objects in the NDS database, which the trustees can then access or manage. Because they are similar, it is often easy for a beginning administrator to forget that NDS security is separate from file system security, and that with only one exception, assigning rights in the NDS system has no effect on file system security. The one exception is when a trustee is made a Supervisor of the Server object, in which case the trustee will be automatically granted Supervisor rights to all volumes on that server. You will learn more about how this works later in this section.

By default, NetWare provides most of the NDS security rights users need to work with objects in their containers. However, as network administrator, you will need to work with NDS security to allow users special rights to work with certain objects such as the Directory Map objects you created in Chapter 3, or to access resources in other containers. Conversely, in some cases, you may want to reduce users' rights to prevent the users from being able to modify their personal login scripts or change their print job configuration data. Another use of NDS security is to delegate work by providing a user with the rights necessary to manage users and other objects within certain containers. In this chapter, you will need to use this feature so that Chuck can manage the objects in the AeroDyn division without having rights to the entire network.

NDS security also provides the ability to establish a separate administrator for a container to create a network in which there is not a single networkwide administrator with Supervisor privileges for all objects and data in the entire network. Having multiple network administrators can be important for large organizations and government agencies that do not want to put the entire network under the control of one all-powerful network administrator. In this section, you will learn what a CNA is required to know about NDS security rights and inheritance, along with how to use NetWare Administrator to view, assign, or modify these rights.

NDS Rights

As you learned in Chapter 2, each object in the NDS database contains certain fields of information called **properties**. One property that exists for all objects is called the Access Control List. The **Access Control List (ACL)** is a multivalued property that contains the names of users, groups, or containers that have been given rights to the object. In addition to user, group, and container objects, NetWare includes two special objects named [Root] and [Public] that can be made trustees of another object. The **[Public]** object represents all client computers that are attached to the network and running the requester (Virtual Loadable Module, or VLM) or Novell Client software. The **[Root]** object represents all users defined in the NDS tree. To gain the access rights granted to the [Root] object, a user must first be authenticated by successfully logging in to the NDS tree.

Any user or other object that is placed in the ACL property becomes a **trustee** of that object with certain rights. In Chapter 5, you learned that file system security consists of a single group of eight access rights that controls what operations a user can perform in a directory or file. Rather than having a single group of rights, in NDS security the rights are divided into two categories: object rights and property rights. **Object rights** control what a trustee can do to the object itself, whereas **property rights** determine whether or not a user is allowed to view or change the information fields within the object. Figure 6-2 illustrates the [Root] object's trustee listing showing the object and property rights assigned to the Students group. Notice that trustees of [Root] include the Admin user, the Students group, and [Public]. In addition to the trustees, notice that NDS rights are divided into object rights on the left side of the window and property rights on the right side.

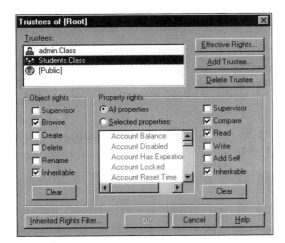

Figure 6-2   NDS rights

Object Rights

As shown in Table 6-1, object rights consist of Browse, Create, Rename, Inheritable, Delete, and Supervisor. The **Browse object right** is similar to the File Scan right in that it allows a user to find the object. Most users need only the Browse right to access objects in a container. If one user is to control other users or manage a container, the network administrator will need to make that user a trustee of the other user(s) or container by assigning additional rights. The **Create object right** applies only to container objects and allows the trustee to create new subcontainer or leaf objects. Having **Rename** and **Delete object rights** allows the trustee to change an object name, delete an object, or move an object to another location. The **Inheritable object right** allows the trustee's assignment to be inherited by leaf objects and other subcontainers. Just as in the file system, the **Supervisor object right** includes all other object rights. In addition, when you assign the Supervisor object right, the trustee will automatically be given Supervisor rights to all of the object's properties. The Supervisor right in NDS security is different from the Supervisor right in file system security because in NDS security, an Inherited Rights Filter (IRF) in a subcontainer or leaf object can reassign or block the Supervisor right. Later in this chapter, you will practice blocking and reassigning Supervisor object rights.

Table 6-1   NDS Object Rights

Right	Description
Supervisor	Grants all access privileges including the Supervisor right to all properties.
Browse	Grants the right to see the object.
Create	Grants the right to create objects in a container.
Delete	Grants the right to delete the object or leaf objects from a container.
Rename	Grants the right to change the name of the object.
Inheritable	Allows the trustee assignment to be inherited by leaf objects and subcontainers.

Property Rights

Property rights control access to an object's information fields, called properties, and include the six rights described in Table 6-2.

Table 6-2   NDS Property Rights

Right	Description
Supervisor	Grants all rights to the property unless blocked by an object's Inherited Rights Filter.
Read	Grants the right to view the values stored in the object's property fields. Includes the Compare right.
Compare	A special case of the Read right that allows the trustee only to compare the value of a property field to a fixed value returning either true or false, without being able to view property contents.
Write	Grants the right to add, change, or remove any value of a property field. Includes the Add Self right.
Add Self	A special case of the Write right that allows the trustee to add or remove himself or herself as a value of the property field. This right is meaningful for properties that contain object lists such as group membership and mailing lists.
Inheritable	Allows the trustee assignment to be inherited by leaf objects and subcontainers.

The two major property rights are Read and Write. The **Read property right** allows the trustee to view values in the property fields, whereas the **Write property right** allows the trustee to change information in the property fields.

The **Compare property right** is a limited version of the Read right that enables the trustee to find an object based on information in the property field without allowing the trustee to actually view the property information. For example, by having the Compare property right available to all users in a container, a trustee could run a command such as NLIST /USER WHERE "City" EQ "Mikana" to see a list of all users who live in the city of Mikana without being able to view the address of a specific user.

The **Add Self property right** is a special case of the Write property right and can be used to allow trustees to make themselves members of a group or remove their usernames in the future. For example, by giving all users the Add Self right to a mail server group, users can make their usernames members of the group to receive copies of all messages, or remove their usernames from the group when they no longer want to receive copies of all email messages. As with the Inheritable object right, the **Inheritable property right** allows the property right(s) in a container trustee assignment to be inherited by leaf objects and subcontainers. You will learn more about inheriting property rights later in this chapter.

Property rights may be assigned to all the object's properties or to just specific properties. Notice in Figure 6-2 that the Property rights box contains two radio buttons: All properties and Selected properties. As the name implies, All properties is a blanket way of granting rights to all the object's properties. In Figure 6-2, the All properties button is selected, indicating that the group Students has been assigned the right to read information from all the [Root] object's properties, and that this right is inheritable to all objects in the tree.

 Be careful when assigning the Write right to All properties. If users have the Write right to the ACL property, they can modify their trustee assignment, even to the point of making themselves a Supervisor of the object. In addition, having the Write property right to the ACL property of the Server object provides the trustee with Supervisor rights to all volumes on that server. This is the one exception where assigning NDS rights affects file system security: Making a user a Supervisor of a Server object grants that user all rights to the file system.

In addition to assigning rights for all properties, you can use the Selected properties button to assign rights to a specific property. Rights assigned with the Selected properties option override the rights assigned through the All properties option. For example, Figure 6-3 illustrates that the Students group has been assigned no rights (no rights have been checked) to the selected Account Balance property. The assignment of no rights to the Account Balance property will override the Read and Compare rights granted to all properties and prevent users in the Students group from reading the Account Balance information of other objects.

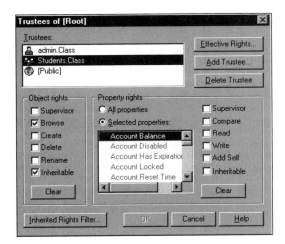

Figure 6-3   Selected property rights

Effective Rights

As you learned in Chapter 5, **effective rights** are the actual rights a user has to an object or property. Effective rights dictate what actions a user can perform with NDS objects. A user's effective rights are a result of one or more of the following factors:

- A trustee assignment made directly to the username
- A trustee assignment made to a group or Organizational Role object to which the user is a member
- A trustee assignment made to the user's parent container
- Container, group, and user rights inherited from a trustee assignment made to a parent container
- Rights blocked by an Inherited Rights Filter applied to a container or leaf object

Because effective rights are determined by a combination of factors, it is sometimes difficult to know what effective rights a user will have to a given container or leaf object. To make it easier to determine effective rights, Novell has included an Effective Rights option in NetWare Administrator that you can use to determine the effective rights a user has to another object. In this section, you will learn how to use NetWare Administrator to display a user's effective rights in a container as well as how to change a user's effective rights using each of the preceding factors.

Trustee Assignment to a User

The most direct way to provide a user with effective rights to an object is by making the user a trustee of the object and then granting the desired access rights. For example, assume Kellie Thiele wants to practice setting up users and working with login scripts. To allow her to do this you agree to create a separate organizational unit for her, named Thiele, and give her Supervisor rights to this container. This will allow her to create the users and login scripts she will need to test the implementation of new software packages.

 In this hands-on activity, you will create a new container for Kellie, grant her Supervisor rights to the new container, and then check her effective rights.

1. If necessary, start your computer and log in using your assigned ##Admin username.

2. Start NetWare Administrator.

3. If necessary, open a browse window for your ##UAS Organization.

4. Create a new container named Thiele as follows:

   a) Click your **##UAS** container to highlight it and press the **[Ins]** key to display the New Object window.

   b) Scroll down and double-click the **Organizational Unit** object type to display the Create Organizational Unit window.

   c) Enter the name **Thiele** in the Organizational Unit name field and click the **Create** button. A new organizational unit named Thiele will be displayed in your ##UAS container.

5. View existing trustee assignments for the Thiele container as follows:

   a) Right-click your **Thiele** organizational unit.

   b) Click the **Trustees of this Object** option. Notice that the Thiele container is a trustee but has been given no object or All properties rights.

   c) Click the **Thiele** Organizational Unit to highlight it.

   d) Click the **Selected properties** button and scroll down the property list. The trustee has been granted rights to any properties that have check marks by them. Click each of the following properties and record the property rights assigned:

   Login Script: _____Read_____

   Print Job Configurations: ____'_____

6. Make Kellie a trustee of Thiele with the Supervisor object rights as follows:

   a) Click the **Add Trustee** button to display the Select Object dialog box.

   b) Double-click the user **KThiele** from the left-hand Available objects window to add Kellie as a trustee of the Thiele container with the default rights shown in Figure 6-4.

   c) Click the **All properties** button and record the default property rights given to the new trustee: _____Compare   read   inheritable_____

   d) Click the **Supervisor** right from the Object rights window. By default, assigning the Supervisor object right also provides the trustee with Supervisor rights to All properties, even though the All properties rights window does not change.

e) To view the new trustee's effective property rights, click the **Effective Rights** button. Notice that KThiele now has the Supervisor right to All properties.

f) Click **Close** to exit the Effective Rights window and then click **OK** to save the trustee assignment.

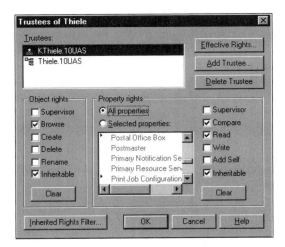

Figure 6-4   KThiele's trustee assignment to Business

7. Check Kellie's effective rights in the Thiele container:

a) Right-click the **Thiele** container and then click the **Trustees of this Object** option to display the Trustees dialog box.

b) Click the **Effective Rights** button to display the Effective Rights dialog box.

c) Click the **browse** button to display the Select Object dialog box.

d) Double-click the user **KThiele** to display her effective rights as shown in Figure 6-5.

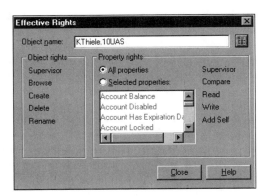

Figure 6-5   KThiele's effective rights to Business

8. Click the **Close** button to exit the Effective Rights dialog box.

9. Click **Cancel** to return to the NetWare Administrator browse window.

Trustee Assignment to a Group

A better way for users to gain effective rights is through membership in a group or through being an occupant of an Organizational Role object. Just as in the file system, giving rights to groups or Organizational Role objects makes security easier to maintain as the network changes or users change job responsibilities. When multiple users need effective rights to an object, you should implement a group trustee assignment. For example, assume all information system users need to be able to create and rename objects in the UAS Organization.

 In this hands-on activity, you will provide the ISMgrs group with a trustee assignment to your ##UAS Organization and then check effective rights for Kellie and your username.

1. If necessary, start your computer, log in using your assigned ##Admin username, and start NetWare Administrator.

2. If necessary, open a browse window for your ##UAS Organization.

3. Make the ISMgrs group a trustee of your ##UAS Organization with Create and Rename rights as follows:

    a) Right-click your ##UAS container and click the **Trustees of this Object** option.

    b) Record current trustees along with object and property rights:

Trustee	Object Rights	Rights to All Properties
_____	_____	_____
_____	_____	

    c) Click the **Add Trustee** button to display the Select Object dialog box.

    d) Double-click your **##UAS** container in the right-hand Browse context window.

    e) Double-click the **ISMgrs** group from the left-hand Available objects window to add it to the Trustees window.

    f) Click the **Create** and **Rename** object rights.

    g) Remove the **Browse** right (click to remove the check mark).

    h) Click **OK** to save your trustee assignment.

4. Check Kellie's effective rights in your ##UAS container as follows:

    a) Right-click your **##UAS** Organization and click the **Trustees of this Object** option.

    b) Click the **Effective Rights** button to display an Effective Rights dialog box.

    c) Click the **browse** button to display the Select Object dialog box.

    d) Use the Browse context window to navigate to your ##UAS container.

    e) Double-click **KThiele** from the left-hand Available objects window to display her effective rights as shown in Figure 6-6.

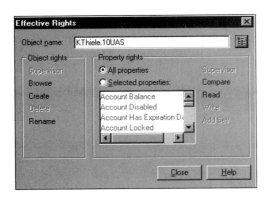

Figure 6-6   KThiele's effective rights from the ISMgrs group

5. Check your username's effective rights to the ##UAS container as follows:

a) Click the **browse** button to display the Select Object dialog box.

b) Double-click your username in the left-hand Available objects windows to display your effective rights. Your effective rights should be the same as Kellie's since you are both members of the ISMgrs group.

6. Click the **Close** button to exit the Effective Rights dialog box.

7. Click **Cancel** to return to the NetWare Administrator browse window.

Trustee Assignment to a Container

When all users in a container need the same effective rights to an object, the best solution is to make the container a trustee of that object and assign it the necessary rights. Just as in the file system, when a container is made a trustee of an object, all users in that container will have the object and property rights that were granted to the container added to their effective rights. In addition, when a container is made a trustee of another object, all subcontainers of that container also receive the same object and property rights as their parent container. As you learned in Chapter 3, a Directory Map object contains a Path property that points to a directory in the file system. By reading the directory path from the Path property, MAP commands can use the Directory Map object to map a drive letter to a specific directory in the file system. As a result, to use a Directory Map object, users must have rights to read the Directory Map object's Path property. For example, before users in the Engineering department can map a drive letter using the EngData Directory Map object, they must have the Read property right to the Path property of the EngData object. Although you could assign this right by making each user a trustee of the Directory Map object with the Read property right, it is much more efficient to make a container or group object a trustee with Read rights to All properties. NetWare provides a fast way to make an NDS trustee assignment by simply dragging the object you want to make a trustee and dropping it on the desired object.

In this hands-on activity, you use the drag and drop method to make the Engineering container a trustee of the EngData Directory Map object and then check effective rights for one or more Engineering users.

1. If necessary, start your workstation, log in using your ##Admin username, and start NetWare Administrator.

2. If necessary, open a browse window to your Engineering container.

3. Follow these steps to make your Engineering container a trustee of the EngData Directory Map object with Read rights to All properties. By giving the Read property right to your Engineering container, you ensure that all users in the Engineering container can read the path stored in the EngData Directory Map object.

a) Click the **Engineering** container to select it.

b) Click the **Engineering** container, and drag and drop the Engineering container on the **EngData** Directory Map object.

c) The Engineering container should now be added to the trustee list for EngData as shown in Figure 6-7. Notice that by default the Engineering container has been given the Browse object right and Read and Compare rights to all properties.

d) Click the **OK** button to save the trustee assignment.

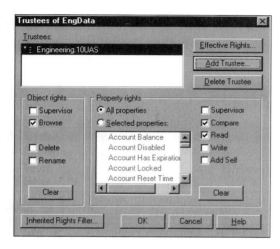

Figure 6-7   Engineering container trustee assignment

4. Use NetWare Administrator to determine the effective rights that users now have to the Directory Map object EngData as follows:

a) Right-click **EngData**.

b) Click the **Trustees of this Object** option to display the Trustees of EngData dialog box.

c) Click the **Effective Rights** button to display the Effective Rights dialog box.

d) Click the **browse** icon to the right of the Object name field to display a Select Object dialog box.

e) Use the right-hand Browse context window to navigate to your Engineering container.

f) Double-click the user object **TRucci** in the left-hand Available objects window. The effective rights of the user Tony Rucci to the EngData Directory Map object will now be highlighted in the Effective Rights dialog box as shown in Figure 6-8. Notice that Tony has the Browse object right along with the Read and Compare rights to All properties.

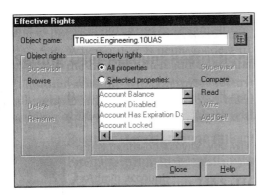

Figure 6-8   TRucci's effective rights to EngData

g) Click the **Selected properties** radio button.

h) Use the scrollbar to scroll down until you see the Path property.

i) Click the **Path** property. Notice that Tony has the necessary Read rights because one of his parent containers—in this case, the ##Engineering container—has been granted Read rights to All properties of the EngData object.

5. Click the **Close** button to exit the Effective Rights dialog box.

6. Click the **Cancel** button to return to the NetWare Administrator browse window. Close the Engineering browse window.

Inherited Rights

To decrease the number of trustee assignments you need to make, NetWare allows trustee object and property rights granted in a container to flow down to any subcontainers or leaf objects within that container. The process of rights flowing down the tree structure is referred to as **inherited rights**. A new feature with NetWare 5 NDS security is that you can use the Inheritable right to specify whether the object and property rights you give a trustee will be inheritable to subcontainers or leaf objects. Just as in the file system, you can block inherited object and property rights using an **Inherited Rights Filter (IRF)**. In addition, with NetWare 5, each individual property has its own IRF that can be used to block rights to just that property. You will use this new feature later when implementing NDS security for Universal Aerospace.

A difference between NDS security and file system security is that with NDS security, you can block Supervisor rights from being inherited by a container or leaf object.

In this hands-on activity, you will observe inherited object rights in action by using NetWare Administrator to check the effective rights that members of the ISMgrs group will inherit as a result of having the Create and Rename rights granted to the Universal Aerospace container. You will then create and use an IRF to block all rights except for Supervisor from being inherited into the Mfg container.

1. If necessary, start your workstation, log in using your ##Admin username, and start NetWare Administrator.

2. If necessary, open a browse window to your ##UAS container.

3. Check Kellie Thiele's effective rights to the Mfg Organizational Unit as follows:

   a) Right-click **Mfg** and click the **Trustees of this Object** option.

   b) Click the **Effective Rights** button to display the Effective Rights dialog box.

   c) Click the **browse** button to display the Select Object dialog box.

   d) Double-click **KThiele** in the left-hand Available objects window. Kellie should have Browse, Create, and Rename rights because of her membership in the ISMgrs group.

   e) Click **Close** to return to the Trustees of Mfg window.

4. Set up an IRF to block all rights except Supervisor from the Mfg container as follows:

   a) Click the **Inherited Rights Filter** button to display the Inherited Rights Filter dialog box.

   b) Remove all object rights except Supervisor and Browse from the IRF by clicking the Create, Delete, and Rename boxes to remove the checks as shown in Figure 6-9.

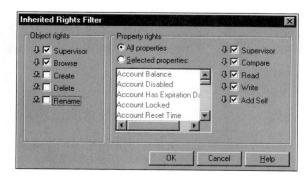

Figure 6-9   Inherited Rights Filter

   c) Click **OK** to save the modified IRF.

   d) Click **OK** to save the modifications to the Mfg container.

5. Now check Kellie's effective rights in the Mfg container as follows:

   a) Right-click **Mfg** and click the **Trustees of this Object** option.

   b) Click the **Effective Rights** button to display the Effective Rights dialog box.

   c) Click the **browse** button to display the Select Object dialog box.

   d) Double-click **KThiele** in the left-hand Available objects window. Kellie should now have only Browse rights to the Mfg container.

6. Click the **Close** button to exit the Effective Rights dialog box.

7. Click the **Cancel** button to return to the NetWare Administrator browse window.

As described earlier, you can use the Inheritable right to control the effective rights a user will inherit into subcontainers and leaf objects. For example, to reduce the number of times you need to log in using the ##Admin username when maintaining objects in the ##UAS container, assume you want your username to have the Supervisor right in the ##UAS Organization but not in the Organizational Units.

In this hands-on activity, you will grant your username the Supervisor object right to your ##UAS container and then use the Inheritable right to prevent the Supervisor right from being inherited by Mfg, Engineering, or Business Organizational Units.

1. If necessary, start your workstation, log in using your ##Admin username, and start NetWare Administrator.

2. If necessary, open a browse window to your ##UAS container.

3. Make your username a trustee of your ##UAS Organization with the Supervisor right, as follows:

    a) Click your username to select it.

    b) Click your username and then drag and drop your username on the ##UAS Organization.

    c) Click the **Supervisor** object right.

    d) Click **OK** to save the trustee assignment.

4. Check your username's effective rights in the Mfg Organizational Unitas follows:

    a) Right-click **Mfg** and click the **Trustees of this Object** option.

    b) Click the **Effective Rights** button to display the Effective Rights dialog box.

    c) Click the **browse** button to display the Select Object dialog box.

    d) Double-click your username in the left-hand Available objects window. Your username should have all rights including the Supervisor object and property rights to the Mfg container.

    e) Click **Close** to return to the Trustees of Mfg window.

    f) Click **Cancel** to return to the NetWare Administrator browse window.

5. Modify your username's trustee assignment to remove the Inheritable object right as follows:

    a) Right-click your ##UAS Organization and click the **Trustees of this Object** option.

    b) Click the trustee assignment for your username.

    c) Remove the check from in front of the **Inheritable** right as shown in Figure 6-10.

    d) Click **OK** to save the trustee assignment.

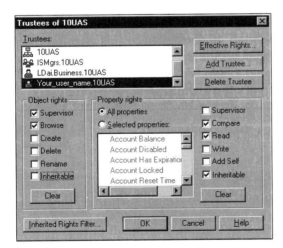

Figure 6-10   Setting the Inheritable right

6. Now check your username's effective rights in the Mfg Organizational Unit:

   a) Right-click **Mfg** and click the **Trustees of this Object** option.

   b) Click the **Effective Rights** button to display the Effective Rights dialog box.

   c) Click the **browse** button to display the Select Object dialog box.

   d) Double-click your username in the left-hand Available objects window. You should now have only the Browse object right along with the Read and Compare property rights. The Create and Rename object rights have been blocked by the IRF you previously modified for the Mfg container.

   e) Click **Close** to return to the Trustees of Mfg window.

   f) Click **Cancel** to return to the NetWare Administrator browse window.

7. Check your username's effective rights in your ##UAS Organization as follows:

   a) Right-click your **##UAS** container and then click the **Trustees of this Object** option.

   b) Click the **Effective Rights** button to display the Effective Rights dialog box.

   c) Click the **browse** button to display the Select Object dialog box.

   d) Use the Browse context window to navigate to your ##UAS container.

   e) Double-click your username in the left-hand Available objects window. Notice that your username still has Supervisor rights to your ##UAS container, but that this right is not inherited by the subcontainers or leaf objects.

8. Click the **Close** button to exit the Effective Rights dialog box.

9. Click the **Cancel** button to return to the NetWare Administrator browse window.

In earlier versions of NetWare 4, selected property rights could not be inherited. This created a lot of work if you wanted to give a user rights to only certain properties such as user addresses or phone numbers. With NetWare 5, Novell allows Organizational Units and leaf objects to inherit selected property rights.

In this hands-on activity, you will observe inherited property rights in action by making the AdmAsst Organizational Role object a trustee of the UAS container with rights to change address information for all users except those in the Mfg container.

1. If necessary, start your workstation, log in using your ##Admin username, and start NetWare Administrator.

2. Make the AdmAsst organizational role object a trustee of your ##UAS container with the Browse object right and Read and Write property rights to the Mailing Label Information property, as follows:

   a) Drag and drop **AdmAsst** on top of your ##UAS organization.

   b) Click the **Selected properties** button and use the scrollbar to scroll down to the Mailing Label Information property. Notice that the properties are listed in alphabetic order.

   c) Click the **Mailing Label Information** property.

   d) Click the check boxes next to the **Read**, **Write**, and **Inheritable** property rights as shown in Figure 6-11. The check mark in front of the Mailing Label Information property indicates that a trustee assignment has been made to this property.

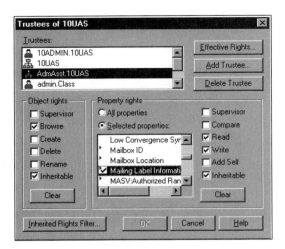

Figure 6-11   Setting selected property rights

    e) Click **OK** to save your trustee assignment.

3. As an occupant of the AdmAsst Organizational Role object, Ira Means should now have the effective rights to maintain mailing label information. Check Ira's effective rights to the Mailing Label Information property for a user in the Mfg Organizational Unit as follows:

    a) Right-click the **Mfg** Organizational Unit and click the **Trustees of this Object** option.

    b) Click the **Effective Rights** button to display the Effective Rights dialog box.

    c) Click the **browse** button to display the Select Object dialog box.

    d) Use the right-hand Browse context window to navigate to your Engineering Organizational Unit.

    e) Double-click IMeans in the left-hand Available objects window.

    f) Click the **Selected properties** button and scroll down to the Mailing Label Information property.

    g) Click the **Mailing Label Information** property and verify that Ira has Compare, Read, Write, and Add Self rights. The Read and Compare rights are inherited from the Read and Compare rights assigned to all properties of the ##UAS container for the AdmAsst Organizational Unit.

    h) Click **Close** and **Cancel** to return to the NetWare Administrator browse window.

4. Now use an Inherited Rights Filter to block the AdmAsst Organizational Role object's inherited rights in the Mfg container as follows:

    a) Right-click the **Mfg** Organizational Unit and click the **Trustees of this Object** option.

    b) Click the **Inherited Rights Filter** button to display the Inherited Rights Filter dialog box.

    c) Click the **Selected properties** button and scroll down to the Mailing Label Information property.

    d) Click the **Mailing Label Information** property and remove the check marks from the **Write** and **Add Self** rights to remove those rights from its IRF as shown in Figure 6-12.

    e) Click **OK** to save the IRF changes.

    f) Click **OK** to save the modifications to the Mfg container.

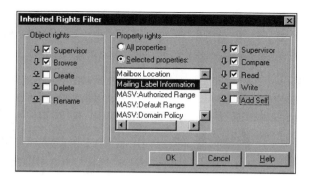

Figure 6-12   Setting a selected property IRF

5. Check Ira's effective rights to the selected address properties of the users in the Mfg Organizational Unit as follows:

a) Right-click the **Mfg** Organizational Unit and click the **Trustees of this Object** option.

b) Click the **Effective Rights** button to display the Effective Rights dialog box.

c) Click the **browse** button to display the Select Object dialog box.

d) Use the right-hand browse context window to navigate to your Engineering Organizational Unit.

e) Double-click **IMeans** in the left-hand Available objects window.

f) Click the **Selected properties** button and scroll down to the Mailing Label Information property.

g) Click the **Mailing Label Information** property and verify that Ira now has only Compare and Read rights.

6. Click the **Close** button to exit the Effective Rights dialog box.

7. Click the **Cancel** button to return to the NetWare Administrator browse window.

NDS Default Rights

The NDS security system is very powerful and flexible, allowing the network administrator to tailor the system to meet special needs. Knowing what rights are available by default and where they come from is important in planning for NDS security needs, as well as in troubleshooting the NDS security system. In this section, you will learn what a CNA needs to know about the NDS default rights as well as how to view trustee assignments using NetWare Administrator.

Initial Installation

When NDS is installed on the first server, the [Public], [Root], and Admin objects are created. The Admin object is assigned the Supervisor object right to the root of the new NDS tree, thereby making Admin a supervisor of the entire network, including all servers. Giving the Supervisor object right to a Server object automatically provides that user with Supervisor rights to the server's volumes and file system as described in Chapter 5. In addition to receiving the Admin user assignment, during installation the [Public] object is given the Browse object right all the way to the root of the tree. This allows an unauthorized user to view all objects in the tree by using the Start menu's Run command CX/T/A from Windows prior to logging in.

Windows Network Neighborhood and Explorer require the user to log in prior to browsing the tree structure. However, all user names can be listed by opening an MS-DOS prompt window and entering the CX/T/A/R command to display all objects in the tree.

If this creates a security problem in your organization, you will need to remove [Public] as a trustee of the root of the tree and then assign the Browse right to individual users, groups, or containers. You can give all users who have logged in to the network rights to browse the entire tree by making the [Root] object a trustee of the root of the tree with Browse object rights.

 In this hands-on activity, you will use NetWare Administrator to record the trustees of the [Root] object along with their object and property rights.

6

1. If necessary, start your workstation, log in using your ##Admin username, and start NetWare Administrator.

2. Open a browse window showing the root of the tree as follows:

   a) Click **View**, **Set Context**.

   b) Click the **Context** field, type **[Root]**, and click **OK**.

3. To check the trustees of the [Root] object, right-click the **[Root]** object and click the **Trustees of this Object** option.

4. Record the trustees of the [Root] object along with their assigned object and property rights in Table 6–3.

Table 6-3   Default Container Trustees

Trustee	Object Rights	Property Rights	
		Property	Rights
Admin user			
[Public]			

5. Click the Cancel button to return to the NetWare Administrator browse window.

6. Exit NetWare Administrator and log out.

Server Installation

When a Server object is installed in the NDS tree, default rights are given the Server object itself and to the [Public] object.

 In this hands-on activity, you will use NetWare Administrator to record the default trustees and their rights.

1. If necessary, start your workstation, log in as Admin, and start NetWare Administrator.

2. Open a browse window to the **Class** organization.

3. Check the trustees of the Server object by right-clicking the **UAS_Host** Server object and then clicking the **Trustees of this Object** option.

4. Record the trustees of the Server object along with their assigned object and property rights in Table 6-4.

Table 6-4   Default Server Trustees

Trustee	Object Rights	Property Rights	
		Property	Rights
Server object			
[Public]			

5. Click the **Cancel** button to return to the NetWare Administrator browse window.

6. Close all browse windows, exit NetWare Administrator, and log out.

In addition to the NDS rights identified in this section, in Chapter 5 you learned that by default the container that houses the Server object is made a trustee of the SYS:Public directory during server installation. This allows all users in the same container as the SYS volume to run NetWare commands on their local server. As a result, to run NetWare commands, users in containers that do not have a Server object must be given file system access rights to a SYS volume as described in Chapter 5.

User Objects

When a new user object is created in NDS, certain necessary property rights are granted automatically to provide the user with access to basic resources on the network. Knowing the default rights assignments for a new user can help in planning and implementing an NDS security system that meets the needs of the organization as well as of the users.

In this hands-on activity, you will use NetWare Administrator to create a new user object for Chuck Botsford and then discover and record the default trustees of Chuck's user object.

1. If necessary, start your workstation, log in using your ##Admin username, and start NetWare Administrator.

2. Open a browse window for your ##UAS Organization as follows:

   a) Click **View**, **Set Context**.

   b) Click the **browse** button to the right of the Context window and then use the up arrow in the Browse context pane to move up one level in the tree.

   c) Double-click your **##UAS** container from the left-hand Available objects window.

   d) Click **OK** to open a ##UAS browse window.

3. Use the T_ISMgrs template to create a username for Chuck Botsford (CBotsford) in your ##UAS container as follows:

   a) Click your **##UAS** Organization.

   b) Click the **Create User object** icon from your toolbar.

   c) Enter **CBotsford** in the Login name field.

d) Enter **Botsford** in the Last name field.

e) Click the **Use Template** box and use the **browse** button to navigate to the T_ISMgrs template. Double-click the **T_ISMgrs** template from the Available objects window.

f) Click the **Create** button to create Chuck's username.

4. Now check and record the trustees of CBotsford as follows:

a) Right-click **CBotsford** and click the **Trustees of this Object** option.

b) Record the trustees of CBotsford along with their assigned object and property rights in Table 6-5.

6

Table 6-5   Default User Trustees

Trustee	Object Rights	Property Rights	
		Property	Rights
CBotsford			
[Public]/[Root]			

5. Click the **Cancel** button to return to the NetWare Administrator browse window.

NDS SECURITY FOR UNIVERSAL AEROSPACE

As with file system security, when setting up NDS security you first need to identify and document the effective rights that users will need to access their resources or perform their management responsibilities. After meeting with Dave and the department managers, Lynn Dai sent out a memo, shown in Figure 6-13, that documents the NDS security requirements you will need to implement in addition to the NetWare 5 defaults.

Memo

To: Network Administrator

From: Lynn Dai

Date: Yesterday

Subject: Notes from the Engineering and Manufacturing NDS Security Meeting

1.   Kellie Thiele will be responsible for maintaining user login scripts for all except in the AeroDyn organization. Users should not be able to change their own login scripts.

2.   The NDS tree structure for the Manufacturing division needs to be modified to accommodate AeroDyn Industries.

3.   A new Information Systems user account needs to be created for Chuck Botsford.

4.   An Organizational Role object named MfgMgr should be created and Chuck made the occupant. The MfgMgr object should have all object rights to manage the Mfg structure with the exception of deleting objects in the UAS.Mfg Organizational Unit. In addition, the MfgMgr object should have Write access to all properties of the Mfg Organizational Unit except for the Access Control List property in the UAS.Mfg Organizational Unit. The MfgMgr object should be limited to Read access in the UAS.Mfg Organizational Unit to prevent members of the group from changing their assigned rights.

5.   All users in the Engineering container need rights to use the EngData Directory Map object.

6.   All users in the ISMgrs group need rights to use the ISData Directory Map object.

7.   All users in the ISMgrs group should have rights to create and rename objects in all AeroDyn containers.

8.   Ira Means should be given rights to create and rename objects in the Engineering container.

Figure 6-13   NDS security memo

Defining Trustee Assignments

The next step will be to define the trustee assignments you will need to make to each NDS object to implement the security plan. NDS security can be complex, so following Novell's general guidelines and cautions can help avoid certain pitfalls and will help you build a secure system that is relatively easy to manage and troubleshoot. To help you with this task, the list of Novell recommendations is shown in Figure 6-14.

6

Novell Security Guidelines

- **Start with the default trustee assignments as described earlier in this chapter.**
  With the exception of the Directory Map and Profile objects, the defaults provided by the NDS system will enable users to access the basic network resources and services within their default container. To keep NDS security assignments to a minimum, attempt to locate objects that users need to access, such as volumes and printers, within the user's default context.

- **Minimize trustee assignments.**
  As with file system security, you can often keep user trustee assignments to a minimum by assigning rights to containers first. Assign rights to groups when you do not want to include all users in a container, or if you want to include selected users from multiple containers. Rather than assigning rights to individual users, consider using Organizational Role objects.

- **Use caution when assigning the Write property right to the Object Trustee (ACL [Access Control List]) property.**
  If users have the Write right to the ACL property of another object, users will be able to create and remove trustees of the object in addition to changing their own trustee assignments. This includes making their usernames or some other user a Supervisor of the object, as well as modifying the object's Inherited Rights Filter. In a worst case scenario, trustees with the Write right to the ACL property of a container could make their username the Supervisor of the container and lock out the Admin user by removing "S" from the container's IRF.

- **Avoid assigning rights using the All properties option.**
  Use caution when assigning a trustee the Write right in the All properties field, as this will give the trustee the ability to change any of the property values including the ACL property. Through inheritance, the All properties rights assigned to a container will flow down to all subcontainer and leaf objects. As a general rule, it is better to assign only the Read right in All properties and use Selected properties when assigning the Write right.

- **Use caution when granting a trustee the Supervisor object right to a container that contains a Server object.**
  When a user has the Supervisor object right to a Server object, the user also becomes a Supervisor of the Server's file system by gaining the Supervisor access right to the root of all volumes (described in Chapter 5). The most common way this problem occurs is when another user is made manager of a container by granting the person the Supervisor object right to that container. If the container happens to contain a Server object, the new trustee will also have all rights to the file system on the server. To prevent a user from accidentally inheriting Supervisor rights to the Server object, you can make the Admin user a Supervisor of the Server object by adding an explicit trustee assignment for Admin, and then remove the Supervisor right from the Server object's Inherited Rights Filter.

- **Use caution when filtering Supervisor rights with an Inherited Rights Filter.**
  NetWare will not allow you to remove the Supervisor rights from an object's IRF until you have added an explicit trustee assignment that has been granted the Supervisor object right for that object. But it is still possible to "shoot yourself in the foot" by adding a user as a trustee with Supervisor rights, removing the Supervisor rights from the IRF, and then later accidentally deleting the user that has the Supervisor trustee assignment. If this has occurred, you would essentially lose control of the container or leaf object because it would have no Supervisor.

Figure 6-14   NDS security guidelines

Using these guidelines along with the NDS Security Worksheet she developed, Jennifer defined the trustee assignments as shown in Figure 6-15.

NDS Security Worksheet

Created by: Jennifer Almquest, Consultant

Date:

Organization or Organizational Unit Name: Universal Aerospace Corporation

Object		Trustee			Property		
Name	Type	Trustee Name/Type	Object Rights	IRF	Property Name	Rights	IRF
EngData.Engineering.##UAS	Directory Map	.Engineering.##UAS/container	B	All.	Path	R	All
ISData.##UAS	Directory Map	.ISMgrs.##UAS/group	B	All	Path	R	All
##UAS	Organization container	.KThiele.##UAS	B	All	Login script	RW	All
All users	User object	The user's name			Login script	R	All
Mfg.##UAS	Organizational Unit container	.MfgMgr.Mfg.##UAS/org role	SBCRD	All			
UAS.Mfg.##UAS	Organizational Unit container	.MFGMgr.Mfg.##UAS/org role	BCR	SBC	Login script All ACL	RW	SR All R
AeroDyn.Mfg.##UAS	Organizational Unit container			S	All		S

Figure 6-15   NDS Security Worksheet

Each row on the NDS Security Worksheet contains the name and object type of an object that needs a special assignment. The Trustee columns contain the name of one or more trustees along with the object and property rights to be assigned. For example, the first two rows contain the names of two Directory Map objects that you created in Chapter 3.

For users to access a Directory Map object, they need to be able to read the Path property. Notice that since all users in the Engineering department need to be able to use the EngData Directory Map object, the Engineering container has been identified as the trustee with Read rights to the Path property. Only Kellie's and Chuck's usernames will be needed to access the ISData Directory Map object. Since Chuck's username will be in the AeroDyn Organizational Unit, Jennifer felt the best way to assign rights to the Path property of ISData is through the ISMgrs group.

To allow Kellie to maintain login scripts, Jennifer has given Kellie the Read, Write, and Inheritable rights to the selected Login Script property of your UAS Organization. This will allow her to maintain login scripts for all users through inheritance. In addition, notice that Jennifer has removed the ability of users to change their own login scripts by modifying their selected Login Script property to only Read.

To allow the user or users occupying the MfgMgr Organization Role object to manage the Manufacturing division, Jennifer has recommended modifying the NDS structure to place both AeroDyn and Universal Aerospace as suborganizational units within Mfg as shown in Figure 6-16. Because of inheritance, the Supervisor object right assigned to the MfgMgr object in the Mfg container will be inherited by the UAS and AeroDyn Organizational Units. As described earlier, the Supervisor object right also provides Supervisor rights to all properties.

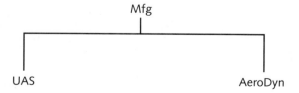

Figure 6-16   Modified Mfg NDS structure

Jennifer explained that even though having the Supervisor right provides all effective rights to the container, she still includes all other rights as well. As described earlier, in NDS security the Supervisor right can be reassigned at a lower level. To prevent the MfgMgr object from deleting objects in the UAS container, Jennifer has reassigned rights to the MfgMgr object in the UAS Organizational Unit that will reduce its effective rights to Browse, Create, and Rename. Notice that Jennifer is using caution in assigning the MfgMgr object Write right to All properties of the UAS Organizational Unit by also including the selected property assignment of Read to the ACL property. Jennifer explained that this will prevent an occupant of MfgMgr from changing his or her trustee assignment.

Notice that the Inherited Rights Filter on the AeroDyn container has been reduced to have just the Supervisor right. This will prevent users in the ISMgr group who have Create rights in the UAS Organization from inheriting Create rights in the AeroDyn division. Reducing the IRF of All properties to just Supervisor will prevent Kellie from changing login scripts for AeroDyn users, as recommended in the security memo shown previously in Figure 6-13.

Making Trustee Assignments

Now that you have reviewed Jennifer's NDS trustee assignment plan, your next step is to implement the trustee assignments and check effective rights using NetWare Administrator. The hands-on activities in this section correspond to the trustee assignments on the NDS Security Worksheet in Figure 6-15. In these activities, you will learn how to use NetWare Administrator to make the NDS trustee assignments on the worksheet as well as learn how you can use inherited rights and filters to modify users' effective rights.

Changing Trustee Assignments for Directory Map Objects

As described in the "Using Directory Map Objects" section of Chapter 3, for the users to access Directory Map objects, you will need to provide the users with a minimum of the Read right to the Path property of these objects. In a previous activity, you made the Engineering container a trustee of the EngData Directory Map object with the Browse object right and Read rights to All properties. This actually gives the Engineering users more rights to EngData than they need.

 In this hands-on activity, you will change the Engineering container's trustee assignment so that the users have Read rights to only the Path property. In addition, you will make the ISMgrs group a trustee of the ISData Directory Map object and then use NetWare Administrator to check effective rights for the users of each object.

1. If necessary, start your workstation, log in using your ##Admin username, and start NetWare Administrator.

2. Open a browse window for your Engineering Organizational Unit.

3. Change the Engineering container's trustee assignment to EngData to have only Read rights to the Path property, as follows:

    a) Right-click the **EngData** Directory Map object and click the **Trustees of this Object** option.

    b) In the Trustees window, click the **Engineering** Organizational Unit.

    c) Remove the checks from the **Read** and **Compare** rights in the All properties area by clicking the associated boxes.

    d) Click the **Selected properties** button and scroll down to the Path property.

    e) Click the **Path** property and then click the box to the left of the **Read** right. A check mark will appear to the left of the Path property, indicating that a trustee assignment has been made to this property.

    f) Click **OK** to save the changes to the trustee assignment.

4. Check effective rights for LJarka to the Path property of the EngData Directory Map object:

   a) Right-click the **EngData** Directory Map object and click the **Trustees of this Object** option.

   b) Click the **Effective Rights** button to display the Effective Rights dialog box.

   c) Click the **browse** button to display the Select Object dialog box.

   d) Double-click **LJarka** from the left-hand Available objects window. Notice that Ira does not have rights to All properties.

   e) Click the **Selected properties** button and scroll down to the Path property.

   f) Click the **Path** property. Ira should have Read and Compare rights to the Path property as shown in Figure 6-17.

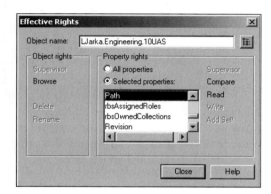

Figure 6-17   IMeans' effective rights to EngData

   g) Click **Close** and **Cancel** to return to the NetWare Administrator browse window.

   h) Close the Engineering browse window.

5. Make ISMgrs a trustee of the ISData Directory Map object with Read rights to the Path property as follows:

   a) If necessary, open your **##UAS** container browse window.

   b) Click your **ISMgrs** group to select it.

   c) Drag and drop the ISMgrs group on top of the **ISData** Directory Map object.

   d) Remove the checks from **Read** and **Compare** rights in All properties by clicking the associated check boxes.

   e) Click the **Selected properties** button and scroll down to the Path property.

   f) Click the **Path** property and then click the check box to the left of the **Read** right. A check mark will appear to the left of the Path property, indicating a trustee assignment has been made to this property.

   g) Click **OK** to save the new trustee assignment.

6. Now check Chuck's effective rights to the Path property of the ISData Directory Map object as follows:

   a) Right-click the **ISData** Directory Map object and click the **Trustees of this Object** option.

   b) Click the **Effective Rights** button to display the Effective Rights dialog box.

   c) Click the **browse** button to display the Select Object dialog box.

   d) Double-click **CBotsford** from the left-hand Available objects window. Record Chuck's Object and All properties rights below.

   Object: _____   All properties: _____

   e) Click the **Selected properties** button and scroll down to the Path property.

   f) Click the **Path** property. Record Chuck's effective rights to the Path property on the following line:

   Path property rights: _____

7. Click the **Close** button to exit the Effective Rights dialog box.

8. Click the **Cancel** button to return to the NetWare Administrator browse window.

Inheriting Selected Property Rights

It is important to remember that with NetWare 5, both Selected and All properties rights may be inherited by subcontainers and leaf objects. This was not true of NetWare 4.x, where only object and All properties rights could be inherited by child containers and leaf objects. Of course, not all leaf objects will inherit certain property rights that are unique to certain objects. For instance, an assignment that gives a trustee rights to change the phone number of a container can be inherited by user objects in that container but has no effect on Printer or Volume objects. Being able to inherit selected property rights can be very useful. For example, Kellie is to maintain login scripts for all containers and users in the UAS Organization. With NetWare 5, you can provide Kellie with Write rights to all Login Script object properties by using the ability of child containers and leaf objects to inherit selected property rights.

In this hands-on activity, you will give Kellie rights to maintain login scripts by providing the ISMgrs group with the Write and Inheritable rights to the Login Script property of your ##UAS container. You will then use NetWare Administrator to check Kellie's effective rights to the Login Script property of Organizational Units and users. In a later activity, you will use an Inherited Rights Filter as specified on the NDS Security Worksheet (Figure 6-15) to block Kellie's effective Login Script property rights from the AeroDyn container.

1. If necessary, start your workstation, log in using your ##Admin username, and start NetWare Administrator.

2. If necessary, open a browse window to your ##UAS Organization.

3. Give your ISMgrs group Write and Inheritable rights to the Login Script property as follows:

   a) Right-click your **##UAS** container and then click **Trustees of this Object**.

   b) Click the **ISMgrs** group.

   c) Click the **Selected properties** button and scroll down to the Login Script property.

   d) Click the **Login Script** property and then click the **Write** and **Inheritable** rights check boxes as shown in Figure 6-18.

   e) Click **OK** to save the trustee assignment.

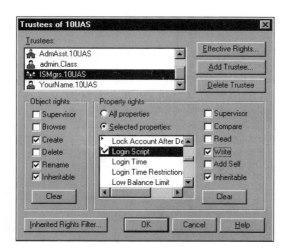

Figure 6-18   KThiele's effective rights to Login Script

4. Check Kellie's effective rights to the Login Script property of the Engineering container by doing the following:

a) Right-click the **Engineering** Organizational Unit and click the **Trustees of this Object** option.

b) Click the Effective Rights button to display the Effective Rights dialog box.

c) Click the **browse** button to display the Select Object dialog box.

d) Double-click **KThiele**.

e) Click the **Selected properties** button and scroll down to the Login Script property.

f) Click the **Login Script** property to display Kellie's effective rights as shown in Figure 6-19.

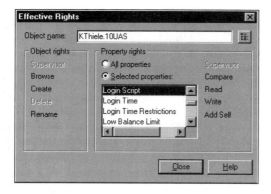

Figure 6-19   KThiele's modified rights to Login Script

5. Click the **Close** button to exit the Effective Rights dialog box.

6. Click the **Cancel** button to return to the NetWare Administrator browse window.

Since Kellie will be managing login scripts, it is important to prevent users from making changes to their personal login scripts that could interfere with system operations. In this hands-on activity, you will prevent users in the Engineering department from changing their login scripts by removing the Write property right from the Login Script property of each user's trustee assignment in the Engineering container.

1. If necessary, start your workstation, log in using your ##Admin username, and start NetWare Administrator.

2. If necessary, open a browse window for your Engineering Organizational Unit.

3. First remove the Write property right from Lianne Jarka's trustee assignment as follows:

    a) Right-click the user **LJarka** and click the **Trustees of this Object** option.

    b) Click the trustee **LJarka**.

    c) Click the **Selected properties** button.

    d) Use the scrollbar under the Selected properties option to scroll down to the Login Script property. Notice that the Login Script property has a check in front of it indicating a trustee assignment to this property.

    e) Click the **Login Script** property.

    f) Click the **Clear** button located under the Property rights to clear any check marks from the Property rights list. Notice that the check is removed from in front of the Login Script property.

    g) Click the **OK** button to change the trustee assignment and return to the browse window. Ira will now be unable to change his Login Script commands.

4. Repeat the preceding process to clear the Login Script property right for all users in the Engineering container.

5. Close the Engineering browse window.

Managing the AeroDyn Container

Since Chuck Botsford has had a lot of experience working with manufacturing applications, he will be responsible for maintaining manufacturing users and resources for both Universal Aerospace and AeroDyn. Without inheritance, you would need to make at least two trustee assignments to grant Chuck Supervisor rights to both the Mfg and AeroDyn containers. As shown previously in Figure 6-16, to use inheritance to reduce the number of trustee assignments, Jennifer has recommended creating a separate container for UAS under the Mfg container and then moving all Universal Aerospace user objects to this new container. To provide Chuck with rights to manage both the UAS and AeroDyn containers, Jennifer recommends making Chuck an occupant of a new MfgMgr Organizational Role object and then assigning the MfgMgr object Supervisor rights to the Mfg container. Because UAS and AeroDyn are subcontainers of Mfg, the trustee assignment you make for the MfgMgr object will be inherited by both the UAS and AeroDyn containers. Although assigning the Supervisor object right will provide the trustee with all other object and property rights, Jennifer recommends specifically assigning all other object and property rights in addition to Supervisor. This way, should Chuck's rights be accidentally blocked by an IRF, he would still be able to manage the object and even restore his Supervisor right because he would still have the Write right to the ACL property.

In this hands-on activity, you will use NetWare Administrator to modify the Mfg tree structure, create an Organizational Role object for Chuck named MfgMgr, and then assign the MfgMgr object all object rights to the Mfg container. You will then use NetWare Administrator to check Chuck's effective rights in the UAS and AeroDyn containers.

1. If necessary, start your workstation, log in using your ##Admin username, and start NetWare Administrator.

2. If you have not previously done so, create a user named CBotsford in your ##UAS Organization.

3. If necessary, open a browse window to your Mfg Organizational Unit.

4. Create Organizational Units for UAS and AeroDyn as follows:

   a) Click the **Mfg** Organizational Unit and press **[Ins]** to display the New Object window.

   b) Scroll down and double-click **Organizational Unit**.

   c) Enter the name **AeroDyn** and click the **Create another Organizational Unit** box.

   d) Click the **Create** button.

   e) Enter the name **UAS** and click **Create**.

   f) Click the **Cancel** button to return to the NetWare Administrator browse window.

5. To move all objects from Mfg into the UAS.Mfg Organizational Unit, follow these steps:

   a) Hold down **[Ctrl]** while clicking each leaf object in your Mfg container so that user and group objects are highlighted.

   b) Click **Object**, **Move**.

   c) Click the **browse** button to the right of the Destination field to display the Select Object dialog box.

   d) Double-click the **UAS** Organizational Unit from the left-hand Available objects window to display the Move dialog box as shown in Figure 6-20.

   e) Click **OK** to move the selected objects. Your Mfg Organizational Unit should now appear like the one shown in Figure 6-21.

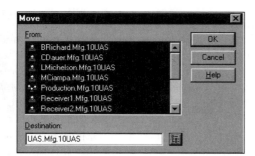

Figure 6-20   Move dialog box

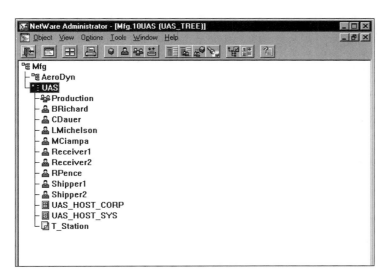

Figure 6-21   Modified Mfg structure

6. Make Chuck Botsford an occupant of the MfgMgr organizational role as follows:

a) Double-click your **MfgMgr** Organizational Role object.

b) Click the **browse** button to the right of the Occupant field to display the Occupant window.

c) Click the **Add** button to display the Select Object dialog box.

d) Use the Browse context window to navigate up to your ##UAS container Select Object dialog box as shown in Figure 6-22.

e) Double-click the user **CBotsford** to add Chuck as the occupant of MfgMgr.

f) Click **OK** to close the occupant screen.

g) Click **OK** to save the Organizational Role object information.

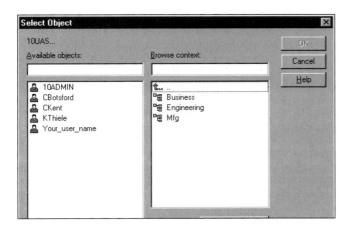

Figure 6-22   UAS container browse window

7. Make the MfgMgr Organizational Role object a trustee of the Mfg container with all rights including Supervisor, as follows:

a) Drag and drop the **MfgMgr** Organizational Role object on top of the Mfg container.

b) Click all rights including the **Supervisor** right in the Object rights and Property rights windows as shown in Figure 6-23.

c) Click **OK** to save the trustee assignment.

Figure 6-23   MfgMgr trustee assignment

 Although assigning the Supervisor right will provide all effective rights, checking all rights will allow the manager to restore his or her rights if he or she is ever accidentally blocked out.

8. Check Chuck's effective rights in the UAS and AeroDyn containers as follows:

a) Right-click the **AeroDyn** Organizational Unit object and click the **Trustees of this Object** option.

b) Click the **Effective Rights** button to display the Effective Rights dialog box.

c) Click the **browse** button to display the Select Object dialog box.

d) Use the right-hand browse frame to navigate to the **##UAS** container.

e) Double-click **CBotsford** from the left-hand Available objects window. Chuck should now have all effective rights in the Mfg container.

f) Click the **Close** and **Cancel** buttons to return to the NetWare Administrator browse window.

g) Repeat Steps 8a through 8f to display Chuck's effective rights in the UAS Organizational Unit.

9. Click the Close button to exit the Effective Rights dialog box.

10. Click the **Cancel** button to return to the NetWare Administrator browse window.

Reassigning the Supervisor Right

As you learned in Chapter 5 on file system security, a new trustee assignment will override an object's inherited object and property rights. In the file system, this is true for all access rights except Supervisor. As described earlier, NDS security is different from file system security in that you can block or reassign the Supervisor right at a lower container or leaf object. For example, Chuck should not have the Delete object right in the UAS.Mfg container. Because he is a trustee of Mfg, he is currently inheriting all rights into both UAS and AeroDyn containers.

 In this hands-on activity, you will reduce Chuck's effective rights in the UAS container by providing him with a new trustee assignment.

1. If necessary, start your workstation, log in using your ##Admin username, and start NetWare Administrator.

2. If necessary, open a window to your Mfg Organizational Unit.

3. Make the MgrMgr Organizational Role object a trustee of the UAS.Mfg Organizational Unit container with Browse, Create, and Rename rights as follows:

   a) Drag and drop the **MfgMgr** object on the UAS.Mfg Organizational Unit.

   b) Click the check boxes for the **Create** and **Rename** object rights.

   c) Click **OK** to save the new trustee assignment and return to the NetWare Administrator browse window.

4. Now check Chuck's effective rights in the UAS Organizational Unit container as follows:

   a) Right-click the **UAS** Organizational Unit and click the **Trustees of this Object** option.

   b) Click the **Effective Rights** button to display the Effective Rights dialog box.

   c) Click the **browse** button to display the Select Object dialog box.

   d) Use the Browse context window to navigate up a level to your **##UAS** container.

   e) Double-click **CBotsford** in the left-hand Available objects window.

5. Notice that Chuck now has only Browse, Create, and Rename object rights. The Supervisor assignment made to the parent container has been reassigned.

6. Click the **Close** button to exit the Effective Rights dialog box.

7. Click the **Cancel** button to return to the NetWare Administrator browse window.

 Removing a trustee assignment for a user can sometimes increase the user's effective rights by allowing the user to inherit rights from the parent container. For example, assume that a new administrator was told that the MfgMgr object was no longer to have rights to the UAS.Mfg container. At first, the solution might seem to be to remove the MfgMgr object as a trustee of the UAS.Mfg container. However, as you can see from doing the previous activity, removing MfgMgr as a trustee of UAS would actually have the opposite effect and increase the object's rights to Supervisor. If you have time, demonstrate this to yourself by removing Chuck's trustee assignment from the UAS Organizational Unit and then checking his effective rights. Remember to restore his trustee assignment before continuing.

Blocking Rights to the AeroDyn Container

As you learned in the previous section, you can change the inherited rights of a trustee by assigning the trustee a different set of object and property rights to a leaf or subcontainer object. Although this is effective for changing a single user's effective rights in a child container or leaf object, it does not block the rights that other users or groups may inherit from the parent container. As described earlier, another alternative is to block inherited rights by using an Inherited Rights Filter (IRF). For example, in a previous activity, the ISMgrs group was granted the Create and Rename rights to your UAS Organization and will therefore inherit these rights to all objects in the AeroDyn and UAS containers.

 In this hands-on activity, you will implement an IRF on the object rights of the AeroDyn container to block the ISMgrs group from inheriting object rights in the AeroDyn container.

1. If necessary, start your workstation, log in using your ##Admin username, and start NetWare Administrator.

2. If necessary, open a browse window to your Mfg Organizational Unit.

3. Modify the IRF on the AeroDyn container to remove all rights except Browse and Supervisor as follows:

   a) Right-click the **AeroDyn** Organizational Unit and click the **Trustees of this Object** option.

   b) Click the **Inherited Rights Filter** button to display the Inherited Rights Filter dialog box.

   c) Remove all object rights from the IRF except for Supervisor and Browse by clicking the **Create**, **Delete**, and **Rename** boxes.

   d) Click **OK** to save the modified IRF.

   e) Click **OK** to save the changes to the AeroDyn container.

4. Check Kellie's effective rights to the AeroDyn container as follows:

   a) Right-click the **AeroDyn** Organizational Unit and click the **Trustees of this Object** option.

   b) Click the **Effective Rights** button to display the Effective Rights dialog box.

   c) Click the **browse** button to display the Select Object dialog box.

   d) Use the Browse context window to browse up to the **##UAS** Organization.

   e) Double-click **KThiele**.

   f) Click **Selected properties** and scroll down to the Login Script property.

   g) Click the **Login Script** property to display Kellie's Effective Rights dialog box shown in Figure 6-24. Notice that Kellie is still inheriting her selected rights to maintain login scripts that you granted her previously in the ##UAS container.

   h) Click **Close** to return to the Trustees of AeroDyn window.

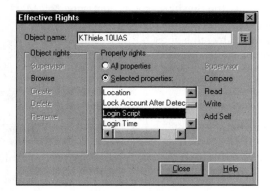

Figure 6-24   KThiele's Effective Rights dialog box

5. Block Kellie's rights to maintain login scripts in the AeroDyn container as follows:

   a) Click the **Inherited Rights Filter** button to display the Inherited Rights Filter dialog box.

   b) Click the **Selected properties** button and scroll down to the Login Script property.

   c) Click the **Login Script** property and remove the **Write** and **Add Self** rights.

   d) Click **OK** to save the modified IRF.

   e) Click **OK** to save the changes to the AeroDyn container.

6. Repeat Step 4 to verify that Kellie's rights to maintain login scripts in the AeroDyn container have been blocked.

7. Check Chuck's effective rights to the AeroDyn container as follows:

   a) Right-click the **AeroDyn** Organizational Unit and click the **Trustees of this Object** option.

   b) Click the **Effective Rights** button to display the Effective Rights dialog box.

   c) Click the **browse** button to display the Select Object dialog box.

   d) Use the Browse context window to browse up to the **##UAS** Organization.

   e) Double-click **CBotsford** and verify that Chuck has all object and property rights.

8. Click the **Close** button to exit the Effective Rights dialog box.

9. Click the **Cancel** button to return to the NetWare Administrator browse window.

Setting Up an Independent Container Administrator

Because NetWare 5 allows you to use an IRF to block the Supervisor right, it is possible to set up a container administered by a user other than the main Admin user. Of course, misuse of this capability can cause some major problems. To prevent accidentally blocking your Admin user, the NetWare operating system requires you to establish a user with Supervisor rights in a container before removing the Supervisor rights from the IRF. Without this safety check, thoughtlessly removing the Supervisor right from the IRF of a container or leaf object would mean that no one, including the network administrator, would have rights to manage that container or leaf object. As a result, before you can use an IRF to block the Supervisor rights from a container, you first need to use an explicit trustee assignment to grant another object or the main Admin user the Supervisor rights to the container. For example, assume AeroDyn wants to have a private container within its manufacturing division, and that only the MfgMgr Organizational Role object will access and manage the container.

 In this hands-on activity, you will use NetWare Administrator to make the MfgMgr Organizational Role object, along with the classroom administrator, the only Supervisors of the new container. You will then verify the results of the IRF by checking your effective rights and then log in as Chuck to restore your ##Admin's Supervisor rights to the new container.

1. If necessary, start your workstation, log in using your ##Admin username, and start NetWare Administrator.

2. If necessary, open a browse window to your Mfg Organizational Unit.

3. Create a container named Private within your AeroDyn.Mfg Organizational Unit.

4. Attempt to remove the Supervisor right from the new container as follows:

   a) Right-click the **Private** container.

   b) Click the **Trustees of this Object** option to display the Trustees of Private window.

   c) Click the **Inherited Rights Filter** button to display the IRF dialog box.

   d) To prevent the Supervisor rights from being inherited by the user object, click the box to the left of the **Supervisor** object to remove the check mark. Notice the error message indicating you cannot block out the Supervisor rights unless you first make an explicit assignment of Supervisor rights to another user.

   e) Click the **OK** button to exit the Error window.

   f) Click **Cancel** to return to the Trustees of Private window.

5. Make your MfgMgr Organizational Role object, along with the classroom Admin user, trustees of the Private container with Supervisor rights, as follows:

   a) Click the **Add Trustee** button to display the Select Object dialog box.

   b) Use the Browse context window to navigate up to your Mfg Organizational Unit.

   c) Double-click your **MfgMgr** Organizational Role object.

   d) Click all object and property rights including the **Supervisor** right.

   e) Click the **Add Trustee** button to display the Select Object dialog box.

   f) Use the Browse context window to navigate to the **Class** Organization.

   g) Double-click the **Admin** username to add Admin as a backup trustee.

   h) Click the **Supervisor** right in both the Object amd All Properties panes.

 Placing the Classroom Admin user as a trustee of your Private container will allow your instructor to verify your work.

6. Now remove all rights except Browse from the IRF of the Private container as follows:

   a) Click the **Inherited Rights Filter** button located at the bottom of the Trustees of Private window.

   b) To prevent the Supervisor rights from being inherited by the Private container, click the box to the left of the **Supervisor** object to remove the check mark. NetWare now allows the Supervisor right to be removed from the IRF because an explicit trustee with the Supervisor right has been added to an existing trustee. Remove all object rights except Browse and then remove all property rights as shown in Figure 6-25.

   c) To save the new IRF, click **OK**.

   d) To complete the change, click the **OK** button in the Trustees of Private window.

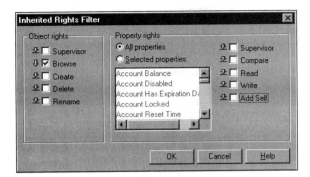

Figure 6-25   Private container IRF

6

7. Attempt to check your effective rights in the Private container. Notice that your ##Admin user cannot access the Private container.

8. Log out.

9. Log in as **CBotsford**.

10. Start NetWare Administrator.

11. Make your ##Admin user a trustee of the Private container as follows:

    a) Click your **##Admin** user to select it.

    b) Open the **Mfg** container.

    c) Click your **##Admin** user and then drag and drop your ##Admin user on top of the **Private** container.

    d) Click the **Supervisor** object right.

    e) Click **OK** to save the trustee assignment.

12. Log out.

13. Log in using your **##Admin** username.

14. Verify that you have all effective rights in the Private container.

15. Close all windows and exit NetWare Administrator.

Congratulations! Dave Heise is pleased with your progress on integrating AeroDyn into the network and has promised you a raise on your next paycheck. Chuck is now ready to begin setting up the AeroDyn manufacturing users. The work of a network administrator is never dull! In the exercises at the end of the chapter, you will finish setting up NDS security for the Business division. In Chapter 7, you'll move on to setting up network printing.

CHAPTER SUMMARY

❑ The Novell Directory Services database, or NDS, is the backbone of the NetWare network, providing access to all network objects. As a result, it is very important that a network administrator know how to implement the NDS security system properly to provide users with rights to access and manage the objects for which they are responsible. NDS security consists of object and property rights that are assigned to trustees. Each object in the NDS database has an Access Control List (ACL) property. You make an object a trustee of another object by placing the trustee's name in the ACL property of the object. Object rights consist of Supervisor, Browse, Create, Delete, and Rename. Property rights consist of Supervisor, Read, Compare, Write, and Add Self. A trustee granted the Supervisor object right automatically is granted the Supervisor right to all properties. Special trustee objects include

[Public] and [Root]. The [Public] object represents all clients that have run the VLM (Virtual Loadable Module) requester and attached to the network but have not yet logged in. The [Root] object represents all network objects, including clients, that have logged in using authorized usernames. Object and property rights assigned to a trustee of a container may flow down from the container to leaf and subcontainer objects, unless reassigned or blocked by an Inherited Rights Filter (IRF). Effective rights consist of the actual rights a user has to an object as a result of a combination of explicit trustee assignments, inherited rights, group memberships, or rights assigned to the user's container object. As a CNA, you will need to know how to use NetWare Administrator to grant trustees object and property rights, as well as establish IRFs, and view effective rights.

❑ Default rights play an important role in managing NDS security. Upon initial installation, the Admin user is assigned the Supervisor rights to the root of the NDS tree, and the [Public] object is assigned Browse rights. The Server object's default trustees include the installer of the Server object (usually the Admin user) and Server, which are given the Supervisor object right, and [Public], which is given the Read right to the Messaging Server property. Newly created users' default trustees include the user, who is given the Read right to all properties, along with Write rights to the Login Script and Print Job configuration properties; [Root], which is granted the Read property right to the Network Address and group membership properties; and the [Public] object, which is granted the Read property right to the Default Server property. In addition to having default assignments, any user needing to access a Directory Map object must have the Read right to the Path property.

KEY TERMS

Access Control List (ACL) — A property of each object that contains a trustee list for that object.

Add Self property right — A special case of the Write property right that allows trustees to add or remove themselves from a group.

Browse object right — A right that allows a trustee to view leaf objects and containers in the container where this right is granted.

Compare property right — A right of the Read right enabling the trustee to find an object without viewing the property information.

Create object right — A right that allows a trustee to create new leaf objects and containers in the container where this right is granted.

Delete object right — A right that allows a trustee to delete leaf objects and subcontainers in the container where this right is granted.

effective rights — The actual object and property rights a user has to a container or other leaf object.

Inheritable (object/property) right — An object or property right that allows the rights assigned to a trustee of a container to be inherited by child containers and leaf objects.

inherited rights — Object or All Property rights that flow down to other containers or leaf objects.

Inherited Rights Filter (IRF) — A property of all objects that contains a list of Object and All properties rights that the object can inherit er can do with an object. These rights consist of Browse, Create, Delete, Rename, and Supervisor.

properties — Fields that contain information about an object.

property rights — Rights that control what actions a trustee can perform on the information in the object's property fields. These rights include Read, Compare, Write, Add Self, and Supervisor.

[Public] — A special group object, created by NetWare during installation, that consists of all client computers that are attached to the network.

Read property right — A right that allows the trustee to view the contents of the object's property fields.

Rename object — Grants the right to change the name of the object. right

[Root] — A special container object that is the parent container for all other objects in the NDS tree structure. All users that have logged in to the NDS tree are part of the [Root] container.

6

Supervisor object right — An object right that provides a user with all object and property rights to the container or leaf object. Having the Supervisor object right automatically provides the trustee with the Supervisor property right. The Supervisor object right can be revoked from other objects or subcontainers within the container where it was assigned.

Supervisor property right — A property right that provides the trustee with all rights to all properties of the object.

trustee — A user or other object that is given access rights in another object's Access Control List.

Write property right — Grants the right to add, change, or remove any value of the property.

REVIEW QUESTIONS

1. Identify which of the following are controlled by NDS security.
   a. Access to the SYS:Public directory *NO*
   b. The ability to create new users *yes*
   c. The right to supervise the NetWare server *yes*
   d. The ability to change login scripts *yes*
   e. The ability to remove jobs from the print queue *NO*

2. When creating a Directory Map object, what security assignment will users need to use the Directory Map object?

3. The ———————————— security system allows users to view, access, create, and modify objects in the Novell Directory Services tree.

4. Having the ———————————— right to the ———————————— property of the Server object is the one exception to the rule that NDS security does not affect file system security.

5. In the preceding exception, what rights would the trustee of the Server object have in the SYS volume?

6. Any object placed in the ———————————— of another object becomes a trustee of that object with certain ———————————— and ———————————— rights.

7. The ———————————— object represents all users whose workstations are attached to the network.

8. The ———————————— object represents all authorized users in the network tree.

9. List the six object rights:

10. List the two major property rights:

11. List the two property rights that are special cases of the two major property rights:

12. List two ways in which property rights can be assigned:

13. Describe one advantage of granting the Supervisor object right, as compared to the other object rights: _____

14. The process of rights flowing down the NDS structure is referred to as

_____ .

15. True or false: Only the All properties rights will flow down from a container object to all the leaf objects.

16. The actual NDS rights a user has to an object are referred to as the

_____ rights.

17. List five ways a user may gain rights to an NDS object:

_____   _____

_____   _____

_____

18. A(n) _____ is a property of every object, and consists of the object and property rights that the object can inherit from its parent container.

19. List the two default property rights a user has to his or her own user object:

_____   _____

20. By default, all clients have _____ rights to the NDS tree.

21. Assigning a user the Supervisor object right to the _____ object would give a user all rights to the file system.

22. A user could also obtain all rights to the file system by having the _____ property right to the _____ property of the Server object.

23. Identify the security problem associated with each of the following:

Assigning a user the Supervisor rights to a container that houses the Server object:

_____

_____

Assigning a user the Write right to All properties:

_____

_____

Removing Supervisor rights from a container's Inherited Rights Filter:

_____

_____

The Universal Aerospace Project

Your raise came through as Dave promised. It is good to be appreciated, but the pressure is on to get the network fully operational, and your next step is to complete securing the system by applying what you learned about NDS security to the Business division. In the following exercises, you define and implement the NDS trustee assignments necessary to provide Business and Marketing users in the Business container with the rights they need to access and manage the resources for which they are responsible.

Step 1: Defining Trustee Assignments

Figure 6-26 contains a memo you recently received from Lynn Dai summarizing the results of the meeting on NDS security you had with the Business and Marketing department managers. In this exercise, you use this information to fill out an NDS Trustee Worksheet (see Appendix B) showing the trustee assignments along with any Inherited Rights Filters you will need to implement these requirements.

Memo

To: Network Administrator

From: Lynn Dai

Date: Yesterday

Subject: Notes from the Business and Marketing NDS Security Meeting

1. A new container needs to be established for AeroDyn office staff.

2. Only Chuck and your ##Admin user should have rights to create, rename, or delete objects in the AeroDyn office staff container.

3. Lynn Dai should have rights to maintain address information on all users in the AeroDyn containers.

4. While Kellie Thiele has rights to maintain login scripts for all UAS users, only Chuck Botsford should have rights to maintain login scripts in the AeroDyn staff container.

5. All users in the Business container need rights to use their corresponding Directory Map objects.

6. The design engineers (Ira Means, Tony Rucci, and Paul Alm) along with the Desktop Publishing staff (Diana Brady, Bradley Dahl, and Julie DamRau) need to be able to use the PubData Directory Map object.

Figure 6-26   NDS business security memo

Step 2: Implementing Trustee Assignments

After you have verified your NDS trustee rights plan with your instructor, use NetWare Administrator to implement the trustee assignments.

Step 3: Instructor Checkout

Have your instructor verify your trustee assignments and initial that he or she is satisfied that you have successfully implemented the trustee assignments.

Instructor checkout: _____   Date: _____

Additional Exercises

These exercises are included to give you more practice working with NetWare Administrator and the NDS system and to help you pass the CNA exam. It is assumed that you have already completed the previous Universal Aerospace projects.

Exercise 6-1: Preventing [Public] Browsing

By default, the [Public] object is given Browse rights to the root of the NDS tree structure. This means that any user or intruder can display all objects in the NDS tree by using the command **CX/R/A/T**.

Allowing a client computer to display all objects before logging in can create a potential security problem since an intruder could easily learn valid login names and then attempt to guess the appropriate password. To allow only authorized users who have logged into the network to view the objects in the NDS tree structure, you need to use an Inherited Rights Filter (IRF) to block the Browse right from being inherited by your ##UAS container. Then you can assign the [Root] object Browse rights to the ##UAS container by following these steps:

1. Log in using the assigned ##Admin username.
2. Start NetWare Administrator.
3. Right-click the **##UAS** container and then click the **Trustees of this Object** option.
4. Click the **Inherited Rights Filter** button at the bottom of the window.
5. Remove **Browse** from the inherited object rights. Click **OK**.
6. Click the **Add Trustee** button to add a trustee to the ##UAS container.
7. Click **[Root]** in the Select Object entry box.
8. Click the **OK** button to add [Root] as a trustee with Browse rights.
9. Click the **OK** button to save and exit the Trustee of ##UAS window.
10. Exit NetWare Administrator.
11. Log out of the network.
12. Open a DOS window.
13. Change to your F drive.
14. Change your context to the [Root] of the classroom tree by entering the **CX /R [Enter]** command.
15. Use the **CX /R/T/A** command to verify that a client cannot see the objects without logging in.
16. If required by your instructor, use the **CX /R/T/A > PRN** command to print a copy of your work.
17. Exit the DOS window and log out.

Exercise 6-2: Assigning Rights through All Properties

One of the guidelines described near the end of this chapter cautioned you about the potential security problem created when a user receives the Write right to the object trustees' (ACL) property. This can happen accidentally when a user or other object is made a trustee and given the Write right to All properties.

Assume you want to allow Lynn Dai to maintain information on all users in the Business container. One way to do this is to make the user LDai a trustee of the Business container with the Write right to All properties. The Write right to All properties in the Business container will then flow down by inheritance to all user objects. By following the steps in this exercise, you will see how giving LDai the Write right to All properties allows her to become a Supervisor of the Business container and then block out the network administrator.

1. Log in using the assigned ##Admin username.
2. Start NetWare Administrator.
3. Right-click the **Business** container and then select the **Trustees of this Object** option.
4. Click the **Add Trustee** button and add **LDai** as a trustee.
5. Click the **All properties** button and then assign the Write right by clicking the check box to the left of the **Write** right.
6. Click the **OK** button to save the assignment.
7. Close NetWare Administrator.
8. Log out of the network.
9. Change the current context to the Business container and log in as **LDai**.

10. Start NetWare Administrator.

11. Right-click the **Business** container and click **Trustees of this Object**.

12. Click the **LDai** trustee and then click the **Supervisor** object right.

13. Click the **Inherited Rights Filter** button and remove the **Supervisor** object right from the IRF.

14. Click the **OK** button to save your modification to the IRF.

15. Click **OK** to save your trustee assignment and return to the browse window.

16. Right-click the **Business** container and click **Trustees of this Object**.

17. Check the effective rights of your ##Admin user and record them in the following blanks:

    ##Admin object rights: _____

    ##Admin All properties rights: _____

18. Briefly summarize what happened to your ##Admin user rights:

    _____

    _____

19. Close the Effective Rights dialog box.

20. Click the **Inherited Rights Filter** button and restore the **Supervisor** right.

21. Click **OK** to save the IRF.

22. Record your ##Admin user's effective right to the Business container on the following lines:

    ##Admin object rights: _____

    ##Admin All properties rights: _____

23. Log out of the network.

24. Briefly summarize why assigning the Write property right to All properties can cause a security problem:

    _____

    _____

6

7

IMPLEMENTING NETWORK PRINTING

After reading this chapter and completing the exercises, you will be able to:

♦ Describe the print queue system used by previous versions of NetWare

♦ Identify and describe NDPS components along with their relationship to each other

♦ Define a network printing environment for the Universal Aerospace Corporation

♦ Use NetWare Administrator to create, configure, and work with public access and controlled access network printers

♦ Describe the process needed to load NDPS server and client software components

♦ Use the CAPTURE command to direct output to a queue

♦ Direct output from a client to an NDPS network printer

♦ Customize a network printing environment to use forms and special printer setup modes

♦ Manage the NDPS environment

This morning, you have been informed that the new printers Dave Heise ordered are currently in the receiving area. Setting up these printers and attaching them to the network will be the focus of your work in this chapter. As described in Chapter 1, sharing printers is an important benefit of implementing a network. Network printing provides cost savings, increased workspace for users, and multiple printer selection options. To become a NetWare CNA, you must know how to use NetWare's new Novell Distributed Print Services (NDPS) and how to set up, customize, and maintain the printing environment on your network. This chapter discusses the printing concepts and skills you need to understand the NDPS components and to use NetWare utilities to implement a network printing environment for Universal Aerospace.

NETWORK PRINTING OVERVIEW

The basic function of network printing is to take output from applications running on client computers and direct that output to a shared printer attached to the network. Since a printer can print output from only one application at a time, network printing also functions to control the flow of output from the application to the printer. This is usually accomplished by sending output from an application running on a client computer to a print queue on the server where it is held until the network printer it needs is available. The process of sending output from a client computer to a print queue is referred to as **spooling**. When a network printer finishes printing the output for one application, it retrieves the next application's printer output from the print queue. Because of print spooling, applications can quickly send their output to a network printer and continue processing information without having to wait for the output to be printed physically.

NetWare 5 provides two ways to implement network printing. The first method, called **queue-based printing**, has been available since NetWare 3, and is designed to support simple printers and DOS-based applications. Today's printing needs are much more sophisticated, involving complex network-aware printers along with Windows-based applications designed to run on networks. Because of the more complex printing needs, setting up and maintaining queue-based printing on today's networks has become a headache for many network administrators. To make setting up and maintaining network printers more efficient, Novell, Hewlett-Packard (HP), and Xerox teamed up to create a more manageable network printing system called **Novell Distributed Print Services (NDPS)** that can take advantage of more sophisticated printers and Windows-based applications.

In this chapter, you will first learn how to set up a simple printing environment using queue-based printers, then you will learn how to implement the new NDPS to set up network printing for the Universal Aerospace network.

Queue-Based Printing

Before implementing a queue-based printing environment for your organization, you need to understand the basic components of queue-based printing and how they work together. In this section, you will learn about the following four queue-based printing objects and how they are implemented in a NetWare printing environment:

- Print queues
- Print servers
- Printers
- Clients

Print Queues

A **print queue** is an NDS network object that represents a network holding area used to store output from workstations in a form that is ready to be sent directly to a printer. As shown in Figure 7-1, a print queue allows multiple workstations on a network to use the same printer by storing the printer output from each client as a separate print job. After being stored in the print queue, print jobs are then printed one at a time as the printer becomes available.

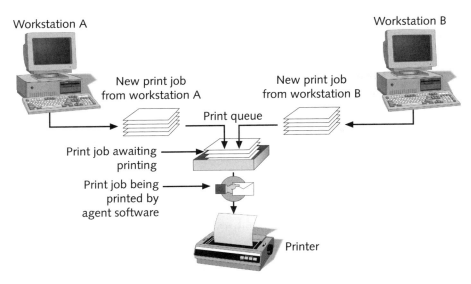

Figure 7-1   Print queues

In queue-based printing, print jobs are actually files containing output formatted for a specific printer. In many ways, having a client send output to a print queue is very similar to storing files on a volume. For example, when a user saves a file on the server, the data is transferred from the client to the server and then stored in a file located within the specified directory. Since an application's printer output is actually data being transmitted to the printer, placing a job in a print queue involves a similar process in which the printer data from the application is stored in a file called a print job. Just as data files are stored in directories, print job files are located in special print queue directories as illustrated in Figure 7-2.

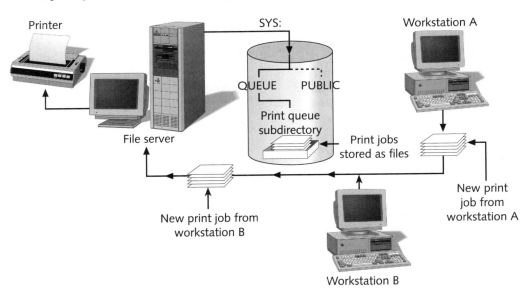

Figure 7-2   NetWare print queue

On a NetWare queue-based printing system, print queues are actually subdirectories of the Queues directory and may be placed on any volume. As described later in this section, you create print queues using NetWare Administrator. When setting up a NetWare queue-based printing environment, you create at least one print queue for each networked printer. Once print jobs have been stored in the print queue, they are printed by the printer assigned to the print queue in the sequence they were received. After a job has been printed, it is automatically deleted from the print queue.

In Windows 95/98, you can set up printers with the Add Printer Wizard to direct their output to the NetWare print queues associated with those printers. DOS-based applications can direct their output to a print queue using the NetWare CAPTURE command.

One of the tasks involved in administering network printing is managing jobs in the print queues. By default, the network administrator who created the print queue is made a print queue operator. A print queue operator can rearrange the sequence of print jobs, remove a print job, or place a print job on hold. In addition to designating this task to the network administrator by default, NetWare allows other users to be print queue operators. You may wish to honor other users in your organization with the title of print queue operator to delegate the work of managing jobs on several print queues.

Printers

Although there is an almost unlimited number of different printer models and configurations, most printers commonly found on networks can be grouped into three general types: dot matrix, laser, and ink jet. Because each of these printer types requires a different print job format, as a network administrator it is important to be aware of the types and models of the printers that are used on your network so that you can correctly configure network printing to ensure that the correct output is sent to the printer for which it was created. For example, a word processing program may be installed to support both dot matrix and laser printers. When a user selects a laser printer and prints a document, the network printing configuration must be set up to ensure that the output will be sent to the laser printer for which it was formatted.

Printers can be attached to the network in one of three ways: local attachment to the print server, remote attachment through a workstation, or direct attachment to the network cable. Figure 7-3 illustrates each of these printer attachment methods.

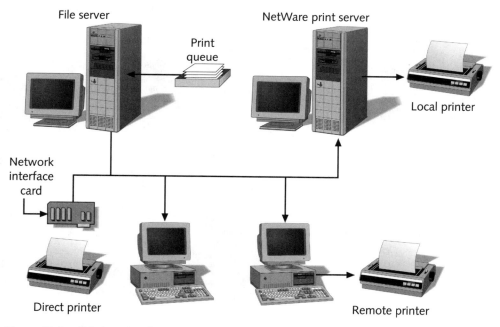

Figure 7-3   Printer attachment methods

You must consider the printer attachment method when configuring the network printing environment, as each attachment method has certain advantages and will affect the way printers are distributed on the network. Many network administrators use a combination of printer attachments based on the type of printer and its use. In this section, you will learn about each of the printer attachment options and how they affect network printing.

Remote Attachment **Remote printers** are attached to other clients on the network. These printers are called **manual load printers** because software has to be manually loaded on the client computer to connect its printer to the print server. Once the software has been loaded on the client, print jobs may be sent to its remote printer, using the network cable to transmit packets of printed data from the print server to the client that has the remote printer attached. NetWare includes a Windows 95/98 utility called NPTWIN95 that can be loaded on a client computer that has a network printer attached. The NPTWIN95 program receives the packets of printer output directed to it from the print server and then prints the output on the attached network printer without interfering with anyone who may be using that Windows 95/98 client for other processing. The advantage of using remote manual load printers attached to client computers is that a convenient location for the printer can be selected, making it easier for users to obtain their output. The disadvantages associated with manual load printers include the additional setup time to load the NPTWIN95 software, the need to leave on the client computer to access the network printers, and the possible decrease in printing performance of large graphical print jobs due to applications running on the client computer as well as the extra load on the network cable created when sending printer output from the print queue on the server to the network printer attached to the workstation.

Local Attachment **Locally attached printers** are attached directly to one of the printer ports of the server that is running the print server program (PSERVER.NLM). These printers are referred to in NetWare as **automatic load printers** because output is sent directly from the print server to the local printers through the ports on the server computer. Automatic load printers can be attached to the **parallel (LPTn)** or **serial (COMn)** ports of the server that is running the print server software. The advantages of automatic load printers as compared to remote printers include higher printing performance than remote printers and less network traffic. Higher printing performance is obtained through less software overhead since the print server does not have to communicate with a client computer running the NPTWIN95 software. Locally attached printers reduce network traffic because print jobs do not need to be sent from the print server to a printer attached to a client somewhere on the network.

Direct Attachment A rapidly growing alternative to using remote printers attached to a client computer is to attach the printer directly to the network cable by obtaining a special network card for the printer or by using a dedicated print server device such as Intel's NetPort or HP's JetDirect products. Dedicated print server devices have a network port and one or more printer ports along with built-in software that allows these devices to receive print jobs off the network and then print them on the attached printer or printers. Many high-speed laser printers today have an option that includes a network card that allows the printer to be attached directly to the network cable. With the direct attachment option, the printer may become its own print server and be able to print jobs directly from a NetWare print queue. The direct printer attachment is often used with high-speed laser printers that need to be placed on the network, but do not operate efficiently when attached as remote printers.

The main disadvantage of directly attaching printers to the network is the cost and availability of the network attachment option for each printer. Another possible disadvantage of making each directly attached printer its own print server is the need to use an additional network connection for each print server. Since your NetWare license supports a limited number of network connections, having several direct-attachment printers acting as independent print servers could potentially cause your server to reach the maximum limit of the NetWare license. If this happens, additional users will not be allowed to log in. You can usually get around the use of extra license connections by configuring the directly attached printers as remote printers controlled through a common NetWare print server as described in the following section.

Print Server

A **print server** takes print jobs from print queues located on NetWare servers and sends them to the assigned printer as shown in Figure 7-4.

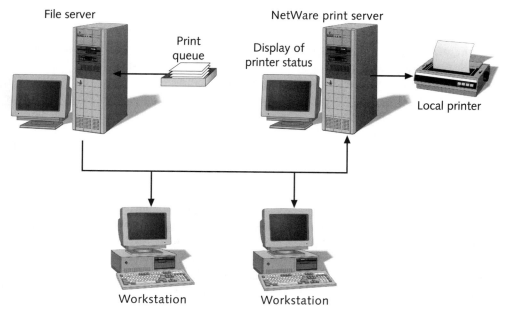

Figure 7-4 NetWare print server

Printers can be attached directly to the print server as is the case with local printers, attached remotely through a client running the NPTWIN95 software, or attached directly to the network through a device such as the Intel NetPort or the HP JetDirect. In addition to printing, print servers are responsible for sending control commands to the printers and reporting printer status to the print server operator. In NetWare queue-based printing, each print server is defined by an NDS Print Server object that contains the name of the print server along with the names of up to 255 Printer objects. After you create and configure the Print Server object, you can load the NetWare print server software and run it as a nondedicated print server from the file server computer by loading the PSERVER.NLM program.

Setting Up Queue-Based Printing

Setting up a simple queue-based network printing system involves the following five basic steps:

1. Define the network printers and how they will be attached.

2. Create a print queue for each printer.

3. Create an NDS Printer object to represent each printer.

4. Define a Print Server object to send output from the print queues to the corresponding printer.

5. Load the necessary print server and remote printer software.

In the hands-on activities in the following sections, you will perform each of these steps to share the printer attached to your classroom server. Because only one print server can be loaded on your classroom server at one time, you will need to coordinate the final step of loading and testing your print server with other students in the class.

Define the Network Printers

Prior to setting up any network printing system, it is important to identify the type, location, name, and attachment method of printers. For example, assume that you have just received the new printer HP LaserJet Postscript printer that you and Kellie want to share. Since the NetWare server is located near both of your offices, you decide initially to attach the printer locally to the server to avoid having to run additional software on your workstations. Although you plan to develop a more sophisticated naming scheme for the Universal Aerospace printers in the near future, initially you plan to name this printer IS_P and the associated print queue IS_Q. Since the printer will be attached directly to the NetWare server, you will use the local attachment method to the LPT1 port of your server. Table 7-1 contains the information you will need to set up a locally attached printer named IS_P on the LPT1 port of your server. You will learn more about planning a network printing system later in this chapter.

Table 7-1   Print Server Definition Form

Print Server Definition Form							
Print Server Name: ##UAS-PS							
Context: ##UAS							
Operators: ##Admin							
Printer Name	Make/Model	Port and Interrupt	Location	Users	Print Queue Name/Volume	NDS Context	Operator
IS_P	HP LaserJet 5si Postscript	LPT1 Polled	Server AutoLoad	ISMgrs Group	IS_Q/Corp volume	.##UAS	Your Username KThiele

Create the Print Queue

Now that you have defined the name and NDS contexts of the Printer, Print Queue, and Print Server objects, you are ready to use NetWare Administrator to create the queue-based printing objects.

In this hands-on activity, you use NetWare Administrator to create the IS_Q Print Queue object identified previously in Table 7-1.

1. Start your computer and log in to the network using your assigned ##Admin username.

2. Start NetWare Administrator and if necessary, open a browse window for your ##UAS Organization.

3. Create a Print Queue object named IS_Q in your ##UAS Organization as follows:

   a) Click your **##UAS** Organization and press **[Ins]** to display the New Object dialog box.

   b) Scroll down and double-click the **Print Queue** object to display the Create Print Queue dialog box shown in Figure 7-5.

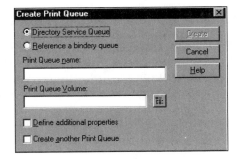

Figure 7-5   Create Print Queue dialog box

   c) Enter **IS_Q** in the Print Queue name field.

   d) Click the **browse** button located to the right of the Print Queue Volume field.

e) Double-click the **UAS_HOST_CORP** volume object from the left-hand Available objects window.

f) Click **Create** to create the print queue and return to the NetWare Administrator browse window.

4. Add yourself and Kellie as print queue operators as follows:

a) Double-click your newly created Print Queue object to display the Print Queue Identification window shown in Figure 7-6.

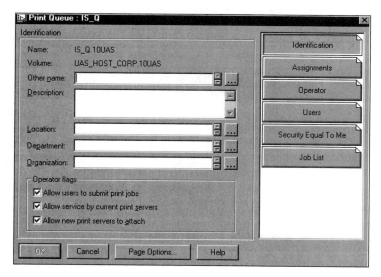

Figure 7-6   Print Queue Identification window

b) Click the **Operator** button and click **Add** to display the Select Object dialog box.

c) Hold down **[Ctrl]** while you click your username and **KThiele**.

d) Click **OK** to add both users as print queue operators.

5. Add the ISMgrs group as print queue users as follows:

a) Click the **Users** button to display existing users. Record the print queue users on the following lines:

_____

_____

b) Notice that by default the container where the print queue is located is made a user of the print queue. Because your ##UAS Organization is a user, all users in ##UAS as well as users in the Engineering, Mfg, and Business containers can send output to this print queue. To limit the use of the print queue to members of the ISMgrs group only, click the **##UAS** user and click **Delete**.

c) Click the **Add** button to display the Select Object dialog box.

d) Double-click the **ISMgrs** group to add it as a user of the print queue.

6. Click **OK** to save your changes and return to the NetWare Administrator browse window.

Create the Printer Object

Now that you have created the print queue and defined the users and operators, the next step is to create and define the Printer object, including the printer attachment method, the port and interrupt to be used, and the print queue from which the printer will get its output.

In this hands-on activity, you use NetWare Administrator to create and define the IS_P Printer object identified in Table 7-1.

1. If necessary, start your computer, log in using your assigned ##Admin username, and start NetWare Administrator.

2. Create a Printer object named IS_P as follows:

   a) Highlight your **##UAS** container and press **[Ins]** to display the New Object dialog box.

   b) Scroll down and double-click the **Printer (Non NDPS)** object to display the Create Printer dialog box.

   c) Enter **IS_P** in the Printer name field.

   d) Click the **Define additional properties** check box.

   e) Click the **Create** button to create the Printer object and display the Printer (Non NDPS) Identification window shown in Figure 7-7.

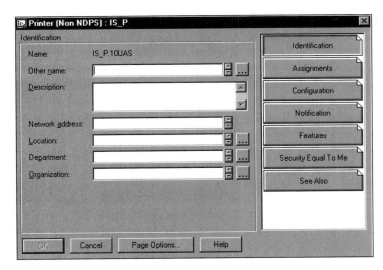

Figure 7-7   Non NDPS Printer Identification window

3. To enable your newly created Printer object to obtain output, identify which print queue the printer will use as follows:

   a) Click the **Assignments** button to display the Print Queues pane. Notice that initially there are no print queues attached to the printer.

   b) Click the **Add** button to display the Select Object dialog box.

   c) Double-click your **IS_Q** print queue from the left-hand Available objects window. The IS_Q should now appear in the Print Queues pane.

4. The final step in configuring the printer object is to define the attachment method along with the printer port and interrupt as follows:

a) Click the **Configuration** button to display the Configuration window shown in Figure 7-8. Notice that by default the printer is defined as a parallel printer with a text banner type. The service interval of 5 defines that the print server will check the print queue every five seconds to see whether there are any jobs to be printed. By default, the printer will start with form type 0 mounted. The Minimize form changes within print queues setting tells the printer to print all jobs with form number 0 before checking for jobs with form number 1, and so on.

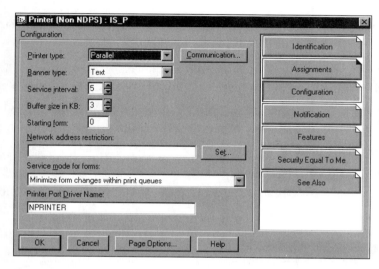

Figure 7-8   Printer Configuration window

b) To set the attachment method and port information, click the **Communication** button to display the Parallel Communication pane. Notice that the default port is LPT1 with the Polled interrupt setting. Using the polled method, the computer will frequently check the printer to see whether it is ready. Using the polled method prevents the printer from interrupting the computer processor every time it is ready to print and can provide better server performance.

c) Notice that by default the printer is defined as a manual load or remote printer. Since IS_P will be attached directly to the server, click the **Autoload (Local to Print Server)** button.

d) Click **OK** to save your changes and return to the Printer Configuration window.

e) Now that the printer configuration has been defined, click **OK** to return to the NetWare Administrator browse window.

Create a Print Server Object

As described previously, queue-based printing requires a print server to send output from a print queue to the appropriate network printer. To work, the print server software needs to know what printers it controls as well as who the print server operators and users are. You supply the names of the printers, operators, and users to the print server software by creating and configuring an NDS Print Server object.

In this hands-on activity, you create a Print Server object for your ##UAS container and then configure it to manage your IS_P printer.

1. If necessary, start your computer, log in using your assigned ##Admin username, and start NetWare Administrator.

2. Create a Print Server object named UAS_PS in your ##UAS container as follows:

   a) Click your **##UAS** container to highlight it.

   b) Press **[Ins]** to display the New Object dialog box.

   c) Scroll down and double-click **Print Server (Non NDPS)** to display the Create Print Server dialog box.

   d) Enter **UAS_PS** in the Print Server name field and click the **Define additional properties** check box.

   e) Click the **Create** button to create the Print Server object and display the Identification window.

   f) Click the **Assignments** button to display the Printers dialog box.

   g) Click the **Add** button to display the Select Object dialog box.

   h) Double-click the **IS_P** printer from the left-hand Available objects window to add your printer to the Printers dialog box.

   i) Click the **Users** button and record the users of the print server on the following line:

   _____

   j) Click the **Operators** button and record the name of the print queue operator on the following line:

   _____

3. Click **OK** to save your print server configuration and return to the NetWare Administrator browse window.

4. Exit NetWare Administrator.

There are two methods you can use to send output from your Windows 95/98 client to your print queue. The first method is to create a network printer using the Add Printer function. The second method is to redirect a local printer port to the NetWare print queue. The disadvantage of redirecting a local printer port to a NetWare print queue is that you have to be sure the network printer uses the same print driver as the local printer. If you send output to a network printer that is formatted for another type of printer, you may generate a lot of garbage output. As a result, it is usually preferred to create a network printer that uses the correct print driver for the queue you have selected.

In this hands-on activity, you create a Printer object that will send output to your IS_Q print queue.

1. If necessary, start your computer and log in using your assigned ##Admin username.

2. Click the **Start** button, point to **Settings**, and then click **Printers** to display the Printers dialog box.

3. Double-click the **Add Printer** icon to start the Add Printer Wizard and click **Next** to continue.

4. Click the **Network printer** button and click **Next**.

5. Click the **Browse** button under the Network path or queue name field to display a Browse for Printer window.

6. Double-click your **##UAS** Organization to display your Printer and Print Queue objects.

7. Click your **IS_Q** Print Queue object and click **OK** to display your print queue in the Network path or queue name field.

8. Click **No** in response to the "Do you print from MS-DOS based programs?" question.

9. Click **Next** to display the printer selection window.

10. Click the printer Manufacturer and Printer identified for your classroom printer and click **Next** to continue.

11. If you receive the message that the driver is already installed, click the **Keep existing driver (recommended)** option and then click **Next** to display the printer name field.

12. Enter **IS_P** for the printer name and click **No** if asked whether to use this as the default printer.

13. Click **Next** to continue.

14. Select the option to **Print a test page** and click **Finish** to copy any necessary files and return to the Printers dialog box. (Note: If Windows cannot find the files on your local disk, you will be asked to insert the Windows 95 CD-ROM.)

15. Click **Yes** in response to the "Did the test page print correctly?" question. Your new printer should now appear in the Printers dialog box. Note that in Steps 15 and 19, the printer will not produce output yet. Close the printer window.

16. To test the printer, start Wordpad and create a simple document.

17. Save the document on the G:\Shared directory with the name **ISPDemo**.

18. Print the document to your IS_P printer.

19. Exit Wordpad

20. Verify that the output is in the print queue as follows:

    a) Start NetWare Administrator.

    b) Double-click your **IS_Q** Print Queue object to display the Print Queue Identification window.

    c) Click the **Job List** button to display all jobs in the print queue. Your new entry should be listed. Record your Job Name on the following line:

    _____

    d) Click **Cancel** to return to the NetWare Administrator browse window.

    e) Exit NetWare Administrator.

Load and Test the Print Server Software

Before network printing can start, you need to run the print server software on the NetWare server. Since there can be only one print server running on a NetWare server at one time, you will need to coordinate this activity with the other students in your class.

In this hands-on activity, you will load your print server on the UAS_HOST NetWare server and retrieve your output.

1. Wait for your turn to access the server console, if necessary.

2. Enter the following command on the server console: **PSERVER .CN=UAS_PS.O=##UAS**. After the print server loads, the console will display an Available Options menu as shown in Figure 7-9.

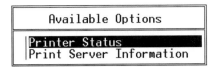

Figure 7-9   Print Server Available Options

3. Highlight the **Printer Status** option and press **[Enter]** to display a printer list.

4. Press **[Enter]** to display a printer status window similar to the one shown in Figure 7-10. Your documents should now be printing on the classroom printer.

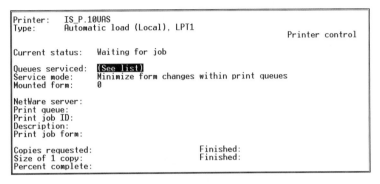

Figure 7-10   Print Server status window

5. Use the **right-arrow** key to highlight the Printer Control option and press **[Enter]** to display a printer control menu.

6. Highlight the **Form Feed** option and press **[Enter]** to eject a page.

7. Press **[Esc]** twice to return to the Available Options menu.

8. Perform the following steps to unload your print server:

   a) Highlight the **Print Server Information** option and press **[Enter]** to display the Printer Server Information and Status window.

   b) Press **[Enter]** to display the Print Server Status Options menu.

   c) Highlight the **Unload after active print jobs** and press **[Enter]** to unload your print server and return to the console screen.

9. Retrieve your output from the classroom printer.

NOVELL DISTRIBUTED PRINT SERVICES

As described previously, NetWare 5 includes the Novell Distributed Print Services (NDPS) system. NDPS is the result of a joint effort between Novell, Hewlett-Packard, and Xerox to develop a truly distributed network printing system based on the International Standards Organization (ISO) 10175 Document Printing Application (DPA) standard. Since most printer manufacturers support this standard, NDPS will support existing and future printer products. NDPS is an improvement over queue-based printing solutions because it makes network printing easier to configure, use, and manage. As you learned in the previous section, with queue-based printing you need to create at least three objects (Print Queue, Printer, and Print Server) to set up network printing. In addition, you need to be sure that each printer is properly configured to get its output from the correct print queue and that workstations are set up to use the correct print queues. NDPS is designed to simplify this system by taking advantage of new client software and more sophisticated printers. Rather than creating Print Queue and Printer objects, the NDPS printing system represents each printer with a printer agent that can send out packets to client computers on the network identifying itself as a network printer.

An NDPS-compatible printer has built-in printer agent software that allows you simply to connect the NDPS printer to the network to make it available to all users. Once connected to the network, the NDPS printer will communicate directly with NDPS-compatible clients, allowing users to send output directly to the printer through the printer agent. NDPS also makes it easier to install printers on user computers by automatically downloading the necessary printer drivers. In addition, NDPS allows users to easily check printer status.

Since most printers currently on the market do not have built-in printer agents, Novell has supplied printer **gateway** software that you can run on your NetWare server to manage non-NDPS-compatible printers. Using the gateway software, you can attach non-NDPS printers to the network using the local or remote attachment methods described in the "Setting Up Queue-Based Printing" section. The gateway software acts as the printer agent for the local and remote printers. Another advantage of NDPS is the way in which print drivers are managed. Using NDPS, you do not need to install printer drivers on each client as you did in queue-based printing. With NDPS printing, the printer driver is automatically downloaded to your client when you select the printer. Users will also benefit from NDPS printing. For example, NDPS allows users to view printer status quickly to send jobs to printers that are not as busy. In addition, with NDPS, users can search the network for printers with certain capabilities such as printing color documents. In this section, you will learn how to set up and configure a NetWare NDPS printing system that will meet the needs of the Universal Aerospace users.

Before implementing the NDPS network printing environment for the Universal Aerospace network, you should understand the basic components of NDPS and how they work together. The basic components are:

- Printers (public access and controlled access)
- Printer agents
- NDPS Manager
- Brokers
- Gateways
- Clients
- Print queues

Printers

Most organizations have a variety of types of printers that need to be attached to the network and shared. For example, at Universal Aerospace, each department has color ink jet printers along with Postscript laser printers that need to be attached to the network and shared by all the department users. When using NDPS, printers can be classified as either public access or controlled access. As the name implies, **public access printers** are available to anyone with an attachment to the network. These printers are the easiest to set up since they do not require a corresponding NDS object. **Controlled access printers** provide more security and manageability, but for each controlled access printer, you will need to create and configure an NDS object and then provide access to that object to the appropriate users or groups. In this chapter, you will define and install both public access and controlled access printers for the Universal Aerospace network users.

For example, suppose that to experiment with the new NDPS system, you have decided to replace the queue-based printing system you are currently using with the new NDPS printing system. As with queue-based printing, one of the first decisions is how the printer will be attached to the network. As described earlier, NDPS-compatible printers can be attached directly to the network cable and contain their own printer agent to which client computers can send output. Since the IS_P printer you have set up to share with queue-based printing is not NDPS-compatible, you will need to attach it using one of the methods described in the queue-based printing section. For this example, assume that because the NetWare server is not very accessible, you want to relocate the printer from the server and attach it to your workstation. Another decision is who will be able to send output to the printer. Public access printers are available to all users running an NDPS-compatible client. Since you want to be able to restrict access to the printer, you will need to make the printer a controlled access printer.

Printer Agents

As described earlier, **printer agents (PAs)** are software that represent network printers and form the core of the NDPS architecture. To configure and manage NDPS, you will need to understand and work with printer agents. Each physical printer on the network is to be represented by a printer agent. As described earlier, when a system uses NDPS-compatible printers, the printer itself contains the printer agent. For non-NDPS printers, such as the one attached to your workstation, the gateway running on a NetWare server contains the printer agent.

A printer agent acts as a liaison between the physical network printer and the client computer, as shown in Figure 7-11. When a user prints to a network printer, the output first goes to the printer agent that represents that printer, which spools the output to a file until the printer is ready. When the printer is available, the printer agent will transmit the output along with any special configuration commands, from the print spool file to the network printer.

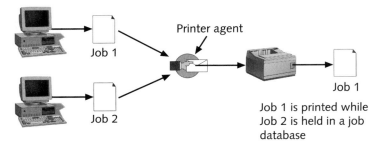

Figure 7-11   Printer agent

 The printer agent can also access other network services that enhance basic printing. For example, a print job configuration may require that the user be notified about the print job's status and completion using a pop-up window or email message. To provide this notification, the printer agent would use a new service called **Event Notification Service (ENS)**. You will learn more about setting up the Event Notification Service later in this chapter. The printer agent submits the user request along with updated status information to ENS. ENS then uses the specified method to send a notification to the user.

To spool printer output and work with other network services, printer agents need to store or have access to basic printer information including the printer's name, location, status, scheduling method, and configurations. As network administrator, it will be your responsibility to set up and configure printer agents for each of your networked printers. When setting up NDPS, you can either create printer agents to represent your network printers, or you can use Printer Agents created for you by third-party software gateways such as the HP or Xerox gateways described later in this section.

For example, to use NDPS to send print jobs from other networked computers to your printer, you will need to have a printer agent for your printer. However, since your HP LaserJet printer is not an NDPS-compatible printer with its own embedded printer agent, you will need to create and load an NDPS Manager to act as a printer agent for your non-NDPS printer.

NDPS Manager

As described earlier, non-NDPS printers do not have their own printer agents built in, and as a result a gateway is necessary to act as a printer agent for non-NDPS printers. **NDPS Manager** consists of software along with an NDS object that is used to create and manage printer agents for non-NDPS printers. One of the functions of the NDPS Manager software is to act as a printer agent gateway. In addition to acting as printer agent gateway, the NDPS Manager provides printer agents with shared access to resources such as scheduling algorithms. The NDPS Manager object is a temporary component of NDPS. When all printers on your network have embedded printer agents, it will no longer be necessary to create and load NDPS Manager. Figure 7-12 shows the relationship between NDPS Manager, printer agents, and the physical printers.

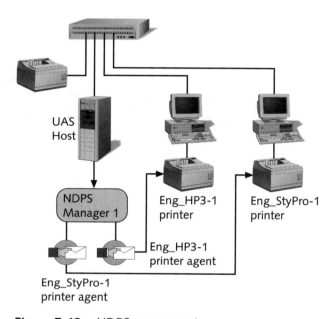

Figure 7-12   NDPS components

 As with print servers, only one NDPS Manager can be loaded on a NetWare server at one time.

Although there is no limit on the number of printer agents that can be controlled from one NDPS Manager, a large network may have multiple NDPS Managers running on separate NetWare servers to delegate administrative tasks or reduce network traffic across routers and wide area networks as illustrated in Figure 7-13.

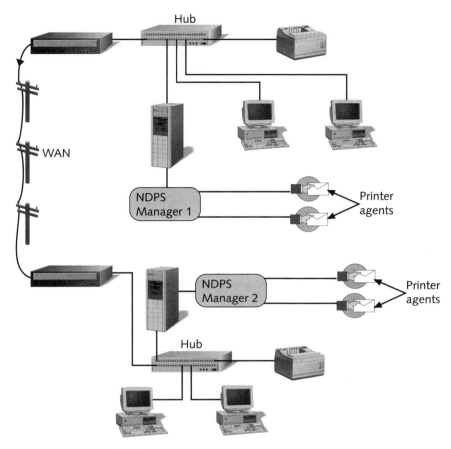

Figure 7-13 Multiple NDPS Managers

In this hands-on activity, you will use NetWare Administrator to create an NDPS Manager for your ##UAS Organization. Because you need Supervisor rights to the server where the NDPS Manager is located, you may not be able to actually create the NDPS Manager at this time. Instead, you will view information on the Class_NDPS Manager object with which you will be working.

Since the classroom server can have only one NDPS Manager loaded at a time, you will use the Class_NDPS Manager set up by your instructor to create your printer agents rather than using your own NDPS Manager object.

1. If necessary, start your computer and log in using your assigned ##Admin username.

2. If necessary, start NetWare Administrator.

3. Highlight your **##UAS** Organization and press **[Ins]** to display the New Object dialog box.

4. Double-click the **NDPS Manager** object to display the Create NDPS Manager object dialog box.

5. Enter the name **UAS_NDPSM** and then click the **browse** button to the right of the Resident Server field to display the Select Object dialog box.

6. Double-click the **UAS_Host** Alias object in the left-hand Available objects window.

7. To select the volume where the spooled output will be stored, click the **browse** button to the right of the Database Volume field to display the Select Object dialog box.

8. To prevent accidentally filling up the SYS volume, double-click your **UAS_HOST_CORP** volume as the volume on which to store spooled output.

 Whenever possible, you should use a volume other than SYS to store spooled output, to prevent filling up the SYS volume.

9. Click the **Create** button to create the NDPS Manager object. If you do not have Supervisor object rights to the UAS_Host server, you will receive an error message. Click **OK** to continue and then click **Cancel** to exit. In the next steps you will work with the existing NDPS Manager in the Class container.

10. Open a browse window to the Class organization.

11. Double-click the **Class_NDPSM** object to display the NDPS Manager dialog box shown in Figure 7-14. The Net Address field indicates the network and node address of the server running the NDPS Manager software. Description and Location fields are documentary and optional. The Volume field displays the volume where the NDPS database is located. The Status field indicates whether this NDPS Manager is currently running. The Unload button may be used to exit the NDPS Manager program.

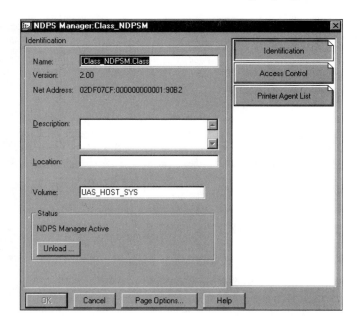

Figure 7-14   NDPS Manager: Class_NDPSM dialog box

Figure 7-15   NDPS Manager Access Control window

12. Click the **Access Control** button to display the Access Control window shown in Figure 7-15. Notice that the group Students along with the Admin user may manage this NDPS Manager. Managers can add and maintain printer agents.

13. Click the **Printer Agent List** button to display the current printer agents and their status as shown in Figure 7-16.

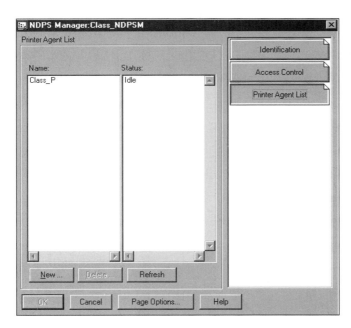

Figure 7-16   NDPS Printer Agent List window

14. Click **Cancel** to return to the NetWare Administrator browse window.

Brokers

NDPS also includes a new NDS object called a Broker. Although the Broker object was developed with NDPS, its services are not limited to printing. The **Broker object** includes server-based software that can provide three services to any network resource:

- *Resource Management Service (RMS).* This service stores network resources such as software drivers, fonts, and forms in a central location and then provides these resources to clients that request them. NDPS uses RMS to download printer drivers and other setup information such as banners to NDPS clients.

- *Event Notification Service (ENS).* As described earlier, the Event Notification Service may be used by printer agents to send printer status messages to users via pop-up windows, email, or a log file.

- *Service Registry Services (SRS).* This service allows public access printers to advertise their presence so they can be accessed by NDPS clients. SRS also maintains printer information such as the device type, device name, and network address. SRS reduces network traffic by eliminating the need for each printer to broadcast its presence on the network by sending out Service Advertising Packets (SAPs) at frequent intervals.

When NDPS is installed on a server, the installation utility ensures that the Broker object is loaded on your network. If a Broker is not running on your network, or if the nearest Broker requires network traffic to go across more than three routers, an additional Broker will be loaded on the new NDPS server.

When NDPS was installed on the Universal Aerospace server, the Broker and NDS objects were automatically installed on the network. A second Broker object will be necessary on the new server planned for the AeroDyn branch since it would not be feasible to share services across the wide area network.

 In this hands-on activity, you will use NetWare Administrator to view information on the Broker installed on your network.

1. If necessary, start your computer and log in using your assigned ##Admin username.

2. If necessary, start NetWare Administrator and open a browse window to the Class organization.

3. Double-click the **UAS_HOST_BROKER** object to display the Broker Identification window shown in Figure 7-17.

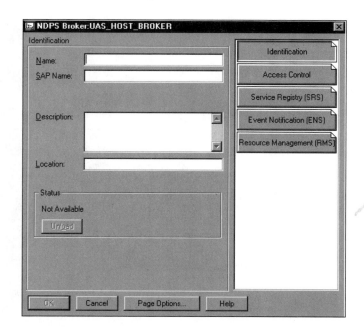

Figure 7-17   Broker Identification window

4. Click the **Service Registry (SRS)** button and list any SRS names on the following line:

_____

5. Click the **Event Notification (ENS)** button and list any currently loaded ENS methods on the following line:

_____

6. Click the **Resource Management (RMS)** button and list the resource path, if any, on the following line:

_____

7. Click **Cancel** to return to the NetWare Administrator browse window.

Gateways

Now that you have viewed the NDPS Manager and Broker for your network, you are almost ready to create a printer agent to manage the printer on your computer. However, as described earlier in this chapter, for the printer agent to access a non-NDPS printer attached to your client, NDPS needs to have a gateway defined in the NDPS Manager as shown in Figure 7-18.

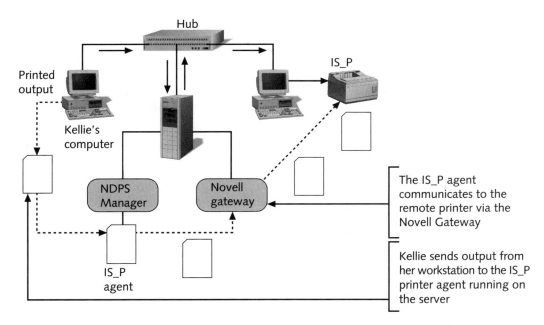

Figure 7-18   NDPS gateway

As you can see in the figure, gateways can be used to connect non–NDPS printers to their associated printer agents running on the NDPS Manager. When you create a printer agent for a printer that does not have an embedded printer agent, you need to select and configure the associated gateway with the printer's make, model, and attachment method (remote, local, or direct). Since the printer attached to your client computer does not have an embedded printer agent, you will need to use a gateway to send output from the printer agent running on the NDPS Manager to the printer remotely attached to your client. Gateways ensure that printer agents can communicate with physical printers regardless of the attachment method or port used to connect the printer to the network. As part of the NDPS Manager, gateways are temporary components of NDPS.

NetWare 5 is currently shipping with three gateways: the Hewlett-Packard (HP) gateway, the Xerox gateway, and the Novell gateway. Using Novell's System Development Kit (SDK), other OEM companies are developing gateways for their printers along with snap-in modules for NetWare Administrator. The snap-in modules are necessary to allow the administrator to use printer-specific management utilities to manage these OEM printers from NetWare Administrator.

The HP and Xerox Gateways

The HP gateway software connects printer agents to printers that attach to the network via an HP JetDirect print server or an HP JetDirect card. The HP gateway can be configured to locate all printers attached to the network via the HP JetDirect print server or JetDirect card and then automatically create printer agents for each of these printers. On a large network with many directly attached printers, this can be much quicker than manually creating printer agents for each printer. The Xerox gateway is similar in function to the HP gateway except that it is designed to find and configure Xerox printer products.

The Novell Gateway

The Novell gateway consists of two major components: the Print Device Subsystem (PDS) and the Port Handler (PH). The Print Device Subsystem translates control information such as commands for landscape or duplex printing to the appropriate escape code sequence for the printer. The Port Handler is responsible for directing output to the appropriate physical printer, using one of the following methods:

- *Local ports.* The Port Handler allows printer agents to communicate with printers attached to the gateway computer's parallel or serial port.
- *Remote printers.* The Port Handler provides communication between a printer agent and a remote printer. The remote printer may either be attached to a client computer running remote printer software, or directly attached via a dedicated print server device such as HP's JetDirect or Intel's NetPort.
- *Print queue.* For devices that support printing only from the earlier queue-based system, the Port Handler can send printer output from a printer agent to a specified print queue that is serviced by a QueueServer or PrintServer device such as earlier versions of Intel's NetPort or HP's JetDirect products.

Since the HP LaserJet Postscript printer you received for the IS department is not an NDPS-compatible printer, to attach it as a remote printer on your workstation's LPT port, you will need to configure your printer agent to use the Novell gateway to communicate with your printer.

 In this hands-on activity, you will use NetWare Administrator to create an NDPS controlled access printer named ##IS_NDPS for a remotely attached HP LaserJet 5Si printer. You will configure the printer for access by members of the ISMgrs group only, and then use Printer Control to check the printer's status.

1. Before doing these steps, Class_NDPSM must be loaded at the console.

2. If necessary, start your computer and log in using your assigned **##Admin** username.

3. Start NetWare Administrator and open a browse window to your **##UAS** container.

4. Click your **##UAS** container to highlight it.

5. Press **[Ins]** to display the New Object dialog box.

6. Double-click the NDPS Printer object type to display the Create NDPS Printer dialog box shown in Figure 7-19.

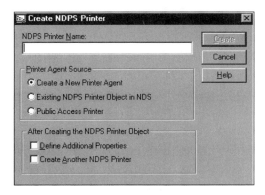

Figure 7-19   Create NDPS Printer dialog box

7. Enter ##**IS_NDPS** in the NDPS Printer Name field and verify that the **Create a New Printer Agent** button is selected.

8. Click the **Define Additional Properties** check box and then click the **Create** button to display the Create Printer Agent dialog box shown in Figure 7-20.

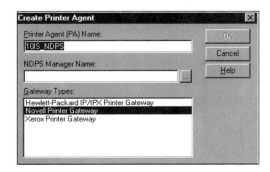

Figure 7-20   Create Printer Agent dialog box

9. Click the **browse** button to the right of the NDPS Manager Name field to display the Select Object dialog box.

10. Use the Browse context pane to navigate to the Class container.

11. Double-click the **Class_NDPSM** object from the left-hand Available objects window.

12. Verify that the **Novell Printer Gateway** is highlighted and then click the **OK** button to display the Configure Novell PDS for Printer Agent dialog box shown in Figure 7-21.

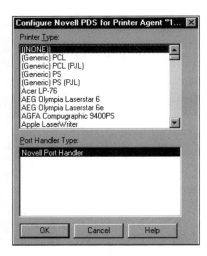

Figure 7-21   Configure Novell PDS for Printer Agent dialog box

13. Scroll to and click your printer type from the Printer Type list box.

14. Click **OK** to display the Configure Port Handler for Printer Agent dialog box shown in Figure 7-22.

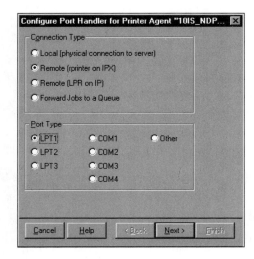

Figure 7-22   Configure the Port Handler's connection and port type

15. Select the connection type **Remote (rprinter on IPX)** and the **LPT1** port type used to connect the printer to your client.

16. Click **Next** to display the next Configure Port Handler for Printer Agent dialog box shown in Figure 7-23. You can use this dialog box to change the assigned printer number or restrict the printer to a specific network card address.

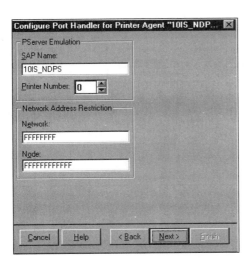

Figure 7-23   Configure the Port Handler's printer number and network address

17. Click **Next** to display the next Configure Port Handler for Printer Agent dialog box shown in Figure 7-24, where you can set the controller type and interrupts. This screen is used to identify the interrupt used by the client computer to monitor the printer port you selected in Step 15. Unless you are sure of the interrupt number used by your client's computer's LPT port, select **None (polled mode)**.

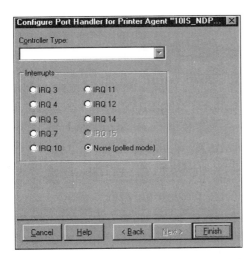

Figure 7-24   Configure the Port Handler's interrupts

18. Click **Finish** to create the printer agent for your ##IS_NDPS printer. A wait message will then be displayed while the system creates your printer agent.

19. Since your printer is not currently connected using the NTPWIN95 software, you will receive a message indicating that the printer needs attention. You will correct this problem later by loading the NPTWIN95 software. At this time, click **OK** to continue.

20. Once the printer agent is created, you are presented with the Select Printer Drivers dialog box. You use this dialog box to identify the printer driver to be used by the client when formatting output for this printer.

21. For Windows 95 and 98 clients, click the **Windows 95/98 Driver** tab and select the appropriate driver for your printer. (Note: If you have a printer attached to your workstation, use the printer type identified by your instructor.) You can also click the Windows 3.1 Driver and

Windows NT Driver tabs to select printer drivers for users accessing the printer from those client operating systems.

22. Click **Continue** to display the Information – NDPS summary window. If you are satisfied with the selections, click **OK** to display the Printer Control window for your ##IS_NDPS printer as shown in Figure 7-25. Click the **Status** button to display the printer state. Notice that the printer state is currently "Printer Not Connected." This state exists because you have not yet loaded the NPTWIN95 software. Click **Close**.

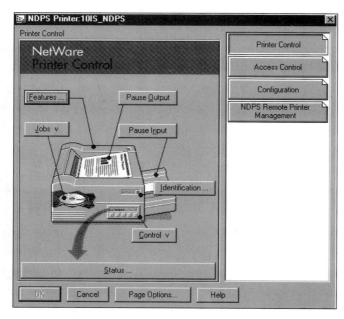

Figure 7-25   Printer Control window

23. Click the **Access Control** button to display the Access Control window shown in Figure 7-26.

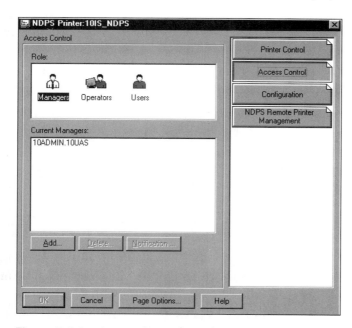

Figure 7-26   Access Control window

24. Click the **Users** icon to display the users who will be allowed to send output to the printer. Notice that your ##UAS Organization along with your ##Admin user are valid users of the printer.

25. Make only the ISMgrs group valid printer users as follows:

   a) Click your **##UAS** container in the Current Users window, click the **Delete** button, and click **OK** to confirm the deletion.

   b) Double-click the **Users** icon to display the Select Object dialog box.

   c) Double-click the **ISMgrs** group from the left-hand Available objects window to add ISMgrs to the Current Users window.

26. Make your username an operator of the printer as follows:

   a) Double-click the **Operators** icon to display the Select Object dialog box.

   b) Double-click your username from the left-hand Available objects window to add it to the Current Managers window.

27. Click the **Printer Control** button to return to the Printer Control window.

28. Click **OK** to save your changes and return to the NetWare Administrator browse window.

29. Exit NetWare Administrator.

Clients

One of the most important components of the NDPS environment is the client computer. Client computers are responsible for formatting application output and routing it to the appropriate printer agent. In addition to requiring the proper printer driver, for a client computer to directly communicate with printer agents, it needs to have the NDPS client software that is included with NetWare 5 installed. The NDPS client component is usually installed with the client software as described in Chapter 2. In addition to installing the NDPS option with your client software, you will also need to create an NDPS Printer object in the Windows client for each NDPS printer to which the user will be sending output. Novell provides a utility called the Novell Printer Manager that you can use to create and manage NDPS-compatible Printer objects from the Windows 95/98 client. Users can also use the Novell Printer Manager utility to select and install additional network printers to which they have access. The Novell Printer Manager utility will automatically install the selected printer and download the correct printer driver to the user's workstation.

In addition to requiring the NDPS Printer objects, Windows 95/98 client computers that have remote printers attached to them will also need to have the NPTWIN95 remote printer software loaded for the printer attached to their port to communicate with the printer agent running on the server. In this section, you will learn how to configure the remote printer software as well as install and download printer drivers.

Loading Remote Printer Software

Now that all the major NDPS components are in place, you are almost ready to share the printer attached to your computer with Kellie. However, before Kellie can send output to your printer, you will need to use the Novell Printer Manager utility to create an NDPS Printer object on Kellie's computer and then load the NPTWIN95 remote printer software on your workstation.

 In this hands-on activity, you will load the Windows 95 remote printer software on your computer and then verify the status of your printer agent.

   1. If necessary, start your computer and log in using your assigned ##Admin username.

   2. Be sure a printer is properly attached to your workstation and is ready to print. If necessary, test the printer to be sure it is working properly.

3. Create a shortcut to the NTPWIN95 remote printer software as follows:

   a) Use **My Computer** to browse to the \Public\Win95 directory on your F drive.

   b) Drag and drop the **NPTWIN95** program onto your desktop to create a shortcut. The NPTWIN95 program should now appear on your desktop.

   c) Close all windows.

4. Double-click the **NPTWIN95** shortcut to display the Add Network Printer dialog box as shown in Figure 7-27.

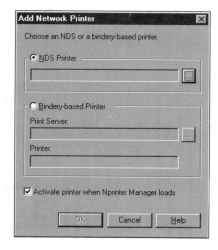

Figure 7-27   Add Network Printer dialog box

5. To attach the printer agent, click the **Bindery-based Printer** option.

6. Click the **browse** button to the right of the Print Server field to display the Print Servers and Printers dialog box. Your ##IS_NDPS printer should appear in the Active Print Server window.

7. Double-click your **##IS_NDPS** print server to display the IS_NDPS printer in the Attached Printers window.

8. Double-click your **##IS_NDPS** printer from the Attached Printers window.

9. Verify that the **Activate printer when Nprinter Manager loads** check box is selected and click **OK** to load the ##IS_NDPS remote printer as shown in Figure 7-28.

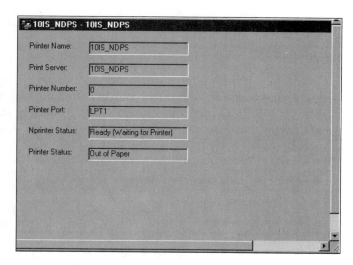

Figure 7-28   Activating a printer

10. Minimize the NetWare Nprinter Manager window.

11. If necessary, start NetWare Administrator and open a browse window for your ##UAS Organization.

12. Double-click your **##IS_NDPS** printer object to display the Printer Control dialog box.

13. Click the **Status** button to display your printer status. The status should be changed to "Idle." If you have an error message, be sure your printer cable is properly connected, and that the printer is on and ready with paper properly loaded.

14. Click **Close** to return to the Printer Control dialog box.

15. Click **Cancel** to return to the NetWare Administrator browse window.

16. Exit NetWare Administrator.

Configuring Clients for NDPS

The user's workstation that will be sending its output to a shared printer is the last, but perhaps the most important, component of NetWare printing since all print jobs originate and are formatted at the client computer. Modern printers require output to be formatted in a language that they are designed to process. Printer drivers on the client computer are responsible for the correct formatting of application output. As a result, each different type of printer requires its own printer drivers to be installed on the client workstation. As described earlier, the Novell Printer Manager utility is used to create NDPS printers on client computers.

 In this hands-on activity, assume you are working at Kellie's computer. You will use the Novell Printer Manager utility to install an NDPS printer to print to your ##IS_NDPS printer. If possible, you should coordinate this activity with another student in the lab. The other student's computer will play the role of Kellie's workstation. You can then log in from your partner's computer and use the Novell Printer Manager to create an NDPS printer for your printer agent on your partner's computer. You will then be able to send output from your partner's computer to the printer attached to your workstation. Your partner can create an NDPS printer for his or her printer agent on your computer and send output from your workstation to the printer attached to his or her workstation.

1. Be sure the NPTWIN95 software is loaded on your workstation as described in the previous hands-on activity.

2. Log in from your partner's computer using the KThiele username.

3. Create a shortcut for the Novell Printer Manager utility as follows:

   a) Use **My Computer** to browse to the **F:\Public\Win32** directory.

   b) Drag and drop the **Nwpmw32** program on your desktop.

   c) Close all windows.

4. Use the Novell Printer Manager utility to install a printer that represents your ##IS_NDPS printer as follows. (Remember that you are installing an NDPS printer on someone else's client computer and want to send output to the ##IS_NDPS printer attached to your computer.)

   a) Start the Novell Printer Manager utility.

   b) Click **Printer**, **New** to display the Novell Printers dialog box.

   c) Click the **Add** button to display the Available Printers window as shown in Figure 7-29.

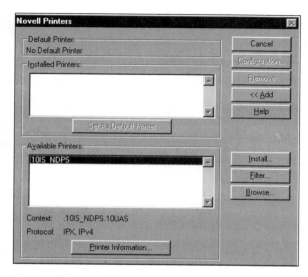

Figure 7-29   Adding an NDPS printer to a client

d) Click your **##IS_NDPS** printer and click the **Install** button to display the Novell Printers – Install window.

e) Click **OK** to install the printer and download the associated printer driver. The ##IS_NDSP printer should then appear in the Installed Printers window.

f) Click **Close** to return to the Novell Printer Manager dialog box. The ##IS_NDPS printer should now have an icon displayed in the Printer Manager window as shown in Figure 7-30.

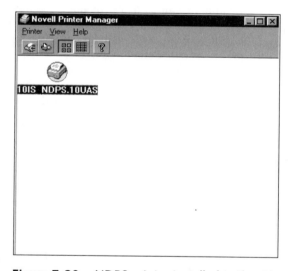

Figure 7-30   NDPS printer installed in the Novell Printer Manager dialog box

5. Make your ##IS_NDPS printer the default printer for the other user's computer as follows:

a) Highlight your **##IS_NDPS** printer and click **Printer**, **Set as Default**.

b) Exit the Novell Printer Manager utility.

6. Print a test document to the ##IS_NDPS printer as follows:

a) Click **Start**, point to **Programs**, point to **Accessories**, then click **Wordpad** to start the Wordpad word processor.

b) Create a simple document that includes your name and lists the steps necessary to install an NDPS printer on a client.

c) Save the document on your G:\Shared directory using the name **NDPStest.doc**.

d) Click **File**, **Print** or click the **Printer** icon to send your output to the network printer.

e) Exit Wordpad.

7. View your printer's jobs as follows:

a) If necessary, start the Novell Printer Manager (Nwpmw32) utility.

b) Double-click your **##IS_NDPS** printer object to display the Novell Job Manager window as shown in Figure 7-31.

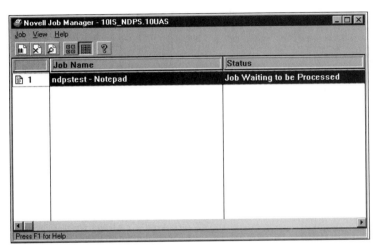

Figure 7-31 Novell Job Manager dialog box

c) Exit Novell Printer Manager.

Print Queues in NetWare 5

Because not all client computers and print devices will initially be compatible with NDPS, and because many organizations will be upgrading from earlier versions of NetWare that use queue-based printing, NetWare 5 has backward compatibility with the use of print queues. As described earlier in this chapter, a print queue is an NDS (Novell Directory Services) network object that represents a network holding area used to store output from workstations in a form that is ready to be sent directly to a printer. Because NDPS printers can also be configured to obtain output from print queues, client computers that have not yet been updated to support NDPS can send output to NDPS printers by redirecting output to the appropriate print queue. For example, because Novell does not ship an NDPS client for DOS and Windows 3.1x with NetWare 5, you would need to set up print queues for computers running these operating systems to print to NDPS printers.

In addition to supporting non-NDPS clients, print queues can also be used to allow NDPS clients to send output to non-NDPS print devices such as earlier versions of HP's JetDirect or Intel's NetPort print servers. For example, an NDPS client would send its job to the printer agent representing the printer attached to a JetDirect print server. The printer agent would then place the print job in the print queue serviced by the JetDirect print server. The JetDirect print server gets the print job from the print queue and sends it to the printer as soon as it is available.

Assume Kellie has a computer that she uses to test software, but that the computer does not support the NDPS client and therefore cannot send output to the laser printer now that you have converted it to use NDPS printing. For Kellie's computer to access the laser printer, you will need to configure your ##IS_NDSP printer agent to print any jobs placed in the IS_Q print queue you created earlier in this chapter.

In this hands-on activity, you will configure your ##IS_NDPS printer to get jobs from the IS_Q print queue.

1. If necessary, start your computer and log in using your assigned ##Admin username.

2. If necessary, double-click your **NPTWIN95** icon to attach your workstation to the ##IS_NDPS printer agent. (If you checked the option for "Activate printer when Nprinter Manager loads" in an earlier hands-on exercise, NPTWIN95 should automatically attach to your printer agent when you start it. If NPTWIN95 is running on your computer, you will receive a message that informs you that the Nprinter file NPTWIN95 is already loaded.) Click **OK** to continue.

3. Start NetWare Administrator.

4. Configure your NDPS printer agent to pull jobs from the newly created print queue as follows:

    a) Double-click your ##**IS_NDPS** printer object to display the Printer Control window.

    b) Click the **Jobs v** button to display a menu that includes Job List and Spooling options.

    c) Click the **Spooling Configuration** option to display the Spooling Configuration dialog box shown in Figure 7-32.

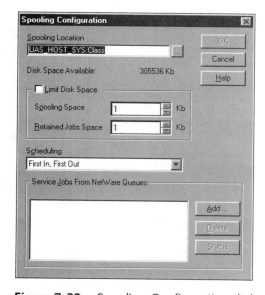

Figure 7-32 Spooling Configuration dialog box

    d) Click the **Add** button to the right of the Service Jobs From NetWare Queues area to display the Select Object dialog box.

    e) Double-click your **IS_Q** object from the left-hand Available objects window.

    f) Click **OK** to save your changes and return to the Printer Control window.

    g) Click **Cancel** to return to the NetWare Administrator browse window.

    h) Exit NetWare Administrator.

Now that you have configured your NDPS printer to get jobs from a print queue, DOS and Windows 3.1 clients can send output to your printer. At the beginning of the chapter, you learned that you can use the CAPTURE command in queue-based printing to redirect output from a client computer to a printer or print queue. As you will learn in the next chapter, in addition to working with NDPS clients, the CAPTURE command can also be useful in login scripts to help automate the user's printing environment. As a CNA, you should know the basic syntax of the CAPTURE command and be able to use it to redirect output to a print queue. The syntax of a CAPTURE command to send output to a print queue is:

CAPTURE Q = queuename [option list]

Table 7-2 contains a list of all the CAPTURE command options.

Table 7-2 CAPTURE Command Options

Option	Syntax	Description
Notify	NOTI	Causes a message to be sent to the user who submitted the print job when the job has been printed. By default, the sending user will not be notified.
Queue	Q=queuename	Specifies the name of the print queue where you want the output to be placed.
Job	J=jobname	Specifying a specific PRINTCON job will cause the NPRINT command to get all unspecified parameters from the given print configuration job name.
Form	F=formname or ##	Specifies the form type to be used. The default form type is 0.
Copies	C=#	Specifies the number of copies of the job to place in the print queue.
Tabs	T=#	Specifies the number of spaces to leave for each tab code encountered. The default is eight.
NoTabs	NT	Specifies that the byte stream output format is to be used with no tab codes expanded.
NoBanner	NB	Specifies that no banner page is to be printed. By default, a banner page will be printed.
Name	NAM=text	Specifies the name to appear in the upper part of the banner page. The default is the username.
Banner	B=text	Specifies the name to appear in the bottom part of the banner page. By default, the filename is used.
FormFeed	FF	By default, this option is enabled, causing the printer to eject a page after printing the file listing.
NoFormFeed	NFF	Disables the form feed after the file has printed. Output from the next print job can then start printing on the same page.
Show	SH	Displays the current capture status of the printer ports.
Timeout	TI=#	Determines when the application is done printing based on no printed output being sent within the specified time period. For example, a TI=5 parameter would tell the system that the print job is complete if no output is received in a five-second period.
Autoendcap	A	Causes the job to be printed when the application ends. For example, you might print three spreadsheets and not receive any output until you exit the spreadsheet program, at which time all three printouts would be generated.
Local	L=#	Specifies the number of the LPT port to be rerouted to the print queue. By default, LPT1 is redirected.

Table 7-2   CAPTURE Command Options (continued)

Option	Syntax	Description
Keep	K	Specifies that the job should be kept on the print queue in the event the workstation crashes before the output is complete. If you do not include the Keep parameter and the workstation hangs during the capture process, the NetWare server will discard the data it has received.
End Capture	EC [L=#] [ALL]	Returns the port specified in the L=# parameter to the local operating system. Replace # with 1, 2, or 3, representing the number of the LPT port. If only the EC parameter is specified, the LPT1 port returns to local mode. You can return all ports (LPT1, LPT2, and LPT3) to local mode by using the EC ALL parameters.

In this hands-on activity, you will simulate Kellie sending output from a non-NDPS client to your ##IS_NDPS printer by using the DOS CAPTURE command with the options shown in Table 7-2.

1. If necessary, start your computer and log in as KThiele.

2. Remove any existing jobs for the ##IS_NDPS printer as follows:

   a) Start the Novell Printer Manager utility. Create a shortcut if this has not already been done.

   b) Double-click your **##IS_NDPS** printer to display a Job Manager showing any existing print jobs.

   c) Use **[Del]** to remove any existing print jobs.

   d) Close the Job Manager window and exit the Novell Printer Manager utility.

3. Use the CAPTURE command to redirect output to your IS_Q print queue as follows:

   a) Open a DOS window (click **Start**, point to **Programs**, click **MS-DOS Prompt**).

   b) Change to your F drive.

   c) Use the following CAPTURE command to redirect output to the IS_Q print queue:

   CAPTURE Q=IS_Q NB TI=5 NT [Enter]

   d) On the following line, record the message you receive from the CAPTURE command:

   _____

   e) Enter **CAPTURE SH** to display your current capture status.

4. Send output to your ##IS_NDPS printer by entering the following command from the DOS prompt:

   DIR C:\ > PRN [Enter]

5. Log out.

DEFINING A PRINTING ENVIRONMENT

Now that you have had a chance to become more familiar with setting up NDPS printing components, it's time to apply this new knowledge to implementing the new network printers for Universal Aerospace. The first task a network administrator needs to perform when establishing a network printing environment is to define the printing needs to be supported on the network, which involves these steps:

1. Define the printing requirements of each user's applications.

2. Determine printer types, locations, and attachment methods.

3. Define names for all printers and identify any required print queues.

4. Plan the NDS context for each printer object.

In this section, you will learn about each of these steps and how to apply them to defining a network printer environment for the Universal Aerospace organization using the NDPS definition form developed by the NetWare consultant, Jennifer.

Define Printer Requirements

The first step in defining a printing environment is to identify the number and types of network printers and print queues that will be needed by the organization. To do so, you analyze each user's application software and printing needs. Table 7-3 contains a summary of the printing needs identified for Engineering and Manufacturing users in Universal Aerospace.

Table 7-3   Engineering/Manufacturing Printing Needs

Engineering	The department's HP LaserJet 5Si Postscript printer will be attached to Ira Means's computer and used by all designers to print correspondence and instruction manuals. While waiting for the hardware to attach the Engineering department's HP Color LaserJet printer, the department will initially need to attach the printer to Lianne Jarka's computer, to be shared by all users in the Engineering department and Publishing groups.
Manufacturing	Until its printer can be directly attached to the network using a JetConnect box, the Manufacturing department will have its HP LaserJet 5Si Postscript printer attached to its shipping computer. The shipping software will use the LaserJet printer to print packing slips as well as inventory reports. Russ Pence will manage the printer.

After you have identified the printing needs for an organization, the next step is to identify each network printer and how it will be attached to the print server. The NDPS Definition Form, shown in Figure 7-33, has been used to identify the printers in the Engineering department.

NDPS Definition Form

Created by: Jennifer Almquest, Consultant

Date:

NDPS Manager: Class NDPSM

NDS Context: .##Class

Server: UAS Host

Database Volume: Corp

Managers: ##Admin

Printer Name	Make/Model	Port and Interrupt	Location	Users	Print Queue Name/Volume	NDS Context	Operator
##ENG-HPColJet	HP Color LaserJet 5	LPT1 Int7	Remote	Engineering container, Publishing group		.Engineering.##UAS	IMeans Ljarka ##Admin
##ENG-HP5si-1	HP LaserJet 5Si Postscript	LPT1 Int 7	Remote	Engineering container	Eng-HP5si-Q Corp Volume	.Engineering.##UAS	IMeans ##Admin
##Mfg-HP5si-1	HP LaserJet 5Si Postscript	LPT1 Int 7	Remote	UAS Mfg container	Mfg-HP5si-Q Corp Volume	.UAS.Mfg.##UAS	MfgMgr ##Admin
##UAS-Public	See Instructor	See Instructor	See Instructor	See Instructor	See Instructor	Public Access Printer	See Instructor

Figure 7-33   NDPS Definition Form

The top part of the NDPS Definition Form identifies the name of the NDPS Manager object, as well as the NetWare server that will run the NDPSM software. Since an NDPS Manager can support an unlimited number of printer agents, one server running the NDPS Manager software is usually sufficient for most organizations. The exception to this is when the organization's network is connected over a wide area network. For example, because the AeroDyn division is connected across a T1 line, Jennifer recommends that a separate NDPS Definition Form be filled out for the AeroDyn Manufacturing department.

The NDPS Definition Form includes columns that allow you to identify the printer model along with the users and applications for each network printer that will be attached to a print server. To keep the printing system as simple as possible, Jennifer recommends that Universal Aerospace standardize the make and model of the printers to be used on the network when purchasing new equipment.

After analyzing the user needs in the Engineering department, Jennifer recommended placing two Engineering printers on the network: a color laser printer for use in printing graphs and presentation material, and a laser printer to be used for generating word processing documents and reports. She also recommended that the Manufacturing department initially have one laser printer to print packing slips and shipping reports. In addition, all networked computers should have access to the color laser printer attached to the server computer. To simplify setup and maintenance, Jennifer has recommended that you make the color laser printer a public-access printer.

Determine Printer Location and Attachment Method

After you have identified the printers that will meet the projected printing requirements of users, the next consideration is the physical location of the printers, including how they will be attached to the network. There are several rules you should consider when planning where and how to attach the printers to the network:

- Attempt to place the printer close to the user who is most responsible for it.

- Determine whether the printer is to be a local printer attached to the server, a remote printer attached to a client, or a printer directly attached to the network.

- Identify what printer port and interrupt each printer is going to use.

- Avoid attaching remote printers to clients that are not running 32-bit operating systems such as Windows 95, 98, or NT.

- Attach your printers directly if your network will employ heavily used high-speed printers or if you cannot find a client that will not conflict with the remote printer software.

The NDPS Definition Form, shown earlier in Figure 7-33, shows how Jennifer has identified the printer attachment and location information for each printer in the Engineering and Manufacturing departments. Notice that the form shows the printer port and interrupt to be used to connect the printer to the network. The port and interrupt usage, the type and location information, and the other properties shown in the NDPS Definition Form are important printer properties that you should supply when creating the printer agents.

Define Printer Names

An important consideration in keeping your printing system as simple as possible is selecting printer (and print queue) names that will allow you to identify quickly the printer when working with the printing environment. One way to create meaningful printer and print queue names is to define one- to six-character codes that identify the printer's location, model, and number. Each printer name would then consist of the codes for location, model, and number separated by dashes (-) or underscores (_). For example, the consultant has suggested the printer name ##ENG-HP5si-1 to identify the first Hewlett-Packard LaserJet 5Si laser printer installed in the Engineering department.

The ## preceding the printer names is necessary for all students to share the same NDPS Manager program.

If additional HP5Si laser printers are installed in the future in the Engineering department, their names would be ##ENG-HP5si-2 and ##ENG-HP5si-3. Using this system, the Engineering department's HP Color LaserJet 5 color laserjet printer will be named ##ENG-HP ColJet.

Notice that the NDPS Definition Form contains a column for print queues. If a printer agent is required to support non-NDPS clients, you will need to create a print queue. In this case, the print queue name should be the same as the printer agent name, with the last characters being a hyphen and the letter Q. As described earlier in this chapter, each print queue consists of a subdirectory within a directory named Queues. Because any NetWare volume can be used to store print queues, when defining print queues, you need to assign each print queue to a NetWare volume where its Queues directory will be located.

To prevent print queues that contain many large print jobs from filling up the SYS volume, Novell recommends that you place large print queues on a volume other than SYS.

In addition to using printer names when creating the printer agents and queues, it is a good idea to label each printer in the office physically with its assigned name. This will make it easier for both the network administrator and users to identify the printers when working with the printing system.

Plan the NDS Context

As with all network objects, printers, print queues, and print servers need to be defined in NDS. Before you can implement network printing, you need to plan where you will place printing objects in the NDS structure. Placing printers and print queues in the same container as users provides convenient access, since you can then select the printer by its name without having to specify its context. For example, if the ##ENG_HP5si-1 laser printer object is placed in the Engineering container, then all users in the Engineering department could send output to the printer. Users whose current NDS context is located in another department's container would have to browse to the printer or use a distinguished name for the printer. Another reason for placing printer and print queue objects in the container where they are most frequently accessed is that by default the container in which a print queue is located becomes a user of that print queue and printer. If necessary, you can make other users, groups, or containers users of a print queue object through NetWare Administrator as described in the following section. Notice in the

NDPS Definition Form shown previously in Figure 7–33 that Jennifer has recommended placing the printers in the Engineering or Manufacturing departments and then providing the Publishing group with rights to use the Engineering laser printer.

The NDPS Manager object is accessed from the NetWare server and can service printers and users in any container. On the top line of the NDPS Definition Form, Jennifer has recommended that the NDPS Manager object be located in the UAS Organization container, along with the NetWare Server object.

SETTING UP THE PRINTING ENVIRONMENT

Once the printing components and their location in NDS have been defined, you can continue implementing the network printing environment by using either NetWare Administrator or PCONSOLE to create and configure NDS objects for print queues, printers, and the print server by following these steps:

1. Create and load the NDPS Manager.

2. Create and configure printer agents.

3. Create print queues for non-NDPS clients.

4. Load necessary remote printer software.

5. Configure printers on client computers.

To become a NetWare CNA, you need to know how to use NetWare Administrator to set up an NDPS printing environment. In this section, you will learn how to use NetWare Administrator to perform each of the tasks necessary to set up the printing environment identified by the NetWare consultant for the Engineering and Manufacturing departments.

Creating and Loading the NDPS Manager

Prior to creating and configuring a printer agent for each of your printers, you need to create an NDPS Manager object in your NDS Directory tree and then load the NDPS Manager (NDPSM) software on the selected server. After you have created the NDPS Manager object and loaded the NDPSM software, you can use NetWare Administrator or the server console to create and configure your printer agents. Since your classroom server can have only one NDPS Manager running, in this simulation you will use the Class_NDPSM Manager object rather than creating and loading your own NDPS Manager as described in the following optional hands-on activity.

In this optional hands-on activity, you will use NetWare Administrator to create an NDPS Manager object in your UAS Organization. Since the following hands-on activities will use the existing Class_NDPSM Manager to create and configure printer agents, you should skip this activity unless instructed to do it. To create an NDPS Manager object, you will have to log in to the network using a username that has Supervisor rights to the classroom server object. As a result, you will have to check with your instructor for proper access rights before attempting to perform the following activity.

1. If necessary, start your computer and log in using the username with administrator privileges provided by your instructor.

2. Start NetWare Administrator and open a browse window for your ##UAS Organization.

3. Highlight your **##UAS** Organization and press **[Ins]** to display the Create New Object dialog box.

4. Double-click the **NDPS Manager** object to display the Create NDPS Manager Object dialog box.

5. Enter **##UAS_NDPSM** in the NDPS Manager Name field.

6. Click the **browse** button to the right of the Resident Server field to display the Select Object dialog box.

7. Double-click your **UAS_HOST** Alias object from the left-hand Available objects window.

8. Click the **browse** button to the right of the Database Volume field to display all volumes on the UAS_HOST server.

9. Because you do not want to fill up your SYS volume accidentally, it is recommended to select another data volume, such as the CORP volume, to store the print job database. However, since your CORP volume may have limited space, in this simulation double-click the **UAS_HOST_SYS** volume to display the Create NDPS Manager Object dialog box shown in Figure 7–34.

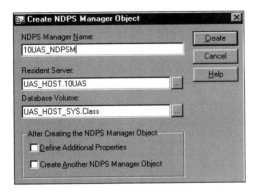

Figure 7-34 Create NDPS Manager Object dialog box

10. Click **Create** to create your new NDPS Manager object and return to your ##UAS browse window.

Once the NDPS Manager object is created, you will have to enter the following command on the server console to load the NDPSM software on the assigned server. (To load the NDPS Manager each time the server is booted, you will need to place the command in the server's startup files as described in Chapter 10.)

NDPSM .##UAS_NDPSM.##UAS [Enter]

Creating and Configuring Printer Agents

Once the NDPS Manager has been loaded on your network, you can create the four printer agents for the Engineering and Manufacturing departments identified on the NDPS Definition Form in Figure 7–33. Since it is probably not practical for you to load the NDPS Manager you created in the previous activity, you will need to use the Class_NDPSM Manager object when you create your printer agents. Notice that one of the printers identified on the NDPS Definition Form is a public access printer available to all clients. Since your classroom network already has a locally attached public access printer, you can use it as your UAS public access printer.

In this hands-on activity, you will create controlled access printer agents for the ##ENG-HP5si-1, ##ENG-HPColJet, and ##MFG-HP5si-1 printers.

1. Before beginning, ensure that the Class_NDPSM is loaded on the server console.

2. If necessary, start your computer and log in using your assigned ##Admin username.

3. Start NetWare Administrator and open a browse window for your ##UAS Organization.

4. Create the ##ENG–HP5si–1 controlled access printer as follows:

   a) Open a browse window for your Engineering container.

   b) Click your **Engineering** container and press **[Ins]** to display the New Object dialog box.

   c) Scroll down and double-click the **NDPS Printer** object to display the Create NDPS Printer dialog box shown previously in Figure 7-19.

   d) Enter the name **##ENG–HP5si–1** in the NDPS Printer Name field.

   e) Click the **Define Additional Properties** check box and click the **Create** button to display the Create Printer Agent dialog box shown previously in Figure 7-20.

   f) Click the **browse** button to the right of the NDPS Manager Name field to display the Select Object dialog box.

   g) Use the right-hand browse context window to navigate up to the **Class** Organization.

   h) Double-click the **Class_NDPSM** object in the left-hand Available objects window.

   i) Click **OK** to display the Printer Type selection window.

   j) Click the printer type that best matches the printer type attached to your workstation. If your printer type is not listed, you can change it later.

   k) Click **OK** to display the Connection Type window.

   l) Click **Remote (rprinter on IPX)** and **LPT1**.

   m) Click **Next** to display the default Emulation and Network Address Restriction window.

   n) Click **Next** to accept the defaults and display the Interrupts window.

   o) Click **None** unless otherwise instructed.

   p) Click **Finish** to create the printer agent and display the Printer Driver selection window. If you get an error message indicating the printer needs attention, click **OK** to continue.

   q) Click the **Windows 3.1 Driver** tab and click the printer driver that best matches your printer. Ask your instructor if you are not sure.

   r) Click the **Windows 95/98** tab and click the suggested printer driver that best matches your printer.

   s) If necessary, click the **Windows NT 4 Driver** tab and click the suggested printer driver that best matches your printer.

   t) Click **Continue** to display a summary of the printer drivers you have selected.

   u) If necessary, click **OK** to create the printer agent and display the Printer Control window.

   v) Click **Access Control** to display the Access Control window as shown previously in Figure 7-26.

   w) Click the **Operators** icon to display the current operators.

   x) Click the **Add** button to display the Select Object dialog box.

   y) Double-click **IMeans** to make Ira Means an operator. Now both Ira and the ##Admin user are operators, as defined on the NDPS Definition Form.

   z) Click **OK** to save your changes and return to the NetWare Administrator browse window.

5. Follow the procedure from Step 4 to create the ##ENG–HPColJet controlled access printer. Also follow these steps to make LJarka an operator.

6. Create the ##MFG-HP5si-1 controlled access printer in the .UAS.Mfg.##UAS container as identified in the NDPS Definition Form shown in Figure 7-33.

7. Create the public access printer to which all workstations can send jobs, as follows:

   a) Open a browse window to the Class container.

   b) Double-click the **Class_NDPSM** Manager object to display the NDPS Manager Information window.

   c) Click the **Printer Agent List** button to display the printer agent list window showing all printer agents managed by the Class_NDPSM Manager.

   d) Click the **New** button to display a Create Printer Agent dialog box similar to the one shown previously in Figure 7-20.

   e) Enter the name **##UAS-Public** as shown on the NDPS Printer Definition Form in Figure 7-33.

   f) Click **OK** to display a Printer Type window similar to the one shown previously in Figure 7-21.

   g) Select the printer type for an HP LaserJet 5Si Postscript printer or select the printer type identified by your instructor for the classroom printer. Then click **OK** to continue.

   h) Click a connection type of **Local** with a port of **LPT1** and click **Next** to continue to display the Configure Port Handler for Printer Agent dialog box.

   i) Click **Finish** to load the public access printer. Click **OK** when you receive the "Printer needs attention" error message window.

   j) Select the suggested printer drivers for Windows 3.1 and Windows 95/98 and click **Continue**. Click **OK**. Your printer should now appear in the Class-NDPSM Printer Agent List window.

   k) Click **Cancel** to close the NDPS Manager dialog box and return to the NetWare Administrator browse window.

8. View the status of each printer as follows:

   a) Open a browse window for the Engineering container.

   b) Double-click the **##ENG-HP5si-1** object to display a printer control page similar to the one shown previously in Figure 7-25.

   c) Click the **Status** button. Because you have not yet loaded the remote printer software on a client, the printer status should be "Printer Not Connected."

   d) Click **Close** to return to the Printer Control window.

   e) Click **Access Control** to view information in the Access Control window, then click **Printer Control** to return to the Printer Control window. Use the **Configuration** and **NDPS Remote Printer Management** buttons to view those respective windows as well.

   f) Click **Cancel** to return to the NetWare Administrator browse window.

After the printer agents are created, the NDPS Manager on the server console will display a list of printer agents and their status as shown in Figure 7-35.

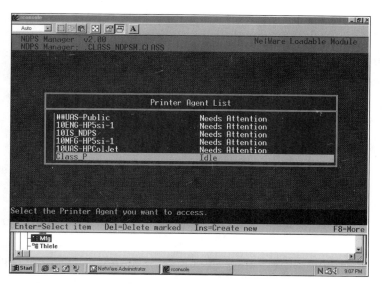

Figure 7-35   Sample NDPS Manager status window

Creating Print Queues for Non-NDPS Clients

Assume that currently there is an older DOS computer in the Receiving department that runs a simple word processing program used to print work orders. Since this computer will not be updated to the NDPS client software, you will need to create a print queue and associate it with the ##MFG-HP5si-1 laser printer.

In this hands-on activity, you will create print queues for the Manufacturing and Engineering printers and then associate them with the corresponding printer agent.

1. If necessary, start your computer and log in using your assigned ##Admin username.

2. If necessary, start NetWare Administrator and open a browse window for your **##UAS** Organization.

3. Create a print queue named ##MFG-HP5si-1 in your .UAS.Mfg.##UAS Organizational Unit as follows:

   a) If necessary, open a browse window to your **UAS.Mfg** organizational unit.

   b) Click your **UAS**.**Mfg.##UAS** Organizational Unit to highlight it.

   c) Click the **Create Print Queue object** icon from the toolbar to display the Create Print Queue dialog box.

   d) Enter the name **##MFG-HP5si-Q** in the Print Queue name field.

   e) Click the **browse** button to the right of the Print Queue Volume field and use the Browse context window to navigate up to your ##UAS container.

   f) Double-click **UAS_HOST_CORP** in the Available objects window.

   g) Click **Create** to create the ##MFG-HP5si-Q print queue.

4. Configure the ##MFG-HP5si-1 printer to look for jobs in the ##MFG-HP5si-Q print queue as follows:

   a) Double-click your **##MFG-HP5si-1** printer to display the Printer Control page.

   b) Click the **Jobs v** button to display a pop-up menu.

c) Click **Spooling Configuration** from the Jobs menu to display the Spooling Configuration dialog box.

d) Click **Add** to display the Select Object dialog box.

e) Use the Browse context window to navigate to your UAS.Mfg organizational unit.

f) Double-click **##MFG-HP5si-Q** from the left-hand Available objects window.

g) Click **OK** to save the change to the Spooling Configuration dialog box.

h) Click **Cancel** to return to the NetWare Administrator browse window.

5. Create a print queue named ##ENG-HP5si-Q in your Engineering Organizational Unit as follows:

a) If necessary, open a browse window to your Engineering container.

b) Click your **Engineering** Organizational Unit to highlight it.

c) Click the **Create Print Queue object** icon from the toolbar to display the Create Print Queue dialog box.

d) Enter the name **##ENG-HP5si-Q** in the Print Queue name field.

e) Click the **browse** button to the right of the Print Queue Volume name field and use the browse context window to navigate up to your ##UAS container.

f) Double-click **UAS_HOST_CORP** in the Available objects window.

g) Click **Create** to create the ##ENG-HP5si-Q print queue.

6. Configure the ##ENG-HP5si-1 printer to look for jobs in the ##ENG-HP5si-Q print queue as follows:

a) Double-click your **##ENG-HP5si-1** printer to display the Printer Control page.

b) Click the **Jobs** button to display a pop-up menu.

c) Click **Spooling Configuration** from the Jobs menu to display the Spooling Configuration dialog box.

d) Click **Add** to display the Select Object dialog box.

e) Double-click **##ENG-HP5si-Q** from the left-hand Available objects window.

f) Click **OK** to save the change to the Spooling Configuration dialog box.

g) Click **Cancel** to return to the NetWare Administrator browse window.

7. Exit NetWare Administrator.

Loading Remote Printing Software

As described previously, when printer agents are first created, they display the "Needs Attention" message until they are connected to the remote printer's client. To connect remote printers to Windows 95 or Windows 98 clients, you need to use the NTPWIN95 software as you did to connect the ##IS_NDPS printer in the previous section.

 In this hands-on activity, you will test the configuration for each of your remote printers by loading the remote printer software for a printer and then using NetWare Administrator to check the status of that printer.

1. If necessary, start your computer and log in using your assigned ##Admin username.

2. Start the NPTWIN95 remote printer software from your desktop. Notice that it automatically connects to your ##IS_NDPS printer.

3. Disconnect your ##IS_NDPS printer as follows:

   a) Click the **Printers** option to display the printer options.

   b) Click the **Remove** option to display the Nprinter warning asking whether you want to remove the ##IS_NDPS printer from service. Click **Yes** to remove the printer. You will receive a NetWare Alert message box informing you that Nprinter is unloaded. Click **Close** to continue. Your NetWare Nprinter Manager windows will now be blank.

4. Load the remote printer software for the ##ENG-HP5si-1 printer as follows:

   a) Click **Printers**, **Add**.

   b) Click the **Bindery-based Printer** option.

   c) Click the **browse** button to the right of the Print Server field to display the Print Servers and Printers window.

   d) Click the **##ENG-HP5si-1** print server from the left-hand Active Print Servers window.

   e) Click the **##ENG-HP5si-1** printer from the right-hand Attached Printer window.

   f) Click the **OK** button to select the printer.

   g) Click the **Activate printer when Nprinter Manager loads** check box to remove the check. This will prevent this remote printer from attaching to your computer each time you start the NPTWIN95 program.

   h) Click **OK** to load the remote printer software on your client.

   i) Minimize the NPTWIN95 window.

5. Now check the status of your ##ENG-HP5si-1 printer as follows:

   a) If necessary, start NetWare Administrator and open a browse window to the Engineering Organizational Unit.

   b) Double-click your **##ENG-HP5si-1** printer to display the Printer Control page.

   c) Click the **Status** button. If your printer is turned on and ready, the status shows "Idle." If there is no printer attached, the status will show "Out of paper."

   d) Click **Close** and then click **Cancel** to return to the NetWare Administrator browse window.

6. Unload the remote printer driver as follows:

   a) Restore the NPTWIN95 software.

   b) Click **Printers**, **Remove**.

   c) Click **Yes** to remove the connection to your ##ENG-HP5si-1 printer.

7. Repeat Steps 4 through 6 to connect to the ##ENG-HPColJet-1 printer and check its status.

8. Repeat Steps 4 through 6 to connect to the ##MFG-HP5si-1 printer and check its status.

Configuring Printers on Client Computers

As you learned in the previous section, for users to access NDPS printers, they need to have installed on their workstations the NDPS client software along with NDPS printer drivers they will access. Assuming that the NetWare 5 client has been installed on each user's computer, there are two ways in which you can install the printer drivers for the NDPS printers. In the previous section, you learned how a user can use the Novell Printer Manager to select and install a printer to which he or she has access. Installing NDPS printers in this manner can be a time-consuming task, or require special user training to allow the users to install their own printers. To speed up and simplify the task of installing NDPS printers on user workstations, Novell has enabled NDPS to install printers automatically on user workstations when users log in.

In this hands-on activity, you will use NetWare Administrator to configure the Engineering and Mfg containers to install the appropriate printers automatically for the users in those containers when they log in.

1. If necessary, start your computer and log in using your assigned ##Admin username.

2. Start NetWare Administrator and open a browse window for your **##UAS** Organization.

3. Select printers to be automatically installed on all client computers when they log in, as follows:

   a) Right-click the **Engineering** container and click the **Details** option.

   b) Click the **NDPS Remote Printer Management** button to display the NDPS Remote Printer Management window shown in Figure 7-36.

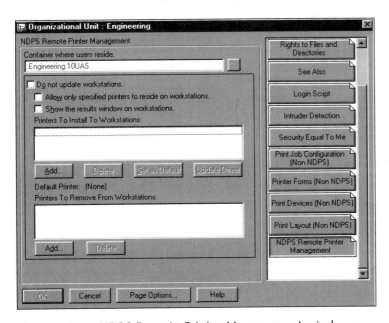

Figure 7-36 NDPS Remote Printer Management window

   c) Click the **Add** button under the Printers To Install To Workstations window to display the Available Printers options.

   d) Click the **##ENG–HP5si–1** printer and click **OK**.

   e) Click the **##ENG–HP5si–1** printer from the Printers To Install To Workstations window and then click the **Update Driver** button.

   f) Click **OK** to the Notice window saying that the driver for the printer will be copied to the workstations the next time users in this container log in.

   g) Click the **Set as Default** button to make the ##ENG–HP5si-1 printer the default for all Engineering workstations.

   h) Click **OK** to save the changes and return to the NetWare Administrator browse window.

4. Exit NetWare Administrator and log out.

5. To install the printer automatically, log in as a user as follows:

   a) Click the **Advanced** button and change the context to **Engineering.##UAS**.

   b) Enter **IMeans** in the Username field.

   c) If necessary, enter Ira's password.

   d) Click **OK** to log in. If asked to change your password, click **No** and notice the number of grace logins that are left.

   e) If necessary, click **Cancel** when asked to change the Windows password. A message window will appear showing that the new printer has been installed on the workstation.

6. Add the ##ENG-HPColJet printer:

   a) Start the Novell Printer Manager utility (Nwpmw32).

   b) Click **Printer, New** to display the Installed Printers window. Notice that the ##ENG-HP5si-1 printer has automatically been installed for you.

   c) Click the **Add** button to display the Available Printers window.

   d) Double-click the **##ENG-HPColJet** printer to display the Novell Printers – Install window.

   e) Click **OK** to install the printer using the default configuration.

   f) Click **Close** to return to the Novell Printer Manager window.

7. Check error messages as follows. Both printers should display error messages.

   a) Right-click a printer and click **Information** to display the "Printer not connected" error message.

   b) Click **Close** to return to the Novell Printer Manager window.

8. Exit Novell Printer Manager.

9. Log out.

Testing Printer Configurations

Before advertising the fact that you have set up the network printing environment for the Engineering users, you will want to test each printer along with your client installation to be sure they work as expected.

 In this hands-on activity, you will test your NDPS setup by loading the remote software for each printer and then sending output to that printer.

1. If necessary, start your computer.

2. Log in as **LJarka**.

3. Start the NetWare Nprinter Manager software (NPTWIN95). If Nprinter Manager is already running, you will receive an error message. In this case, you simply need to restore the running Nprinter Manager from the taskbar.

4. Use NetWare Nprinter Manager (NPTWIN95) to remove any attached remote printers as follows:

   a) If no remote printers are currently loaded on your client, skip to Step 5.

   b) Click **Printers, Remove** to display the Nprinter confirmation window. Click **Yes** to remove the current remote printer. A NetWare Alert message window informing you that Nprinter has been unloaded will then be displayed. Click **Close** to continue.

5. Attach the ##ENG-HP5si-1 remote printer to your workstation as follows:

 a) Click **Printers**, **Add** to display the Add Network Printer window.

 b) Click the **Bindery-based Printer** button.

 c) Click the **browse** button to the right of the Print Server field to display the Print Servers and Printers window.

 d) Click **##ENG-HP5si-1** from the Active Print Servers window.

 e) Double-click **##ENG-HP5si-1** from the Attached Printers window.

 f) Click the **Activate printer when Nprinter Manager loads** check box to remove the check mark.

 g) Click **OK** to load the remote printer software.

 h) Minimize NetWare Nprinter Manager.

6. Make the ##ENG-HP5si-1 printer the default:

 a) Start the Novell Printer Manager utility (Nwpmw32) from your desktop.

 b) Right-click the **##ENG-HP5si-1** printer and click the **Set as Default** option.

7. Create and print a document describing the steps necessary to use Novell Printer Manager to install a new printer to the ##ENG-HP5si-1 printer as follows:

 a) Start Wordpad (click **Start**, point to **Programs**, point to **Accessories**, click **Wordpad**).

 b) Create a simple document describing the steps necessary for a user to use Novell Printer Manager (Nwpmw32) to install a network printer on a workstation.

 c) Save the document in your G:\Shared directory with the name **Nwpmw32.doc**.

 d) Print the document.

 e) Close Wordpad.

8. Repeat Steps 4 through 7 to test your ##ENG-HPColJet printer.

9. Close all windows and log out.

MANAGING NETWORK PRINTING

After setting up the NDPS printing environment, an ongoing task is to manage the network printers and print jobs. To prevent the network administrator from becoming bogged down in the details of maintaining day-to-day printing needs, it is important to train users to manage network printers and to set up special configurations that meet special printing needs.

In this section, you will learn how to use Novell Printer Manager to perform common network printing management tasks as well as how to create printer configurations that can make it easier for users to deal with special printing needs.

Controlling Print Queue Workflow

You have learned that network printing requires printer output from an application to be stored as a job in a print queue until the printer agent sends the job to a network printer. Until they have been printed, jobs in a printer can be viewed or modified using NetWare Administrator or Novell Printer Manager. For example, if you have a high-priority print job, the print queue operator can rearrange the print job sequence to cause that job to be printed next. If output is sent to the wrong print queue, it can be deleted or moved to another printer. If you decide you want two copies of a job printed instead of one, you can change the print job attributes to increase the number of copies. A large print job that is not needed until tomorrow could be placed on hold. Two common types of job holds that can be applied are Retain Job and User Hold. Retain Job holds are used when you want NDPS to print the job automatically at a later time. User Holds allow the user or operator to prevent the job from printing until the hold is removed. In the following hands-on activities, you will learn how to retain jobs and apply User Holds.

 In this hands-on activity, you use the Novell Printer Manager utility to practice working with printer jobs on your ##ENG-HP5si-1 printer.

1. If necessary, start your computer and log in using your assigned ##Admin username.

2. Start NetWare Nprinter Manager (NPTWIN95) and attach your client to the ##ENG-HP5si-1 remote printer.

3. Start NetWare Administrator.

4. Use the Printer Control window to pause your ##ENG-HP5si-1 printer as follows:

   a) Open a browse window to your Engineering container.

   b) Double-click the **##ENG-HP5si-1** printer.

   c) Click the **Pause Output** button.

   d) Click **Cancel** to return to the NetWare Administrator browse window.

   e) Exit NetWare Administrator.

5. Open Nwpmw32.exe and set the ##ENG-HP5si-1 printer as the default. Now send three print jobs to the ##ENG-HP5si-1 printer as follows:

   a) Start Wordpad.

   b) Retrieve the instructions you saved in the previous activity.

   c) Print the document.

   d) Create a new document describing today's weather. Include the date, your name, the temperature, the sky (sunny, cloudy, partly cloudy, and so on), and any precipitation.

   e) Save the document in your G:\Shared directory with the name of **Weather.doc**.

   f) Print the document.

   g) Create a document that defines the following acronyms: NDPS, NDS, CNE, and CNA.

   h) Save the document in your G:\Shared directory with the name **Acronym.doc**.

   i) Print the document and close Wordpad.

6. Restore the Novell Printer Manager (Nwpmw32) on your desktop.

7. Check error messages as follows:

   a) Notice that the icon for your ##ENG-HP5si-1 printer has changed to an exclamation point.

   b) Right-click your **##ENG-HP5si-1** printer and click **Information** to display the message. The message should inform you that the printer is paused or waiting for paper. Click **Close**.

8. View your print jobs and change the second print job to print two copies and retain the job for one day, as follows:

   a) Double-click your **##ENG-HP5si-1** printer to display the Job Manager window.

   b) Double-click your second print job to display the Job Configuration dialog box shown in Figure 7-37.

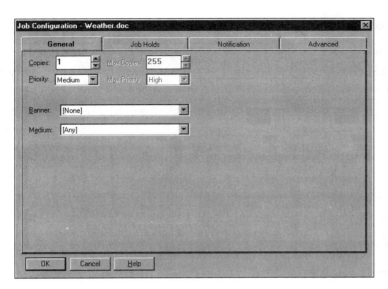

Figure 7-37   Job Configuration dialog box

   c) To print a Banner page containing your username and print job name prior to the output, click the scroll button to the right of the Banner field and then click the **Auto Select** option.

   d) Change the number of copies to two by clicking the **up arrow** to the right of the Copies field.

   e) To retain the print job so that it does not print until tomorrow, click the **Job Holds** tab and then click the **Retain Job For** box. Click the **Days** button to the right of the Retain Job for field to retain the job for one day.

   f) Click the **Notification** tab to display the print job notification parameters. You can use this configuration tab to control what notification message is sent to users and operators. For example, to send an error message to the printer operator, click the **Plus** box to the left of the Printer option and then click both the **Errors** and **Warnings** boxes to place an *X* in each check box.

   g) Click the **Advanced** tab to view print job properties including Modification time, Total Bytes, Job State, and Document Type.

   h) Click **OK** to return to the Novell Job Manager dialog box.

9. Place your first job on user hold as follows:

   a) Double-click your first job, click the **Job Holds** tab, and then click the **User Hold** box.

   b) Click **OK** to return to the Novell Job Manager dialog box.

10. Make the last job you added print first, as follows:

   a) Right-click the last job in the Job List window and then click the **Reorder** option to display the Job Position field.

   b) Enter **1** in the Job Position field.

   c) Click **OK** to return to the Job List window.

   d) If necessary, use the scrollbar to view the date and time the print jobs were submitted. The latest job should now be on the top of the Job List.

11. Change the second print job to print in five minutes as follows:

   a) Click the second print job and then click the **Job** menu.

   b) Click the **Configuration** option to display the Job Configuration dialog box.

c) Click the **Job Holds** tab and then click the **Delay Printing Until** box.

d) Click the **User Hold** check box to remove the check mark.

e) Enter today's date in the MM/DD/YYYY field, and the time you want the job to print (five minutes from now) in the HH:MM field.

f) Click **OK** to save the configuration changes. Close the Novell Job Manager and Novell Printer Manager windows.

12. Use the Printer Control window to resume the ##ENG-HP5si-1 printer as follows:

a) Start NetWare Administrator.

b) Double-click your **##ENG-HP5si-1** printer to display the Printer Control window.

c) Click the **Resume Output** button.

13. Close the Printer Control window and return to the NetWare Administrator browse window.

Managing Printers and Print Jobs

To keep a printer running, an operator may need to perform a variety of tasks including mounting forms, aborting a runaway print job, starting and stopping printing, or advancing paper. With manual load printers, the users of client computers are normally made printer operators so they can quickly respond to needs and problems that may arise on the printer attached to their workstations.

In this hands-on activity, you learn how to use the Printer Control window in NetWare Administrator to do a form feed and mount different media.

1. If necessary, start your computer and log in using your assigned ##Admin username.

2. Open the Printer Control page as follows:

a) Set the ##MFG-HP5si-1 printer as the default printer and ensure that Nprinter is running. Minimize all windows.

b) Start NetWare Administrator and open a browse window to your UAS.Mfg Organizational Unit.

c) Double-click the **##MFG-HP5si-1** printer to display the Printer Control page.

3. Print a form feed as follows:

a) Click the **Control** button to display a menu consisting of Reset, Form Feed, Mount Media, Statistics, and Set Defaults options.

b) Click the **Form Feed** option to advance one piece of paper through the printer.

4. Change the media to North American Legal White paper as follows:

a) Click the **Control** button and then click the **Mount Media** option. Click the Supported Media button to list all available media types for the printer.

b) Click the **North American Legal White** option. Click **OK**.

c) Click **OK** to save your media change.

5. Click **Cancel** to close the Printer Control page and return to the NetWare Administrator browse window.

6. Close all windows.

CREATING PRINT JOB CONFIGURATIONS

Once the network printing system is operational, the next task of a network administrator is to customize the printing environment to make it easier to use, as well as meet any special printing needs of user applications. In this chapter, you have learned that print jobs can be customized to include number of copies, a banner, delayed printing, special notification, and printer drivers. **Print job configurations** allow the user to set these parameters before sending a job to the printer. When you create a printer agent, a set of default print job parameters is established for jobs sent to that printer. Later you can either change these defaults or add more configuration options from which users can select.

For example, assume that Kellie has recently upgraded her computer to start either Windows NT or Windows 98. However, when you created the ##IS_NDPS printer, you did not define a printer driver for Windows NT. For her to add the ##IS_NDPS printer to her Windows NT client, you will need to add a print driver to the ##IS_NDPS printer.

In this hands-on activity, you will use NetWare Administrator to change the default print configuration of your ##IS_NDPS printer to include a Windows NT driver.

1. If necessary, start your computer and log in using your assigned ##Admin username.

2. If necessary, start NetWare Administrator and open a browse window to your ##UAS container.

3. Double-click your **##IS_NDPS** printer to display the Printer Control page.

4. Click the **Configuration** button.

5. Click the **[Default Printer Configuration]** option and click the **Modify** button to display the Printer Defaults dialog box as shown in Figure 7-38.

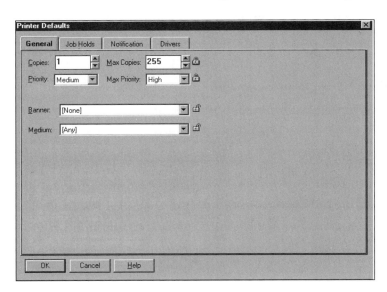

Figure 7-38   Printer Defaults dialog box

6. Click the **Drivers** tab and then click the **WinNT 4** icon.

7. Click the **HP LaserJet 5Si** printer in the list of Available Drivers and click **OK** to return to the Configuration dialog box.

8. Click **OK** to save your changes and return to the NetWare Administrator browse window.

9. Exit NetWare Administrator and log out.

Network printing setups are called **print configurations**. Each printer can have several printer configurations that are maintained in NDS by the NetWare Administrator utility. Having multiple configurations for a printer allows a user to select a special setup that may include a banner, multiple copies, user hold options, or special drivers. For example, assume the Engineering department wants to create a configuration that will be used to put print jobs on user hold and then print them during the night.

In this hands-on activity, you will create a print configuration named UserHold for the ##ENG-HPColJet printer.

1. If necessary, start your computer and log in using your assigned ##Admin username.

2. If necessary, start NetWare Administrator and open a browse window for the Engineering Organizational Unit.

3. Create a UserHold print job configuration for your ##ENG-HPColJet printer as follows:

    a) Double-click the **##ENG-HPColJet** printer to display the Printer Control page.

    b) Click the **Configuration** button.

    c) Click the **Create** button and enter the name **UserHold** in the Configuration Name field.

    d) Click **OK** to display the Printer Configuration — UserHold window.

    e) Click the **Job Holds** tab and then click the **User Hold** box.

    f) Click **OK** to save the configuration and return to the Configuration window.

    g) Click **OK** to return to the NetWare Administrator browse window.

4. Exit NetWare Administrator.

5. Add the new UserHold print job configuration to the client as follows:

    a) Start the Novell Printer Manager utility (Nwpmw32).

    b) Click **Printers, New**.

    c) Click **Add** to display the Available Printers window.

    d) Use the **Browse** button to display the Select Object dialog box.

    e) Use the Browse context window to navigate to the Engineering container.

    f) Double-click the **##ENG-HPColJet** printer in the left-hand Available objects window.

    g) Click the **Install** button to display the Novell Printers – Install dialog box.

    h) Change the name to **##ENG-HPColHold.Engineering.**

    i) Click **UserHold** in the Novell Printers — Install dialog box as shown in Figure 7-39 to select the UserHold configuration you just created.

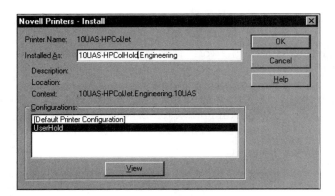

Figure 7-39   UserHold configuration

    j) Click **OK** to add the new printer.

    k) Click **Close** to return to the Novell Printer Manager dialog box. The ##ENG-HPColHold printer should now appear in the installed printer window.

6. Print a job to the ENG-HPColHold printer as follows:

    a) Start Wordpad and create a document that includes the title **Delayed Printout** along with your name and date.

    b) Save your document in the G:\Shared directory with the name **Delayed.doc**.

    c) Click **File**, **Print**.

    d) Select the **##ENG–HPColHold** printer from the Name field.

    e) Click **OK** to send your output to the ##ENG-HPColHold printer.

    f) Exit Wordpad.

7. Now check the job list as follows. The new print job should be automatically placed on user hold.

    a) Start or restore the Novell Printer Manager utility (Nwpmw32).

    b) Double-click the **##ENG-HPColHold** printer to display the Novell Job Manager window.

    c) Double-click the latest print job to display the Job Configuration window.

    d) Click the **Job Holds** tab to see that the User Hold box is checked. You could release the job by clicking the User Hold check box to remove the check mark.

8. Click **OK** to return to the Novell Printer Manager dialog box.

9. Close all windows and log out.

It's been a lot of work, but the printers for the Engineering and Manufacturing departments are installed and ready for the users. Tomorrow you plan to train the Engineering users and Russ Pence in the Receiving department on how to select and control the network printers using the Novell Printer Manager and NetWare Administrator. What you've learned in setting up printing for Engineering and Manufacturing should make the Business and Marketing printing setup go a lot easier.

CHAPTER SUMMARY

❑ One of the most important and challenging tasks for a network administrator is setting up and maintaining a network printing environment that will provide users with access to a variety of printers. In previous versions of NetWare, Novell has supported network printing through a queue-based printing system. Queue-based printing requires creating Print Queue, Printer, and Print Server objects. When configuring queue-based printers, you must be sure to configure each printer to get its jobs from its corresponding print queue. You then must add all printers to the Print Server object and then load the PSERVER module on the server.

❑ In cooperation with Hewlett-Packard (HP) and Xerox, Novell has developed a new network printing environment called Novell Distributed Printing Services (NPDS). As a CNA, you will be expected to know the printing concepts and utilities that make up NDPS and be competent to set up and maintain a NetWare printing environment consisting of an NDPS Manager, printer agents, gateways, brokers, print queues, and client workstations.

❑ Printer agents are software that make up the core of NDPS. Client computers send formatted printer output to printer agents, which then control the physical printer. When setting up NDPS, you need to create and configure one printer agent for each physical printer. In the future, printer agents will be embedded in printers, making the task of setting up and managing networked printers much easier. Today, to send output to NDPS printers, the printer agent software needs to run on a server. The component that is used to create and run printer agents is called the NDPS Manager. Gateways allow NDPS printers to be remotely attached to client computers, locally attached to the server, or attached directly using such products as HP JetDirect or the Xerox NetPort. Since not all clients will immediately be compatible with NDPS, Novell has provided backward compatibility with older clients through the use of print queues. Print queues consist of a directory on the file system used to hold print jobs until the printer is ready to use them. An NDS Print Queue object needs to be defined for each print queue and must include a name and volume properties. An NDPS Printer object defines a physical printer on the network and must contain the name, printer type, location, port, interrupt, and print queue properties.

❑ The first task in establishing the printer environment is to define the printing requirements for each user's applications, determining the types and number of printers necessary to meet these requirements, and the location of the printers on the network and whether they will be locally attached to the print server or remotely attached to printer ports on the workstations. An important step in defining the printer environment is to develop a naming system for printers and print queues that will make it easier for the user to identify the printer location, type of printer, and method of attachment.

❑ After defining the printing environment, the next step is to install the printing system. NetWare Administrator is used to perform most of the work involved in setting up and maintaining the NetWare printing system. To install the printing system initially, you need to create the NDPS Manager followed by the printer agents. The printer configuration may include a notification list consisting of usernames to receive printer messages.

❑ After installing the network printing environment, the network administrator will need to focus attention on the customization and day-to-day management of network printing. Managing network printing involves monitoring network printer status, controlling printers, and working with printer agents. In addition to maintaining the printer agents and configurations, NetWare Administrator and the Novell Printer Manager utility may be used by managers to provide such printer controls as mounting new media, stopping and starting a printer, and sending out form feeds.

COMMAND SUMMARY

Command	Syntax	Definition
CAPTURE	CAPTURE [*options*]	The CAPTURE command is used to redirect output from an LPT printer port to the specified print queue. The CAPTURE command contains options to determine when a print job is complete by using either a Timeout factor or AUTOENDCAP to release the print job when the application program ends. Table 7-2 lists CAPTURE command options.

KEY TERMS

automatic load printer — A printer attached to the server running print server or NDPS Manager software.

Broker object — An NDPS component that is responsible for sending printer messages and notifications.

controlled access printer — An NDPS printer that exists as an object in the NDS tree. By default, only users in the same container as the controlled access printer can send output to it.

Event Notification Service (ENS) — An NDPS broker service that is used by printer agents to send messages to workstations, users, or e-mail addresses.

gateway — The NDPS component that acts as a printer agent to allow printers that do not have embedded printer agents to work with NDPS.

local printer — A printer that is attached directly to a printer port of the server computer or to a port on the workstation.

manual load printer — A remote printer attached to a port of a networked workstation and controlled by the print server.

NDPS Manager — The NDPS component that manages the printer agent gateways for printers that do not have an embedded printer agent.

Novell Distributed Print Services (NDPS) — A new printing system developed by Hewlett-Packard and Novell to provide more convenient configuration and access to network printers.

parallel port (LPTn) — A common printer port used on personal computers. Parallel ports require thicker cables to transmit several bits of information at one time.

print configurations — Printer setup commands that include banners, number of copies, user hold options, and special drivers to be applied to print jobs. Each printer can have multiple print configurations for different types of print jobs.

printer agent (PA) — The software component of NDPS that transfers output from the client and controls the physical printer.

print job configurations — Network printing setups or entities in a print queue similar to configurations files that are entities in a directory. Print jobs contain data and printing parameters in a format that a print server can send to a printer.

print queue — A holding area where print jobs are kept until the printer is available to print them. In NetWare, a print queue is a subdirectory of the SYS:System directory.

print server — A component of a queue-based printing that manages network printers by sending jobs from print queues to the appropriate network printer.

public access printer — An NDPS printer that is attached to the network but does not have an NDS object in the tree. Any user attached to the network can send output to a public access printer without even having to log in to the network.

queue-based printing — An older NetWare printing system based on associating print queues with printers and print servers.

remote printer — A printer attached to a port of a networked workstation and controlled by the print server.

serial port (COMn) — A port often used to connect communication devices such as modems and printers in order to send signals over longer cables. Serial ports send only one bit of data at a time, so serial cables may consist of only a few wires.

spooling — The process of directing printer output from an application to a print queue.

REVIEW QUESTIONS

1. List the three components of a queue-based printing system:

   _____

   _____

   _____

2. A print server can control up to _____ printers.

3. A printer attached to the server is referred to as a(n) _____ attached printer.

4. A manual load printer is one that is attached to a(n) _____ computer.

5. Printers that are attached to the network using their own built-in network cards are called _____ attachment printers.

6. _____ is the queue-based printing component that holds printed output until the printer is ready to print.

7. _____ is the NDPS printing component that manages each physical printer.

8. The _____ is an NDPS component that connects physical printers attached to client computers to printer agents.

9. _____ must be running before you can create printer agents.

10. A network printer attached to a client is called a(n) _____ printer.

11. List four steps required to set up a networked printing environment, in the sequence they should be performed:

    _____

    _____

    _____

    _____

12. In addition to NetWare Administrator, the _____ utility can be used to manage network printers.

13. Write a CAPTURE command that will send output to the print queue named MFG-HP5si-Q with a timeout of five seconds, no banner, no form feed, and no tabs.

14. The _____ utility allows a printer attached to a Windows 95/98 client to be used as a remote NDPS printer.

15. A(n) _____ is used to connect printers that do not have embedded printer agents to NDPS.

16. _____ printers advertise themselves on the network, can be used by any client attached to the network, and do not have a corresponding NDS object.

17. _____ is an NDPS object that manages notification messages.

18. The _____ utility would be used to create a public access printer on your NDPS Manager.

19. The _____ utility is used to add an NDPS printer to a Windows 95 client.

20. A user would probably use the _____ utility to view jobs waiting to be printed.

21. List the two options from the Printer Control window that you would use to add a print queue to an NDPS printer:

_____

_____

The Universal Aerospace Project

In this chapter, you have been working with the NetWare consultant, Jennifer, to define and implement network printing for the Engineering and Manufacturing departments. In the following steps, you will set up and test network printing for Accounting, Sales, and Desktop Publishing users at Universal Aerospace.

Step 1: Define Business Printing Needs

Use an NDPS Definition Form provided by your instructor (see also Appendix B) to define each printer and print queue along with operators and users that are necessary to meet the printing needs for the Accounting, Sales, and Desktop Publishing departments, as defined in Table 7-4. If your lab has a laser printer attached to the network, use that for the Business department rather than the HP LaserJet identified in the table.

Table 7-4   Accounting, Sales, and Desktop Publishing Network Printer Needs

Department/User	Network Printing Needs
Accounting department	All accounting users should have access to the HP LaserJet 5Si Postscript printer on Amy Pan's computer.
Terry Blackwell	Except for correspondence, which is printed on the department's HP LaserJet 5Si Postscript, Terry Blackwell will need a new dot matrix printer to replace his current Epson LQ-2170 printer he uses for accounting reports. He has asked you to recommend a new dot matrix printer that will be compatible with the drivers that come with NetWare 5 NDPS. Both he and Amy Pan should be able to control the printer and change printer forms. Occasionally Terry needs to print spreadsheet output in landscape format to fit all columns on the paper. Since it is difficult to set these codes in the spreadsheet software, he would like you to automate this process.
Amy Pan	Amy uses the department's HP LaserJet 5Si Postscript printer attached to her computer to print correspondence. In addition to printing accounting reports, Amy Pan uses special forms in the Epson LQ-2170 printer to print payroll checks and W-2 forms.
George Perez	George Perez uses the department's HP LaserJet 5Si Postscript printer to print correspondence. In addition, George will need access to the dot matrix printer to print accounting and inventory reports.
Sales department	The Sales department will share an HP LaserJet 5Si Postscript printer attached to Laura Hiller's computer for correspondence, reports, and graphics output.
Laura Hiller	Laura Hiller will be responsible for operating the HP LaserJet 5Si printer attached to her workstation.

Table 7-4   Accounting, Sales, and Desktop Publishing Network Printer Needs (cont.)

Department/User	Network Printing Needs
Desktop Publishing department	An HP LaserJet 5Si laser printer will be attached to Diana Brady's computer and shared by Desktop Publishing users to print manuals and sales flyers.
Diana Brady	Diana Brady will be responsible for changing forms and controlling the HP LaserJet 5Si Postscript printer attached to her computer. In addition, occasionally Diana wants to send output to the Engineering department's ENG-HPColJet printer.
Bradley Dahl	Bradley Dahl uses the HP LaserJet 5Si Postscript printer on Diana's desk for most output. Like Diana, he occasionally sends output to the Engineering color printer.
Lynn Dai	Since the HP LaserJet 5Si Postscript printer has a paper tray dedicated to company letterhead, Lynn Dai normally uses this printer for most of her correspondence printing.

Select a dot matrix printer for the Accounting department that has a printer driver included in the NetWare 5 NDPS printer type list. Record the name and model of the printer in your NDPS Printer Definition Form.

Upon completion of your NDPS Definition Form, have your instructor verify your completed form against the master. Be sure to include your assigned student number prior to your printer names to keep them separate from other student printer names. To complete projects in later chapters, make any necessary changes to include all printer information included in the master NDPS Definition Form.

Step 2: Set Up Network Printing

In this step, you will apply what you learned in this chapter in using NetWare Administrator to create NDPS printer objects in the Business container for the printer agents and print queues defined on your NDPS Definition Form.

1. Use NetWare Administrator to create the NDPS printer objects in the Business container.

2. Use NetWare Administrator to create a print queue for each of the printers.

3. For each printer, use NetWare Administrator to call up a Printer Control window and add the appropriate print queue.

Step 3: Test Your Printing Setup

In this part of the project, you will test each of your Business department printers by loading the Nprinter Manager for each printer and then sending output to the printer and viewing the jobs on the print queue. Since you probably do not actually have an HP LaserJet attached to your computer, you will only be able to view the jobs in the print queue and the printer status to verify the network printing setup.

1. If necessary, start your computer and log in using your assigned ##Admin username.

2. Start the Novell Printer Manager utility and use the Printers menu to add each of your Business printers to your client. Check the status of each printer and record the status of each printer in Table 7-5.

Table 7-5   Business Printer Test Results

Department Printer	Printer Name	Initial Status	New Status
Accounting LaserJet 5Si			
Accounting dot matrix printer			
Sales LaserJet 5Si			
Publishing LaserJet 5Si			

3. Start Wordpad and create a simple document that includes a "This is a test" message.

4. Minimize Wordpad.

5. Perform the following process for each of the printers you previously listed:

   a) Start or restore the Nprinter Manager software (NPTWIN95) and remove the current printer.

   b) Add the printer to Nprinter Manager.

   c) Restore the Novell Printer Manager utility and check the status of the printer. Record the new status in Table 7-5.

   d) Restore Wordpad and modify the message to include the name of the printer you are testing.

   e) Send the document to the printer.

   f) Minimize Wordpad.

   g) Restore the Novell Printer Manager utility and double-click the printer. Verify that the test document is in the printer job list.

   h) Close the Novell Job Manager window and minimize the Novell Printer Manager utility.

6. Have your instructor verify your printer setup by looking in each printer's job list and then signing off on the following line:

   Instructor signoff: ———————————————————— Date: ————————————————

7

8

IMPLEMENTING NETWARE LOGIN SCRIPTS

After reading this chapter and completing the exercises, you will be able to:
- Identify the four types of login script files and how they are used
- Identify the purpose and correct syntax of login script commands
- Identify the recommended login script commands
- Write container login scripts to meet the needs of an organization
- Write profile and user login scripts to meet special processing needs of users

Now that you have completed setting up the network printers, the major components of the network are all in place. The next challenge for you as a network administrator is to make the network system you have established easy to access and maintain. To accomplish this, you will need to have a consistent environment that can be managed from a central location. With NetWare 5, Novell has provided the tools to create a centralized and consistent environment through the use of login scripts and Z.E.N.works. Login scripts consist of commands that enable users to access network services by establishing drive pointers, providing informational messages, directing printer output to network printers, and running special programs. Z.E.N.works is a tool to centrally monitor and manage workstations and applications.

Because establishing the user environment plays such an important part in the network administrator's job, Novell requires CNAs to be familiar with login scripts and Z.E.N.works. In this chapter, you will learn to create and maintain login scripts. In Chapter 9, you will learn how you can use Z.E.N.works to help you centrally configure and manage workstations and applications across the network.

As you have learned in previous chapters, unless you select the option to reconnect drive pointers and printers when you log in, any drive mapping or network printer commands you establish during a network session are effective only until you log out of the network. The next time you log in, it is necessary to reconnect each drive pointer or network printer you want to use. Using Windows to reconnect drive pointers automatically when the user logs in can create problems when other users attempt to log in from that workstation. Requiring users to reestablish their drive pointers not only requires them to have technical knowledge about the system but also takes time away from productive work and can cause problems when users try to access software or files. To solve these problems, Novell has provided login scripts that can be used to establish a consistent network environment each time a user logs in. As shown in Figure 8-1, a NetWare login script consists of a set of NetWare login command statements that are processed by the Novell NetWare client when a user logs in.

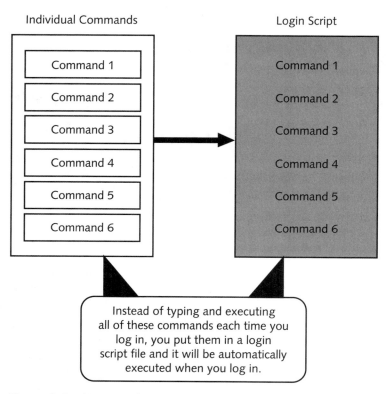

Figure 8-1   NetWare login script

Types of Login Scripts

To understand how NetWare stores and processes login scripts, you first need to be aware of the types of login scripts and their purpose. To provide for maximum flexibility, NetWare contains four types of login scripts: container, profile, user, and default. Having multiple login scripts is important because it enables the network administrator to provide a standard environment for all users while still allowing flexibility to meet individual user needs. **Container login scripts** allow the network administrator to provide standard setups for all users in a container. **Profile login scripts** are special NDS objects that contain login commands that are common to multiple users no matter what container their user object exists in. In addition to providing container and profile login scripts, NetWare allows for individual user requirements by providing each user object with a **user login script** that may contain additional statements that are executed for that user after the container and profile login script commands. The **default login script** is a set of commands that establish a default working environment for each user who does not have a user login script defined. To become a CNA, it will be necessary for you to know how these login script files work together to set up a reliable and efficient login script system for the network. Figure 8-2 contains a flow-chart that illustrates the relationship among the NetWare login scripts.

Once a login script is created for a container, its commands are performed by the users in that container when they log in to the network. Once all commands in the container login script have been executed, NetWare will next determine whether the user is assigned to a Profile object. If the user object has a profile script defined, NetWare will perform any login script commands included in the profile script. After NetWare checks for a profile, the last step is to execute the commands in either the user login script or the default login script. To stop the default login script commands from being executed, you will need either to create a personal login script for each user containing at least the EXIT command, or include the NO_DEFAULT command in the container login script as described later in this chapter. In this section, you will learn about the purpose and function of container, user, and default login scripts; profile login scripts will be covered in more detail later in the chapter.

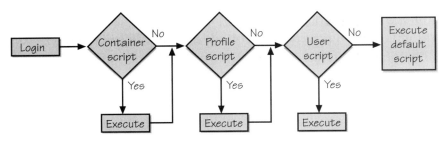

Figure 8-2   NetWare login script execution

Container Login Scripts

Each container object has a Login Script property that may be used to enter login script commands that will be executed for each User object housed in that container. Whenever a user logs in to the network, the Novell NetWare Client software looks for login script commands in that user's container. Only the login script commands included in the user's home container are executed; login script commands contained in parent containers are not executed. For example, login script commands placed in your ##UAS container will not be executed by users in the .Engineering.##UAS or .Business.##UAS containers. This means that each container's login script should include all the commands needed to set up a standard working environment for all the users in that container. Your Universal Aerospace organization has users in four different containers: the ##UAS container, the Engineering container, the Mfg container, and the Business container. As a result, you will need to create container login scripts for each of these containers. An important purpose of container login scripts is to map a search drive to the Public directory as well as set up drive pointers to each volume the users in that container will access.

User Login Scripts

The user login script is located in the Login Script property of each User object. Unless the EXIT command is executed in the container or profile login script, the LOGIN.EXE program will execute any login script commands located in the user's Login Script property. Unless the NO_DEFAULT command has been executed, when no login script commands exist in the user's Login Script property, the LOGIN.EXE program will execute the Default login script commands.

By default, either the network administrator or the user can access and maintain the user login script by using NetWare Administrator to select the Login Script property from the user's information screen. If you do not want users to be able to modify their own login script commands, you can use Selected property rights from NetWare Administrator to remove the Write property right from the user's Login Script property as described later in this chapter.

Placing commands in user login scripts makes maintaining the login script environment more difficult since making changes may require accessing many separate user login script files. As a result, many network administrators prefer to place most commands in container or profile login scripts to reduce the need for user login scripts whenever possible.

Default Login Scripts

The default login script consists of several login script commands that are built into the Novell NetWare Client software. If a user login script file does not exist for the user currently logging in, the NetWare

Client will execute the default login script commands. The purpose of the default login script is to provide basic drive mappings for users initially until a system login script has been established. The statements that make up the default login script for the NetWare Client include the following:

`MAP *1:=SYS:`   (maps the first network drive to the SYS volume)

`MAP INS S1:=SYS:PUBLIC`   (maps the first search drive to the Public directory)

Once the network administrator has established a container login script that includes the basic drive mappings for the network, it is important to prevent the default login script from executing, since its execution would cause drive mappings made in the container login script to be either overwritten or duplicated.

NetWare provides three basic ways to stop the default login script from being executed:

- Place the NO_DEFAULT statement in the container login script.

- Provide a user login script for each user on the network even if the user login script contains only the EXIT command.

- Include an EXIT command in the container login script. The EXIT command ends the login script process and therefore prevents the execution of all profile, user, or default login scripts. Placing the EXIT command in the container login script is not normally a good option since it also prevents the execution of profile login scripts.

Although many network administrators avoid large or complex login scripts, others actually prefer having one large container login script program rather than having lots of user and profile login scripts that require administrators to look in many different places when trying to maintain the login script environment. Based on your network environment and personal preference, you will need to decide on the method that is best for you and your network.

LOGIN SCRIPT PROGRAMMING

Creating login scripts is much like writing programs with any programming language. To write login scripts, you need to learn the valid commands along with the syntax or rules used to format the commands. In addition, like any other programming language, login script commands allow the use of variables that can be used to allow one command to be used for multiple values. In the following sections, you will learn how to use login script commands and variables to create sophisticated login scripts that can automate many functions as well as provide the user with announcements and other messages.

The command statements in a login script file form a program that is processed by the Novell NetWare client software. The software on the client computer processes the login script file only after authenticating a user successfully by prompting the user to provide a valid username and optional password to the network. The Novell NetWare client login window contains an Advanced button that you can use to control the processing of login script commands.

Figure 8-3 illustrates a simple container login script program similar to the one you entered for your ##UAS Organization in Chapter 3. Notice that the script contains statements to display a greeting message and establish a network environment by mapping drive pointers and directing output to a default network print queue. The # symbol ahead of the CAPTURE command is a special login script command that tells the system to run the CAPTURE program. (Placing CAPTURE statements in the login script may be necessary if the user needs to access network printers from non-NDPS clients as described in Chapter 7.)

8

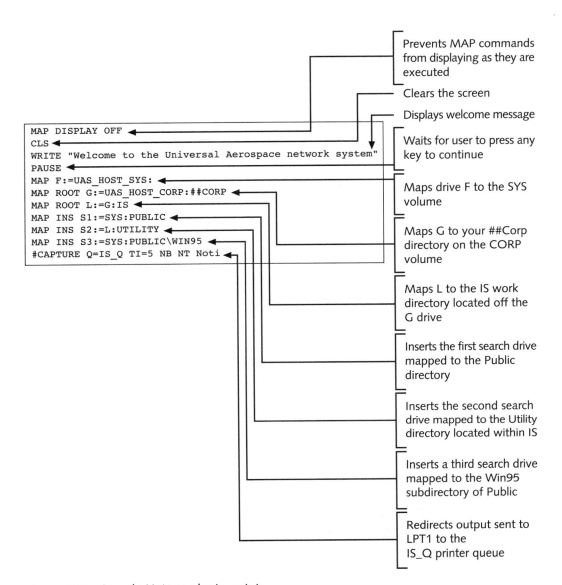

Figure 8-3 Sample Netware login script

 In this hands-on activity, you will modify the login script you entered in Chapter 3 to contain the commands shown in Figure 8-3 and then practice using the client login script options to run the login script when you log in.

1. If necessary, start your computer and log in using your assigned ##Admin username.

2. Start NetWare Administrator and open a browse window for your ##UAS container.

3. Modify your ##UAS Organization as follows:

   a) Right-click your **##UAS** Organization and click the **Details** option.

   b) Click the **Login Script** button.

   c) Modify the login script commands to appear as shown in Figure 8-4.

   d) Click **OK** to save the login script and return to the NetWare Administrator browse window.

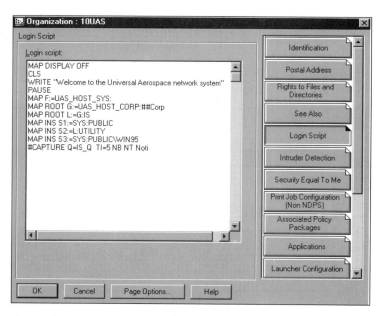

Figure 8-4   Entering a user login script

4. Exit NetWare Administrator and log out.

5. Set up the Novell NetWare client to display your login script results and not automatically close the login screen, as follows:

   a) Enter your ##Admin username and password.

   b) Click the **Advanced** button and click the **Script** tab to display the screen shown in Figure 8-5.

   c) Click the **Close automatically** check box to remove the check mark.

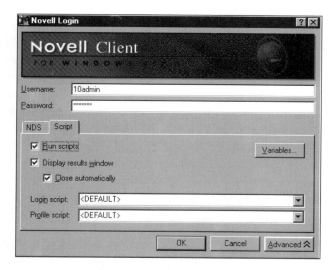

Figure 8-5   Advanced login Script tab

6. Click **OK** to log in. A Results window will be displayed with the welcome message.

7. Press the **space bar** to continue. The Results window will be displayed showing the CAPTURE command as well as a list of drive mappings.

Even though the container script includes the MAP DISPLAY OFF command, the drive mappings are still displayed as a result of the default login script. Later in this chapter, you will learn how you can prevent the default login script from running.

8. Click the **Close** button to close the Results window.

9. Log out.

10. Repeat the login process with the NetWare client. This time, you will reset the client to close the Results window automatically, as follows:

    a) If necessary, enter your ##Admin username and password.

    b) Click the **Advanced** button and click the **Script** tab to display the script window.

    c) Click the **Close automatically** check box to add a check mark.

11. Click **OK** to log in. The Results window should be displayed with the welcome message.

12. Press any key to complete the log in and automatically close the Results window.

13. Log out.

Login Script Variables

Login script programs consist of a limited number of command statements in the NetWare login script language. As a CNA, you will need to know how to use the NetWare login script language to design and write login scripts for your organization.

As with other programming languages, the NetWare login script language allows the use of variables within many of the command statements. A **login script variable** is a reserved word in the login script language whose value may change for each user logging in. By properly using login script variables, you can write a login script program that will work for many different users and workstations. In this section, you will learn what a CNA needs to know about login script variables and commands to design and write login script programs for the Universal Aerospace Corporation.

Login script variables play an important role in writing login script programs by allowing login script statements to meet the needs of many different users. Because login script variables are an important part of many command statements, to learn the NetWare login script language, you should first know about login script variables and how you can use them in login script command statements.

Login script variables can be divided into types based on their usage: date variables, time variables, user variables, workstation variables, and user-defined variables. In this section, you will learn about the use of each of these login variable types along with the specific variables associated with each type.

Date Variables

Date variables contain information about the current month, day of the week, and year in a variety of formats as shown in Table 8-1.

Table 8-1   Date Variables

Variable	Description
DAY	The day number of the current month. Possible values range from "01" to "31".
DAY_OF_WEEK	The name of the current day of the week. Possible values are "Monday", "Tuesday", "Wednesday", etc.
MONTH	The number of the current month. Possible values range from "01" for January to "12" for December.
MONTH_NAME	The name of the current month. Possible values range from "January" to "December".
NDAY_OF_WEEK	The current weekday number, ranging from "1" for Sunday to "7" for Saturday.
SHORT_YEAR	The last two digits of the current year; for example, "95" or "96".
YEAR	The full four-digit year; for example, "1995" or "1996".

Date variables can be valuable when displaying current date information or checking for a specific day to perform certain instructions. For example, the Engineering users need to meet at 10:00 a.m. each Monday to review weekly work projects. Using the DAY_OF_WEEK variable, you can write login script commands to display a message on Monday morning reminding the users of the meeting. When using date variables, it is important to note that the value of date variables is stored as an ASCII string of a fixed length. For example, the DAY variable contains the day number of the current month and ranges from 01 to 31, whereas the NDAY_OF_WEEK variable contains values ranging from 1 to 7.

Time Variables

The **time variables** shown in Table 8-2 provide a variety of ways to view or check the login time.

Table 8-2   Time Variables

Variable	Description
AM_PM	Day or night (a.m. or p.m.).
GREETING_TIME	The welcome message to display. Possible values are "Morning", "Afternoon", or "Evening".
HOUR	The current hour of day or night in the range of "01" through "12".
HOUR24	The current hour in 24-hour mode ranging from "01" for 1 a.m. through "24" for 12 a.m.
MINUTE	The current minute in the range of "00" through "59".
SECOND	The current second in the range of "00" through "59".

The GREETING_TIME variable is most often used in WRITE statements to display welcome messages. The difference between the HOUR24 variable and the HOUR variable is that the HOUR variable requires the use of the AM_PM variable to determine whether the specified time is before or after noon. The HOUR24 variable uses a 24-hour clock, where hour 12 is noon, and hour 13 is 1 p.m. When you are checking for a specific time, the HOUR24 variable is often easier to use. For example, if you want all users who log in before 3:00 p.m. to be notified of a special meeting, you could write login script commands that use the HOUR24 variable to compare the current login hour to 15. If HOUR24 is less than 15, the login script commands could display a message regarding the meeting.

User Variables

The **user variables** shown in Table 8-3 allow you to view or check the user's login name, full name, or hexadecimal user ID given to the user in the bindery files.

Table 8-3   User Variables

Variable	Description
FULL_NAME	The user's full name as defined from SYSCON or USERDEF.
LOGIN_NAME	The user's unique login name.
USER_ID	The hexadecimal number assigned by NetWare for the user login name.

The LOGIN_NAME variable is commonly used to map a drive letter to a user's home directory from within the system login script, provided the name of the user home directories is the same as the user's login name. You can use the FULL_NAME variable to personalize greeting messages by including the user's name as part of the message.

Workstation Variables

The **workstation variables** are shown in Table 8-4. The MACHINE, OS, and OS_VERSION variables are most commonly used in the system login script when mapping a search drive to the correct DOS version used on the workstation. The STATION variable contains the connection number assigned to the user's workstation. Software packages sometimes use this variable to separate the user's temporary files by including the station number as part of the temporary filename. For example, some network administrators use the STATION variable to separate temporary files when creating menus, as described in Chapter 9. The P_STATION variable contains the actual node address of the workstation logging in and can be used in login script files to cause certain processing to be performed on specific workstations. For example, suppose only workstation address DC03D7D27 is used to run the new CAD software. In the login script, you could write commands to use the P_STATION variable to check for the station address DC03D7D27 and then set up the necessary drive mappings and start the CAD software. The NETWORK_ADDRESS variable may be used to display or check the address of the network card of the user who is currently logging in.

Table 8-4   Workstation Variables

Variable	Description
OS	The workstation's operating system. The default value is "MSDOS".
OS_VERSION	The version of DOS being used on the workstation that is processing the login script. An example value is "V6.20".
MACHINE	The long machine name that may be assigned in the SHELL.CFG or NET.CFG file. The default value is "IBM_PC".
P_STATION	The node address of the network card in the workstation. The value is expressed as a 12-digit hexadecimal value.
SMACHINE	The short machine name that may be assigned in the SHELL.CFG or NET.CFG file. The default value is "IBM".
STATION	The connection number of the current station.
SHELL_TYPE	The workstation's shell version number.
NETWORK_ADDRESS	The network address of the cabling system to which the user's workstation is attached. The value is expressed as an eight-digit hexadecimal number.
FILE_SERVER	The name of the current file server.

8

Workstation variables are most often used to allow drive mappings for software utility directories to be established according to the client computer's hardware or operating system.

User-Defined Variables

Based upon the workstation or applications they need to run, more advanced network users may want to modify certain login script parameters when they log in. **User-defined variables** provide a method users can use to enter parameters that will be used by their login scripts. User-defined variables are represented using a number preceded by a percent sign. When you click the Variables button on the Script tab of the Novell Client login window, the NetWare client allows you to enter four user-defined variables as shown in Figure 8-6. Since the first variable parameter, %1, is reserved for system use, the user variables start with %2. For example, when testing software for different departments, Kellie Thiele needs to be able to modify the drive mapping for drive letter L to point to the departments' shared work directory. To allow her to select the department's directory path when she logs in, she decides to use the %2 user-defined variable to represent the department name. She then enters the following command in her personal login script that will map drive letter L to the department's name contained in the %2 variable:

```
MAP ROOT L:=UAS_HOST_CORP:##Corp\%2
```

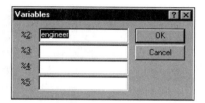

Figure 8-6   User-defined variables

Now when she logs in, the client computer will execute all commands in the ##UAS container and then perform the MAP command, substituting the department name she specified in the login window for the %2. For example, if she enters "Engineer" for %2 in the Variables dialog box, the MAP command would become:

```
MAP ROOT L:=UAS_HOST_CORP:##Corp\Engineer
```

In the next section, you will create a login script for Kellie that uses the %2 variable.

Using Login Script Variables

As described previously, a login script variable is a reserved word that will be replaced with an actual value when the login script is processed. To learn how login script variables work, we'll examine the use of a login script variable to display the current date in the greeting message and assign a drive pointer to the home directory for each user in your ##UAS Organization. To assign a drive pointer to each user's home directory without the use of login script variables, you would have to create a separate login script for each user containing a MAP command to the user's home directory as shown in Figure 8-7.

Script for Kellie

MAP DISPLAY OFF
WRITE "Welcome to the Universal Aerospace network system"
MAP INS S1:=UAS_HOST_SYS:PUBLIC
MAP F:=UAS_HOST_SYS:
MAP G:=UAS_HOST_CORP:##Corp
#CAPTURE Q=IS_Q NB NT TI=5
MAP ROOT H:=UAS_HOST_CORP:\##Corp\IS\KThiele
DRIVE H:

Script for your user

MAP DISPLAY OFF
WRITE "Welcome to the Universal Aerospace network system"
MAP INS S1:=UAS_HOST_SYS:PUBLIC
MAP F:=UAS_HOST_SYS:
MAP G:=UAS_HOST_CORP:##Corp
#CAPTURE Q=IS_Q NB NT TI=5
MAP ROOT H:=UAS_HOST_CORP:##Corp\IS\yourname
DRIVE H:

Script for Chuck

MAP DISPLAY OFF
WRITE "Welcome to the Universal Aerospace network system"
MAP INS S1:=UAS_HOST_SYS:PUBLIC
MAP F:=UAS_HOST_SYS:
MAP G:=UAS_HOST_CORP:##Corp
#CAPTURE Q=IS_Q NB NT TI=5
MAP ROOT H:=UAS_HOST_CORP:\##Corp\IS\CBotsford
DRIVE H:

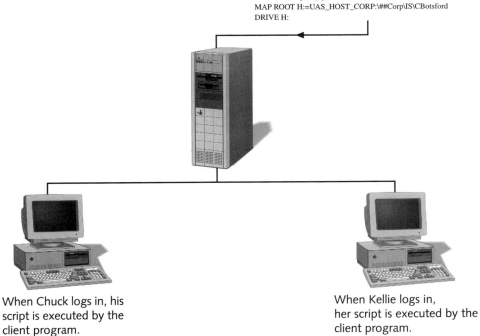

When Chuck logs in, his
script is executed by the
client program.

When Kellie logs in,
her script is executed by the
client program.

Figure 8-7   Using individual user login scripts

As you can see, creating a separate login script for each user involves a lot of extra work and redundancy. An alternative is to create a single login script that will work for all users in the Engineering container. Notice in Figure 8-7 that each user's directory name is the same as the user's login name. As you learned in Chapter 4, when you create new users, by default each user's home directory is given the same name as the user's login name. This is important because when each user's home directory has the same name as the user's login name, you can substantially shorten the number of statements in the login script by using the LOGIN_NAME variable in the MAP command statement as shown in Figure 8-8.

```
MAP DISPLAY OFF
CLS
WRITE "Good %GREETING_TIME, %LOGIN_NAME."
WRITE "Welcome to the Universal Aerospace network system"
PAUSE
MAP F:=UAS_HOST_SYS:
MAP ROOT G:=UAS_HOST_CORP:##CORP
Rem
Rem The following command maps drive letter H: to the user's home directory
Rem
MAP ROOT H:=UAS_HOST_CORP:##CORP\IS\%LOGIN_NAME
MAP ROOT L:=G:IS
MAP INS S1:=SYS:PUBLIC
MAP INS S2:=L:UTILITY
MAP INS S3:=SYS:PUBLIC\WIN95
```

Figure 8-8   Using the %LOGIN_NAME variable

A container login script is stored in the NDS database and will be processed when any user in the container logs in to the network. (The different types of login scripts are discussed later in this chapter.) The percent sign (%) in front of the variable name is necessary to tell the NetWare client software to substitute the user's login name in place of the LOGIN_NAME variable during the login process. In addition to the percent sign, notice that the login script variable name is entered in all uppercase.

Because many login script command statements require variable names to be capitalized, it is a good practice to capitalize all login script variable names.

Thus, when Kellie logs in, the NetWare client software running on her computer replaces the %LOGIN_NAME variable with the username KThiele. The H drive letter will then be mapped to the IS\KThiele directory. When Chuck Botsford logs in, the NetWare client on his computer replaces the %LOGIN_NAME variable with the username CBotsford, causing his H drive letter to be mapped to the IS\CBotsford directory.

In this hands-on activity, you will modify the login script for your ##UAS container to include the login script variables in commands to map drive letter H to each user's home directory by using the %LOGIN_NAME variable.

1. If necessary, start your computer and log in using your assigned ##Admin username.

2. Start NetWare Administrator and open a browse window for your ##UAS container.

3. Modify your ##UAS Organization as follows:

   a) Right-click your **##UAS** Organization and click the **Details** option.

   b) Click the **Login Script** button.

   c) Modify the login script commands to add the following command as shown in Figure 8-8:

      ```
      MAP ROOT H:=UAS_HOST_CORP:##Corp\IS\%LOGIN_NAME
      ```

   d) Click **OK** to save your login script changes and return to the NetWare Administrator browse window.

4. Exit NetWare Administrator and log out.

5. Log in as **KThiele**.

6. Use Windows Explorer to verify that Kellie has drive letter H mapped to her home directory.

7. Exit Windows Explorer and log out.

8. Log in using your assigned ##Admin username. Notice the error message that displays when the system attempts to map drive letter H to your ##Admin home directory. This message displays because there is no ##Admin subdirectory in the IS directory. You will learn how to correct this problem later in this chapter.

9. Close your login script window.

 As described earlier, Kellie needs to have the flexibility to change her L drive mapping to the shared directory for the department where she is testing the software. In this hands-on activity, you will enter a user login script for Kellie that contains a user-defined variable to map the L drive to the department directory she specifies by using the %2 login script variable.

1. If necessary, start your computer and log in using your assigned ##Admin username.

2. Note the error message generated when the computer attempts to map a drive to the ##Admin home directory. This is caused because there is not an ##Admin home directory in the IS directory structure. Later in this chapter, you will learn how to correct this problem using an IF statement.

3. Start NetWare Administrator.

4. Enter a MAP ROOT command in Kellie's login script as follows:

   a) If necessary, open a browse window for your ##UAS Organization.

   b) Double-click **KThiele** and click the **Login Script** button.

   c) Enter the following login script command in Kellie's login script window:

   ```
   MAP ROOT L:=UAS_HOST_CORP:##CORP\%2
   ```

   d) Click **OK** to save the changes.

5. To test her software, Kellie will need to have Read, Create, Write, Modify, and File Scan rights to the department Shared directories. In this step, you will check Kellie's effective rights to the Engineer\Shared directory, as follows:

   a) Open a browse window for the ##Corp\Engineer directory.

   b) Right-click the **Shared** directory and click the **Details** option.

   c) Click the **Trustees of this Directory** button.

   d) Click the **Effective Rights** button to display the Effective Rights dialog box.

   e) Click the **browse** button to display the Select Object dialog box.

   f) Double-click **KThiele** in the left-hand Available objects window and verify that Kellie has all rights to the Shared directory except Supervisor and Access Control. Click **Close** and **Cancel** to return to the NetWare Administrator browse window.

6. If Kellie does not have Read, Create, Write, Modify, and File Scan rights in the Engineer\Shared directory, you will need to give her these rights as follows:

   a) Right-click your **##Corp\Engineer\Shared** directory and click the **Details** option.

   b) Click the **Trustees of this Directory** button.

   c) Click the **Add Trustee** button to display the Select Object dialog box.

   d) Double-click the **ISMgrs** group to add it as a trustee.

   e) Click the **Read**, **Write**, **Create**, **Modify**, and **File Scan** rights.

   f) Click **OK** to save the trustee assignment.

7. Repeat Step 5 to check Kellie's effective rights.

8. Close NetWare Administrator and log out.

9. Log in as KThiele and specify the Engineer directory as follows:

   a) Enter **KThiele** in the Username field.

   b) If necessary, enter Kellie's password in the Password field.

   c) Click the **Advanced** button and click the **Script** tab.

   d) Remove the check from the **Close automatically** check box.

   e) Click the **Variables** button to display the Variables page.

   f) Enter **engineer** in the %2 field as shown in Figure 8-6.

   g) Click **OK** to return to the Script page.

10. Click **OK** to log in and display the Results screen shown in Figure 8-9. Notice that the drive mappings are not displayed after the CAPTURE command. This is because when a user has a personal login script, the client does not perform the default script. You will learn more about the order of login script execution later in this chapter.

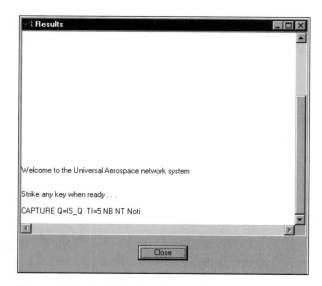

Figure 8-9   Kellie's Results window

11. Check your drive mappings as follows:

   a) Start Windows Explorer and click the plus symbol (+) to the left of the L drive. You should now see the Engineer Shared and CAD subdirectories.

   b) Close Windows Explorer.

12. Log out.

13. Log in as **KThiele** and set your L drive to the Mfg directory.

14. Use Windows Explorer to check your drive mappings. The L drive should now allow Kellie to see the Mfg\Shared directory.

15. Close Windows Explorer and log out.

Writing Login Script Commands

As described earlier, in many ways, creating login scripts is very similar to writing a computer program. As in any programming language, there are certain valid commands that can be used to cause the computer to perform certain processing. In addition, as with any programming language, when you are writing login script commands, you must follow certain rules for the commands to be processed. These rules are commonly referred to as the **syntax** of the programming language. In this section, you will learn about the valid syntax of each of the NetWare login script commands and see examples of how to use each command to perform common login functions. Before studying the login script commands, it is important to be aware of the following general rules that apply to all login script commands:

- You can place only valid login script command statements and comments in a login script file.

- Login script command lines can be a maximum of 150 characters.

- Long commands can be allowed to "wrap" to the next line if there is not enough room on one line.

- The Novell NetWare client reads the login script commands one line at a time, and only one command is allowed on any command line.

- Commands can be entered in either upper- or lowercase letters, except for variables that are enclosed in quotation marks which must be preceded by a percent sign (%) and typed in uppercase letters.

- You enter comments by preceding the text with either the command REM, an asterisk (*), or a semicolon (;).

CLS

The CLS command is used simply to clear the screen. Normally it is a good idea to precede messages by clearing the screen and then using the FIRE PHASERS command to make a sound that will get the users' attention and make the message easier to read. You may want to follow the message with another CLS to remove the message from the screen. If you do this, be sure to follow the message with a PAUSE; otherwise, the user will not get time to read it.

MAP

The MAP command is perhaps the most important login script command since it is necessary to use it to set up automatically both regular and search drive mappings that a user needs to access files and software in the NetWare environment. The syntax and use of the MAP login script command are very similar to that of the MAP command-line utility described in Chapter 3, except that with the login script version, you can use identifier variables and relative drive letters as part of the MAP command syntax, as follows:

    MAP [option] [drive:=path[;drive:=path]]

You can replace [option] with one of the parameters shown in Table 8-5.

Table 8-5   MAP Command Options

Optional Parameter	Description
ROOT	This option is used to make a drive appear as the root of a volume to DOS and application programs.
INS	This option is used with search drives to insert a new search drive at the sequence number you specify and then renumber any existing search drives.
DEL	This option is used to remove the specified regular or search drive mapping.

The [*drive:*] parameter must be replaced with a valid network, local, or search drive. In addition to using a specific drive letter, you can use a relative drive specification such as *1: to indicate the first network drive, *2: for the second network drive, and so on. If the workstation's first network drive letter is F, *1: will be replaced with F, and *2: will be replaced with G. On the other hand, if a workstation's first network drive is L, *1: will be replaced with L, and *2: will be replaced with J. Replace [*path*] with a full directory path beginning with a DOS drive letter or NetWare volume name.

With the login script version of the MAP command, you can place additional drive mappings on the same line by separating them with semicolons (;). For example, if you want to map the F drive to the SYS volume and the G drive letter to the DATA volume, you can do so by specifying the following MAP command: MAP F:=SYS:; G:=DATA:.

As described previously, login script variables can be included in the MAP statement. Commonly used variables include %LOGIN_NAME, %OS, %OS_VERSION, and %MACHINE. The %MACHINE, %OS, and %OS_VERSION variables are often used for DOS- and Windows 3.11–based clients to map a search drive to a specific DOS directory based on the version of DOS being used on the workstation logging in. The DOS requester or shell program determines the values for these variables. These variables often contain certain default values as described previously in Table 8-4. If you used the default values for %MACHINE, %OS, and %OS_VERSION when creating a directory structure for your DOS software versions as shown in Figure 8-10, you could use the following MAP command statement in a container login script to map the second search drive to the appropriate DOS version for the workstation currently logging in:

```
MAP S2:=SYS:PUBLIC\%MACHINE\%OS\%OS_VERSION
```

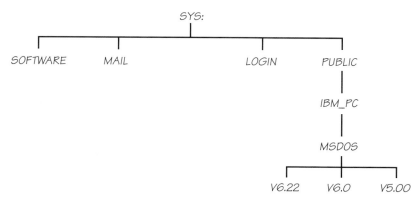

Figure 8-10   Sample DOS directory structure

 The DOS commands that come with Windows 95/98 are stored in the Windows\Command directory. It is not recommended to place them on the server.

Other special MAP command statements include MAP DISPLAY OFF and MAP ERRORS OFF. The MAP DISPLAY OFF command is used to prevent the MAP commands from displaying on the user workstation as they are executed. This MAP command is often included at the beginning of a login script command to reduce the amount of information that is displayed on the user workstations. You can use the MAP ERRORS OFF command to prevent error messages generated by MAP commands that specify invalid paths from being displayed on a user's workstation. This command is useful if you include drive mapping commands in a login script that you know will not be valid for all users. Rather than have users confused by receiving error messages that do not affect them, you can include the MAP ERRORS OFF command before the MAP commands that contain the invalid drive paths.

NO_DEFAULT

The NO_DEFAULT login script command prevents the default login script commands from being executed when users do not have their own login scripts. However, once you implement a login script system, running the default login script can cause multiple drive mappings and messages. As a result, it is important to include the NO_DEFAULT statement at the beginning of each container's login script to prevent the default script from running.

In this hands-on activity, you will modify your ##UAS container login script to include the NO_DEFAULT login script command and then test the command by logging back in as your ##Admin user and observing that the extra MAP commands are no longer being displayed.

1. If necessary, start your computer and log in using your assigned ##Admin username. Notice the MAP commands that are displayed after the CAPTURE command. These MAP commands are a result of the default login script being executed.

2. Start NetWare Administrator and if necessary, open a browse window for your ##UAS container.

3. Right-click your **##UAS** Organization and click the **Details** option.

4. Click the **Login Script** button to display your existing login script.

5. Add the following command to the beginning of your ##UAS container login script:

   NO_DEFAULT

6. Click **OK** to save the changes and return to the NetWare Administrator browse window.

7. Exit NetWare Administrator and log out.

8. Log in using your assigned ##Admin username. Notice that the extra MAP commands are no longer displayed after the CAPTURE command.

CONTEXT

As you learned in Chapter 2, accessing network resources is much easier when the current context of your client is set to the container that holds the objects you need to use. You usually do so by specifying the context using the Advanced button on the Novell Client login window. However, if a user logs in using his or her distinguished username, the current context of the client will not be changed. The CONTEXT login script command allows you to change the current context of the client computer to the default container when a user logs in. For example, to test software, Kellie often needs to log in from other users' workstations. To allow her to use her distinguished name rather than selecting the context from the Novell Client login window each time she logs in, you could include the CONTEXT .O=10UAS command in her personal login script.

In this hands-on activity, you will add the CONTEXT command to Kellie's user login script and then test the command by logging in using Kellie's distinguished username.

1. If necessary, log in using your assigned ##Admin username.

2. Start NetWare Administrator.

3. Double-click Kellie's **KThiele** username.

4. Click the **Login Script** button.

5. Add the following CONTEXT command to the beginning of Kellie's user login script:

   CONTEXT .O=##UAS.

6. Click **OK** to save the changes.

7. Exit NetWare Administrator and log out.

8. Assume you are at Ira Means's workstation and want to log in as Kellie. Take the following steps:

   a) To simulate being at Ira's workstation, at the login screen click the **Advanced** button and enter **.Engineering.##UAS** in the Context field.

   b) Enter Kellie's distinguished login name, **.KThiele.##UAS** and password, and click **OK** to log in.

c) Click **Continue** and notice that the context is changed from Engineering.##UAS to .##UAS.

d) Click **Close** to close the Results window.

9. Log out.

WRITE

The WRITE command is used to place simple messages enclosed in quotation marks (" ") on the screen of the workstation. In addition to including text, messages may also contain identifier variables and special control strings as described in the WRITE command syntax:

```
WRITE "text [control string] [%variable]"
```

Common login script variables that are often used with the WRITE statement include %GREETING_TIME and %FULL_NAME. The %GREETING_TIME variable contains the current time expressed as either "Morning", "Afternoon", or "Evening". For example, many network administrators include a WRITE statement with the following greeting message at the beginning of a login script to display the login time and the user's full name:

```
WRITE "Good %GREETING_TIME %FULL_NAME"
```

Important messages that you want to be sure all users see and acknowledge should be followed with the PAUSE statement, as follows:

```
WRITE "File server will be coming down today, March 1, at 5:00 p.m.,
for a maintenance call."
PAUSE
```

 In this hands-on activity, you will modify your ##UAS container login script to add a command that will write the greeting time prior to the welcome message.

1. If necessary, start your computer. Use the **Advanced** button on the login screen to change the context back to your ##UAS container, then log in using your assigned ##Admin username.

2. Start NetWare Administrator.

3. Right-click your **##UAS** container and click the **Details** option.

4. Click the **Login Script** button.

5. Add the following command immediately before your current Write statement:

   WRITE "Good %GREETING_TIME %FULL_NAME"

6. Click **OK** to save the login script change and return to the NetWare Administrator browse window.

7. Double-click your **##Admin** username.

8. Click the **Identification** button and enter in the Full Name field the name by which you want to be identified.

9. Click **OK** to save your change and return to the NetWare Administrator browse window.

10. Any user who has no entry in the Full Name field will have the word "Unknown" displayed in place of his or her full name. As a result, you should repeat Steps 7 and 8 for each of your users to make an entry in the Full Name field of each of your users.

11. Exit NetWare Administrator and log out.

12. Log in using your assigned ##Admin username and verify that your name is now displayed in the greeting.

13. Log out.

DISPLAY and FDISPLAY

The DISPLAY and FDISPLAY commands are used to show the contents of an ASCII text file on the screen during the execution of the login script. The proper syntax of either command is:

```
[F]DISPLAY [directory path] filename
```

If the *filename* specified is in the current directory, or if a search drive has been established to the directory containing the *filename*, the directory path is not needed. However, usually you will want to place messages in their own subdirectory and will therefore need to include the complete path along with the filename. For example, to show the WELCOME.MSG file stored in the PUBLIC\MESSAGE directory, you could place the FDISPLAY command in the container login script as follows:

```
MAP INS S1:=SYS:PUBLIC
FDISPLAY SYS:PUBLIC\MESSAGE\WELCOME.MSG
PAUSE
```

 An error message will be displayed if the file specified in the DISPLAY command does not exist.

It is important to follow the DISPLAY or FDISPLAY command with a PAUSE statement to allow the user time to read the message file. The difference between DISPLAY and FDISPLAY is that the FDISPLAY command "filters" and formats the contents of the specified filename so that only the ASCII text itself is displayed. FDISPLAY will not display tabs. The DISPLAY command, on the other hand, will display the exact characters contained in the file including "garbage" characters such as printer or word processing edit codes. As a result, it is generally preferred to use the FDISPLAY command when displaying files that have been created with word processing packages; however, if you use a word processing package, be sure to save the file in ASCII text format; otherwise, probably not even FDISPLAY will be able to read it.

For example, assume that the company president would like a daily reminder file that lists activities scheduled for each day of the week. The administrative assistant, Ira Means, would be responsible for maintaining files for the Engineering and Manufacturing users. The files would be located in the corresponding department's shared directory so all users have access to them. Assume that Kellie has agreed to maintain daily files for the IS department and modify the ##UAS container login script.

 In this hands-on activity, you will test the system by logging in using your ##Admin username and then creating simple text files for each day of the week in your ##Corp\Shared directory. You will then modify the ##UAS container login script to display the contents of the day's text file and finally test the system by logging back in as KThiele.

1. If necessary, start your computer and log in using your assigned ##Admin user name.

2. Start NetWare Administrator.

3. Use NetWare Administrator to create a Messages subdirectory within your ##Corp\Shared directory as follows:

   a) Open a browse window for your ##Corp\Shared directory.

   b) Create a subdirectory within your ##Corp\Shared directory named **Messages**.

4. Create a text file for Monday as follows:

   a) Click **File**, point to **New**, then click **Text Document** to create a text document named **Monday.txt**.

   b) Double-click the **Monday** text file and enter a brief message indicating that today is Monday.

   c) Save the document.

5. Repeat Step 4 to create text files named **Tuesday.txt**, **Wednesday.txt**, **Thursday.txt**, and **Friday.txt**. Close the Shared directory window.

6. Modify the ##UAS container login script to display the day's text file as follows:

   a) Start NetWare Administrator.

   b) Right-click your **##UAS** container and click the **Details** option.

   c) Click the **Login Script** button to display the existing login script.

   d) Enter the following commands at the end of the login script:

   ```
   CLS
   DISPLAY G:\Shared\Messages\%DAY_OF_WEEK.txt
   PAUSE
   ```

   e) Click **OK** to save the changes and return to the NetWare Administrator browse window.

   f) Exit NetWare Administrator.

7. Test your system by logging in as **KThiele** with **IS** in the %2 variable field. The day's message should be displayed in the Results window.

8. Close the Results window and use Windows Explorer to verify that the L: drive letter is mapped to the IS directory as specified by the %2 variable.

9. Log out.

(Execute a DOS Program)

The external program execution (#) command is used to load and run an .EXE or .COM program without exiting the Novell NetWare Client. Upon completion of the program, the next login script command line will be executed. The syntax of the # command is as follows:

```
# [path] filename [parameters]
```

You can optionally replace [*path*] with a full directory path using either a DOS drive letter or NetWare volume name to specify the location of the DOS program. If a network drive letter is used in the path, be sure a previous login script MAP command is used to map the drive letter to a valid NetWare path. You must replace *filename* with the name of the .COM or .EXE program you want executed. The extension is not needed. Depending upon the program you are running, you may replace [*parameters*] with any parameters that are to be passed to the specified program.

The external program execution character (#) is important because it lets you run other command-line utilities or DOS commands from inside the login script. For example, a common use of the # command is to run the CAPTURE program to establish a default network printer for DOS and Windows 3.11 clients. Since CAPTURE is not a login script command, the # command can be used to run the CAPTURE command with the appropriate parameters.

IF ...THEN ...ELSE

Many network administrators use the IF login statement to customize a login script for specific users or groups as well as to perform special processing when a certain condition such as a specific day, time, or station exits. The syntax of a simple IF statement is:

```
IF condition THEN command
```

The *condition* parameter is replaced with a conditional statement that has a value of either true or false. Conditional statements usually consist of an identifier variable and a value enclosed in quotation marks. Examples of several common conditional statements are shown in Table 8-6.

Table 8-6   Common Conditional Statements

Condition	Description
MEMBER OF "group"	This statement is true if the user is a member of the specified group.
DAY_OF_WEEK="Monday"	This statement is true if the name of the day is MONDAY. Possible values range from SUNDAY through SATURDAY. Upper- or lowercase letters may be used.
DAY="05"	This statement is true on the fifth day of the month; valid day values range from "01" to "31". It is necessary to include the leading zero for day numbers less than 9.
MONTH="June"	This statement would be true for the month of June. You can replace "June" with any valid month name from January to December. Either upper- or lowercase is accepted.
NDAY_OF_WEEK="1"	This statement is true on Sunday, which is the first day of the week. Valid weekday numbers range from "1" to "7".

The *command* parameter may be replaced with any valid login script command statement. For example, you can write a simple IF statement with a single condition as: IF DAY_OF_WEEK = "FRIDAY" THEN WRITE "Hurrah it's Friday!"

More complex IF statements can consist of multiple commands followed by the END statement. The syntax of a multiple statement IF command is:

```
IF condition THEN
        command 1
        command 2
        command n
    END
```

When you use a multiple-command IF statement, all commands between the IF statement and the END statement are performed when the condition is true. For example, to prevent the error message created when your ##UAS Organization's login script attempts to map a home directory when the ##Admin user logs in, you can use an IF command similar to the following:

```
IF MEMBER OF "ISMgrs" THEN BEGIN
    MAP ROOT H: = UAS_HOST_CORP:##CORP\IS\%LOGIN_NAME
END
```

Sometimes it is desirable to combine multiple conditions using AND or OR. When you use OR to connect two conditions, the login command statements will be performed if either condition is true. For example, if you want all members of either the Publishing or Sales groups to be informed of a weekly meeting, you could use the statement IF MEMBER OF "SALES" OR MEMBER OF "PUBLISH" in the previous IF statement.

The word AND is used when you want both statements to be true before processing the commands. For example, suppose you want to remind all Sales users of a meeting on Friday morning. Before displaying the reminder, you would want to make sure the user is a member of the Business department, the day is Friday, and the login time is before noon. To do this, you could use AND to connect these three conditions with the statement IF MEMBER OF "SALES" AND DAY_OF_WEEK="FRIDAY" AND HOUR24 < "12" THEN.

The optional word ELSE is an important feature of the IF statement because it allows you to perform either one set of commands or another based on the condition. For example, the following ...IF...ELSE command could be used if all members of the Sales department need to have their I drive pointer mapped to the Engineer\Shared directory, whereas all other users should have their I drive pointer mapped to the Business\Shared directory:

```
IF MEMBER OF "SALES" THEN
  MAP I: = UAS_HOST_CORP:ENGINEER\SHARED
ELSE
  MAP I: = UAS_HOST_CORP:BUSINESS\SHARED
END
```

In this hands-on activity, you will correct the error message received when logging in using your ##Admin username. You will modify your ##UAS Organization's login script to map drive H to the user's home directory only when the user logging in is a member of the ISMgrs group.

1. If necessary, start your computer and log in using your assigned ##Admin username.

2. Start NetWare Administrator.

3. Right-click your **##UAS** container and click the **Details** option.

4. Click the **Login Script** button.

5. Add IF and END commands around your drive mapping to the user's home directory as shown here:

```
IF Member of "ISMgrs" THEN BEGIN
     MAP ROOT H:=UAS_HOST_CORP:##CORP\IS\%LOGIN_NAME
END
```

6. Click **OK** to save the changes.

7. Exit NetWare Administrator and log out.

8. Log in as the user **KThiele**.

9. Start Windows Explorer and verify that your H drive is mapped to Kellie's home directory.

10. Exit Windows Explorer and log out.

11. Log in using your assigned ##Admin username. Notice that no drive mapping error message is received.

DRIVE

The DRIVE command is used to set the default drive for DOS and Windows 3.11 clients to use after the user logs in. The proper syntax for the DRIVE command is:

```
DRIVE drive:
```

You need to replace *drive* with either a local or a network drive letter. If a network drive letter is being used, be sure the drive letter has been mapped to a directory path where the user has the necessary access rights. Most network administrators use the DRIVE command near the end of the login script to place the user in either their home directory drive, or a drive location from which the menu system is run.

The DRIVE statement has no effect on Windows 95, 98, or NT clients.

EXIT

The EXIT command stops execution of the login script and returns control to the client computer. Because the EXIT command ends login script program execution and returns control to the client computer, no additional login script commands will be processed after the EXIT command is executed. When working with DOS and Windows 3.11 clients, you can also use the EXIT command to pass a command to DOS. For example, you can use the EXIT command to start Windows automatically by using the following syntax:

```
EXIT "WIN"
```

You can replace "WIN" with any statement up to a maximum length of 14 characters you want passed to the DOS command prompt.

FIRE PHASERS

The purpose of the FIRE PHASERS command is to make a noise with the PC speaker to alert the operator of a message or condition encountered in the login process. You can control the length of the phaser blast by including a sound with the following command:

```
FIRE [PHASERS] n [TIMES]
```

You can replace *n* with a number from 1 to 9 representing how many successive times the phaser sound will be made. The words PHASERS and TIMES are optional and may be omitted from the FIRE login script command. The FIRE PHASERS command is often used with the IF statement to notify the user of a certain condition. For example, you could use the FIRE PHASERS statement in a nested IF statement to remind the user of a special meeting time, as follows:

```
IF DAY_OF_WEEK = "Tuesday" AND "HOUR24" < "11" THEN
    WRITE "Department meeting at 11:30"
    FIRE PHASERS 2 TIMES
    PAUSE
END
IF LOGIN_NAME = "SUPERVISOR" THEN
    FIRE 5
END
```

REM

The REM command may be used along with either the asterisk (*) or the semicolon (;) to place a comment line in the login script. The login process will skip any line that begins with REM, REMARK, *, or ;. Using comments in your login script can make the script much easier for you or another administrator to read and understand. Placing a comment on the same line as other login script commands will cause errors when the script is executed. It is a good idea to use REM statements to proceed your login script with a brief description along with a comment identifying the function of each section in the script, as shown later in this chapter.

SET

The SET command may be used to place values in the DOS environment space for later use by programs or batch files. Each value placed in the DOS environment space can be assigned to a variable name as shown in the following syntax:

```
[DOS] SET variable="value"
```

The *variable* parameter must be replaced with a unique and meaningful name that represents the data to be stored. The variable name must consist of a single word with eight or less characters. You can replace *"value"* with any character string or with a login script variable preceded by a percent sign (%). The word DOS is optional and may be omitted from the SET login script command.

Profile Login Scripts

The purpose of a profile login script is to allow you to create a standard set of login commands that only certain selected users will perform. You set up profile login scripts by creating a Profile object in a container and then entering the login script command into the Login Script property of the Profile object.

Because profile login scripts are not a property of the container object, they have the advantage of being available to users in any container by providing the users with Read property rights to the Profile object's Login Script property.

For example, as identified in Chapter 5, all users in the WebMgr group (currently KThiele, CBotsford, CKent, and your username) have access to the IS\Web directory. To make accessing the files in the Web directory easier, Julie has recommended assigning drive printer I (for *Internet*) to the directory for all the users who need to work with the Web directory. Rather than placing these MAP commands in the UAS, Engineering, and Business container login scripts, it will be easier for you to create a Profile object in your ##UAS container that contains the commands that are common to all users in the WebMgr group. To allow users to use the profile login script, you next use NetWare Administrator to give the WebMgr group the Read property right to the Profile object's Login Script property. You can now assign the Profile object to the Profile Login Script property of each user of the Desktop Publishing and Engineering departments.

 In this hands-on activity, you will create a Profile object named WebProfile in your ##UAS container and then assign the object to Kellie Thiele's login script.

1. If necessary, start your computer and log in using your assigned ##Admin username.

2. Start NetWare Administrator and open a browse window for your ##UAS container.

3. Create a Profile object named WebProfile that maps drive I to the IS\Web directory, as follows:

   a) Click your **##UAS** container and click the **Create a new object** icon from the toolbar to display the New Object dialog box.

   b) Scroll down and double-click the **Profile** object to display the Create Profile dialog box.

   c) Enter **WebProfile** in the Profile name field and click the **Define additional properties** button.

   d) Click the **Create** button to create the new WebProfile object and display the Profile Identification dialog box.

   e) Click the **Login Script** button.

   f) Click in the login script window and enter the following command:

      MAP ROOT I:=UAS_HOST_CORP:##Corp\IS\Web

   g) Click **OK** to save the login script and return to the NetWare Administrator window.

4. Grant the WebMgr group rights to read the Path property:

   a) Right-click the **WebProfile** object and click the **Trustees of this Object** option.

   b) Click the **Add Trustee** button to display the Select Object dialog box.

   c) Double-click the **WebMgr** group from the left-hand Available objects window. Notice that by default the WebMgr group is given Read and Compare rights to All properties, which includes the Path property.

   d) Click **Read** to remove the Read right from All properties.

   e) Click the **Selected properties** option and scroll down to the Path property.

   f) Click the **Path** property and then click the **Read** right. Notice that a check mark is placed to the left of the Path property.

   g) Click **OK** to save the trustee assignment and return to the NetWare Administrator browse window.

5. Assign the WebProfile object to Kellie:

   a) Double-click **KThiele** and click the **Login Script** button.

   b) Click the **browse** button to the right of the Profile field to display the Select Object dialog box.

   c) Double-click the **WebProfile** object from the left-hand Available objects window to place WebProfile in the Profile field as shown in Figure 8-11.

   d) Click **OK** to save the profile script assignment and return to the NetWare Administrator browse window.

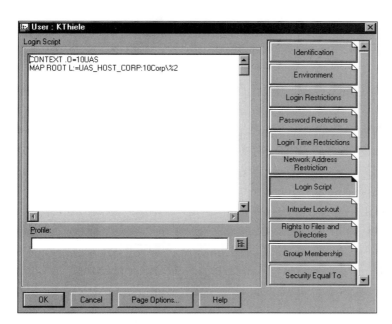

Figure 8-11   Specifying a profile for Kellie

6. Repeat Step 5 to assign the WebProfile object to JDamRau.

7. Exit NetWare Administrator and log out.

8. Log in as **KThiele**.

9. Start Windows Explorer and verify that drive I is mapped to the IS/Web directory.

10. Exit Windows Explorer and log out.

IMPLEMENTING LOGIN SCRIPTS

Once you understand the syntax and function of the login script commands along with the way in which login scripts are stored and executed, the next task is to apply login scripts to setting up a network environment for each user's workstation when he or she logs in. Implementing a login script system for your network requires three basic steps:

1. Identify the login script requirements for each container and user.

2. Write and enter the script commands.

3. Test the login script by logging in as various users.

In this section, you will learn how to apply these steps by implementing login scripts for the users in the Engineering department.

Identifying Login Script Requirements

To design a login script system for Universal Aerospace, the consultant, Jennifer, started by identifying the user drive mapping, non-NDPS printer queue usage, and messages, as shown in Figure 8-12.

Drive Mappings				
Users	Drive	Path	Container Script	Profile Script Name/Context
All	F:	UAS_HOST_SYS:	All containers	
All	G:	UAS_HOST_CORP:##Corp	All containers	
All	S1:	UAS_HOST_SYS:Public	All containers	
Engineering	H:	UAS_HOST_CORP:##Corp\Engineer\login_name	Engineering Container	
Engineering	L:	UAS_HOST_CORP:##Corp\Engineer	Engineering Container	
Uas.Mfg	H:	UAS_HOST_CORP:##Corp\Mfg\login_name	.uas.Mfg Container	
Uas.Mfg	L:	UAS_HOST_CORP:##Corp\Mfg	.uas.Mfg Container	
Engineering and Uas.Mfg users	S:	UAS_HOST_CORP:##Corp\Engineer\Shared		EngShared Engineering.## UAS
Design group	P:	UAS_HOST_CORP:##Corp\Manuals	Engineering Container	

Non-NDPS Printers		
Users	Port	Print Queue
UAS.Mfg	LPT1	##MFG-HP5si-Q

Messages				
Users	Description	Container Script	Profile Script/Context
All	Login greeting message	All Containers	
All	Display a daily message file (monday.msg, tuesday.msg, ...) created by Lynn Dai and stored in the Corp:##UAS\Shared\Message directory.	All Containers	
Engineering	Weekly design meeting on Monday morning at 9:00 a.m.	Engineering container	
Engineering and UAS.Mfg	Monthly meeting held at 9:00 a.m. on the first Wednesday of each month to discuss documentation and promotional needs		EngShared/ Engineering.## UAS

Figure 8-12   Engineering/Manufacturing login requirements

The first section identifies the standard drive mappings for use on the network as well as the name of the container or profile login script where the mapping will be performed. Drive letters such as F, G, and S1 are common to all users in the company and are therefore included in all container scripts. Notice that the H and L drive mappings are dependent upon department and are therefore different in the Engineering and UAS.Mfg container login scripts. Jennifer has also identified a profile login script named EngShared to be used to provide users in both Mfg and Engineering containers with common login script commands and messages. Notice that in addition to including a common drive letter for each volume, each container login script will map an H drive to the user's home directory and an L drive to the department's directory.

The "Non-NDPS Printers" section is used to define print queues that CAPTURE commands will automatically assign to the indicated printer port when the users log in. Because the client computer handles NDPS printers, no login scripts commands are necessary for them.

The "Messages" section defines any message needs for each group of users along with the login script where the message will be placed. Notice that the EngShared profile login script will be used to send a message to users in both the Engineering and Mfg containers regarding the weekly meeting.

Writing Login Scripts

After you have identified login requirements, the next step is to plan and write the necessary login script commands. To write the login script commands for the Engineering container, Jennifer used login script worksheets as shown in Figure 8-13.

Container Login Script Form (Page 1 of 2)
Designer: Jennifer Almquest, Consultant
Date:
Container Context: Engineering.##UAS
REM Preliminary Commands *NO_DEFAULT* *MAP DISPLAY OFF* *MAP INS S1:=UAS_HOST_SYS:PUBLIC* *CLS* *WRITE "Good%GREETING_TIME, %LOGIN_NAME"* *DISPLAY UAS_HOST_CORP:##Corp\SHARED\MESSAGES\%DAY_OF_WEEK.MSG* *PAUSE*
REM DOS Setup *SET UNAME="%LOGIN_NAME"* *SET STATION="%STATION"*
REM Common Application *CONTEXT .Engineering.##UAS* *MAP F:=UAS_HOST_SYS:* *MAP ROOT G:=UAS_HOST_CORP:##Corp* *MAP ROOT H:=G:ENGINEER\%LOGIN_NAME* *MAP ROOT L:=EngData*
REM Mapping for <u>Design</u>_____**Workgroup** *IF MEMBER OF "DESIGN" THEN* *   MAP ROOT P:=UAS_HOST_CORP:##Corp\MANUALS* *END*
REM End of Login Script Commands *DRIVE H:*

Figure 8-13   Login script worksheets

Container Login Script Form (Page 2 of 2)
Container Context: UAS.Mfg.##UAS
REM Preliminary Commands *NO_DEFAULT* *MAP DISPLAY OFF* *MAP INS S1:=UAS_HOST_SYS:PUBLIC* *CLS* *WRITE "Good%GREETING_TIME, %LOGIN_NAME"* *DISPLAY UAS_HOST_CORP:##Corp\SHARED\MESSAGES\%DAY_OF_WEEK.MSG* *PAUSE*
REM DOS Setup *SET UNAME="%LOGIN-NAME"* *SET STATION="%STATION"*
REM Common Application *CONTEXT .UAS.Mfg.##UAS* *MAP F:=UAS_HOST_SYS:* *MAP ROOT G:=UAS_HOST_CORP:##Corp* *MAP ROOT H:=G:Mfg/%LOGIN_NAME* *MAP ROOT L:=MfgData* *#CAPTURE Q=##MFG-HP5si-Q NB NT TI=5 NFF*
REM Mapping for _____ Workgroup
REM End of Login Script Commands *DRIVE H:*

Figure 8-13   Login script worksheets (continued)

The worksheets are divided into sections using REM statements to define the start of each section. The "Preliminary Commands" section contains any initializing commands such as NO_DEFAULT, MAP DISPLAY OFF, and MAP S1:=UAS_HOST_SYS:PUBLIC. In addition, this section can be used to clear the screen and display a greeting message to the user. Notice how the CLS command is used to clear the screen prior to displaying messages. Use the "DOS Setup" section if you are planning to map a search drive to a network DOS directory or include any SET commands needed to store information in the workstation environment space. In the example, SET commands are included to store such workstation information as username, connection number, and station address. This information will then be available for use in batch files.

The "Common Application" section contains drive mappings and printer redirection commands for all users in the container. Notice the use of the EngData Directory Map object created in Chapter 4 to map drive L to the Engineer structure. Using the Directory Map object would allow the Engineer directory to be changed to another volume without modifying the login script. In addition to the drive mappings, notice the #CAPTURE command used in the Mfg container script to redirect output from LPT1 to the ##MFG-HP5si-Q print queue for Manufacturing users.

The "Mapping for Workgroup" sections are used to contain login script commands that are performed only for users who are members of the specified groups. In the Engineering container form, if a user is a member of the Design workgroup, he or she will receive a P drive mapping to the Publish\Shared directory.

The "End of Login Script Commands" section may be used to contain any commands that all users will perform before exiting the login script. In the example, the DRIVE H: command will place all users in their home directory before exiting the container login script.

Figure 8-14 shows the profile script form developed by Jennifer for the Engineering department's EngShared profile. The form identifies the profile login script commands along with the name of the profile and all users to whom the profile is to be assigned. The form for the EngShared profile script maps a root drive S to the Shared Engineering directory and includes a reminder for the weekly meeting. Notice that the profile script is to be assigned to all users in the Engineering department as well as Russ Pence from the Mfg department.

Profile Login Script Form		
Created by: Jennifer Almquest, Consultant		
Date:		
Container Context: Engineering.##UAS		
Profile Object Name: EngShared		
Users:		
IMeans	LJarka	TRucci
RPence	PAlm	

MAP S:=UAS_HOST_CORP:##Corp\Engineer\Shared
 	
IF DAY_OF-WEEK="Monday" AND HOUR24 < "09"THEN
    FIRE 2
    WRITE "Remember meeting at 9:00 a.m. in Conference Room 100"
    PAUSE
END		

Figure 8-14   Profile script worksheet

Entering Login Scripts

Defining and writing the login script commands can be the most difficult part of setting up the user environment, especially if you're not a programmer. Although the Engineering login scripts have been written for you, in the projects at the end of the chapter, you will get the opportunity to create your own login script programs for the Business users. Once the login script programs have been completed, you can begin the relatively fun part of using the NetWare utilities to enter, test, and print each of your login scripts. As a CNA, you will need to learn how to use NetWare Administrator to implement and maintain container, profile, and user login scripts. In this section, you will use NetWare Administrator to enter and print each of the login scripts created for the Engineering container.

 It is important to realize that despite your best efforts, network administrators are human (well, most of them anyway) and make mistakes. As you know, computers are very intolerant of errors, and as a result, you can expect to receive some error messages and encounter commands that do not work correctly the first time. As a result, some tips to help you test and debug your login scripts are provided in the next section.

Entering the Container Login Script

The first task in setting up your login script system is to enter and test the container login scripts. After you have the container login scripts working correctly, you can proceed to enter and test the profile and user login scripts.

In this hands-on activity, you use NetWare Administrator to enter and print the container login script commands for the Engineering and UAS.Mfg containers.

1. If necessary, start your computer and log in using your assigned ##Admin username.

2. Start NetWare Administrator and open a browse window for your ##UAS container.

3. Enter the Engineering container login script as follows:

   a) Right-click the **Engineering** container and select the **Details** option to display the Identification window.

   b) Click the **Login Script** window and enter the login script commands shown in Figure 8-13.

   c) Click **OK** to save the container login script and return to the browse window. Check for UAS_HOST_CORP and UAS_HOST_SYS volume objects in the Engineering container and create them if necessary.

4. Enter the UAS.Mfg container login script shown in Figure 8-13 as follows:

   a) Open your **Mfg** container by double-clicking it.

   b) Right-click the **UAS** container located within your Mfg container and select the **Details** option to display the Identification window.

   c) Click the **Login Script** window and enter the login script commands shown in Figure 8-13.

   d) Click **OK** to save the container login script and return to the browse window. Check for UAS_HOST_CORP and UAS_HOST_SYS volume objects in the Engineering container and create them if necessary.

5. Minimize your NetWare Administrator window.

6. Document your Engineering and Mfg container login scripts as follows:

   a) Open a DOS window.

   b) To print the Engineering container login script, first change your default context to your ##UAS container by entering the following commands:

   ```
   F: [Enter]
   CX .10UAS [Enter]
   ```

   c) Print your Engineering container login script by entering the following command:

   ```
   NLIST "Organizational Unit" = Engineering SHOW "Login Script" > PRN
   ```

   d) Print your Mfg container login script by entering the following commands:

   ```
   CX mfg
   NLIST "Organizational Unit" = .UAS.Mfg SHOW "Login Script" > PRN
   ```

   e) Type **EXIT** and press **[Enter]** to return to Windows.

Entering the Profile Login Script

Entering a Profile login script requires that you first create a Profile object and then assign the user the Read property right to the Login Script property.

In this hands-on activity, you use NetWare Administrator to create the EngShared Profile object, assign all users Read rights to the Login Script property, and then enter and print the login script commands.

1. Restore NetWare Administrator.

2. Create the EngShared Profile object as follows:

   a) Highlight the **Engineering** container and press **[Ins]** to display the New Object dialog box.

   b) Double-click the **Profile** object type to display the Create Profile dialog box.

   c) Enter the profile name **EngShared** and click the **Define Additional Properties** check box.

   d) Click **Create** to create the Profile object and display the Identification window.

   e) Click **Login Script** to display the Login Script dialog box.

   f) Click the **Login Script** dialog box and enter the EngShared profile login script shown in Figure 8-14.

   g) Click **OK** to save the profile script and return to the browse window.

3. Provide all users in the Engineering and Mfg containers with Read rights to All properties of the EngShared Profile object as follows:

   a) Right-click the **EngShared** object and click the **Trustees of this Object** option to display the Trustees window.

   b) Click **Add Trustee** to display the Select Object dialog box.

   c) Double-click the **up arrow** in the right-hand browse context window until your Engineering and Mfg containers appear in the left-hand Available objects window.

   d) **[Ctrl]-click** to select both the Engineering and Mfg containers in the left-hand Objects window, and then click **OK** to add them to the Trustees window.

   e) Click **OK** to save the changes and return to the browse window.

   f) Minimize NetWare Administrator.

4. Document the EngShared profile login script as follows:

   a) Open a DOS window.

   b) To print the Profile login script, first change your default context to your Engineering container by typing the following command:

   ```
   CX   .Engineering.##UAS [Enter]
   ```

   c) Enter the following command:

   ```
   NLIST Profile = EngShared SHOW "Login Script" > PRN
   ```

   d) Type **EXIT** and press **[Enter]** to return to Windows.

5. Attach the EngShared profile script to the users indicated on the Profile Login Script worksheet in Figure 8-14 as follows:

   a) Restore NetWare Administrator and double-click **IMeans**.

   b) Click the **Login Script** button.

   c) Click the **browse** button to the right of the Profile script field to display the Select Object dialog box.

   d) Use the Browse context window to navigate to the Engineering container.

   e) Double-click the **EngShared** Profile object.

   f) Click **OK** to save the profile script assignment.

   g) Repeat this process for LJarka, TRucci, PAlm, and RPence.

   h) Exit NetWare Administrator.

6. Log out.

Testing and Debugging Login Scripts

After the login scripts have been entered, you should proceed to test the login script for each container by logging in as a user within that container and then checking to be sure all commands are executed properly. When testing login scripts, do not be discouraged if everything does not work correctly the first time. Although proper planning and design can eliminate many possible problems, small errors due to missing or invalid login script commands, incorrect paths, or lack of user access rights can still be irritating. In this section, you will test the login scripts for the Engineering and Mfg containers and correct any problems.

In this hands-on activity, you test the Engineering container login script by logging in as Lianne Jarka and then verifying drive mappings and printer assignments.

1. Log in as **LJarka**. (Click the **Advanced** button and change the context to **.Engineering.##UAS**, then click **OK** to login.)

2. Use My Computer to check your drive mappings.

3. Use My Computer to check printer redirection.

4. Log out.

A frequent problem when testing login scripts is receiving invalid drive mapping messages. The most common causes for invalid drive messages are either an incorrectly typed path statement in the login script, or insufficient rights for the user in the specified directory path. For example, earlier in this chapter, you created an EngShared profile login script to allow Engineering and Manufacturing users such as Russ Pence to access the Engineer\Shared directory. However, in Chapter 5, Russ Pence was not given access rights to the Engineer\Shared directory and will receive an invalid drive path message when he logs in.

In this hands-on activity, you log in as the user RPence and observe the results of the attempt to map a drive to the Engineer\Shared directory. You then correct the problem by assigning Russ access rights to the directory and finally test your fix by again logging in as Russ.

1. Log in as **RPence**. Notice the error messages as a result of the attempt to map the S drive to the Engineer\Shared directory.

2. Log out of the network.

3. Log in using your ##Admin username.

4. Start NetWare Administrator.

5. Give Russ Pence Read and File Scan rights to the Engineer\Shared directory structure.

6. Exit NetWare Administrator, then log out of the network.

7. Log in as Russ.

8. Verify that the S drive is now mapped to the Engineer\Shared directory.

9. Log out.

CHAPTER SUMMARY

❑ Establishing a workstation environment that makes the network easy to use is one of the primary responsibilities of a network administrator. NetWare provides a powerful way to automate workstation setups through the use of login scripts. NetWare login scripts contain the login script commands used to provide the necessary drive mappings and other workstation setup functions during the login process. Novell has provided a set of commands that may be included in login script files. These commands may be used to map drive letters, set the DOS environment of a workstation, display messages and files, execute other programs, as well as execute certain commands based on whether a given condition is true or false. The use of login script variables with commands allows you to create general-purpose login scripts that work for multiple users.

❏ Login script variables can be divided into several types including date variables such as DAY_OF_WEEK, time variables such as HOUR24, user variables such as LOGIN_NAME, and workstation variables such as OS and OS_VERSION. A common example of using a login script command with a variable is mapping a drive pointer to the home directory of each user by including a command such as MAP ROOT H:=DATA:USERS\%LOGIN_NAME in the login script. The percent sign ahead of a variable name tells NetWare to substitute the value of the variable into the login script command when it is executed.

❏ The Novell NetWare client software can execute four types of NetWare login scripts: the container login script, the profile login script, the user login script, and the default login script. The container login script is a property of the container object and its commands are executed first by all users in that container when they log in. After the container login script has completed, the login script processor looks in the user's object to determine whether the user is assigned to a Profile object. If a Profile object is identified, the login script commands in the Profile object are executed. Last, the system checks for commands in the user Login Script property. If no user login script exists, the login script processor executes the default login script commands stored in the client software. Whenever possible, login script commands should be stored in the container login script. By including the NO_DEFAULT command in the container login script, you can prevent NetWare from executing the default login script statements. If you place the EXIT command at the end of the container login script, the login script processing ends and no profile, user, or default login scripts will be executed. Creating a login script for each user prevents the default login script from running and provides additional security.

❏ The NetWare Administrator utility is used to maintain container, profile, and user login scripts. You create and maintain the container login script by selecting the Login Script property of a container. Implementing a profile login script requires creating a Profile object and then granting users the Read property right to the Login Script property. You create and maintain the user login script by first selecting the user object and then clicking the Login Script button from the Details option. When you are testing login scripts, it is important for the user to have access rights to the directory paths in the MAP statements. By default, only the container in which the server is located is made a trustee of its SYS:Public directory. As a result, a common problem in implementing login scripts for users who are not in the same container as the server is not having rights to the SYS:Public directory. You can easily solve this problem by making the parent container for all users a trustee of the server's SYS volume with Read and File Scan rights.

COMMAND SUMMARY

Command	Syntax	Definition
#	# [path] filename[parameters]	Executes the specified DOS program and returns control back to the login script program.
CONTEXT	CONTEXT context	Specifies the NDS context for the client.
CLS	CLS	Clears the Results window.

DISPLAY	DISPLAY [*directory*] *filename*	Types the contents of the specified file to the screen. If the filename specified is not in the current directory or search drive, include the full NetWare path to the specified filename. DISPLAY will display all characters in the file including tabs and other printer control characters.
DRIVE	DRIVE *drive:*	Sets the specified drive letter as the default DOS drive. Unless you specify this command, the default drive will be set to the first network drive letter, usually F.
EXIT	EXIT *command*	Ends the login script processing and exits the login process. You can replace *command* with a DOS command you want executed after completing the login process.
FDISPLAY	FDISPLAY [*path*] *filename*	Like the DISPLAY command, types the contents of the specified file to the screen; however, the FDISPLAY command will "filter" any tab or printer control characters, making files that contain these control characters more readable.
FIRE PHASERS	FIRE [PHASERS] *n* [TIMES]	Produces a phaser sound on the PC speakers the number of times specified, up to nine.
IF THEN ELSE	IF *condition(s)* THEN *command* ELSE *command* END	Allows you to specify commands that execute only when the specified condition is true. Commands following the ELSE command will be executed if the condition is false. Each IF statement must conclude with an END statement and may contain up to 10 additional nested IF statements.
MAP	MAP [*option*] [drive:=path [; drive=path]]	Creates both regular and search drive mappings from the login script. The path statement may contain identifier variables preceded by percent signs such as %MACHINE, %OS, %OS_VERSION, and %LOGIN_NAME. Special MAP commands include MAP DISPLAY OFF/ON and MAP ERRORS OFF/ON.
NO_DEFAULT	NO_DEFAULT	Prevents the default login script commands from being executed.
PAUSE or WAIT	PAUSE or WAIT	Suspends login script processing until the user presses any key to continue.
REM	REM [*text*] * [*text*] ; [*text*] REMARK [*text*]	Allows comments to be placed in the loging script files.
SET	[DOS] SET *variable*="*value*"	Allows you to place a value in the DOS environment space using the specified variable name. Example: DOS SET PROMPT="pg".

| **WRITE** | WRITE *"text"* | Displays the message string enclosed in quotation marks on the console. Special control codes such as /r for a new line along with identifier variables preceded by percent signs may be included within the quotation marks. |

KEY TERMS

container login script — A login script that is a property of a container object and executed by all users in that container when they log in to the network.

date variables — Login script variables that contain date information such as month, name, day of week, and year.

default login script — Commands stored in the Novell NetWare client which are executed when a user does not have a personal user login script file.

identifier variables — Login script variables that may be used in login script commands to represent such information as the user login name, date, time, and DOS version.

logical variables — Login script variables that have a value of true or false.

login script — A set of commands that are executed when a user successfully logs in to the network.

login script variable — A reserved word in the login script language with a variable value special to the user.

profile login script — NDS objects containing login commands common to multiple users.

syntax — Rules to be followed when writing login script commands.

time variables — Login script variables that contain system time information such as hour, minute, and a.m. or p.m.

user-defined variables — Variables named %1 through %9 that enable users to enter values to be processed by the login script using the Advanced button of the login window.

user login script — Specialized commands that are part of a user object and are executed after the system login script by only a single user.

user variables — Login script variables that contain information about the currently logged in user, such as the user's login name, full name, or user ID.

workstation variables — Login script variables that contain information about the workstation's environment such as machine type, operating system, operating system version, and station node address.

REVIEW QUESTIONS

1. On the following lines, briefly describe the importance of login scripts:

   _____

   _____

2. The NO_DEFAULT command would most likely be found in the _____ login script file.

3. The _____ command would be used to write the contents of an ASCII text file to the display screen.

4. The _____ command is used to display a brief message on the screen.

5. The _____ login script is executed first to standardize the environment for all users in a department directory.

6. The _____ login script is used to provide drive mappings and other setup commands that are common to users in multiple containers.

7. The default login script is executed if there is no _____ login script.

8. The _____ command can be used to stop the default login script from being executed when there is no user login script.

9. In addition to the command used in Question 8, list two other ways you can prevent the default login script commands from being executed:

   _____

   _____

10. Suppose the first network drive on your workstation is L. What drive letter would the MAP *3:=DATA login script command use to access the DATA volume?

    _____

11. In the following space, write a login script command that would display a welcome message containing today's date, including the name of the day, the month, the day, and the year.

    _____

    _____

12. In the following space, write a condition that could be used to determine whether a user is logging in on the third day of the week.

    _____

    _____

13. In the following space, write a MAP command that uses identifier variables to map H as a root drive pointer to the user's home directory located in the DATA:Users directory path.

    _____

    _____

    _____

14. The _____ login script command can be used to change the default drive to the user's home directory on drive H.

15. Assume the home directories for the Sales department are stored in the DATA: Sales\Users directory, and the home directories for the Accounting department are stored in the DATA:Acct directory. Write an IF statement for the container login script that will map H as a root drive to the correct home directory path for each Sales department user.

    _____

    _____

    _____

16. Identify and correct any errors in each of the following login script commands:

    ```
    TURN MAP DISPLAY OFF
    MAP S2=SYS\PUBLIC\%MACHINE\%OS\%OSVERSION
    COMSPEC=S2:\COMMAND.COM
    CAPTURE Q=BUS_HP3_R0_Q1 TI=5 NT NB NFF
    WRITE "Good %Greeting_Time," %Login_name
    ```

17. A user object can have a maximum of _____ profile login scripts associated with it.

18. Identify the sequence that the following login scripts would be executed, by placing a number in front of the login script type.

    _____ Default   _____ Container

    _____ User   _____ Profile

19. To run a profile login script, a user needs to have _____ rights to the _____ property of the Profile object.

20. Write an IF statement that would map drive letter M as a root drive to each user's home directory of the CORP\Mktg structure for all users who are members of the Marketing group.

    _____

The Universal Aerospace Project

Management is happy that already some of the users are logging in and beginning to use the network mail system. However, network usage is hampered because users cannot access network printers and data without proper drive pointer mappings. As a result, to get the Engineering users up and running with their applications, you have been working with the consultant, Jennifer, to develop and implement a login script system. This system is now working well for the Engineering and Manufacturing users; they can log in, start Windows, and get access to their network directories and printers. Your next task is to use what you have learned in setting up the Engineering department to implement login scripts for the users in the Business department. In the following steps of the Universal Aerospace project, you will set up and test container, profile, and user login scripts for the Business department.

Step 1: Writing the Business Container Login Script

In this phase of the project, you will apply what you learned in this chapter to writing a login script for the Business container. To do this, you will need to obtain a container login script form from the instructor (or see Appendix B) and refer to the login script requirements shown in Figure 8-15. Be sure to include a command that will display the daily message file as in the Engineering container script. Notice that each department will need a special workgroup section to map the L drive to the department's directory and set up default printer redirection. Use the Directory Map objects you created in Chapter 3 to map drive letters to each department's directory.

8

Drive Mappings			
Users	**Drive**	**Path**	**Script**
All	F:	UAS_HOST_SYS:	All containers
All	G:	UAS_HOST_CORP:##Corp	All containers
All	S1:	UAS_HOST_SYS:Public	All containers
Accounting	H: L:	UAS_HOST_CORP:##Corp\Business\login_name UAS_HOST_CORP:##Corp\Business	Business container
Publish	H: L:	UAS_HOST_CORP:##Corp\Publish\login_name UAS_HOST_CORP:##Corp\Publish	Business container
Marketing	H: L:	UAS_HOST_CORP:##Corp\Sales\login_name UAS_HOST_CORP:##Corp\Sales	Business container
Desktop	L:	UAS_HOST_CORP:##Corp\Publish	Business container
Publish	S:	UAS_HOST_CORP:##Corp\Engineer\Shared	EngShared profile script
Julie DamRau Lynn Dai Kellie Thiele	I:	UAS_HOST_CORP:##Corp\IS\Web	WebMgr profile script
Accounting	P:	UAS_HOST_CORP:##Corp\Business|Accting	Business container
Marketing	L:	UAS_HOST_CORP:##Corp\Sales	Business container
Ira Means Laura Hiller Terry Blackwell	T:	Inventory system	INVAPP profile script

Non-NDPS Printers		
Users	**Port**	**Print Queue**
Accounting	LPT1	BUS_HP3-1_Q

Messages			
Users	**Description**	**Container Script**	**Profile Script/Context**
Sales Group	Weekly sales meeting on Wednesday at 11:30 a.m.	Business container	Web Mgr profile script
WebMgr group	Monthly design meeting on the first Monday of each month from 8:00 a.m. until 9:00 a.m.		

Figure 8-15   Business/Marketing login script requirements

Step 2: Writing Profile Login Scripts

On the Business/Marketing script requirements in Figure 8-15, the consultant recommended creating an INVAPP profile script. Use the profile login script form found in Appendix B to write the necessary profile login script for the INVAPP Profile object.

Step 3: Identifying User Profile Script Requirements

Use the profile login script form found in Appendix B to write the necessary commands to provide the necessary users with access to the INVAPP and EngShared profile scripts.

Step 4: Checking Off

Before proceeding to enter and test your login scripts, have them reviewed by your instructor and compared to the login script master. Although your commands can vary slightly, be sure to include all the commands in the master login script to perform exercises properly in the remainder of this book.

Instructor checkoff: _____

Step 5: Entering and Testing the Container Login Scripts

Once your login script commands have been checked, enter the login script commands for the Business container.

Step 6: Entering the Profile Scripts

After the container login script has been tested, the next step is to create the INVAPP and WebMgr Profile objects and enter the login script defined in Step 2.

Step 7: Attaching Users to Their Profiles

Attach the WebMgr and INVAPP profile scripts to the users in the Business container as indicated in Figure 8-15. Julie DamRau, Lynn Dai, and Kellie Thiele will be attached to the WebMgr profile, and Ira Means, Laura Hiller, and Terry Blackwell to the INVAPP profile.

Step 8: Creating Message Files

To test your login scripts, you next need to create a message file to contain today's message. If necessary, create a subdirectory within your ##UAS\Shared directory named Message. Use the Windows Notepad application to create a message file that welcomes the user to the network and contains any special announcements you want to include for today. Save this file in your ##UAS\Shared\Message directory. Name the file the same as the current day of the week, such as MONDAY, TUESDAY, or SUNDAY. You can continue to create message files for other days of the week and save them in the same Message directory.

Step 9: Testing Login Scripts

To test your login scripts, you will need to log in as each of your users, correct any errors by changing login script commands or granting additional rights, and then verify the drive mappings and printer port redirection.

Step 10: Documenting Login Scripts

Printing login script programs is important both for documentation as well as maintaining and debugging login script problems. Follow these steps to print copies of each of your login scripts:

1. Log in using your assigned ##Admin username.

2. Open a DOS window.

3. Change your default context to your ##UAS container.

4. Print your Business container login script. On the following line, record the command you use:

_____

5. Change the current context to your Business container.

6. Print your INVAPP and WebMgr profile login scripts. On the following line, record the command you use:

_____

Step 11: Checking Out

If requested by your instructor, label all your printouts and assemble them in the sequence generated. Turn in your user test screens and login script printouts for grading.

If required, demonstrate logging in as Terry Blackwell and Diana Brady and have your instructor or lab assistant sign on the following line when satisfactory.

Completion signoff: _____

Additional Exercise

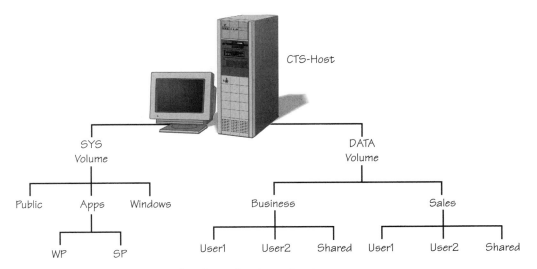

The following exercise is not necessary to implement your login script system for the Universal Aerospace Corporation, but is included to give you more practice working with NetWare Administrator and login scripts to help you pass your CNA exam and become a more competent network administrator.

In this exercise, use the login script forms described in this chapter to write a login script system for the Computer Technology Company. Use the directory structure shown in Figure 8-16, and make sure the script meets the following objectives:

- Include search drives to the Public, WP, and SP directories.

- Include a drive mapping to each volume of the CTS=Host server.

- For all Business users, map a root drive to the user's home directory, map a root drive to the Business\Shared directory, and capture printed output to the BUS-LASER-Q print queue.

- For all Sales users, map a root drive to the user's home directory, map a root drive to the Sales\Shared directory, and when the users log in prior to noon on Monday, display a message reminding users of the weekly sales meeting in Conference Room 212 at 10:00 a.m.

- Include a root drive mapping to their department directory in the DATA volume.

- Before noon on Monday, a message should be displayed for all Business department users reminding them of the weekly business meeting in Conference Room 210 at 10:30 a.m.

Figure 8-16   Computer Technology directory structure

9

MANAGING USER ENVIRONMENTS WITH Z.E.N.WORKS

After reading this chapter and completing the exercises, you will be able to:

♦ Identify the benefits of Z.E.N.works as well as its software and hardware requirements

♦ Install Z.E.N.works on servers and workstations

♦ Use the Application Launcher to automate installation and access to software over the network

♦ Use Z.E.N.works to create Workstation objects

♦ Use Z.E.N.works to manage user desktop environments

♦ Understand how to use Z.E.N.works to manage workstations remotely

In Chapter 8, you learned how to use login scripts to help make a consistent, standardized environment for users each time they log in to the network. However, login scripts are only part of the solution to making the network easy to use and maintain. Making the network easy to use requires that users have access to the applications they need from any workstation on which they work. In the past, the network administrator had to install applications and modify workstation configurations on many different computers to accommodate the computing needs of the various people who used those machines.

Novell's new Z.E.N.works starter pack that comes bundled with NetWare 5 provides users with easy mobility among workstations, and network administrators with the ability to centrally monitor and manage software and workstation configuration. The Z.E.N.works starter pack includes tools to manage applications and user desktop environments. The full version of Z.E.N.works may be purchased for either NetWare 5 or NetWare 4.11 and includes tools that allow you to control and manage remote workstations in addition to performing a hardware and configuration inventory of all workstations imported into the NDS tree. In this chapter, you will learn how to install Z.E.N.works and how to use it to install and configure applications and manage workstations and desktop user environments.

Now that the network services are set up, your next task will be to configure each workstation for the applications users will need to access. In this chapter, you will use Novell's new Zero Effort Networks (Z.E.N.works) to help with this task.

Z.E.N.WORKS OVERVIEW

The actual cost of hardware and software is only a small part of the total cost of owning a computer. In addition to the physical and software components, the cost of ownership includes the ongoing costs of maintaining and upgrading the computer hardware, software installation and configuration, troubleshooting, and user support and training. The total cost of computer ownership is becoming a major concern for many organizations.

Although the Windows environment makes it easy for users to interact with and personalize their desktop computers, because of its complexity, it can actually increase the total cost of ownership. This is due to the increased time required by network administrators to initially configure and then manage and support Windows environments. In addition, configuration time can also be increased when users move among workstations yet want to access the same desktop environment. In a large network, another concern is providing help desk support for users when they have problems or questions.

With NetWare 5, Novell bundles a new tool called **Zero Effort Networks (Z.E.N.works)**. With Z.E.N.works, you can make the network easier for users as well as reduce the time you have to spend at each user workstation. In addition, Z.E.N.works contains a remote control capability that allows you to provide a secure way to take control of a client computer's display, keyboard, and mouse to help a user fix a problem or change a workstation's configuration without having to go physically to that workstation. The Z.E.N.works product consists of client and server components that allow network administrators to reduce the time and redundancy of workstation configuration and management by using Novell Directory Services (NDS) to centralize configuration information for applications, users, and workstations.

Benefits and Functions

Z.E.N.works has benefits in each of the following areas of network management:

- *Application management.* Z.E.N.works includes Novell's **Application Launcher** software, which allows you to distribute, upgrade, and manage applications centrally on any Windows-based workstation attached to your network.

- *Workstation management.* The Workstation Manager component allows you to store user and desktop configurations for Windows workstations in NDS. Because Z.E.N.works uses NDS to extend Windows features such as policies, printers, and user profiles, these features are manageable from a centralized location using NetWare Administrator.

- *Remote control.* Z.E.N.works allows you to manage and interact with workstations securely from a remote location. This makes troubleshooting user problems as well as changing configurations much more convenient on large networks.

Hardware and Software Requirements

To use Z.E.N.works, your server must be running NetWare 4.11 or higher, and workstations (Windows 3.1, 95/98, or NT) need to have the NetWare client installed on them. Keep in mind that these are *minimum* hardware requirements:

- Processor: 486/33 or higher

- Memory: 16 MB (for Windows 95); 24 MB (for Windows NT)

- Hard disk space: 4 MB (workstation); 24 MB (full installation)

In addition, to configure and manage Z.E.N.works, you will need to use the 32-bit version of NetWare Administrator, as you have been throughout this book.

INSTALLING Z.E.N.WORKS

Prior to taking advantage of the Z.E.N.works features, you need to install Z.E.N.works on your server and update the client on the workstations. Your instructor has already installed Z.E.N.works on your server and copied the Z.E.N.works files from the NetWare client CD-ROM to the Public directory by going through the following process:

1. Log in to the network from your workstation using the Admin username to give Supervisor rights to the server or servers.

2. Insert the Novell Client CD-ROM in the CD-ROM drive of the workstation. The WinSetup software automatically starts and displays the Clients and language selection screen. Click **English** and the setup program will display the options shown in Figure 9-1.

Figure 9-1   Initial client installation window

3. Click the option **Install Z.E.N.works**. After displaying a welcome screen, a license agreement window for the Z.E.N.works Starter Pack is displayed.

4. After confirming the license agreement, the installation program gives you options to do a Typical, Compact, or Custom installation as shown in Figure 9-2. Verify that the **Typical** option is selected and click **Next** to display a list of servers to install.

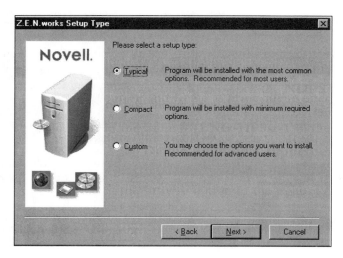

Figure 9-2   Z.E.N.works Setup Type dialog box

5. Verify that your server and tree are checked, and then click **Next** to display a language selection window. The language window may be blank if you are installing the default English language.

6. Click **Next** to install the program using English, the default language, and display a summary window similar to the one shown in Figure 9–3 showing the options you have selected. View the options and then click **Next** to continue.

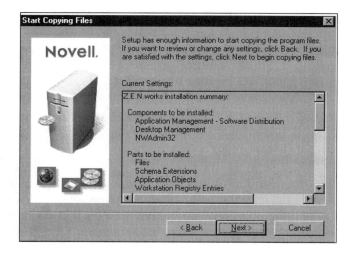

Figure 9-3   Z.E.N.works installation summary window

7. The installation program will now copy files to the server and workstation and then display a Context selection window as shown in Figure 9–4.

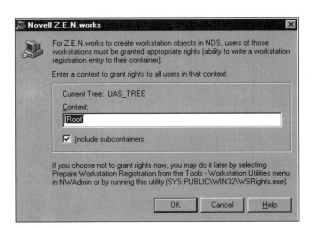

Figure 9-4   Context selection window

8. Click **OK** to select the default [Root] container and display a Z.E.N.works Auto-Registration successful window. Click **OK** to close the window and display a completion screen allowing you to view the Read Me and Setup Log files as shown in Figure 9-5.

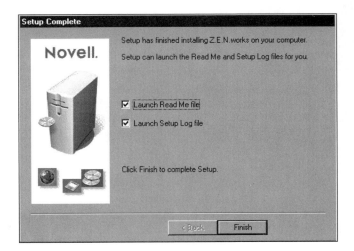

Figure 9-5   Setup Complete dialog box

9. When you click the **Finish** button, you can choose to view the Readme.txt and Setuplog.txt files to obtain more information and document your setup options, or you can remove the checks from these options and click **Finish** again to display a Congratulations on Installing Z.E.N.works window. Click the **Exit** icon to end the setup program and return to the desktop.

After Z.E.N.works has been installed on the server, the next step is to upgrade workstation computers with the new Z.E.N.works client software. In this hands-on activity, you will install the new Z.E.N.works client on your workstation.

1. If necessary, start your computer and log in using your assigned ##Admin username.

2. Use My Computer or Windows Explorer to browse to the F:\Public\Client\Win95\ibm_enu directory and start the **Setup** program by double-clicking it.

3. Click **Yes** to agree to the license agreement and display the installation options window.

4. Click the **Custom** option and click the **Install** button to display the Client Installation Protocol Preference dialog box shown in Figure 9-6.

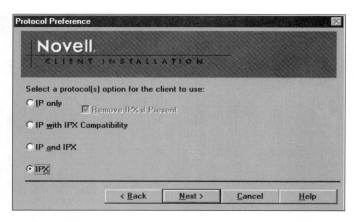

Figure 9-6   Client Installation Protocol Preference dialog box

> 5. Click the **IPX** button and click **Next** to display the login establishment options shown in Figure 9–7.

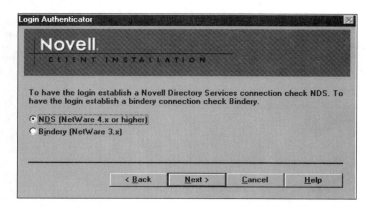

Figure 9-7   Login authentication options

> 6. Click **NDS (NetWare 4.x or higher)** and click **Next** to display the optional component selection window shown in Figure 9-8.

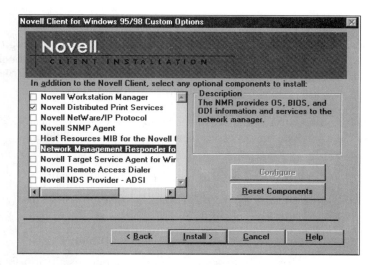

Figure 9-8   Optional component selection window

7. Click the check boxes for **Novell Workstation Manager**, **Novell Distributed Print Services**, and **Network Management Responder** and click **Install** to remove the existing Novell client and copy files for the new client installation.

8. After all client files have been installed, click the **Reboot** button to restart your workstation.

9. Log in using your assigned ##Admin username.

MANAGING APPLICATIONS

Now that Z.E.N.works is installed, your next concern in setting up the Universal Aerospace network is installing and configuring applications on each Windows workstation. Prior to Z.E.N.works, installing applications required physically going to each workstation and installing and configuring the application software needed on that workstation. It also meant possible administration headaches with proper transfer of configuration files and other files necessary to run the applications.

During the installation process, program files and **Dynamic Link Libraries (DLLs)** are copied to the workstation, and the system configuration files are modified. DLLs contain subprograms that are called by an application to perform certain operations, and are often placed in the Windows\System directory or in a subdirectory of the application. Often problems with running applications occur because of missing or wrong versions of certain application DLLs.

Whereas Windows 3.x uses .INI files to store configurations, Windows 95, 98, and NT store system configuration information in a database called the **Registry**. After installation, the job of maintaining workstation configurations can be an ongoing task since software upgrades will need to be applied, and problems resulting from corrupt or changed system configurations must be fixed.

Because application installation and management tasks can take so much of a network administrator's time, Novell has included the Application Launcher utility as part of Z.E.N.works to help you distribute and manage applications. The Application Launcher consists of four major components:

- A snap-in component for NetWare Administrator. A **snap-in** is a DLL that extends the capabilities of a Windows program. APPSNP32.DLL is a snap-in that allows NetWare Administrator to work with Application objects and properties.

- A snapshot utility to record configuration changes. A **snapshot** is a record of configuration information at a particular point in time, including Registry settings and the names of system and application files. The **snAppShot** utility creates snapshots of configuration settings before and after installing applications. These snapshots are used to create Application Object Templates (AOTs), discussed later in the chapter.

- Application objects in the NDS tree. An **Application object** is an NDS object that is used to store an application's configuration information and determine which users and workstations may use the application.

- Two components that allow for the delivery of applications to user workstations: Application Launcher Window and Application Launcher Explorer.

In the following sections, you will learn about each of these components in the process of distributing and configuring the Netscape Navigator browser application for users at Universal Aerospace.

The NetWare Administrator Snap-In

To work with the Application Launcher, the 32-bit version of NetWare Administrator needs the APPSNP32.DLL snap-in program. This snap-in program is placed in the SYS:Public\Win32\Snapins directory of the server when you install Z.E.N.works as described in the last section. The APPSNP32 snap-in extends the capabilities of NetWare Administrator, allowing you to create and display Application objects, and providing an additional property page for container, group, and user objects. When Application Launcher properties are set at the container or group level, they affect all users in that container or group.

The snAppShot Utility

When you install an application on a Windows 95/98 or Windows NT workstation, certain files such as DLLs, along with executable and other support files, may be copied to the workstation. In addition, most applications require special configuration settings that are stored in the Windows Registry. As a result of the required DLLs and Registry settings, in the past it has not been possible to run many applications directly from a shared application directory on a server without first running the installation software on the workstation. The Application Launcher provides a solution to this problem through the use of the snAppShot utility. The snAppShot utility allows you take a "snapshot" of the Windows workstation prior to installing the application. The snapshot includes Registry settings along with the names of system and application files on the workstation. After the application has been installed, the snAppShot utility takes another picture of the workstation's configuration and then uses the two snapshots to produce an **Application Object Template (AOT)** file. The Application Launcher uses the AOT file to determine what Registry settings and system files need to be copied to the workstation to run the application from the network. In addition to including configuration settings and system file names, the AOT file also contains the name of the Application object and the path where you want to store the AOT and installation files. As a result, prior to running the snAppShot utility, you need to define the name you want to use for the Application object and decide where the application and AOT files will be stored.

After consulting with Kellie Thiele, you have decided that it would be easiest to name the Application object "Netscape." Since you already have an Apps directory in your ##Corp volume, Kellie has suggested using that directory to store the Netscape Navigator installation files as well. In addition to defining a location for the installation files, you also need to decide where you want the application to run from. You can either run the application from the workstation's local drive, or from a shared directory on the network. To provide greater speed and save network disk storage, Jennifer, the NetWare consultant, has recommended that you run most applications from the workstation's local hard drive. Although it will take a little longer to set up applications on the local hard drive, the setup is simpler and running the applications locally will also decrease network traffic.

 In this hands-on activity, you will create a Netscape directory and then use the snAppShot utility to create an AOT file necessary to distribute the Netscape Navigator application to the local hard drives of user workstations.

1. If necessary, start your computer and log in using your assigned ##Admin username.

2. Create a subdirectory in Apps named Netscape, as follows:

   a) Double-click **My Computer** and open your **##Corp** directory.

   b) Double-click your **Apps** folder and click **File**, then point to **New**.

   c) Click the **Folder** option and enter the name **Netscape**.

   d) Close all windows.

3. Verify that you have drive G mapped to your ##Corp directory as follows:

   a) Start Windows Explorer.

   b) Expand drive G to verify that it contains the Universal Aerospace directories you created.

   c) Exit Windows Explorer.

4. Start the snAppShot program as follows:

   a) Click **Start**, **Run**.

   b) Browse to the F:\Public\Snapshot directory and double-click **Snapshot.exe**.

   c) Click **OK** to start the snAppShot program and display the Novell snAppShot dialog box shown in Figure 9-9.

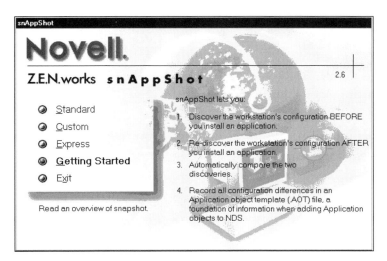

Figure 9-9   Novell snAppShot dialog box

5. Click **Standard** to display a window where you can enter the NDS Application object name and icon title as shown in Figure 9-10. You will create the Application object later.

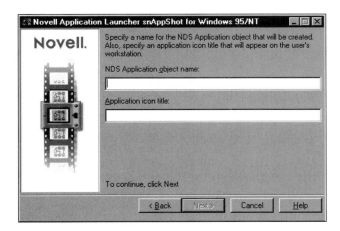

Figure 9-10   Naming the Application object

6. Type **Netscape** in the NDS Application object name field and then click in the **Application icon title** field. Notice that the name you typed in the object name field is automatically duplicated in the title field. Click **Next** to accept the object name and icon title and display the Application file(s) location window.

7. The Application file(s) location field is used to specify where to place the application installation and AOT files needed to create an application object. Use the folder icon to the right of the field to browse to the Netscape directory you just created, or enter **G:\Apps\Netscape** as shown in Figure 9-11 to store the installation files in the folder you created in Step 2.

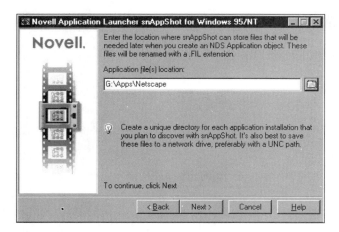

Figure 9-11   Application file(s) location window

8. Click **Next** to display the AOT file location window shown in Figure 9-12. You could use this window to change the location of the AOT file created by the snAppShot utility.

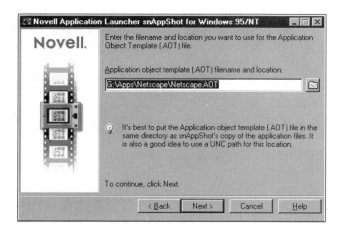

Figure 9-12   AOT file location window

9. Click **Next** to accept the same directory for the AOT file as used to store the installation files.

10. The snAppShot utility will next ask which drives you want to scan during the snapshot. In addition to the C drive, you should also include the G drive directory by clicking the **Add** button and then selecting your **g:** drive as shown in Figure 9-13.

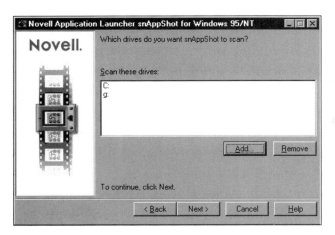

Figure 9-13 Specifying drives to scan

11. Click **Next** to display a summary window. Scroll through the summary windows to view your selected settings.

12. After verifying that all your selections are correct on the summary window, click **Next** to begin the snapshot scanning process. After the scanning process is complete, the snAppShot utility will display the application installation window shown in Figure 9-14.

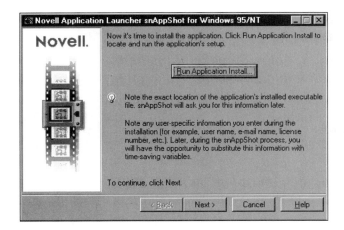

Figure 9-14 Installing the application

13. Click the **Run Application Install** button and use the Select Setup program window to browse to the F:\Software.cti\Netscape\Win32\English directory and double-click the **N32e404** setup program. The setup program will start while the snAppShot utility waits in the background.

14. Click **Yes** to start the Netscape installation process by displaying a Welcome screen. Click **Next** to show the license agreement. Click **Yes** to accept the license agreement and follow the default Typical installation options. In the Destination Directory field, accept the default directory path. Record the path on the following line. You will need to refer to it later. _____

15. Click **Next** and then click **Yes** if asked whether you want to create the directory.

16. After selecting the destination directory, click **Next** to accept the default program folder, and then click **Install** to copy files and perform the installation process.

17. Click **No** when asked whether you want to view the README file now.

18. Click **OK** to the "Setup is complete" message.

19. After installation is complete, a window showing the Netscape icons will be displayed along with the Application Launcher window. Close the Netscape window and then click **Next** on the Application Launcher window to display the install directory selection window as shown in Figure 9-15.

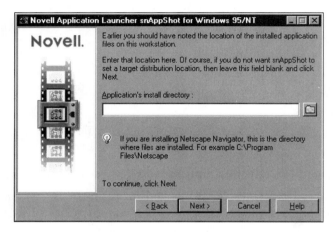

Figure 9-15 Specifying the application's install directory

20. Click the folder icon to the right of the Application's install directory field to select the directory you recorded in Step 14 and click **OK** to return to the Application's install directory field.

21. Click **Next** to perform the after-installation snapshot process. This may be a good time for a break, as the scanning process will probably take several minutes.

22. After the snapshot has been scanned, a Completion Summary screen will be displayed identifying the name and location of the AOT and installation files along with steps on how to create the Application object. After you have reviewed the information, record the application installation steps on the following lines.

_____

_____

_____

_____

23. Click **Finish** to return to the Windows desktop. You are now ready to create and configure the Netscape Application object.

Application Objects

The Application Launcher stores configuration and user access information in **Application objects** located within the NDS tree. This information is used when an application is accessed from a user's workstation. For example, an Application object contains properties that identify the application along with a path to its executable files, the required workstation environment, the drive letters that need to be mapped, Windows Registry settings, the users who are allowed to run the application, and the rights users will need in the application directory. You will need to create an Application object for each application managed by the Application Launcher. When you create an Application object using an AOT file, you then need to configure the object to supply the path to the executable file that starts the application as well as provide a list of groups or containers that are associated with the application. When users who are members of one of the specified groups or containers log in, they will see the application icon in the Application Launcher window.

In this hands-on activity, you will use NetWare Administrator to create an Application object for Netscape using the AOT file created in the previous activity.

1. If necessary, start your computer and log in using your assigned ##Admin username.

2. Start NetWare Administrator and, if necessary, open a browse window for your ##UAS Organization.

3. Highlight your ##UAS container and press **[Ins]** to display the New Object dialog box.

4. Double-click the **Application** object class to display the Create Application Object dialog box.

5. Click the **Create an Application object with an .aot/.axt file** option as shown in Figure 9-16 and click **Next** to display the Path to .aot/.axt file window.

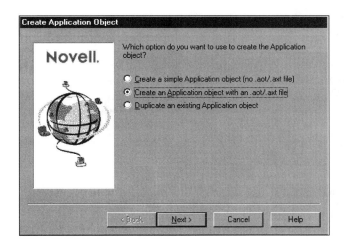

Figure 9-16   Creating an Application object

6. When entering the path to the .aot/.axt file, you can either use a drive letter or specify a complete Universal Naming Convention (UNC) path. The UNC path specifies the server name, preceded by two backslashes, along with the volume name and all directories separated by backslashes. For example, the UNC path to your Netscape directory would be written as \\UAS_HOST\Corp\##Corp\Apps\Netscape. Since you have the G drive letter mapped to the ##Corp directory, you can shorten the path to G:\Apps\Netscape by using the G drive letter.

Although using a drive letter provides for a shorter path, it also requires that you map G to the directory containing the Apps\Netscape directory. The advantage of using a UNC path is that the user's workstation does not require a specific drive letter such as G to be mapped to the ##Corp directory.

In this example, use the **browse** button to browse to your G:\Apps\Netscape directory and then double-click the **Netscape.AOT** file to insert that path in the field as shown in Figure 9-17.

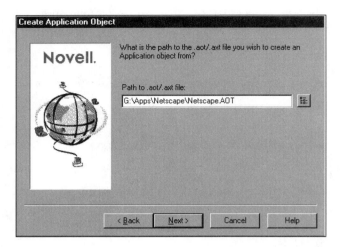

Figure 9-17   Specifying the path to the AOT file

7. Click **Next** to display the Customize the new Application object window. The SOURCE_PATH field should contain the G:\Apps\Netscape directory that contains the installation files. If you want to run the program from the client's local drive, use the browse button next to the TARGET_PATH text box to select the directory on the client where the files should be installed. Since you want to run the Netscape application from the client's local driver, verify that the TARGET_PATH field contains C:\Program Files\netscape as shown in Figure 9-18 and then click **Next** to display the summary screen.

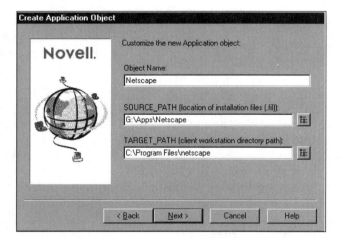

Figure 9-18   Customizing the Application object

8. After reviewing the summary screen, click **Finish** to create the new Application object and return to the NetWare Administrator browse window.

The Netscape Application object should now appear in your ##UAS Organization container. However, for users to use the Application object, you next need to connect the Netscape Application object to an executable file and associate it with all users in your ##UAS Organization.

In this hands-on activity, you will use NetWare Administrator to view the Netscape Application object setting and configure it for all users in your Universal Aerospace Organization.

1. From the NetWare Administrator browse window, right-click your **Netscape** Application object and click **Details** to display the Application Identification page shown in Figure 9-19.

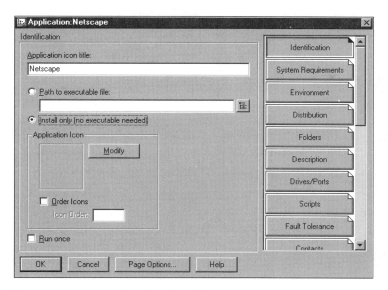

Figure 9-19   Application Identification page

2. Click the **Path to executable file** option button and then either enter or use the **browse** button to specify the path to the Netscape program you recorded in Step 14 of the previous installation activity. In addition to specifying the path, you also need to add Windows 95/98 as the client system requirement. Only clients that meet the requirements you specify will display the application icon. Follow these steps to set Windows 95/98 as the required client operating system for the Netscape application:

a) Click the **System Requirements** button to display the window shown in Figure 9-20.

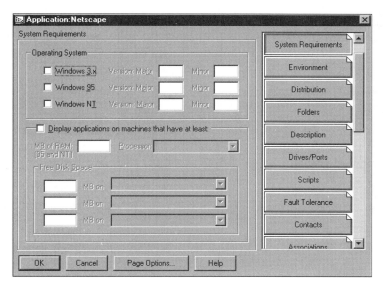

Figure 9-20   System Requirements page

b) Click the **Windows 95** box to specify that the client computer must have Windows 95/98 to run the Netscape application. You can also use this page to specify other minimum machine requirements such as megabytes of RAM, processor type, and free disk space.

3. Next you need to associate the application with the users who will have access to it. To do this, scroll down and click the **Associations** button on the right of the screen.

4. Add your ##UAS container as an object that can use this application by following these steps:

   a) Click **Add** to display the Select Object dialog box.

   b) Use the Browse context window to navigate to your ##UAS container.

   c) Double-click your **##UAS** container from the left-hand Available objects window.

5. Assume you want users to be able to save downloaded files in your ##Corp\Shared directory. To make this more convenient, you could have Application Launcher map the S drive to the Shared directory each time Netscape starts by following these steps:

   a) Click the **Drives/Ports** button to display the Drives/Ports window.

   b) Click the **Add** button under the Drives to be mapped pane to display the Drive to be mapped dialog box shown in Figure 9-21.

Figure 9-21   Drive to be mapped dialog box

   c) Click the list arrow to the right of the Option field and click the **Drive** option.

   d) Click the list arrow to the right of the Drive field and click the **S:** drive.

   e) Enter **UAS_HOST_CORP:##Corp\Shared** in the Path field and click **OK**. The new drive mapping should now appear in the Drives pane.

6. Another useful feature of the Application Launcher is automatically providing authorized users of an application with rights to a directory. For example, assume users will need Read, Write, Create, and File Scan rights to the Netscape directory. Follow these steps to provide all users with these rights in the Netscape application directory:

   a) Scroll down and click the **File Rights** button and then click the **Add** button to display the Select Object dialog box.

   b) Use the Browse context window to navigate to your ##Corp\Apps directory and then double-click your **Netscape** directory from the left-hand Available objects window to add the Netscape directory to the File Rights page as shown in Figure 9-22.

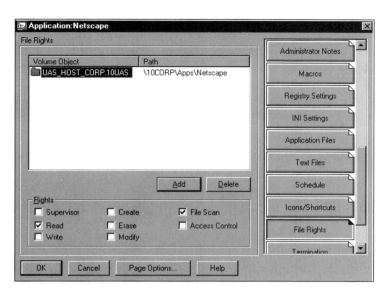

Figure 9-22   File Rights page

c) Click to select the **Write** and **Create** check box in the Rights area.

7. As you can see, an Application object contains many customizable settings. Three other settings you should be familiar with are the Registry Settings, Application Files, and Macros. Follow these steps to view information on these settings:

a) Click the **Registry Settings** button and then expand the HKEY_LOCAL_MACHINE | Software | Netscape key to look for settings pertaining to Netscape. These are the configuration settings that the Application Launcher will need to make to a workstation running this application for the first time. Record the version number of your Netscape software here: _____. Click the **Application Files** button to see all files that need to be verified on the client workstation or application directory to run the application.

b) Scroll up and click the **Macros** button to record the source and target directories on the following lines:

Source directory: _____

Target directory: _____

8. Click **OK** to save your configuration changes and return to the NetWare Administrator browse window. Exit NetWare Administrator.

Now that the Netscape Application object is configured, you can deliver Netscape to each user's workstation as described in the next section.

Delivering the Application

For a user to run applications that he or she has been assigned to, the Application Launcher software needs to be run from the user's workstation. After a user logs in, the Application Launcher software displays icons for the applications that have been set up for the user. The Application Launcher software consists of a wrapper program component and a launcher component. The **wrapper program** determines which launcher program to run based on the client computer's operating system. The **launcher program** displays the Application Launcher window with the application icons for the client, and determines whether an application needs to be installed or updated before running.

If you have a network with Windows 3.x and Windows 95/98 client computers, you should use the NAL.EXE wrapper program located in the SYS:Public directory. If a client is using Windows 3.1x, the wrapper program will execute the NALW31.EXE launcher; for clients running Windows 95/98 or NT, the wrapper program will execute the NALWIN32.EXE launcher. If your network consists of only Windows 95/98 or NT clients, you may wish to use the NAL Explorer wrapper program rather than the NAL.EXE wrapper described in this chapter. NAL Explorer can be used to deliver applications to Windows Explorer, the Start menu, System Tray, or Desktop.

You can start the wrapper software, NAL.EXE, either by selecting it from the desktop or by automatically starting it from a login script when the user logs in. When the NAL.EXE software loads, it first checks the operating system of the local computer and then loads either the NALW31.EXE or NALWIN32.EXE launcher program. The launcher program then determines the Application objects to which the user has access and displays a window showing all applications the user has been authorized to run. When the user selects an application, the launcher determines whether the application is installed on the workstation. If this is the first time the user has run the application from this workstation, the application will automatically be installed using the AOT file created by the snAppShot utility. The next time a user runs this application from the workstation, Application Launcher will detect that the application has been installed and, after checking the configuration, start the application. If Application Launcher senses that the application configuration has been damaged, or files are missing or corrupt, it will automatically correct the application configuration and copy any damaged or missing files. For example, suppose a user accidentally deletes a DLL file that an Application Launcher-managed application needs to start successfully. The Application Launcher will detect that the application is damaged, and will recopy the deleted file from the installation directory.

Prior to using the Application Launcher to install Netscape Navigator on all the user computers, it is a good idea first to test your plan. Since Kellie is anxious to have Netscape on her desktop, she is willing to have you run a test of the installation on her computer.

In this hands-on activity, you will modify the login script for your UAS container to run the Application Launcher software automatically. You will then log in as Kellie and start the Netscape Navigator application to verify that it will install correctly. You can then modify the container login scripts for the Engineering department to install Netscape Navigator on all Engineering workstations.

1. If necessary, start your computer and log in using your assigned ##Admin username.

2. To simulate using Kellie's computer, you will first need to follow these steps to uninstall Netscape from your computer:

   a) Double-click **My Computer** and start **Control Panel**.

   b) Double-click **Add/Remove Programs**.

   c) Click **Netscape Navigator** and click the **Add/Remove** button.

   d) Click **Yes** when asked to uninstall Netscape Navigator.

   e) After Netscape has been removed, close the Control Panel windows and return to the desktop.

3. Modify your ##UAS container login script to start the Application Launcher as follows:

   a) Start or restore NetWare Administrator.

   b) Right-click your **##UAS** Organization and click **Details**.

   c) Click the **Login Script** button.

   d) Add the following line to the end of your login script (remember that the # is necessary to run an external program from a login script): **#NAL**.

   e) Click **OK** to save your changes.

4. Exit NetWare Administrator and log out.

5. Log in as KThiele. The login script should start the NAL program and display the Application Launcher window containing the Netscape application icon as shown in Figure 9-23.

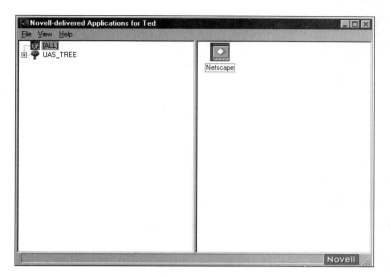

Figure 9-23   Novell Application Launcher window

6. Double-click the **Netscape** application to start it. The installation process may ask whether you want to verify the setup of the application. In this case, click **Yes** to start the application setup process. After the installation is completed, you will be asked to restart your computer. The next time you log in as Kellie, you will be able to run the Netscape application.

MANAGING WORKSTATIONS

In addition to installing and configuring applications on each workstation, network administrators need to be able to maintain a consistent desktop environment and to keep track of the hardware and software configurations of each client. The key to managing Windows desktop environments is through using policies. **Policies** are powerful Windows desktop management tools that allow user workstations to be customized for individual user needs. However, when you are implementing a network with many Windows computers, managing workstation and user policies can be a time-consuming chore using the POLEDIT program provided by Microsoft. Z.E.N.works makes Windows policies both easier to manage and more powerful by adding Policy Package objects to NDS.

Policy Package objects allow you to manage the way users access their workstations and connect to the network. There are two types of policy packages: Workstation policies and User policies. Workstation policies allow you to configure settings such as the path to the Windows setup files, file and printer sharing, workstation passwords, and run options. Run options can be used to configure what applications will be automatically run on a workstation regardless of which user logs in from the workstation. For example, you could use a Workstation policy package to configure workstations to start automatically the Application Launcher (NAL.EXE) rather than placing the command in a container login script. User policy packages affect a user's access to the workstation and the user's desktop restrictions regardless of where the user logs in to the network. User policy packages can be used to define restrictions such as hiding the Entire Network option in Network Neighborhood, or hiding commands such as Run or Find. In addition, you can use the User policy package to define a desktop environment including wallpaper, screen saver, sounds, and colors. One application of policy packages is to insert workstations into the NDS tree. Once Workstation objects are created in your NDS tree, you can use them to manage configuration and access. In this section, you will learn how to create Workstation and User policy packages and then use these packages to register the networked computers and set up desktop environments.

Creating a User Policy Package

To automate the process of importing and registering workstations, you first need to set up a User policy package that enables automatic importing of workstations into the NDS tree.

 In this hands-on activity, you will use NetWare Administrator to create an NDS User Policy Package object in your ##UAS container that will enable importing workstations into the NDS tree.

1. If necessary, start your computer and log in using your assigned ##Admin username.

2. Start NetWare Administrator.

3. Highlight your ##UAS container and press **[Ins]** or click the **Create a new object** icon from the toolbar to display the New Object dialog box.

4. Double-click the **Policy Package** object type to display the Create Policy Package dialog box.

5. Click the drop-down list arrow to the right of the Select policy package type field and click **WIN95 User Package**.

6. Enter the name **Workstation Importer** in the Name field as shown in Figure 9-24.

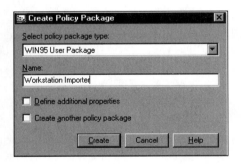

Figure 9-24   Create Policy Package dialog box

7. Click the **Create** button to create the User Policy Package object and return to the NetWare Administrator browse window. The User Policy Package object named Workstation Importer should now appear in your ##UAS Organization.

Registering and Importing a Workstation

After you have created the User Policy Package object, you next need to enable the workstation import policy so that the workstation from which the user logs in will be automatically placed in the NDS tree. To do this, you will need to supply the container in which you want to place the Workstation object along with the object's name. The default naming scheme is to combine the Windows computer name with the workstation's network address. Although this method will produce a unique name, it is rather long and difficult to use or identify. In addition to naming the Workstation object, you will also need to associate the User policy package with a user, group, or container. When a user who is a member of the associated group or container logs in, an NDS object representing the workstation import policy will be automatically created. You can then use this Workstation Import Policy object to register the workstation.

 In this hands-on activity, you will configure the User Policy Package object you created in the previous activity to import the workstation into the same context as the User object. You will then test the process by logging in and viewing the Workstation object in the NDS tree.

1. If necessary, start your computer, log in to the network using your assigned ##Admin username, and start NetWare Administrator.

2. Double-click the **Workstation Importer** User Policy Package object you created in the previous activity to display the Policies page shown in Figure 9-25.

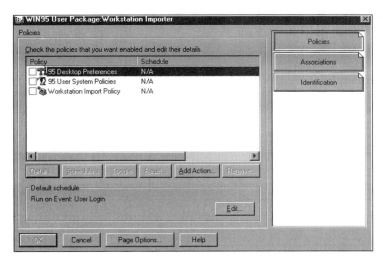

Figure 9-25   Workstation Importer Policies page

3. Double-click the **Workstation Import Policy** option in the Policy area to display the Workstation Import Policy dialog box shown in Figure 9-26. Notice that the option to allow importing of workstations into the user container is set by default.

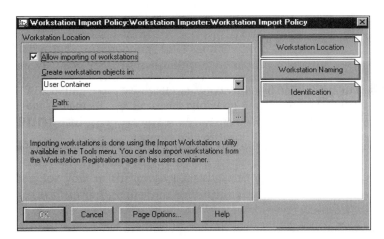

Figure 9-26   Workstation Location page

4. Click the **Workstation Naming** button to display the window shown in Figure 9-27.

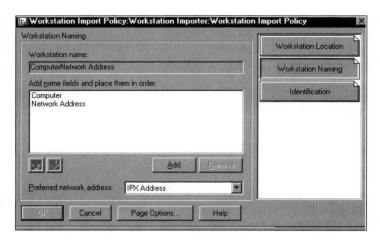

Figure 9-27   Workstation Naming page

5. To remove the network address from the workstation name, click the **Network Address** entry in the name fields area and then click the **Remove** button. You can optionally use the **Add** button to append additional information to the workstation name to ensure that it is unique in the container.

6. Click **OK** to save your Workstation Naming information and return to the Policies page shown earlier in Figure 9-25.

7. To associate the user package with all users in your Organization, click the **Associations** button to display the Associations page.

8. Click the **Add** button to display the Select Object dialog box.

9. Use the right-hand Browse context window to navigate to your ##UAS container.

10. Double-click your **##UAS** container from the left-hand Available objects window to add the container to the Associations page. Whenever a user in the ##UAS structure logs in, a Workstation Import Policy object will be created in the same container as the User object.

11. Click **OK** to save your configuration information and return to the NetWare Administrator browse window.

12. Modify your ##UAS container login script to run the Registration program as follows:

   a) Right-click your **##UAS** container and click the **Details** option.

   b) Click the **Login Script** button and enter the following command prior to the #NAL command:

   #WSREG32

   c) Click **OK** to save the login script changes and return to the NetWare Administrator browse window.

13. Exit NetWare Administrator and log out.

14. Log in using your assigned ##Admin username.

15. Start NetWare Administrator and open a browse window to your ##UAS container.

16. Right-click your **##UAS** container and click the **Details** option.

17. Click the **Workstation Registration** button to display the registered workstations as shown in Figure 9-28. Although your screen will look slightly different, you should notice that your workstation is now registered to be imported.

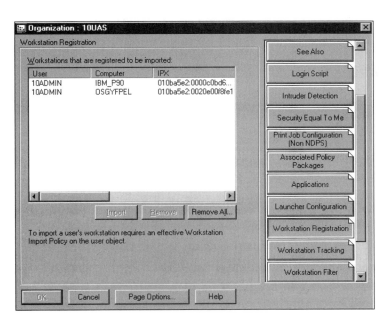

Figure 9-28   Workstation Registration page

18. Click **Cancel** to return to the NetWare Administrator browse window.

19. To import the workstation, click **Tools**, **Import Workstations** to display the Import Workstations dialog box shown in Figure 9-29.

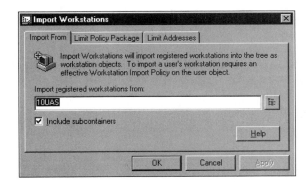

Figure 9-29   Import Workstations dialog box

20. Click **OK** to accept the default container and to create the Workstation object.

21. Click **Close** to acknowledge the Import Complete window and return to the NetWare Administrator browse window.

22. Close and open your ##UAS container to display your Workstation object.

Creating a Standard User Desktop

There are many times when a network administrator may want to maintain a standard desktop environment for a user or group of users no matter which workstation they log in from.

In this hands-on activity, you will create a standard workstation environment for all users in the Engineering container that will hide the Network Neighborhood application and provide a standard wallpaper and screen saver.

1. If necessary, start your computer and log in using your assigned ##Admin username.

2. Start NetWare Administrator.

3. Copy the UAS.BMP file from the F:\Software.cti\Design directory to your Engineer\Shared directory as follows:

   a) Use My Computer or Windows Explorer to browse to the F:\Software.cti\Design directory.

   b) Click the **Uas.bmp** file and then click **Edit**, **Copy**.

   c) Close the F:\Software.cti\Design window.

   d) Use My Computer or Windows Explorer to browse to your G:\Engineer\Shared directory.

   e) Click **Edit**, **Paste** to copy the Uas.bmp file into the Shared directory.

   f) Close the G:\Engineer\Shared directory window.

4. Create a User policy package for the Engineering container as follows:

   a) In NetWare Administrator, highlight your **Engineering** container and press **[Ins]** or click the **Create a new object** icon.

   b) Double-click **Policy Package** to display the New Policy dialog box.

   c) Select **WIN95 User Package** from the Select policy package type field, and enter the name **Engineer User Policy** in the Name field.

   d) Click **Create**.

5. Remove Network Neighborhood from the desktop options:

   a) Double-click the **Engineer User Policy** object you just created to display the User Policy window.

   b) Click the **95 User System Policies** check box and click the **Details** button to display the User System Policies window shown in Figure 9-30.

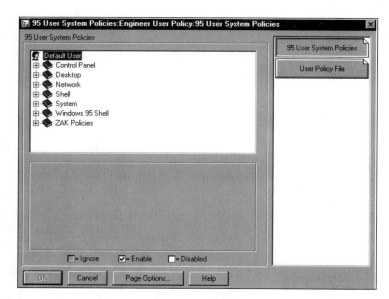

Figure 9-30   Engineer User Policy window

   c) Click the **+** to the left of the Shell option to display the Restrictions tag.

   d) Click the **+** to the left of the Restrictions tag to display the system restrictions.

e) Click the check box to the left of the **Hide Network Neighborhood** option.

f) Click **OK** to return to the User Policy window.

6. Set wallpaper and screen saver options as follows:

a) Remove the check from the **95 User System Policies** check box.

b) Click the **95 Desktop Preferences** check box and click **Details** to display the Control Panel Desktop Preferences icons shown in Figure 9-31.

Figure 9-31   Desktop Preferences icons

c) Double-click the **Display** icon to display the Display Properties dialog box.

d) Click the **Wallpaper** check box, use the browse button to the left of the Path and file name field to navigate to the G:\Engineer\Shared directory, and double-click the **Uas.bmp** file to use it for the Engineering department wallpaper, as shown in Figure 9-32.

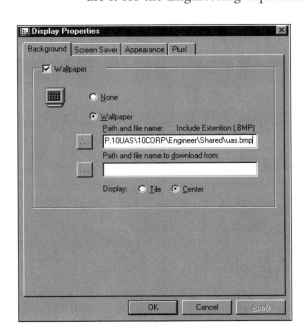

Figure 9-32   Display Properties dialog box

     e) Click the **Screen Saver** tab, click the **Screen Saver** drop-down list arrow, and select any screen saver from the C:\Windows\System directory.

     f) Click the **Appearance** tab, click the **Color Scheme** drop-down list arrow, and select the **Maple** color scheme.

     g) Click **OK** to save your changes and return to the Desktop Preferences window.

     h) Click **OK** to return to the User Policy window.

7. Associate your Engineer User Policy object with all users in the Engineering container:

     a) Click the **Associations** button to display the Associations window.

     b) Click **Add** to display the Select Object dialog box.

     c) Use the Browse context window to navigate to your Engineering container. Double-click the **Engineering** Organizational Unit from the left-hand Available objects window.

8. Click **OK** to save your User Policy Package object and return to the NetWare Administrator window.

9. Log out.

10. Log in as a user in your Engineering container. The workstation desktop should now reflect the changes you made to the Engineer User Profile object.

11. Log out.

REMOTE MANAGEMENT OF WORKSTATIONS

In addition to assisting you in managing applications and workstation environments, Z.E.N.works can also be very useful in helping you to provide support to your users. When a user has a problem, it is often difficult to determine the solution while speaking to the user over the phone. As a result, you often find that you have to go to the user's workstation to see the problem and then help the user correct it. To reduce the amount of time you have to spend traveling to users' workstations to fix their problems, Z.E.N.works provides a remote control option. The remote control facility allows you to view the user's screen as well as take control of the workstation's keyboard and mouse to help a user get through a problem or fix a workstation's configuration. In addition to offering the remote control function, Z.E.N.works also allows you to store user identification information, such as the user's name and context, in the User Policy package. This identification information can then be displayed when a user contacts you for help.

Although there are other good remote control programs on the market, most of these are not secure and can generate a lot of extra network traffic. Because Z.E.N.works uses NDS security, only administrators with the necessary rights can remotely control a workstation. Z.E.N.works reduces network traffic by using the IP or IPX address of workstations stored in NDS to locate workstations, rather than sending out advertising packets as is the case for most remote control programs.

To use the remote control program for Z.E.N.works, you need to obtain the full version of Z.E.N.works and then install an agent program on the Windows workstation you want to control. The remote control agent used for Windows 3.1x and Windows 95/98 is WUSER.EXE, whereas Windows NT workstations require the WUSER32.EXE program. The appropriate program can be run either from the login script or through a Workstation Policy package.

CHAPTER SUMMARY

❑ Installing and maintaining applications as well as managing workstation environments can take a lot of a network administrator's time. As a result, Novell developed the Zero Effort Networking, or Z.E.N.works, product. Z.E.N.works can help you manage your user environments in three ways: installation and configuration of applications, management and registration of workstations, and remote control of client computers. Application management is performed through the Novell Application Launcher. To use the Application Launcher, you first need to install Z.E.N.works on your network server. After the Application Launcher has been installed, your NDS schema is updated to include Application objects along with additional user and container properties.

❑ In addition, installing Z.E.N.works updates the 32-bit NetWare Administrator program, NWADMN32.EXE, with a snap-in program called snAppShot that allows you to manage Application objects and Application Launcher properties. After you install Z.E.N.works, installing and delivering applications to a workstation involves three steps. First you need to run the snAppShot program to create an Application Object Template (AOT) file. The AOT file contains snapshots of the workstation environment before and after the installation of the software. In addition, the AOT file contains application configuration and installation information that NetWare Administrator uses when creating Application objects. After using the snAppShot utility to install your application on one workstation, the second step in the NAL process is to use NetWare Administrator to create and configure an Application object. Configuring the Application object involves providing the path to the executable file used to start the application along with identifying the client operating system requirements and associating the application with the appropriate containers, groups, or users. After the Application object has been created and configured, the third and final step is to modify container or user login scripts to run the NAL Window (NAL.EXE) program. The NAL.EXE program will check the client operating system and then run the Application Launcher, which displays application icons for all applications to which the user has access. When a user starts an application, the Application Launcher will compare the workstation configuration to the snapshot and determine whether the application needs to be installed or updated. The first time a user selects an application from that workstation, the Application Launcher will automatically install and configure the workstation to run the application.

❑ In addition to installing and maintaining application software, network administrators often have the job of managing user desktop environments and documenting client computer configurations. Z.E.N.works can be a great asset in these areas by allowing you to create user and workstation profiles as well as import Workstation objects into NDS. User profile packages can be associated with users, groups, or containers and allow you to customize and restrict the user's workstation environment through the use of Windows policies stored in the NDS database. A Workstation policy package can be associated with workstation or container objects and can be used to automatically run system programs and register workstations for inventory and management. Before you can apply a workstation policy to a workstation, you first need to import the workstation into NDS. Importing a workstation requires that you first enable the Workstation Import property of a User Policy Package object. When a user associated with the policy package logs in, the workstation will be registered in that user's container. After workstations are registered, you can use NetWare Administrator to import the workstation into NDS.

❑ Another useful option of Z.E.N.works (included with the full package but not the starter package) is the help facility, which includes a secure remote control capability. To use the remote control facility, you need first to enable remote control in a user policy or workstation policy. Next you need to run an agent program (WUSER for Windows 95/98 computers, WUSER32 for Windows NT) from a login script or through NAL. After the workstation logs in and the agent program is loaded, you can select the workstation from NetWare Administrator and use the remote control tool to view or take control of the selected client computer.

KEY TERMS

Application Launcher — The Z.E.N.works component that is used to manage and distribute applications from the NDS tree.

Application object — An NDS object that is used to store an application's configuration information and determine what users and workstations may start the application.

Application Object Template (AOT) — A file that is used to create an Application object using configuration information from snapshots taken before and after installation.

Dynamic Link Library (DLL) — A file that contains subprograms that are used by an application to perform certain operations.

launcher program — The Application Launcher component that displays the Application Launcher window and determines whether an application needs to be installed or updated before running.

policies — Files on Windows 95/98 and Windows NT workstations that contain data on the workstation and user configuration.

Policy Package object — An NDS object that holds Windows 95/98 and Windows NT configuration information in the NDS database.

Registry — A database of system and application configuration information stored on Windows 95/98 and Windows NT systems.

snap-in — A DLL that is an extension to a Windows program such as NetWare Administrator. The APPSNP32.DLL snap-in allows NetWare Administrator to work with Application objects and properties.

snAppShot — A utility used to create the Application Object Template (AOT) from snapshots taken before and after installing an application.

snapshot — A process that records application configuration information including Registry settings along with the names of system and application files.

wrapper program — The Application Launcher component that is run from a login script and determines which launcher program to run based on the client computer's operating system.

Zero Effort Networking (Z.E.N.works) — Zero Effort Networking administration package that provides tools that allow a network administrator to manage applications and workstation environments from the NDS tree.

REVIEW QUESTIONS

1. Z.E.N.works will run on a NetWare 4.11 server. True or False?

2. To install Z.E.N.works, you must have _____ rights to the root of the NDS tree.

3. To configure and manage Z.E.N.works, you need to run the _____ version of NetWare Administrator from the _____ directory of your default server.

4. A(n) _____ contains subprograms that are called by an application to perform certain operations.

5. In Windows 95 and 98, system configuration information is stored in a database called the _____.

6. List four components of the Novell Application Launcher system.

   _____

   _____

   _____

   _____

7. The _____ utility allows you to take a snapshot of the Windows workstation configuration.

8. The _____ is used by NAL to determine what configuration settings and system files need to be copied to the workstation to run an application.

9. List the three steps involved in using NAL to deliver an application to a user's workstation.

_____

_____

_____

10. NAL stores configuration and user access information in _____ within the NDS tree.

11. _____ is the wrapper program that can work with either Windows 3.1x or Windows 95/98.

12. _____ is the launcher program used with Windows 95/98 or NT.

13. The launcher program will automatically install an application when

_____

14. To open the Application Launcher window automatically whenever a user from the Engineering department logs in, you should place the _____ command in the _____ login script.

15. After you create an Application object, what three configuration tasks do you need to perform before the application can be selected from a user workstation?

_____

_____

_____

16. _____ are powerful Windows desktop tools that allow you to customize a workstation environment.

17. List the two types of policies offered by Z.E.N.works.

_____

_____

18. List the three steps necessary to import a workstation into NDS.

_____

_____

_____

19. To register a workstation, you can place the _____ program in a login script.

20. The _____ policy package can be used to set up a screen saver on a workstation each time a user logs in.

21. Describe the two steps necessary to use remote control to manage another workstation.

_____

_____

The Universal AerospaceProject

You have successfully used the Application Launcher to get Netscape Navigator running on Kellie's computer, and you will use this procedure to set up that application for all users in the Engineering and Business departments. In addition, there are some other applications such as word processing and spreadsheet programs that need to be installed. In the following steps, you will modify the container login scripts to bring up the Application Launcher for all users. In addition, your instructor will identify a word processing and spreadsheet package for installation through the Application Launcher.

Step 1: Modifying Login Scripts

In this step, do the following:

1. Modify the Engineering, Manufacturing, and Business container login scripts to run the Novell Application Launcher (NAL) software automatically.

2. Verify that your login scripts work by logging in as a user from each department.

3. Verify to your instructor or lab assistant that all your users have access to the Netscape Navigator application. Upon completion, have your instructor or lab assistant initial the following line:

Instructor checkoff: _____   Date: _____

Step 2: Installing a Word Processing Application

All network users will need to be able to access a centralized word processing application. Your instructor will supply you with the name and location of the word processing software he or she wants you to install for your Universal Aerospace network. Follow these steps to install the software using the snAppShot software:

1. Determine the location for the NAL installation files and record the path on the following line:

   _____

2. Check with your instructor to determine whether to run the application from your local workstation's hard drive or from the server. If running the application from the server, select a different path for the application files than the one you recorded in Step 1 and record the path in the following space:

   _____

3. Start the snAppShot application and supply the file locations for the first snapshot scan.

4. Install the application software by running the application's setup program from the path specified by your instructor.

5. Perform the final snapshot scan using the directory you specified to install the application as recorded in Step 2.

6. Create an Application object in your ##UAS container.

7. Configure the Application object to enter the path to the executable file for the application, the Windows 95/98 operating system, and access for all users in your organization.

8. Uninstall the application from your workstation.

9. Log out.

10. Log in using your ##Admin username. The new application icon should appear in the Application Launcher window.

11. Install the application by double-clicking its icon.

12. If necessary, restart your computer, log in using your ##Admin username, and run the application. If the application will not start, be sure the Path to executable field includes the entire path to the executable file, including the volume name, if necessary.

13. Have your instructor check your application installation and initial the following line.

Instructor checkoff: _____   Date: _____

Step 3: Installing a Spreadsheet Application

Assume that the Accounting department recently purchased a new spreadsheet that is to be used only by Terry Blackwell, George Perez, Paul Alm, and Amy Pan. You may wish to create a group named SPUSER and add the selected users to this group. In this exercise, you will need to follow these steps to install a spreadsheet application as specified by your instructor for use by only the specified users:

1. Determine the location for the Application Launcher installation files and record the path on the following line:

   _____

2. Check with your instructor to determine whether to run the application from your local workstation's hard drive or from the server. If running the application from the server, select a different path for the application files than the one you recorded in Step 1 and record the path in the following space:

   _____

3. Start the snAppShot application and supply the file locations for the first snapshot scan.

4. Install the spreadsheet application software by running its setup program from the path specified by your instructor.

5. Perform the final snapshot scan using the directory you specified to install the application as recorded in Step 2.

6. Create an Application object in your ##Business container.

7. Configure the Application object to enter the path to the executable file, the Windows 95/98 operating system, and access for the specified users. If possible, use group accounts or containers to reduce the number of individual names.

8. Uninstall the application from your workstation.

9. Log out.

10. Log in using your ##Admin username. The new application icon should appear in the Application Launcher window.

11. Install the application by double-clicking it.

12. If necessary, restart your computer, log in using your ##Admin username, and run the application. If the application will not start, be sure the Path to executable field includes the entire path to the executable file, including the volume name, if necessary.

13. Verify that the spreadsheet application appears only when the selected users log in on your workstation.

14. Have your instructor check your spreadsheet application installation and initial the following line.

    Instructor checkoff: _____   Date: _____

Step 4: Create Desktop Profiles

After seeing how well the standard desktop profile worked for the Manufacturing department, Dave Heise would like you to implement unique profiles for each of the departments. To help you do this, Jennifer has supplied you with the form shown in Figure 9-33 that she uses to define user profiles (A copy of this form can also be found in Appendix B.). Fill out the form and then create and test the user profiles. After you complete these tasks, have your instructor or lab assistant check your work and initial the following line:

Instructor checkoff: _____   Date: _____

User Profile Worksheet					
Company/Department:					
Date:					
Created by:					
Profile Name	Context	Associations	Wallpaper	Screen Saver	Desktop Scheme

Figure 9-33   User Profile Worksheet

10

OPERATING THE SERVER CONSOLE

After reading this chapter and completing the exercises, you will be able to:

♦ Describe essential NetWare console commands and NetWare Loadable Modules (NLMs)

♦ Use NetWare console commands to secure the server console

♦ Use Java utilities to view server statistics and create a user

♦ Use remote console management to access the server console from a workstation attached to the network

♦ Configure workstations to access the network using the TCP/IP protocol

♦ Use the VREPAIR NLM to fix volume problems

♦ Use the SMS (Storage Management System) storage system to back up network data

With NetWare, most of the activities necessary to set up and maintain the network occur at the workstation. However, there are times when it is necessary to access the server console to shut down the server or start it up, back up network data, install products such as the Web Server, and secure the server from unauthorized access. The server console has taken on new importance in NetWare 5 with its ability to run Java applications and with the introduction of the ConsoleOne utility.

Because of the importance of the server console to maintaining the network, Novell requires CNAs to be familiar with basic console commands as well as the ConsoleOne utility. In addition, because servers are often kept in secure locations and therefore may sometimes be rather inaccessible, NetWare can access the server console from a client computer. In this chapter, you will learn how to use console commands and utilities that are important to monitoring, backing up, and securing the server. In addition, you will learn how to implement the NetWare remote console facility to access the server console from a client workstation or through a modem.

CONSOLE OPERATIONS

Server operations consist of using commands that can be divided into two major categories: console commands and NLMs. **Console commands** are part of the NetWare server operating system kernel program (SERVER.EXE) and therefore are always in the memory of the server computer. Because console commands are integrated into the SERVER.EXE kernel program, when you enter a console command, the system immediately executes it without loading any additional software. **NetWare Loadable Modules (NLMs)** are external programs that are loaded into the memory of the server computer and add functionality to the NetWare kernel operating system. To work successfully with the server console, it is important to know how to use the common console commands and NLMs. In this section, you will learn what a CNA needs to know about using console commands and NLMs to perform common server console operations.

Starting the Server

As described in Appendix A, a NetWare server contains at least two disk partitions: one for DOS and one for NetWare. Initially, a NetWare server starts from the DOS partition (the C drive). As illustrated in Figure 10-1, the NetWare server consists of the SERVER kernel software along with several NLMs.

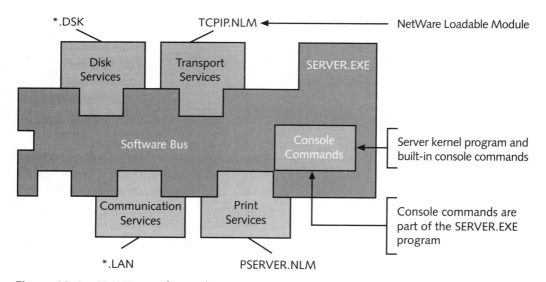

Figure 10-1 NetWare software bus

The SERVER.EXE program provides the core NetWare services such as file sharing and provides a software bus for NLMs. Most network services such as Novell Distributed Print Services (NDPS) and Novell Directory Services (NDS), along with device drivers, are provided through loading NLMs.

To bring up the server, you start by running the SERVER.EXE program from the DOS partition. During installation, the SERVER.EXE program along with its many support files and NLMs are stored on the DOS partition in a directory named Nwserver. To bring up the server, you need to change your current directory to Nwserver and run the SERVER program as follows:

```
C:\>cd nwserver
C:\nwserver>server
```

During server installation a new AUTOEXEC.BAT file is created which contains the CD\NWSERVER and SERVER startup commands. However, when configuring server hardware, it is sometimes desirable to be able to exit the server boot process to go directly to the DOS prompt. For this reason, after completing the Universal Aerospace server installation, Eric Kenton modified the AUTOEXEC.BAT file of the server computer to include the following commands, which give the operator an option to exit to DOS prior to starting the server.

```
CLS
CD\NWSERVER
ECHO Press any key to start the server or Ctrl Break to exit to DOS
PAUSE
SERVER
```

 The PAUSE statement provides the console operator with the option of exiting to DOS without starting the server. This can be useful for troubleshooting or upgrading software, but after successful completion of these tasks, you may wish to remove this command so that the SERVER program will immediately load when the computer starts.

As the SERVER program is loading, it reads commands from the STARTUP.NCF file also located in the Nwserver directory. This file contains the names of the disk drivers and other configuration commands as shown in Figure 10-2.

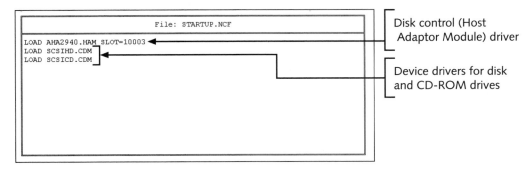

Figure 10-2   Startup NetWare control file

After the SERVER program has loaded its disk drivers, it mounts the SYS volume and continues to read commands from the AUTOEXEC.NCF file stored in the System directory of the SYS volume. As illustrated in Figure 10-3, the AUTOEXEC.NCF file contains commands that identify the server's name, internal address, and any NLMs, such as the network card drivers, that must be loaded for server operation.

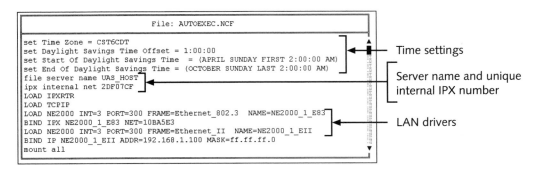

Figure 10-3   Autoexec NetWare control file

The appearance of the console screen after the server starts depends upon the NLMs that are loaded. Figure 10-4 shows the Universal Aerospace server console screen after startup. The screen displays the Broker window that was loaded as part of NDPS. Although some NLMs, such as the Broker, display information on the console as shown in Figure 10-4, many NLMs such as disk and LAN drivers simply provide operating system extensions and need no separate console screen.

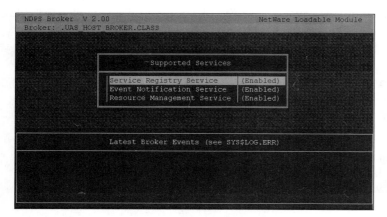

Figure 10-4 Initial console screen

You can use the [Ctrl] + [Esc] key combination to view a window showing all NLM screens from which you can select, as shown in Figure 10-5.

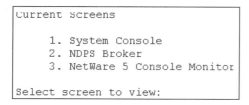

Figure 10-5 Console selection screen

You can now enter the number of the screen you want to view. For example, to change to the System Console screen, you would enter 1 and press [Enter] to display the console prompt as shown in Figure 10-6. An alternate way to switch between console screens is to use the [Alt] + [Esc] combination to rotate screens until you come to the screen you want.

Your console screen may show different modules based on your server's configuration.

Figure 10-6 Console prompt

Console Commands

To operate a server console effectively, you will need to know how to use the basic console commands that are built into the NetWare operating system. As a result, to become an effective CNA, you should know the purpose and use of each of the console commands identified in Table 10-1. This section describes the most common console commands you will need to know and provides examples of using the commands to perform common server operations.

Table 10-1   Essential Console Commands

Command Syntax	Description
ADD NAME SPACE *name* [TO VOLUME] *volume_name*	Adds space to a volume's directory entry table to support other operating system file-naming conventions. Replace *name* with MAC or OS2. Replace *volume_name* with the volume to which the specified name space is to be added.
BIND *protocol* TO *driver\board_name* [*driver_parameters*]	Attaches a protocol to a LAN card. Replace *protocol* with protocol name (such as IPX or IP). Replace *driver\board_name* with either the name of the card drive program or an optional name assigned to the network board. You can optionally replace *drive_parameters* with the hardware settings that identify the network interface card (such as I/O port and Interrupt).
BROADCAST	Sends the specified message to all currently logged-in users.
CLS/OFF	Clears the file server console screen.
CONFIG	Displays configuration information about each network card including hardware settings, network address, protocol, and frame type.
DISABLE /ENABLE LOGIN	Prevents or enables new user logins.
DISPLAY SERVERS	Displays all servers in the file server's router table including the number of routers (hops) to get to each server.
DOWN	Closes all files and volumes, disconnects all users, and takes the file server off-line.
LOAD [*path*]*module_name* [*parameters*]	Loads a NetWare Loadable Module (NLM) in the file server's RAM. Optionally replace *path* with the DOS or NetWare path leading to the directory containing the module to be loaded. Replace *module_name* with the name of the NLM you wish to load. Optional *parameters* may be entered depending upon the module being loaded.
MEMORY	Displays the total amount of memory available to the file server computer.
MODULES	Lists all currently loaded modules starting with the last module loaded.
MOUNT *volume_name* [All] DISMOUNT *volume_name*	Places a volume on- or off-line. Replace *volume_name* with the name of the volume you want mounted or *ALL* to mount all NetWare volumes.
SEND *"message"* [TO] *username\connection_number*	Sends a message to a specified user. Replace *message* with a message line you want sent and replace *username\connection_number* with either the name of the currently logged-in user or the connection number assigned to the user. The *connection_number* can be obtained from the Connection option of the MONITOR NLM.
SET TIME	Allows you to change the file server's current system date and time.

10

Table 10-1   Essential Console Commands (continued)

Command Syntax	Description
UNBIND *protocol* [FROM] *LAN_driver\board_name*	Removes a protocol from a LAN card. Replace protocol with the name of the protocol stack (such as IPX) you wish to remove from the card. Replace *LAN_driver\board_name* with either the name of the driver program that has been loaded for the network card, or the name assigned to the network card by the LOAD command.
UNLOAD *module_name*	Removes a NetWare Loadable Module from memory and returns the memory space to the operating system. Replace *module_name* with the name of the currently loaded module as given in the MODULES command.

BIND [protocol] TO [driver]

The BIND command attaches a protocol stack to a network card and is necessary to allow workstations using that protocol to communicate with the file server. Replace the *protocol* parameter with the name of the protocol stack you want to attach to the network card. Replace *driver* with the name of the network card. For example, you can bind the TCP/IP protocol to the NE2000 card driver by entering the command BIND IP TO NE2000 and then supplying the network address as shown in Figure 10-7.

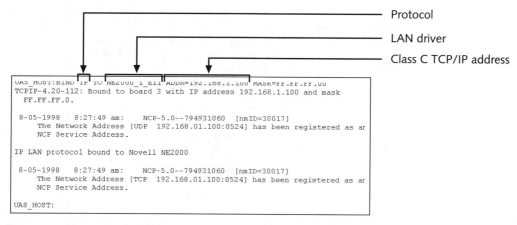

Protocol
LAN driver
Class C TCP/IP address

```
UAS_HOST:BIND IP TO NE2000_1_E11 ADDR=192.168.1.100 MASK=FF.FF.FF.00
TCPIP-4.20-112: Bound to board 3 with IP address 192.168.1.100 and mask
    FF.FF.FF.0.

8-05-1998   8:27:49 am:    NCP-5.0--794931060  [nmID=30017]
    The Network Address [UDP  192.168.01.100:0524] has been registered as an
    NCP Service Address.

IP LAN protocol bound to Novell NE2000

8-05-1998   8:27:49 am:    NCP-5.0--794931060  [nmID=30017]
    The Network Address [TCP  192.168.01.100:0524] has been registered as an
    NCP Service Address.

UAS_HOST:
```

Figure 10-7   Sample BIND command

CONFIG

The CONFIG command displays information about the server and network card configuration as shown in Figures 10-8 and 10-9.

```
File server name: UAS_HOST
IPX internal network number: 02DF07CF
Server Up Time:  2 Days 1 Hour 25 Minutes 49 Seconds

Novell NE2000
      Version 3.65a   December 22, 1997
      Hardware setting: I/O ports 300h to 31Fh, Interrupt 3h
      Node address: 002035567FB3
      Frame type: ETHERNET_802.3
      Board name: NE2000_1_E83
      LAN protocol: IPX network 010BA5E3

Novell NE2000
      Version 3.65a   December 22, 1997
      Hardware setting: I/O ports 300h to 31Fh, Interrupt 3h
      Node address: 002035567FB3
      Frame type: ETHERNET_802.2
      Board name: NE2000_1_E82
      LAN protocol: IPX network 010BA5E2
<Press ESC to terminate or any other key to continue>
```

Figure 10-8   Sample CONFIG command, screen 1

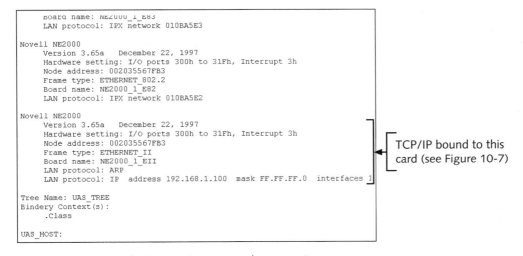

Figure 10-9   Sample CONFIG command, screen 2

Notice that in addition to displaying the file server's name and internal network address, the CONFIG command displays the following information about each network adapter in the file server:

- Name of the LAN driver
- Board name assigned when the LAN driver was loaded
- Current hardware settings including interrupt, I/O port, memory address, and Direct Memory Access (DMA) channel
- Node (station) address assigned to the network adapter
- Protocol stack that was bound to the network adapter
- Network address of the cabling scheme for the network adapter
- Frame type assigned to the network adapter

You should use the CONFIG command before installing memory boards or network adapters in the server so that you have a current list of all hardware settings on the existing boards. This will help you to select unique interrupt and I/O address settings for the new cards. In addition, you can use the CONFIG command to determine the network address of a cable system prior to adding another server to the network.

If you accidentally bring up another server using a different network address for the same cable system, router configuration errors between the servers will interfere with network communications.

DISPLAY SERVERS

The DISPLAY SERVERS command is useful to determine whether the server is properly attached to a multiserver network. When a server first attaches to a network, it sends a broadcast to all machines on the network, advertising its presence. From these broadcasts, the servers and workstations on the network build **router tables** that include the names of all servers and routers on the network. The DISPLAY SERVERS command lists all servers that have been inserted into the router table, as shown in Figure 10-10.

```
UAS_HOST:DISPLAY SERVERS
   CTS_HOST        1    CTS_HOST        2    CTS_PSERVER   2    UAS_HOST        [
   UAS_HOST        0    UAS_HOST_BRO    0    UAS_TREE____  0    UAS_TREE____    [
There are 8 known services.
UAS_HOST:
```

Figure 10-10   Sample DISPLAY SERVERS command

If a new server does not appear in other server router tables, and the new server does not "see" the other servers on the network, your server is not properly communicating with the network. The most common problems are that the IPX protocol has not been bound to the network card or the network card driver is using a different frame type than the other servers. If the new server shows up on other servers, but no servers are showing up on the new server, it may mean that the network card in the new server has a conflicting interrupt or memory address and cannot receive network packets from other servers. You should use the CONFIG command to check for an overlapping interrupt or memory address.

DISABLE/ENABLE LOGIN

The DISABLE LOGIN command prevents new users from accessing services on the NetWare server. Prior to shutting down the server, you should first issue the DISABLE LOGIN message to prevent any additional users from accessing the server and then use the BROADCAST command to send a message to all existing users, telling them that the server will be shutting down in the specified time period and that they should close all files and log out of the server. If the DISABLE LOGIN command were not issued, new users might log in to the server after the message was broadcast and not be aware the server was shutting down shortly. Another use of the Disable Login command is to temporarily prevent users from logging in while you perform certain maintenance work such as loading new drivers or backing up the system. After the work is complete and the server is ready for use, you can issue the ENABLE LOGIN command to allow users to again log in and use the server.

DOWN

The DOWN command deactivates the NetWare server operating system, removes all workstation connections, and returns the server to the DOS prompt. Before issuing the DOWN command, you should disable new logins and broadcast a message to all users as shown in Figure 10-11. If active sessions exist, the NetWare operating system will issue a warning message asking whether you want to terminate active sessions.

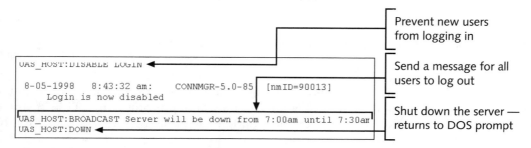

Figure 10-11   Shutting down the server

If you receive this message, you should cancel the DOWN command and use the MONITOR utility described in the next section to determine which connections have open files and then send a message to the user to log out. If no one is at the workstation and data files have been left open, you may need to go to the station to close the file or files and log out the user. In this case, you should be sure to remind the users not to leave their workstation unattended while data files are open.

LOAD

The LOAD command loads an NLM into memory and executes it. By default, the LOAD command will search for the requested module in the SYS:System directory. However, you can specify a different path. Valid paths can include NetWare volume names as well as DOS local drive letters. When a module is loaded into memory, it remains there until the console operator ends the program or uses the UNLOAD command to remove the software from memory. You can place optional parameters after the LOAD command, depending on the needs of the module you are loading.

With NetWare 5, it is no longer necessary to use the LOAD command to run an NLM. By simply typing the name of the NLM, you ensure that the system will automatically perform the load process.

MODULES

The MODULES command lists all the currently loaded modules along with their name, version number, and date. The modules are listed in sequence, starting with the last module loaded and ending with the first module loaded. In addition to listing what modules have been loaded, the MODULES command is also useful for quickly checking the version number and date of a module to determine NetWare compatibility or looking for network problems that are known to be caused by defective versions of certain modules.

MOUNT and DISMOUNT

Mounting a volume is the process of loading information from the volume's directory entry table (DET) into the file server's RAM, thereby making the volume available for access by users and the file server's operating system. The MOUNT command is needed to mount a volume that has been taken off-line using the DISMOUNT command or that did not mount correctly when the file server was started. Normally the MOUNT ALL command is inserted into the file server's AUTOEXEC.NCF startup file during installation and will attempt to mount all volumes when the file server is brought up. However, in some cases, such as after a file server crash, some volumes may not mount due to errors in their File Allocation Tables (FAT) or DET. When this happens, it is necessary to use the VREPAIR module to correct the FAT problem and then use the MOUNT command to bring the repaired volume online. More information regarding the use of the VREPAIR command to fix volume problems is presented later in this chapter.

SEND

The SEND command on the server console is used to send a message to a specific client. The most common use of the SEND command is to request a user to log out prior to shutting down the file server. Messages can be sent to either a user's login name or connection number. For example, to send a message to the user at connection number 9, enter the following command:

```
SEND "Server going down in 5 minutes" TO 9
```

SET TIME

The SET TIME command is used to change the current server time or date. In a multiple server network tree, a single server is designated as a Reference time server. All other servers on the network will synchronize their time to the Reference server. As a result, in a multiple server network, you should change time only at the Reference server. Novell recommends checking the time from DOS or CMOS and then making any corrections before starting the SERVER program. The following commands show several ways of using SET TIME to change the file server's current date and time to 3:00 p.m., October 30, 1999:

```
SET TIME 10/30/99 3:00p
SET TIME October 30, 1999 3:00p
SET TIME October 30, 1999
SET TIME 3:00p
```

UNBIND

The UNBIND command is used to unload a protocol stack from a LAN driver causing the server to stop communicating with other machines using that protocol. The most common use of the UNBIND command is to remove a defective server from the network. For example, assume you have bound the IPX protocol to a LAN driver and used the wrong network number for the cable system. Almost immediately, the servers on the network will begin to complain that another router is calling the network a different name. To stop this problem, you can use the UNBIND command to remove the protocol from the network card and then reissue the BIND command using the correct network address, as shown in Figure 10-12.

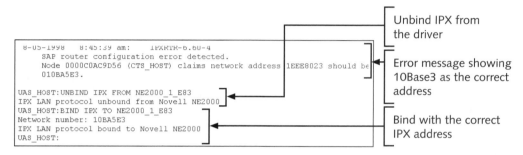

Figure 10-12 Changing a network address

NetWare Loadable Modules (NLMs)

One of the strengths of NetWare is its use of NLMs to add functionality to the core operating system. Because NLMs play such an important role in the tailoring of the NetWare network, it is important that a CNA be familiar with the standard NLMs that are included with the NetWare operating system.

As shown in Table 10-2, NLMs can be classified into four general categories based on their function, with each category having its own extension.

Table 10-2 NLM Categories

Category	Extension	Description
Disk drivers	.HAM and .CDM	Controls access to the NetWare disk partitions. Commands to load these modules are usually placed in the STARTUP.NCF file.
LAN drivers	.LAN	Specifies a LAN driver. Each network card must be controlled by a compatible LAN driver. Commands to load these modules are placed in the AUTOEXEC.NCF file.
Name space	.NAM	Contains logic to support other workstation naming conventions such as are found on Apple Macintosh, OS/2, and UNIX-based computers. Commands to load name space modules are usually placed in the STARTUP.NCF file.
General purpose	.NLM	Adds additional services and functions to the file server's operating system.

In addition to providing the special modules for controlling disk and network cards, NetWare comes with a number of general-purpose NLMs in the SYS:System directory that have the extension .NLM and may be used to provide a wide range of capabilities as shown in Table 10-3. In this section, you will learn about several of these modules that CNAs need to know how to use to manage their network file servers.

Table 10-3   General-Purpose NLMs

NLM	Description
CDROM.NLM	Provides support for CD-ROM commands.
INSTALL.NLM	Enables users to work with NetWare partitions, volumes, and system files.
MONITOR.NLM	Monitors file server performance, hardware status, and memory usage.
NLICLEAR.NLM	Immediately clears the workstation's connection when the corresponding workstation is shut down or restarted.
REMOTE.NLM	Enable users to view and operate the NetWare server console from a remote workstation. Requires a password.
RSPX.NLM	Allows the Remote module to send and receive console screens and commands over the local network cable.
RS232.NLM	Allows the Remote module to send and receive console screens and commands over the Asynchronous port.
UPS.NLM	Enables users to monitor the status of the UPS (uninterruptible power supply) and shut down the server prior to depleting the battery.
VREPAIR.NLM	Checks the specified volume for errors and allows the operator to write corrections to the disk.

Disk Drivers

When you first start the NetWare operating system by running the SERVER.EXE program, the system does not have a way of directly controlling the disk drives on the server computer until a disk driver module is loaded. Accessing the DOS partition of the hard disk and floppy disk drives does not require the disk driver because they are available through the local DOS operating system until you remove it from the computer by using the REMOVE DOS commands. As described in Appendix A, when you install NetWare on the server computer, disk driver modules are copied into the DOS partition. In NetWare 5, disk drivers consist of Host Bus Adapter (HBA) modules and Control Device Modules (CDM). The HBA module manages the disk controller card whereas the CDMs manage the individual devices attached to the card. This arrangement allows the controller card to have different types of devices—such as disk drives, CD-ROMs, and tape systems—attached to it. The commands to load the appropriate HAM and CDM modules for your computer are later placed in the STARTUP.NCF file so that when the SERVER.EXE program starts, it will load the correct disk driver to have access to the NetWare volumes.

LAN Drivers

As described previously, before a server can access the network cable, a LAN driver for the network controller card must be loaded and a protocol bound to that LAN driver. Standard network drivers all have the extension .LAN and may be found in the SYS:System directory after you have installed the NetWare operating system files. If your network card does not use one of the standard drivers, the correct driver software should be included on a disk that comes with the network card. Frame types specify the address format used to send data packets sent over the wire. For example, assume Universal Aerospace has some older workstations that need to use the Ethernet_802.3 packet format. Figure 10-13 shows an example of using LOAD and BIND commands to add a new frame type to the NE2000 Ethernet card driver.

10

```
UAS_HOST:LOAD NE2000 PORT=300 INT=3 FRAME=ETHERNET_802.3 NAME=NE2000_1_E83
Loading module NE2000.LAN
  Previously loaded module was used re-entrantly
UAS_HOST:BIND IPX TO NE2000_1_E83
Network number: 10BA5E3
IPX LAN protocol bound to Novell NE2000

 8-05-1998   9:43:57 am:    RSPX-4.11-28
     Remote console connection granted for 010BA5E2:0000C0BD6D2B

UAS_HOST:
```

Figure 10-13   Adding a new frame type

Name Space Modules

Name space modules add logic to the NetWare operating system that allow it to support non-DOS file-names. By default, NetWare 5 will load the LONG.NAM module to support Windows and OS/2 filenames that may contain up to 255 characters including spaces and special symbols. In addition to loading the LONG.NAM module, NetWare includes a MAC.NAM name module in the SYS:System directory. When using name space support, you must load the necessary modules with the .NAM extension after the disk driver in the STARTUP.NCF file. In addition to loading the .NAM module, you also need to add name space to the volumes where you want to store the long filenames. For example, the commands shown in Figure 10-14 were used to add the name space MAC to the Corp volume.

```
UAS_HOST:LOAD MAC
Loading module MAC.NAM
  NetWare Macintosh Name Space Support
  Version 4.12    March 19, 1998
  Copyright 1998 Novell, Inc.  All rights reserved.
  MAC.NAM does not have any XDC data
  Uni-Processor NLM
  Internal symbol information loaded for MAC.NAM loaded
```

Figure 10-14   Adding name space to a volume

NWCONFIG

The NWCONFIG module shown in Figure 10-15 is used during the initial installation of NetWare on the server computer as described in Appendix A. In addition to using this module during the initial installation process, network administrators may need to use the NWCONFIG module to perform such tasks as adding new disk space to an existing volume, maintaining the STARTUP and AUTOEXEC files, or installing new products and services such as the Web Server or Domain Name Services.

Figure 10-15   NWCONFIG menu

In NetWare 5, the NWCONFIG.NLM module has replaced the INSTALL.NLM module used to configure earlier versions of NetWare.

MONITOR

The MONITOR utility module is one of the most powerful NLMs supplied with the NetWare operating system. In this section, you will learn how to use the MONITOR utility to lock the server console, as well as view server performance, connection information, and disk and network statistics. After you load the MONITOR utility, the main monitor screen displays the version and date of the NetWare operating system. The top half of the screen displays a General Information window, which displays information regarding your server's available memory and performance. The lower half of the screen displays a menu of available options as shown in Figure 10-16.

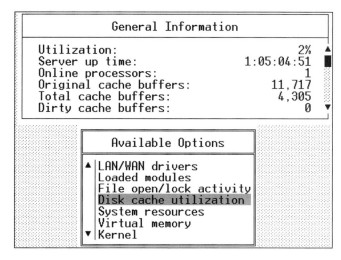

Figure 10-16   MONITOR window

You can view the entire list of options by pressing the Tab key to show all Available Options as shown in Figure 10-17. *Server up time* measures the length of time the server has been running since it was last started. The *Utilization* field shows the percentage of time the processor is busy. In most cases, utilization should be less than 70 percent. The *Original cache buffers* field contains the number of buffers (4 KB blocks) available when the server was first started, whereas the *Total cache buffers* field contains the number of buffers currently available for file caching. If the number of Total cache buffers figure is less than one-third of the Original cache buffers figure, your server is running low on memory and you should either unload modules or add more RAM as soon as possible. The *Dirty cache buffers* field contains a count of the number of buffers that have been modified but are waiting to be written to disk. A large number of dirty cache buffers indicates the disk system is bogging down and a faster disk or an additional disk controller card may be necessary. The *Current disk requests* field shows how many requests for disk access are currently waiting to be processed. As with the dirty cache buffers figure, you can use this number to determine whether disk performance is slowing down the network.

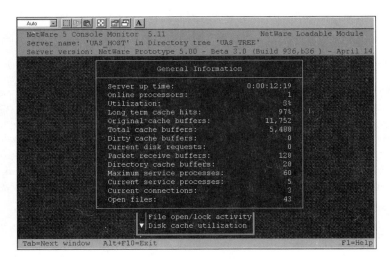

Figure 10-17   Expanded MONITOR window

The value in the *Packet receive buffers* field indicates the number of buffers that have been established to receive packets that have been received by the server and are waiting to be serviced. If this number approaches the default maximum of 400, your file server is falling behind in servicing incoming packets and therefore slowing down the network, so you may need to obtain a faster server, increase the disk speed, or add more memory depending on the other statistics. The *Directory cache buffers* value indicates the number of buffers that have been reserved for disk directory blocks. Increasing the initial number of directory cache buffers available when the server first starts can sometimes improve the performance of the server when it is first started. The *Maximum Service processes* value indicates the number of "task handlers" that have been allocated for station requests. If the number of station requests in the packet receive buffers exceeds a certain limit, the server will add extra task handlers to execute the requests. Of course, this will in turn reduce the amount of memory and processing time for other activities. If the number of service processes approaches the default maximum of 20, and you have a high processor utilization, you may need to unload NLMs or add another file server to decrease the load on the current server. You can use the *Current Connections* field to see quickly how many stations are turned on and connected to the server. A station does not have to be logged in to appear in this statistic, since any computer running the DOS requester or shell uses up a connection on a file server. You can use the *Open files* field to help determine whether any files are currently open prior to shutting down the server.

The Utilization, Total cache buffers, Packet receive buffers, and Dirty cache buffers statistics together can give you a quick picture of your server's health simply by enabling you to verify that the utilization is under 70%, that the total cache buffers are at least 50% of the original cache buffers, and that the dirty cache buffers are less than 30% of the total cache buffers.

In addition to providing the General Information window, the MONITOR utility contains several menu options (shown previously in Figure 10-16) that you can use to view information about the performance and operation of your server. Selecting the *Connections* option will display a window showing all active connections and the username currently logged in. If no user is logged in to a given connection number, the message "NOT-LOGGED-IN" will appear next to the connection number. You can use this option to check for user activity prior to shutting down a server. You can disconnect a user by highlighting the username and pressing the Del key. To view information about any connection, select the connection number and press Enter. The *Volumes* option lists all mounted volumes along with the percentage of the volume space used. The *LAN/WAN drivers* option displays information on all LAN drivers loaded, including driver name, frame type, port, and interrupt. The *System resources* option provides a convenient way to view the percentage of cache buffers used. You can select the *Disk cache utilization* option to view the percentage of memory used for cache buffers as shown in Figure 10-18.

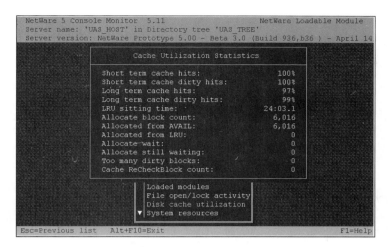

Figure 10-18   Cache memory utilization

Novell recommends that the long-term cache hits should be over 90%. If this figure is less than 90%, adding more memory or unloading NLM will increase server performance.

VREPAIR

The VREPAIR module can often be used to repair the File Allocation Table (FAT) of a volume that cannot be mounted. If your server crashes due to a hardware problem, power failure, or software bug, the server may not restart because of errors in the FAT of the SYS volume. In this situation, you can often use the VREPAIR utility to fix the problems in the FAT to mount the SYS volume and get the server up and running again. Because of the importance of VREPAIR in fixing volume errors as well as checking for volume problems, as a CNA you need to be familiar with how to use VREPAIR both to fix volume problems and check volumes for any errors.

Suppose that during a thunderstorm someone who wishes to remain anonymous turned off the server computer. After bringing the server back up, you want to check the CORP volume to ensure that the data structure has not been damaged. To do this, you call Eric Kenton, the CNE on staff, to get instructions on how to use the VREPAIR utility.

In this example, you follow along with Eric as he explains how to use the VREPAIR utility to remove the MAC name space from the CORP volume and log any error messages to a log file.

1. To use the VREPAIR command to check or fix problems on an existing volume, Eric entered the command VREPAIR to obtain the Volume Repair Utility menu shown in Figure 10-19. Eric explained that if you needed to use VREPAIR to fix a problem that prevents the SYS volume from being mounted, you would need to load the VREPAIR program from the DOS partition by using the command LOAD C:VREPAIR.

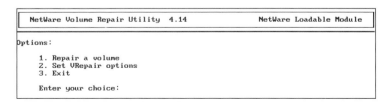

Figure 10-19   VREPAIR menu

2. Next he selects option 2 to view and set the VREPAIR options as shown in Figure 10-20.

```
Current VRepair Configuration:

    Quit if a required VRepair name space support NLM is not loaded.
    Write only changed directory and FAT entries out to disk.
    Write changes immediately to disk.
    Retain deleted files.

Options:

    1. Remove name space support from the volume
    2. Write all directory and FAT entries out to disk
    3. Keep changes in memory for later update
    4. Purge all deleted files
    5. Return to Main Menu

    Enter your choice: 5
```

Figure 10-20   VREPAIR options menu

3. Notice that the currently active settings are displayed on the top of the screen with additional options preceded by numbers listed on the lower half of the screen. Eric first selects option number 1 to remove name space support from the volume and then selects the Macintosh name space.

4. Eric suggests that it is best to select option 3, Keep changes in memory for later update, to give you the option of writing the changes to disk after you have noted all files that are being fixed.

5. After selecting the preceding options, Eric enters option number 5 to return to the main menu.

6. Next Eric selects the Repair a volume option from the main menu to start the volume repairs. Eric explained that if multiple volumes are currently dismounted, VREPAIR will allow you to select the volume to be repaired. If only one volume is currently dismounted, VREPAIR immediately begins scanning that volume. If no volumes have been dismounted, the error message "There are no unmounted volumes" will be displayed. Eric suggests that if you need to dismount a volume, you should use the [Alt] + [Esc] key combination to rotate to the console screen and then use the DISMOUNT command to make the desired volume available to the VREPAIR program. You can then use the [Alt] + [Esc] key combination to rotate back to the VREPAIR menu.

7. Next the VREPAIR utility displays the Current Error Settings menu shown in Figure 10-21.

 Dismounting the SYS or CORP volume may affect other students using the server. Before dismounting any volume, check with your instructor to determine what volume may be dismounted.

```
Current Error Settings:

    Pause after each error.
    Do not log errors to a file.

Options:

    1.  Do not pause after errors
    2.  Log errors to a file
    3.  Stop volume repair
    4.  Continue with volume repair

    Enter your choice: 4
```

Figure 10-21   VREPAIR current error settings

8. Eric selects option 2 to log errors and then enters SYS:System\VLOG.TXT for the log filename.

9. He then selects option 1 to prevent the system from pausing after each error message.

10. Finally he selects option 4 to start the volume repair process.

11. After the volume has been restored, if there are any changes, VREPAIR will pause and ask whether you want to write the repairs to disk as shown in Figure 10-22.

```
Total errors: 169
Current Error Settings:
      Do not pause after each error.
      Do not log errors to a file.
Press <F1> to change error settings.

Start 10:16:01 am
Checking volume CORP:

FAT blocks>...............................................................⁴
Counting directory blocks and checking directory FAT entries.
Mirror mismatches>........................................................⁴
Directories>..............................................................⁴
Files>....................................................................⁴
Trustees>.................................................................⁴
Deleted Files>............................................................⁴
Free blocks>..............................................................⁴
Done checking volume.
Number of FAT repairs: 0
Number of directory repairs: 169
Write repairs to the disk? (Y/N): y
```

Figure 10-22   VREPAIR completion window

12. After changes have been saved to disk, Eric suggests that you run the VREPAIR program again to scan the volume and check for any additional volume problems. He warns that in some cases it may take several passes to fix all problems. When you receive a clean report showing that there are no corrections to write to disk, you can exit the VREPAIR program and mount the volume by entering the command MOUNT CORP [Enter].

SERVER LICENSING

An ongoing concern of every network administrator is having the necessary number of licenses to support users and applications. With NetWare 5, Novell has provided network administrators and software vendors with **Novell Licensing Services (NLS)** to help monitor and control the use of licensed software on your network. As shown in Figure 10-23, NLS consists of License Service Provider (LSP) software that runs on NetWare servers along with NLS client software and license certificates.

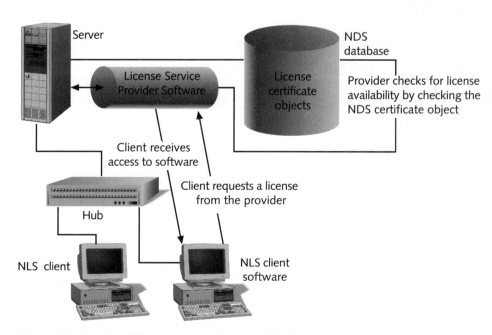

Figure 10-23   NetWare Licensing Services (NLS)

When NLS-enabled software requests a license, the LSP searches the NDS database for a license container object with available licenses. The LSP then checks out a license from the license container object for the requesting software to use. If no licenses are available, an error message is sent to the client requesting to run the software. You can use NetWare Administrator, NLS Manager, or NWCONFIG.NLM to install and create license certificates. NetWare Administrator or NLS Manager can also be used to monitor and manage license usage. In addition, with NLS Manager, you can create a report to view license usage over a selected time period.

At a management meeting, Dave Heise asked whether you could manage the number of users accessing the word processing package to be sure the license agreement was not violated. In this hands-on activity, you will use NetWare Administrator to view the license certificate for your NetWare server.

1. If necessary, start your computer and log in using your assigned ##Admin username.

2. Start NetWare Administrator.

3. Open a browse window for the Class container.

4. Double-click the **Novell+NetWare 5 Conn SCL + 500** container to display the SN: ########## object.

5. Double-click the **SN: #########** certificate to display the General window shown in Figure 10-24.

6. Click the **Policy Information** button to view detailed information about the license agreement.

7. Click **Cancel** to return to the NetWare Administrator browse window.

8. Log out.

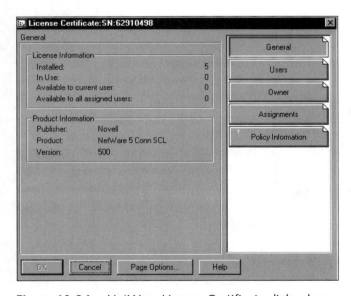

Figure 10-24   NetWare License Certificate dialog box

USING JAVA ON THE SERVER

One of the major new features of NetWare 5 is the ability of the server to run Java applications. The **Java** language was developed by Sun Microsystems and is used to develop Internet applications that can run on multiple platforms including an Internet browser such as Netscape. Having the capability to run Java applications opens up many possibilities for running client/server applications on the NetWare server in the future. A client/server application is one in which at least part of the application runs on the server while the user-interface component runs on the client workstation. The major reason AeroDyn installed NT servers in its Manufacturing department was the ability to run the server-based software. Although NT-based applications are typically limited to the NT platform, one of the strengths of Java applications is that they can run on multiple platforms. As a result, many Internet and client/server applications are being developed in Java to take advantage of operating system platform-independence. As one of the most powerful and fastest Java machines, NetWare 5 is in a good position to be a preferred choice for running Java applications over the Internet as well as on company intranets.

NetWare 5 ships with a Java-based application called **ConsoleOne**. Running Java applications on the server console requires extra hardware resources. Novell recommends at least 48 MB of RAM, a PS/2 or serial mouse, and a PCI video card that conforms to the VESA 1.2 specification or greater. If your video card does not meet VESA 1.2 standards, NetWare will load a default driver that supports only 640-by-480 resolution with 16 colors. To load the Java Virtual Machine (JVM), enter the command JAVA at the console prompt. To run a Java application automatically when the JVM loads, you can enter the command JAVA followed by any options along with the path and name of the application. Names of Java applications are case-sensitive and require long name space support of the volume where the application is stored.

The NetWare Java Virtual Machine provides an APPLET command to view Java applets that are defined as part of an HTML document. Java applets are often used in HTML documents to provide the user with interactive input options. To view a Java applet on the server, enter the command APPLET followed by the path and filename of the HTML document containing the <applet> tag. The APPLET command ignores all other HTML tags and executes only what is contained between the <applet> and </applet> tags. Because other HTML tags are not executed, the applet may appear differently on the console than it will on an actual browser screen.

10

With NetWare 5, Novell has provided a Java GUI console interface. The GUI platform is provided by an implementation of X Windows, allowing Java programs that conform to the Abstract Windowing Toolkit (AWT) to be displayed using the X Windows interface. To load GUI support, you can type the command STARTX at the server console. Although the NetWare GUI is not intended to be a full-featured desktop workstation, it does provide a graphical way to interact with the NetWare console. For example, Eric used the GUI interface to install the TCP/IP product by following these steps:

1. After using the STARTX command to display the GUI console, Eric clicked the Novell button to display a menu containing options for ConsoleOne, Install, Tools, and Exit GUI.

2. He next clicked the Install option to display a list of products already installed.

3. To install additional products, he clicked the new product button and provided the path to the installation CD.

4. Next he selected the product he wanted to install and clicked Next to display a product Summary window. He explained that you can customize any of the selected products by highlighting the product and clicking the Customize button.

5. After any customization is complete, he clicked the Finish button to install the selected product. Once the product was installed, Eric was prompted to restart the server. In case any users were logged in, Eric disabled login and broadcast a message before shutting down the server.

In addition to installing products, you can use the GUI interface to configure video resolution, background, and keyboard configurations.

The ConsoleOne GUI utility provides the administrator with a way to work with NDS objects along with the file system from the server console. In past versions of NetWare, it was necessary to perform all file and user maintenance from a workstation running NetWare Administrator. With the ConsoleOne addition to NetWare 5, Novell has provided the network administrator with a way to manage user and file system objects from the server console. This can prevent you from having to return to a client workstation to create a user or copy a file. For example, Eric recently used ConsoleOne to create a user object named Installer in the UAS container, as follows:

1. First he started the ConsoleOne utility to display the Novell ConsoleOne window shown in Figure 10-25.

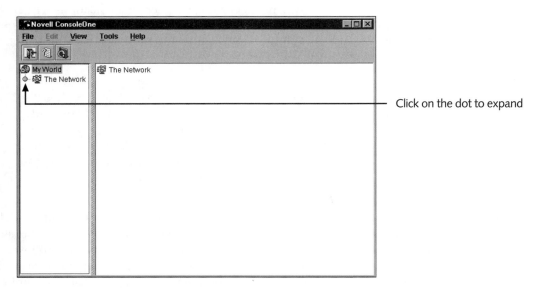

Figure 10-25 ConsoleOne window

2. Next he clicked the **dot** to the left of The Network object to display all services on the network.

3. He then clicked the **dot** to the left of the Novell Directory Services to display any existing trees.

4. In the left window pane, he clicked the **dot** to the left of the UAS_TREE to display a Login window.

5. He next logged in to the UAS_TREE using the Admin user object.

6. In the left window pane, he navigated to your ##UAS container and then used the right mouse button to display a pop-up menu.

7. He then pointed to the **New** option and clicked on the **User** option as shown in Figure 10-26.

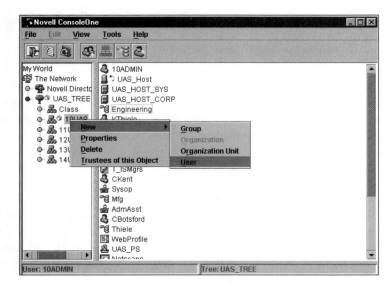

Figure 10-26 ConsoleOne Login window

8. Next he entered the name **Installer** in both the Login and Last name fields.

9. He then clicked **Create** and provided a password in the Create Authentication Secrets window. He then clicked **OK** to complete user creation.

Eric explained that you can modify user property information such as password and time restrictions by right-clicking the username and clicking the Properties option to display the user information window.

SECURING THE SERVER CONSOLE

Securing the server console is necessary to prevent unauthorized users from entering console commands or loading NLMs. Depending upon your organization, the need for server console security can range from keeping the server in a separate room to providing maximum security from intruders who are attempting to get access to your network. Locking the server room is one of the first measures of server security that should be put in place. In addition to locking the server room, the security measures described in this section will allow you to provide extra protection from unauthorized use of console commands.

The SECURE CONSOLE command automatically performs the following security functions intended to prevent several types of breaches in security:

- Prevents NLMs from being loaded from any directory other than the SYS:System directory
- Prevents keyboard entry into the operating system debugger
- Prevents using the SET TIME command to change date and time from the console. (A console operator or supervisor can still change the date and time by using the FCONSOLE utility from a workstation.)

One way an intruder could access or alter information in the file server is to store a special NLM in his or her home directory and then load the NLM from the console. The SECURE CONSOLE command prevents this because it allows NLMs to be loaded only from the SYS:System directory, making it impossible for an intruder to load the naughty module from another directory. For this reason, Novell recommends using the SECURE CONSOLE command since the only way an intruder can load a module after the SECURE CONSOLE command has been issued is to have necessary rights to copy the module into the SYS:System directory. Of course, for this part of the SECURE CONSOLE command to block loading NLMs effectively, you must be sure that no one has rights to SYS:System and that your Admin account is secure.

Certain security and accounting functions depend on date and time for their enforcement. For example, suppose that you secure a payroll clerk's username by a password and by allowing the user to log in only from the workstation in his or her office during regular work hours. Now suppose an intruder has learned the user's password and has access to the user's office on a weekend. Since the intruder has a master key, he or she could gain access to the file server console and use the SET TIME command to change the date and time to a normal weekday, allowing the intruder to log in from the payroll clerk's workstation and access or change the payroll data files.

In addition to the SECURE CONSOLE command, a very effective and easy way to implement security measures is to use the SCRSAVER utility to "lock" the server console, thereby requiring the operator to enter the Admin password to gain access to the console. To prevent unauthorized access to the server console in the future, Eric suggests you implement both console security procedures.

REMOTE CONSOLE MANAGEMENT

Often it is difficult or time-consuming to go to the server console to check server status, make changes, or fix problems with the NetWare operating system. In addition, in some cases, you might have to spend valuable time on the road driving to the locations of the servers you are supporting just to spend a few minutes on the server console. As a result, Novell has provided NetWare with a means of performing console operations from a workstation computer located on the local network or attached through a wide area network via the phone system.

With NetWare 3.12, Novell introduced the **Remote Management Facility (RMF)** to enable a network administrator to manage NetWare servers, version 3.1 and greater, from one location. RMF actually brings the server's console screen to the remote workstation running the RCONSOLE program, allowing network administrators to work with the server as if they were actually at the server computer. In addition to providing the convenience and time savings of being able to manage all servers from one location, the RMF can also help increase server security by allowing the network administrator to remove the monitor and keyboard from the server computer and lock the server in a restricted area where access can be controlled.

You control access to the RMF by assigning a password to each server console. As a result of these measures, only the Admin user or a remote console operator can use the RMF to manage a server's console. As a CNA, it is important to understand how to set up and use the RMF to manage a remote server by performing the following functions:

- Load the necessary NLMs to set up the remote console facility on a NetWare server.
- Use RCONSOLE to access a server from either a remote or locally attached client computer.
- Access the RCONSOLE available options menu.

Setting Up Remote Management

Setting up an RMF connection on a server involves loading the appropriate NLMs for the connection type to be used. Placing commands for the desired connection type in the AUTOEXEC.NCF file causes the server to load remote console management automatically each time the server is started. For a **direct link** connection, place the LOAD REMOTE and LOAD RSPX commands in the AUTOEXEC.NCF file as shown in Figure 10-27.

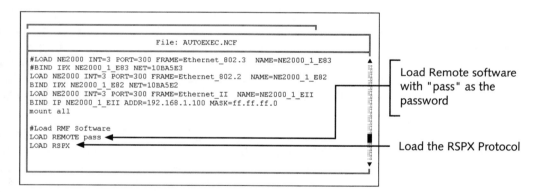

Figure 10-27   Remote console LOAD commands

When loading RMF from the AUTOEXEC.NCF file, it is important to place the LOAD REMOTE command first since RSPX requires the REMOTE module to run. If you use only the LOAD RSPX command, the RSPX software will automatically load the REMOTE module prior to running. However, in this case you will need to enter the password manually from the system console.

Notice the password following the LOAD REMOTE command. If no password is specified, the commands following the LOAD REMOTE command will not be executed until the operator first enters the password to be used by a remote console operator before he or she is granted access to the file server console. Placing a password after the LOAD REMOTE command allows the server to load the remote software automatically and continue without waiting for operator input. For this reason, you should normally include both the LOAD REMOTE [*password*] and LOAD RSPX commands in the AUTOEXEC.NCF file.

Using RCONSOLE

Once the necessary RMF software to support a direct link has been loaded on the server or servers, you can go to any client that meets the necessary hardware requirements and use the RCONSOLE utility to gain access to the console of a server. RCONSOLE provides a number of keystrokes that allow you to perform special functions. Table 10-4 contains a table of the keystrokes you should know to become a CNA.

Table 10-4 RCONSOLE Keystroke Usage

Function Key	Usage
Alt + F1	View the RCONSOLE menu
Alt + F2	Exit RCONSOLE
Alt + F3	Move forward through server console screens
Alt + F4	Move backward through server console screens
Esc	Resume remote console session

In addition to providing access to the server console, the RCONSOLE utility provides a menu of options that can be used to scan directories, transfer files, and shell out to DOS. For example, assume Eric has just brought you a floppy disk containing a new disk driver file that you want to load the next time the server is started. You want to transfer the disk driver file to the server's DOS partition without shutting down the server. Once the new disk driver is in the server's DOS partition, the next time you restart the server it will automatically load the new driver.

In this hands-on activity, you use RCONSOLE to transfer a program to the server's DOS partition to make it accessible to NetWare. To perform this activity, the REMOTE and RSPX modules must be loaded on the server. Refer to the section on Remote Console Management earlier in this chapter on how to load these modules.

1. If necessary, start your client computer and log in using your assigned ##Admin username.

2. On your C drive, use Notepad to create a text file named ##DISK.CDM (where ## represents your student number) that contains your name along with the following message: **This is a test file that represents a disk device controller.**

3. Start NetWare Administrator.

4. Click **Tools, Remote Console**.

5. If you receive a warning message regarding running RCONSOLE from Windows, press **Enter** to continue and display the Connection Type window.

6. Highlight the **LAN** option and press **[Enter]** to display the Available Servers window showing the UAS_HOST server.

7. To access the server, select **UAS_HOST** and then enter the remote password to display the server's MONITOR window.

8. To rotate to the console prompt, use the **[Alt] + [F3]** key combination. You can use the **[Alt] + [F4]** key combination to rotate back to a previous screen.

You should be aware that the Alt + Esc key combination (used to rotate between screens when at the actual server computer) does not work from RCONSOLE.

9. To copy a file to the server's DOS partition, press **[Alt] + [F1]** to display the Available Options menu shown in Figure 10-28.

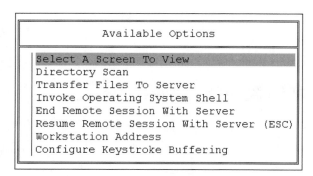

Figure 10-28   RCONSOLE options

10. To view files currently in the server's DOS partition, highlight the **Directory Scan** option and press **[Enter]**.

11. Next enter **C:** in the Target path field and press **[Enter]** to display a window showing all files in the C:\Nwserver directory.

12. Press **[Esc]** twice to return to the Available Options menu.

13. To view the names of the files on the local computer's floppy disk, highlight the **Invoke Operating System Shell** option and press **[Enter]** to display a DOS prompt.

14. Enter the command **DIR C:** to display a directory of all files on your client's disk. Locate the file you saved as ##DISK.CDM.

15. After locating your ##DISK.CDM file, type **EXIT** and press **[Enter]** to return to the Available Options menu.

16. To transfer the file to the server's DOS partition, highlight the **Transfer Files to Server** option and press **[Enter]** to enter the source and target paths as shown in Figure 10-29.

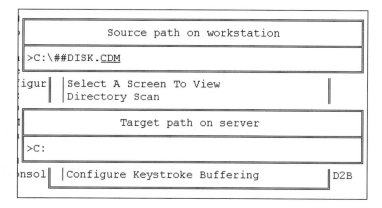

Figure 10-29   Transfer files window

17. After the transfer is complete, highlight the **Directory Scan** option and press **[Enter]** to verify that your ##DISK.CDM file is in the C:\Nwserver directory on the server. Next select the **Resume Remote Session with Server** option to return to the server console screen.

18. Press **[Alt] + [F2]** and respond with **Yes** to exit the server console screen and return to the Available Servers menu.

19. Finally, press **[Esc]** and respond with **Yes** to exit RCONSOLE and return to NetWare Administrator.

BACKING UP NETWORK DATA

An organization's data plays a critical role in today's highly competitive and rapidly changing world of business and industry. A company robbed of its information would certainly suffer major losses and in some cases may be forced out of business. Therefore, as a network administrator in an organization that relies upon the network for data storage and retrieval, you become the "keeper of the flame" in that you will be responsible for much if not all of your organization's critical data files. As a result, management is counting on your knowledge to provide a reliable storage system that is secure from unauthorized access and protected from accidental loss due to equipment failure, operator error, or natural disaster.

In previous chapters, you have learned how the NetWare network can be used to establish a secure directory structure that protects the organization's data from unauthorized access. Another advantage of using the NetWare network operating system is its ability to provide a centralized backup and restore procedure that can protect valuable data from being lost due to equipment failure or operator error. In addition, using NetWare you can implement a disaster recovery procedure that can enable your organization to continue to operate despite the loss of the NetWare server or even an entire building.

Understanding the Storage Management System

NetWare includes a **Storage Management System (SMS)** that allows you to back up even complex networks consisting of data residing on multiple file servers as well as data on DOS and OS/2 workstations. The NetWare server that runs the backup program and has the tape or other backup media attached is referred to as the **host** server. Other servers and client workstations that are being backed up are referred to as **target servers**. Under the SMS system, the term **parent** is used to refer to a data set such as a directory or subdirectory whereas the term **child** refers to a specific data set such as a file or program. SMS uses NLMs on the host server to communicate with modules on target devices reading the information from the target devices and sending it to the backup media, as shown in Figure 10-30.

10

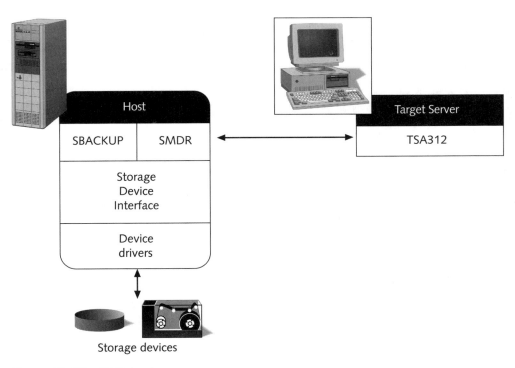

Figure 10-30   SMS backup process

The NetWare SMS consists of the following software components that may be run on NetWare servers as well as DOS or OS/2 workstations:

- Storage device drivers are loaded on the host server and control the mechanical operation of various storage devices and media such as tape drives.

- The Target Server Agents (TSAs) are loaded on the target server or servers and communicate with the SBACKUP program running on the host server. The purpose of the TSA is to get information from the target server's volumes and send it to the SBACKUP program running on the host server. A server can act as both host and target by running both the SBACKUP and TSA software.

- Workstation TSAs are run at the DOS or OS/2 workstations to back up data located on the local drives across the network.

- The enhanced SBACKUP utility is the main software provided with NetWare that runs on the host server or Windows workstation and works with the SMS architecture to control the backup process and transfer data to and from the host server.

Establishing a Backup System

Since having a reliable and tested backup system is one of the best medicines a network administrator can have to ensure a good night's sleep, spending some extra time planning and testing the backup system is well worthwhile. Establishing a successful backup system involves six steps:

1. Determine storage needs.
2. Determine a backup strategy.
3. Assign a backup user.
4. Run the backup software on a scheduled basis.
5. Test the backup.
6. Develop a disaster recovery procedure.

In this section, you will learn how to apply these steps to setting up the backup system for Universal Aerospace.

Determine Storage Needs

The first step in establishing a backup system for your network is to calculate how much data needs to be copied to the backup tape on a daily basis by determining what volumes and directories you plan to back up. If possible, you should then try to obtain an SMS-compatible tape backup system that has sufficient capacity to store your daily backup on one tape cartridge. In a single server environment, the server will act as both the host and target devices, requiring you to load both the SBACKUP and TSA modules on the same server. An advantage of having a server be both host and target devices is that a server backing up its own data runs almost four times faster than a host server backing up data across the network from another target server. As a result, when implementing SMS in a multiple-server environment, you should plan on making the server that has the most amount of data the host system.

Determine a Backup Strategy

Depending on the backup storage needs, one of three backup strategies, shown in Table 10-5, is normally implemented.

Table 10-5 Backup Strategies

Type of Backup	Data to Back Up	Status of "Archive" Attribute
Full	All data, regardless of when or if it has previously been backed up	Cleared
Incremental	Files that have been created or modified since the last Full or Incremental backup	Cleared
Differential	All data that has been modified since the last Full backup	Not cleared

With the **Full backup** strategy, all data is copied to the backup tape each night. This backup strategy will work well for Universal Aerospace since the current size of the files to be included on the backup does not exceed one tape cartridge. The advantage of the Full backup strategy is that should a crash occur, only the previous day's backup needs to be restored. The disadvantage is the need for large tape capacity and the time required to perform each backup.

The **Incremental backup** strategy provides the shortest time for each backup since only the data files that have been changed that day are copied to the backup. With the Incremental backup strategy, a Full backup is made at the beginning of the week and then an Incremental backup is made each day. The disadvantage of this strategy is that all Incremental backup tapes must be restored if data is lost. For example, if a crash occurs on Thursday, you will first need to restore the Monday Full backup followed by the Tuesday and Wednesday Incremental backups.

A compromise between the Full backup and the Incremental is the Differential backup strategy. With the **Differential backup**, all files that have changed since the last Full backup are copied to the tape. This means that the size of the tape backup will increase as the week progresses. The advantage of the Differential strategy is that should a crash occur later in the week, you need to restore only the Full backup and the last day's Differential backup.

Currently, the CNE consultant Eric recommends implementing a Full backup strategy for Universal Aerospace to make a complete backup of all data as well as the NDS database each day. In the future, as the data storage requirements of Universal Aerospace grow beyond the space of one tape cartridge, the consultant recommends implementing a Differential backup strategy to reduce the backup time and eliminate the need for someone to change tapes during the middle of the night.

Assign a Backup User

Although you can log in as Admin to perform the backup procedure, most network administrators prefer to create a separate username to do backups. Creating a separate username has the advantage of allowing you to assign other people to perform the backup procedure as well as limiting the number of times you need to log in to the network as Admin. The username that you create to perform the backup process needs to have the following access rights and privileges:

- To back up the file system, the usernames need to have Read, File Scan, and Modify rights to the volumes and directories that are to be included in the backup. The Modify right is necessary for the backup program to reset the Archive attribute after backing up data files. When assigning these rights to the directory, you need to be aware of any IRFs (Inherited Rights Filters) that may block these rights from a subdirectory that you want to back up.

- To back up the NDS database, the backup username needs to have the Browse object and Read property rights in the containers to be included in the backup.

- The person who is performing the backup needs to know the password used on the host server as well as the passwords assigned to any target servers or clients.

Run the Backup Software

After you have decided on a backup strategy and created any necessary usernames, your next step is to test the SMS installation by backing up your server data and then testing the backup by restoring selected files from the backup tape.

The process that Eric uses to run the SMS backup system from the server console screen is as follows:

1. To load the enhanced SBACKUP utility, Eric first needs to load the Storage Manager Device Redirector software by entering the command LOAD SMDR.

2. The Store Manager next displays a configuration screen asking for the default group context, SDMR context, and Administrator name. Eric presses [Enter] three times to accept the default contexts and Administrator username.

3. After the SMDR software is loaded, Eric next loads the target agents for backing up the NetWare 5 server data and NDS database by entering the following commands:

   LOAD TSA500

   LOAD TSANDS

4. After loading the target service agents, Eric completes the initialization process by loading the Storage Management System Device Interface software using the command LOAD SMSDI.

5. The NetWare 5 SMS uses job queues to enable backup and restore jobs to be stored until they are to be run. Just like a print queue allows a print job waiting for the printer to be available, the job queue allows a job to be entered and then held to be run later that night or when the backup device is available. To load the job queue software, Eric enters the command LOAD QMAN.

6. To load the enhanced SBACKUP software on the server, Eric enters the LOAD SBSC command, followed by the LOAD SBCON command. After he enters these commands, the main backup menu is displayed. To back up data, he next selects the Job Aministration option from the main menu and then selects the Backup option from the Job Selection menu to display the Backup Options screen shown in Figure 10–31.

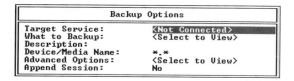

```
            Backup Options
 Target Service:       <Not Connected>
 What to Backup:       <Select to View>
 Description:
 Device/Media Name:    *.*
 Advanced Options:     <Select to View>
 Append Session:       No
```

Figure 10-31 SBACKUP options

7. Next Eric uses the Target Service option to dispay a list of all servers running a Target Service Agent. He then selects the UAS_HOST server and is given the options to back up the file system and Novell Directory. He selects the File System option and then logs in using his Admin user name and password. He then repeats this process to also back up the Novell Directory database containing all user information and rights.

8. After selecting the services to back up, Eric next uses the What to Backup option from the Backup Options menu shown previously in Figure 10-31 to select the volumes and directories to be backed up.

9. Next he uses the Description option to provide a descriptive name for the backup session. By default, the backup program will perform a Full backup. To change the backup type to Incremental or Differential, the backup operator can use the Advanced Options to select the Backup Type field and then select either Incremental or Differential options.

10. Finally he selects the backup media to start the backup process.

Test the Backup

After a successful backup has been completed, the next step in testing your backup system is to try restoring selected files from the backup media. Doing a complete restore is often not feasible due to time constraints as well as the possible loss of data should the restore process fail. As a result, prior to performing a major restore, you should start by restoring test files that are not needed or files that have been copied to another disk storage device. To restore selected files, select the Restore option from the main SBCON menu and then proceed to enter the path to the working directory you used when the backup tape was created. Next select the option Restore from session files and select the session you named previously when the backup was created.

After the restore screen has been completed, start the restore process. The selected files should now be copied back to their appropriate directories. When the restore process has completed, log in from a user workstation and verify that the files have been correctly restored.

Develop a Recovery Procedure

Once the backup system has been tested, the next process in implementing a reliable disaster recovery plan is to develop a tape rotation procedure and backup schedule. A proper multiple tape rotation procedure that provides the ability to save certain backups for a long time period is an important part of a disaster recovery plan, because it provides a way to go back to an earlier backup to recover files as well as a way to store backup tapes from a remote site. It is sometimes important to be able to recover a file from an earlier backup if that file should become corrupted by a software virus, operator error, or software bug, and the damage to the file is not discovered for several days or weeks. If you were rotating your backups among just a few tapes, by the time the error was discovered, a backup copy of the corrupted file would have overwritten the original backup containing the valid file. To help prevent this scenario, the consultant for Universal Aerospace has recommended a tape rotation system consisting of 20 tapes as shown in Figure 10-32.

10

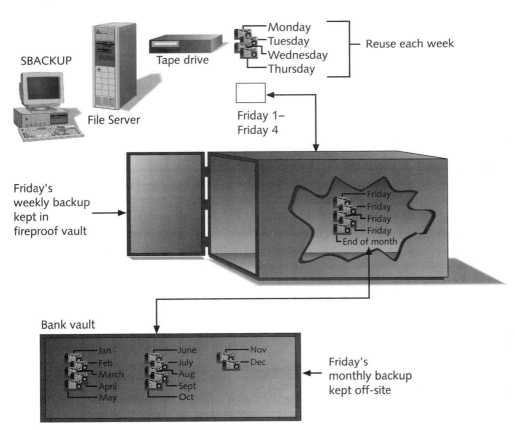

Figure 10-32   Tape rotation procedure

Four tapes are labeled Monday through Thursday and are rotated each week. Four tapes are labeled Friday 1 through Friday 4, with Friday 1 being used on the first Friday of the month, Friday 2 for the second, Friday 3 for the third, and Friday 4 for the fourth. In addition, 12 tapes are labeled January through December. These tapes are rotated each year. On the last Friday of each month, you can use these tapes by replacing the Friday # tape with the appropriate monthly backup. Another alternative, if someone is available to change the tape, is to make the monthly backup on the last Saturday of each month. The storage of the backup tapes is also important in the event of a fire or damage to the building. As a result, many administrators store weekly backups in a fireproof vault and keep monthly backup tapes off-site in a secure location such as a bank safety deposit vault.

The final step in implementing the backup system is to set up a time for the backup to be performed and ensure no users are logged in during the backup process. To prevent interference with user work schedules, many network administrators like the backup to start each night at about 12:00 a.m. To restrict night owls from working late and to prevent users from leaving their workstations logged in during the backup, all user accounts, except the username used to back up the system, should have a time restriction to prevent them from accessing the network between 12:00 a.m. and 5:00 a.m. This provides a five-hour time interval that should be sufficient to create your backup. If extra time is needed, you can set the backup to begin at 11:00 p.m. or possibly go to 6:00 a.m., provided you also set the user time restrictions for the longer backup period.

IMPLEMENTING TCP/IP

During a recent management meeting, Dave explained that his next objective for the network is to provide all users with access to certain company information as well as the Internet from their desktop. As a result, he would like to see the company's network eventually switch from using Novell's proprietary IPX protocol to the Internet standard TCP/IP. He understands that this conversion will take some time and that in the interim the network will need to support both IPX and TCP/IP. Although earlier versions of NetWare supported TCP/IP packet routing, client requests to the NetWare server had to be created in IPX format and then encapsulated within the TCP/IP packet as shown in Figure 10-33.

Figure 10-33   IPX packet encapsulated in TCP/IP

Encapsulating IPX packets within TCP/IP allows communication across an intranet or the Internet, but increases network overhead and complicates network administration. With NetWare 5, Novell enables the server to accept requests formatted directly inside TCP/IP packets as illustrated in Figure 10-34. This capability makes NetWare 5 much more compatible with existing TCP/IP networks such as the Internet. In this section, you will be introduced to the TCP/IP protocol and learn how to configure your workstation to communicate with the server using TCP/IP.

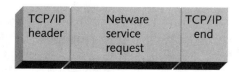

Figure 10-34   Pure TCP/IP packet

TCP/IP Basics

The **Transmission Control Protocol/Internet Protocol (TCP/IP)** was first developed in the 1960s to support communication among mainframe computers in government agencies and educational institutions. The protocol specifications were developed and are still maintained by an independent agency known as the Internet Access Board (IAB). Because TCP/IP was developed to connect a large number of independent organizations, it was designed to support communications between diverse computers and operating systems. In TCP/IP, each computer attached to the network is called a **host** and is assigned a unique address. Routers connect independent networks together and transfer packets from one network to another using the TCP/IP network address.

When connecting your computer to the Internet, you need to be assigned a unique network address by the IAB. Often this is done by connecting your computer to the Internet through an **Internet service provider (ISP)**. The IAB provides each ISP with a range of valid addresses that the ISP can allocate to its customers. For example, Universal Aerospace will be connecting to the Internet through the Unlimited Horizons ISP. Unlimited Horizons has provided you with a range of TCP/IP addresses that you can assign to your workstations and server. TCP/IP addresses consist of 32-bit numbers expressed as four-byte numbers separated by periods, such as 130.57.128.10. Each TCP/IP address contains network and host components as illustrated in Figure 10-35.

10

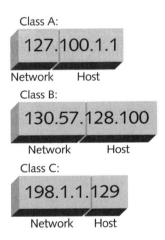

Figure 10-35   TCP/IP address components

Based on the number of bytes in the network component, TCP/IP addresses can be Class A, Class B, or Class C as shown in Table 10-6. A Class A address has the first byte or *octet* reserved for the network address, making the last three bytes available to assign to host computers. Because a Class A address has a three-octet host address, Class A networks can support over 16 million host computers.

Table 10-6   TCP/IP Address Classes

Address Class	Range	Address Bytes	Number of Networks	Host Bytes	Number of Hosts
Class A	1-127	1	127	3	16,777,215
Class B	128-191	2	16,128	2	65,535
Class C	192-223	3	2,097,152	1	254

There are a limited number of Class A network addresses—they are reserved for very large organizations such as the federal government, IBM, and AT&T. A Class B address is evenly divided between a two-octet network address and a two-octet host address. Large organizations and ISPs may be assigned Class B addresses. A Class C address has a three-digit network address and a one-digit host address. This provides the IAB a large number (over 16 million) of Class C addresses to assign for business and home use. However, each Class C network is limited to 255 host computers. In addition to receiving a unique network address, each network must also be assigned a network mask. The **network mask** identifies the network address bits from the host address bits by placing a 1 in each bit that is part of the network address. By applying the mask to a TCP/IP address, a host computer or router can determine what network a packet is destined for. By default, a Class C address would have a network mask of 11111111 11111111 11111111 00000000 in binary or 255.255.255.0 in decimal.

Installing TCP/IP on Clients

When NetWare 5 was installed on the Universal Aerospace server, support for both IPX and TCP/IP was selected as described in Appendix A. During this process, Eric assigned the server an IP address based on the TCP/IP address range provided by the Unlimited Horizons ISP.

 In this hands-on activity, you will modify your client to use the IP address provided by your instructor to communicate on the classroom intranet.

1. If necessary, start your computer.

2. Insert the Novell Client CD-ROM or log in to the network and map a drive to the directory containing the Novell NetWare Client files.

3. If the Client installation program does not automatically start, double-click the **Winsetup.exe** file from the root of the Novell NetWare Client CD-ROM to start the install program and display the Clients and Z.E.N.works Starter Pack window.

4. Click the **English** language button to display the installation options.

5. Click the **Windows 95/98 Client** option to display the Windows 95/98 components window.

6. Click the **Install Novell Client** option to display the Windows 95/98 License agreement window. Click **Yes** to agree to the terms of the license.

7. Click the **Custom** installation method and click **Next** to display the Protocol Preference window.

8. Click the **IP and IPX** option from the Protocol Preference dialog box shown in Figure 10-36 and then click **Next** to display the Login Authenticator window.

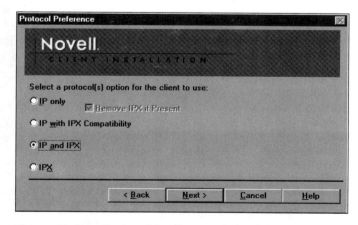

Figure 10-36   Protocol Preference dialog box

9. Click the **NDS** button to access NetWare 4 and NetWare 5 servers and then click **Next** to display the Novell Client for Windows 95/98 Custom Options Optional Components window.

10. Select the **Novell Workstation Manager** and **Novell Distributed Print Services** options and then click the **Install** button. The installation program will first remove your existing client and then copy the NetWare client files and build a driver information database.

11. Click the **Customize** button to display the Network Protocols window.

12. Click **TCP/IP** and then click the **Properties** button to display the TCP/IP Properties dialog box shown in Figure 10-37.

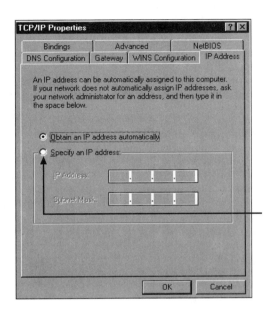 Click here to enter an IP address for this client

Figure 10-37   Network configuration window

13. Click the **Specify an IP address** button and enter the IP address and mask given to you by your instructor.

14. Click **OK** to save the assignment and return to the Configuration menu.

15. Click **OK** to save the settings and build a driver information database.

16. Click **Yes** to restart your computer.

You can test your TCP/IP configuration by using the PING command. The PING command will send a packet to the host identified by the IP Address you enter and then wait for a response. When a response is received, the PING command will display the time required to receive the response. If no packet is received, a timeout error message will be displayed.

 In this hands-on activity, you use the PING command to test your communication to NetWare server

1. Obtain the IP address of your NetWare server from your instructor. You will record this address in Step 4.

2. Log in using your assigned ##Admin username.

3. Open an MS-DOS Prompt window.

4. Enter the command **PING** _____ . _____ . _____ . _____ (the IP address of your server) and press **[Enter]**.

5. If you receive a timeout message, double-check your TCP/IP setup from the previous hands-on exercise to be sure you are using the IP address and mask provided by your instructor. If you still cannot ping your server, work with your instructor to troubleshoot the problem.

6. Type **Exit** and press **[Enter]** to exit the MS-DOS Prompt window.

7. Close any programs and log out.

Congratulations! The Universal Aerospace network is operational. Don't worry, your job is not over. Now that the network is installed, your work really begins. Network systems require continual care and feeding. There are lots of special situations that you will need to deal with as well as the continual line-up of software and hardware upgrades, new applications, and changes in user needs and company procedures. In the exercises at the end of this chapter, you will practice some of the day-to-day tasks you will need to perform.

Chapter Summary

❑ Managing the server computer involves using the console commands and NetWare Loadable Modules (NLMs), as well as being able to use the Java-based ConsoleOne to perform various tasks on the server computer. Console commands are built into the NetWare operating system and can be divided into four categories based upon their use: installation commands, configuration commands, maintenance commands, and security commands. NLMs are external programs that are loaded into the server to control devices and add additional functionality to the server. NLMs may also be divided into four categories based on their three-letter filename extension. Disk drivers have .HAM and .CDM extensions and are needed to allow NetWare to control the attached hard disk drives. LAN drivers have the extension .LAN and are used to attach the file server to a network topology. Name space modules have the extension .NAM and are used to provide NetWare with additional logic necessary to translate file-naming conventions from other workstation operating systems to NetWare's directory system. General-purpose modules have the extension .NLM, and are used to provide other services to the network such as the MONITOR utility that allows you to view file server performance and status, the NWCONFIG module that is used to perform installation processes, or the PSERVER module that allows the file server also to be a print server.

❑ Often the server computer is placed in a location that is not easily accessible, to provide additional security. In addition, a network administrator may often need to manage several servers in different locations. As a result, it is often more convenient to operate the file server console from a workstation in your office than it is to go to the file server computer. The Remote Management Facility (RMF) allows the file server's console to be accessed from other locations on the network by loading the REMOTE and RSPX NetWare Loadable Modules on the servers to be managed and then running the RCONSOLE program from the workstation. This is referred to as a direct link since the network card in the file server and workstation provides for a direct, high-speed communication to the server console. You provide security for the console by setting a password on the REMOTE module and by placing the RCONSOLE software in the SYS:System directory where only the Supervisor has access to it. Network administrators can make users console operators by granting them rights to run the RCONSOLE software and providing them with the necessary REMOTE password. By attaching a modem to a file server and loading the RS232.NLM, you can access the server's console over the dial-up phone line. Using a dial-in connection provides a method of accessing the server from a distant site in addition to providing access to the console in the event of a network failure.

Command Summary

Command	Syntax	Definition
BIND	BIND *protocol TO driver*	Provides a LAN driver with access to a protocol stack. Before a file server can communicate using a LAN driver, a protocol must be identified. TCP/IP is the standard protocol built into NetWare 5; other protocols such as IPX and AppleTalk must first be loaded as NLMs before they can be bound to the network card.

BROADCAST	BROADCAST *message*	Sends the message line to all users logged in to the server.
CLS/OFF	CLS/OFF	Clears the server console screen.
CONFIG	CONFIG	Displays the current server's internal network number along with information about each network card, including the card's hardware settings, the frame type and protocol in use, and the network address assigned to that card.
DISABLE LOGIN	DISABLE LOGIN	Prevents additional users from logging in to the server.
DISMOUNT	DISMOUNT *volume_name\ALL*	Closes a volume and removes it from the network. It is necessary to Dismount a volume before using the VREPAIR utility to check the volume and correct any volume problems.
DISPLAY SERVERS	DISPLAY SERVERS	Displays the name of each network server currently in this server's router table, the number of routers that must be crossed to reach the server, and the average number of ticks (1/18 sec) required to send a packet to this server.
DOWN	DOWN	Removes all attachments to the server, writes all cache blocks to disk, dismounts the volumes, takes the server off-line, and returns to the DOS prompt. You should be sure to use the DOWN command always before shutting off the server computer.
ENABLE LOGIN	ENABLE LOGIN	Reenables the user to log in to the server.
LOAD	LOAD *[path]module_name*	Loads the specified module into the server's memory and executes it. An optional path may be supplied if the specified module is not in the SYS:System directory.
MEMORY	MEMORY	Displays the total amount of memory in the server computer.
MOUNT	MOUNT *volume_name | ALL*	Opens a volume for use on the network by loading directory entry tables (DETs) into memory. A volume must be mounted before it can be accessed on the network. If the SYS volume is not mounted, the server will not show up on the network when you use the SLIST or DISPLAY SERVER commands.
REMOVE DOS	REMOVE DOS	Removes the DOS operating system from memory, providing more memory for file caching and preventing the LOAD command from accessing DOS drives.
SECURE CONSOLE	SECURE CONSOLE	Increases the server's console security by removing DOS from memory, forcing NLMs to be loaded only from SYS:System, preventing the use of the OS debugger program, and not allowing the system time to be changed from the server console.
SEND	SEND *"message"* TO *username\connection*	Sends the message line to a specific user or connection number. As with the DOS workstation, you can use the SEND command from the console.
SET TIME	SET TIME *[m/d/y]* *[hour:min:sec]*	Used by itself, displays the current server time; used with the current date and time, changes the time in the server to the specified time and date.

10

UNBIND	UNBIND *protocol* FROM LAN_*driver*	Removes a protocol stack from a network card, effectively removing the server from that network. The UNBIND command is often used when it is necessary to change the net work address of a server because other servers on that network are using different addresses.
UNLOAD	UNLOAD *module_name*	Removes an NLM from memory and returns its memory to the file cache.

Key Terms

child — A specific data set such as a file or program.

console command — A command function that is built into the NetWare kernel SERVER.EXE program and therefore always in memory.

ConsoleOne — A Java-based application that may be used on a NetWare server console to work with NDS objects.

Differential backup — A backup of all files changed since the last Full backup. When performing a Differential backup, the SBACKUP program will back up all files that have the Archive attribute turned on, but will not reset the Archive attribute, making it easier to restore all data after a disaster.

direct link — A method of using the Remote Management Facility to control the server console from a client by communicating over the network cable system.

Full backup — A backup strategy in which all data is copied to the backup tape during the backup session.

Host — The NetWare server that has a tape drive attached and is running the backup software.

Incremental backup — A back up that includes only files that have been changed (the Archive attribute is on) and then resets the Archive attribute on all files that are backed up.

Internet service provider (ISP) — An organization that provides other individuals and organizations with Internet access services through a telephone connection or wide area network link for a monthly charge.

Java — A programming language developed by Sun Microsystems that is often used to develop Internet applications that run on multiple platforms.

NetWare Loadable Module (NLM) — An external program that can be loaded into the file server's RAM to add additional functionality or control hardware devices such as disk drives and network cards.

network mask — A 32-bit number that is used to determine which bits of an IP address are part of the network address and which bits are part of the computer or node address by placing one bits in the positions of the IP address that are part of the network address and zero bits in the positions of the IP address that are part of the computer or node address.

Novell Licensing Services (NLS) — A NetWare 5 service that allows NetWare to manage the number of licenses on the server as well as other applications that are compatible with Novell Licensing Services.

parent — A data set such as a directory or subdirectory.

Remote Management — A utility included with NetWare v3.12 and

Facility (RMF) — higher to enable users to access server consoles from either a workstation attached to the LAN or through an asynchronous communication link.

router table — A table contained in the memory of each server that contains the name and network address of all available servers.

Storage Management — Several NLMs along with workstation software

System (SMS) — that enables the host computer to back up data from one or more target devices by using the SBACKUP NLM.

target server — A server whose data is being backed up by a host server.

TCP/IP (Transmission Control Protocol/Internet Protocol) — A system of standards and software used for transmitting and routing packets between hosts attached to the Internet or between computers on a local network.

REVIEW QUESTIONS

1. The _____ command is used to provide space on a volume for non-DOS filenames such as Macintosh or OS/2.

2. The _____ command assigns a protocol to a LAN driver.

3. The _____ command would be used to assign a frame type and I/O port to a LAN driver.

4. The _____ command would show total file memory available on the file server computer.

5. The _____ console command would display the network addresses assigned to each LAN in the file server.

6. The _____ console command would let you know whether your newly installed file server can "see" other servers on the network.

7. On the following line, write a console command that would change the server's clock to 11:59 p.m. on December 31, 1999.

   _____

8. In the following space, write the sequence of commands a network administrator should enter before turning off the server computer in the middle of the day.

9. After starting the file server, you notice that the TEXT volume did not mount because of errors in the FAT (File Allocation Table). On the following lines, identify what NLM you could use to fix the volume and then the command necessary to bring the TEXT volume back online.

   _____

   _____

   _____

10. Suppose that after loading the NE2000 Ethernet card driver and binding the IPX protocol with the network address 1EEE8023, your server begins reporting router configuration errors that indicate other servers on the network are using the network address 10BA5E2 for the Ethernet LAN. In the following space, write the commands you could use to correct the problem.

11. The _____ console command will prevent NetWare from loading NLMs from the SYS:Public\NLM directory.

12. In the following space, identify the procedure and commands you would use to shut down your company's server.

13. Record the two console commands used to enable a remote console connection on your server.

   _____

   _____

   _____

14. If the number of Total cache buffers on the MONITOR screen is less than _____ of the Original cache buffers, you need to add more memory to your file server.

10

The Universal Aerospace Project

Management and users are finding the network system a real asset to their productivity and communications. As a result, you want to ensure that the system continues to perform well and that the data is protected. In the following exercises, you will use console commands to document the server environment, determine the server's baseline performance, create a backup user, and then test your backup system by backing up and restoring data.

Step 1: Documenting the Server Environment

An important task for every network administrator is to develop and maintain documentation regarding the network and server configurations. Follow these steps to record the requested server and network information:

1. Use the CONFIG command to record the following server data:

    Server name: _____

    Internal IPX number: _____

    Network card driver: _____

    Interrupt: _____

    Port: _____

    Network address: _____

    Frame type: _____

    Bindery context: _____

2. Use the DISPLAY SERVERS command to record up to two servers on your network on the following lines:

    _____

    _____

3. Use the MEMORY command to record the amount of RAM in your server on the following line:

    _____

4. Use the VOLUMES command to record the name of each volume on your server.

    _____

    _____

    _____

Step 2: Building a Server Baseline

Although the Universal Aerospace network is performing adequately at this time, increased demands as well as equipment failures may cause future performance problems. As a result, to help identify performance problems that may occur in the future, it is important to determine the server's nominal performance by using the MONITOR utility to build a baseline showing server performance during typical work periods. In this exercise, you will use the MONITOR utility over a period of a few days to determine server baseline statistics. To do this exercise, you will need access to the MONITOR utility either from the server console or through the remote console facility. Your instructor will provide you with instructions on accessing the MONITOR utility.

Step 3: Backing Up the Server

Once the network is operational, one of the most important functions of the network administrator is to establish and test a backup system that will provide disaster recovery capability for the organization. In this exercise, you will use the SBACKUP utility to back up your Universal Aerospace file system and NDS containers to a backup medium. Depending on your server hardware and accessibility, your instructor will provide you with instructions on how to perform the backup by loading the necessary device drivers and then running the SBACKUP software as described in this chapter.

NETWARE 5.1 CNA OBJECTIVES

his book originally was written to meet the NetWare 5.0 CNA objectives as of January 1999. With the release of NetWare 5.1, the CNA objectives have been updated to include some of the new features found in NetWare 5.1. Because the NetWare 5.0 CNA test is constantly being revised and updated, you should obtain the latest CNA objectives by checking the Novell Education Web site at *http://education.novell.com* for details. Table A-1 is intended to help you study for the CNA test by relating each of the August 2000 objectives to one or more chapters in this textbook.

Table A-1   NetWare 5.1 CNA Objective Update

Number	CNA Objective	Chapter(s)/Appendix
1	Describe what a network is, and list its components.	1
2	Describe what NetWare is, and list the types of workstations you can use to access it.	1
3	List the responsibilities of a network administrator.	1
4	List the NetWare resources and services you will learn to administer.	1
5	Describe Novell Directory Services (NDS), including the NDS Directory and NDS objects.	1, 2
6	Describe how a workstation communicates with the network.	1
7	Install the Novell Client software.	2
8	Explain and perform the login procedure.	1
9	Install and configure a browser client.	9
10	Create and modify a user account using NetWare Administrator.	2, 4
11	Create a User object with the Java-based Console One utility.	10, B
12	Use the DOS utility UIMPORT to create User objects.	4
13	Describe and establish login security, including login restrictions for users.	4
14	Describe NetWare printing using NDPS.	7
15	Explain the four NDPS components and their functions.	7
16	List the NDPS printer types, and explain the difference between public access printers and controlled access printers.	7
17	Configure the network for NDPS.	7
18	Configure a workstation to print to NDPS printers.	7
19	Manage printer access and print jobs.	7
20	Use utilities to perform file system management tasks	3, 5
21	Access the file system by configuring drive mappings.	3
22	Select the correct utilities for managing the directory structure.	3
23	Select the correct utilities for managing files.	3

Table A-1 NetWare 5.1 CNA Objective Update (continued)

Number	CNA Objective	Chapter(s)/Appendix
24	Manage the use of volume space using NetWare Administrator.	3
25	Explain how file system security works.	5
26	Plan and implement file system security for your organization.	5
27	Plan and implement file and directory attribute security.	5
28	Describe the types of login scripts, and explain how they coordinate at login.	8
29	Design login scripts for containers, user groups, and users.	8
30	Use the MAP command to map network drives from a login script.	3, 8
31	Create, execute, and debug a login script.	8
32	Define NDS security and how it differs from file system security.	6
33	Control access to an object in the NDS tree.	6
34	Determine rights granted to NDS objects.	6
35	Block an object's inherited rights to other NDS objects.	6
36	Determine effective rights.	6
37	Explain guidelines and considerations for implementing NDS security.	6
38	Troubleshoot NDS security problems using NetWare Administrator.	6
39	Explain the benefits of using Application Launcher.	9
40	Explain the components of Application Launcher.	9
41	Distribute applications using Application Launcher and snAppShot.	9
42	Manage applications with Application Launcher.	9
43	Describe the available Z.E.N.works products and their purposes.	9
44	Describe Z.E.N.works policy packages and policies.	9
45	Identify NDS design considerations for Z.E.N.works.	B
46	Register workstations in NDS, and import them into the NDS tree using NetWare Administrator.	9
47	Use policies to configure desktop environment.	9
48	Establish remote control access to workstations on the network.	9, B
49	Set up and use the Help Requester application.	9, B
50	Identify NDS planning guidelines to follow in sample directory structures.	6
51	Provide users with access to resources.	2, 6
52	Create shortcuts to access and manage network resources.	6
53	Identify the actions to take and the rights needed to grant a user access to NDS resources.	6
54	Create login scripts that identify resources in other contexts.	8
55	Describe the function of a NetWare server and its interface, and identify the server components.	1
56	Perform a basic NetWare 5.0 server installation.	B
57	Install the Novell Licensing Service (NLS).	10, C
58	Managing licensing through NLS.	10, B

B

UPGRADING TO AND INSTALLING NETWARE 5.1

Your primary responsibility as a network administrator is to set up and maintain the NetWare network environment after NetWare has been installed on the server(s). The tasks of installing NetWare and configuring the server's computer hardware are often performed by technical support specialists. In addition to providing the Certified Novell Administrator (CNA) program, Novell provides a separate Certified Novell Engineer (CNE) program to certify technical support specialists in planning, installing, and troubleshooting NetWare. Because network administrators do not usually need to install NetWare on the server computer, installing or upgrading NetWare is not a task required to become a CNA. However, a CNA needs to understand the basic installation process and options to be successful in planning and maintaining the network system.

NetWare 5.1 provides several major enhancements to NetWare 5.0 that strengthen its capabilities as an e-commerce platform and Internet server. Although many of these enhancements are directed toward Internet applications and e-commerce, NetWare 5.1 also includes additional management tools and an improved version of NDS, called eDirectory. In this appendix, you will learn about the new NetWare 5.1 enhancements as well as how to upgrade an existing NetWare server or install NetWare 5.1 on a new server.

To better understand how the NetWare 5.1 enhancements can be applied to a business environment, you will be placed in the role of a network administrator for the Universal Aerospace (UAS) company and help it as it upgrades to NetWare 5.1. Universal Aerospace is a fictitious aerospace company that specializes in designing and manufacturing high-tech aerospace components. After obtaining a NASA contract to design and manufacture components for both the International Space Station and Mars Rover projects, Universal Aerospace installed a NetWare 5.0 server with a Novell Directory Services (NDS) tree structure. The tree structure includes separate containers for the users and resources of the Business, Engineering, and Manufacturing Departments, as shown in Figure B-1.

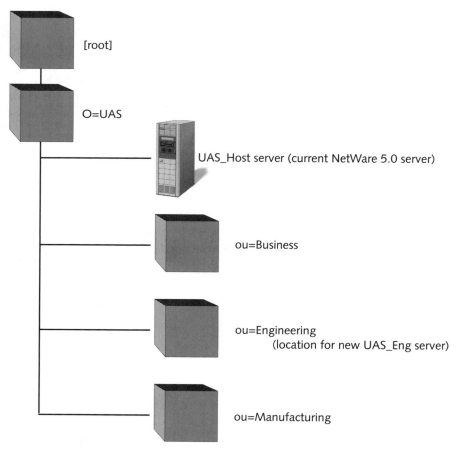

Figure B-1 Universal Aerospace tree containers

In the last year, Universal Aerospace expanded its organization to support the NASA contracts. As part of the expansion project, management would like to add a new server in the Engineering Department. Placing a new server in Engineering will allow the large engineering files and applications to be removed from the UAS_HOST server, thereby providing additional space and capacity on UAS_HOST to accommodate the growth of the Business and Manufacturing Departments. Future expansion plans call for adding another server to support the projected growth of the business and manufacturing applications.

Because the new servers will be installed with NetWare 5.1, the consultant has recommended upgrading the existing UAS_HOST server from NetWare 5.0 to 5.1 to take full advantage of the NetWare 5.1 enhancements. To start, management has asked you to work with the network consultant to develop a proposal listing the benefits of converting to NetWare 5.1, along with a conversion plan and schedule for the next weekly meeting.

After discussing with you the expansion of the Universal Aerospace network, your consultant has recommended that you include the following six advantages of upgrading to NetWare 5.1 in your proposal to management:

- The new NDS version 8 eDirectory system will provide for an almost unlimited number of objects in the NDS tree, along with better performance for reads, writes, and searches. A major advantage gained by Universal Aerospace will be eDirectory's ability to support improved management tasks using ConsoleOne and the new NetWare Management Portal. EDirectory also contains an improved version of the DSREPAIR utility that is important in managing and troubleshooting problems that may occur periodically in NDS networks. In addition, eDirectory's support of a variety of operating systems through an improved version of the Lightweight Directory Access Protocol (LDAP) will be important in helping to integrate the Linux and Windows 2000 applications we discussed. The new BULKLOAD utility improves on the original NetWare 5.0 UIMPORT utility by allowing a variety of NDS objects to be added, modified, or deleted through a batch process.

■ The new NetWare Management Portal provides a browser-based tool that can be used from either Netscape or Internet Explorer to remotely access and manage the company's NetWare volumes, servers, applications, NDS objects, and schemas, as well as monitor server health and hardware, while working from home or traveling to other internet-connected sites.

■ NetWare 5.1 includes a Deployment Manager tool (NWDEPLOY.EXE) that runs on a client and can be used to prepare the existing network before upgrading to NetWare 5.1. In addition, Deployment Manager can be used to update an existing NetWare 5.1 server with products that were not installed during the initial server installation.

■ An important part of the Universal Aerospace network expansion plan is to replace existing dial-up network access with a router to allow users higher-speed access the Internet. Because registered IP addresses are difficult to obtain, assigning each client a registered IP address may not be feasible. In addition, having "live" Internet addresses can allow an intruder to gain access to a client computer through an open internet connection port. NetWare 5.1 provides a solution to these needs through Network Address Translation or NAT. NAT will allow you to use your NetWare 5.1 server as a router between the company's intranet using privately assigned IP addresses and the Internet. Only one registered IP address will need to be assigned to the NetWare 5.1 server's Internet connection. Whenever a client needs to access a service on the Internet, its default gateway setting will direct the packet to the NetWare 5.1 server. NAT running on the NetWare 5.1 server will then replace the client's IP address with its registered IP address and send the packet out to the Internet host. NAT assigns a port number to the connection with the outside host to save connection information. When the Internet host responds, NAT uses the port number assigned to that connection to retrieve the client's information and then send the Internet host's response back to the requesting client. The NetWare 5.1 NAT system eliminates the cost of a dedicated router and effectively isolates the clients from unwanted Internet access, while still providing access to outside services.

■ Although Universal Aerospace currently is not soliciting business on the Internet, NetWare 5.1 contains the following enhancements intended to help businesses develop and manage e-commerce applications. The NetWare 5.1 enhanced Internet and e-commerce capabilities will be important should Universal Aerospace want to develop any of the following Internet services in the future.

- A fully integrated **enterprise web server** that is specifically adapted for maximum performance in the NetWare 5.1 eDirectory environment

- A **NetWare FTP Server** to provide for transfer of files to and from NetWare volumes

- A **NetWare News Server** you can use to host group discussions and forums; the NetWare News Server uses the Network News Transport Protocol (NNTP) to provide compatibility with other NNTP news servers.

- A **NetWare MultiMedia Server**, which provides multimedia streaming capabilities on a NetWare server platform; the NetWare MultiMedia Server supports the WAV, MP3, MPEG-1, and RM file formats.

- A **NetWare Web Search** engine that provides a powerful and customizable search and print solution to let you index information located on a NetWare or web server; the NetWare Web Search engine runs from a super-thin Java client that downloads quickly and yet is powerful enough to perform searches in alternative languages.

- The **IBM WebSphere Application Server** provides a robust and portable environment to deploy and manage Java Applications running under NetWare. Novell is working to integrate NDS and other services and products with IBM WebSphere to ensure an open application server model that leverages the best tools and services available.

■ The **Novell Certificate Authority** service allows your organization to issue digital certificates to clients to provide secure, encrypted transmission for users of your network. The Novell Certificate Server uses Public Key Cryptography consisting of public and private keys to secure e-mail, web servers, and network applications, such as LDAP.

Upgrading an existing network to NetWare 5.1 requires planning and experience. The networking consultant has recommended that your proposal to management include the following four phase approach to upgrading the existing Universal Aerospace network from NetWare 5.0 to 5.1.

1. Prepare for the network upgrade and installation. You will need sufficient time to evaluate server hardware requirements, identify drivers, plan protocol usage, and determine NDS context locations for the new server.

2. Use Deployment Manager to upgrade your existing NetWare 5.0 tree structure to NDS 8 eDirectory and install the NetWare 5.1 Licensing Service (NLS).

3. Install the new NetWare 5.1 server in the Engineering Department.

4. Upgrade existing NetWare 5.0 UAS_HOST server to NetWare 5.1.

After reviewing your recommendation, Universal Aerospace management has given its approval to install a new NetWare 5.1 server in the Engineering Department and upgrade the existing network from NetWare 5.0 to 5.1. Because of your busy schedule and the need to do this quickly, management has agreed to have Eric Kenton from Computer Technology Services upgrade the existing UAS_HOST server to NetWare 5.1 and install NetWare 5.1 on the new Engineering server. In this appendix you will learn the NetWare 5.1 upgrade and installation process by following Eric Kenton as he uses Deployment Manager to upgrade the Universal Aerospace network, installs NetWare 5.1 on the new Engineering server, and then upgrades the existing NetWare 5.0 server to NetWare 5.1.

PREPARING FOR NETWARE INSTALLATION

Just as in other activities, preparation is important to the success of your NetWare server installation. Preparing for NetWare installation involves determining the hardware configuration of the server computer as well as identifying the physical and logical network environment in which the server is to be installed. A NetWare server's hardware environment can become quite complex with two or more disk drives and controllers, multiple volumes, network card configurations, and protocols. To help identify and manage all this information, the Universal Aerospace consultant has prepared a NetWare Server Worksheet as shown in Figure B-2. In this section you will refer to this Worksheet to help you learn how to prepare for a NetWare server installation by identifying the hardware configuration and network information you will need to install NetWare 5.1 successfully.

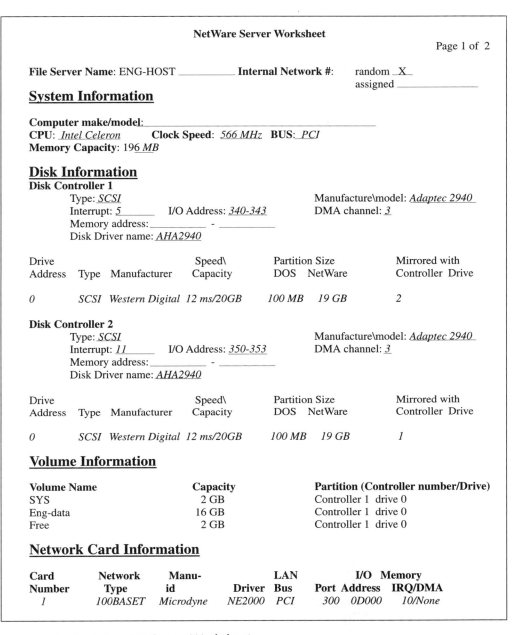

NetWare Server Worksheet

Page 1 of 2

File Server Name: ENG-HOST _____ **Internal Network #**: random _X_

assigned _____

System Information

Computer make/model: _____

CPU: _Intel Celeron_   **Clock Speed**: _566 MHz_   **BUS**: _PCI_

Memory Capacity: 196 _MB_

Disk Information

Disk Controller 1

     Type: _SCSI_   Manufacture\model: _Adaptec 2940_

     Interrupt: _5_   I/O Address: _340-343_   DMA channel: _3_

     Memory address:_____ - _____

     Disk Driver name: _AHA2940_

Drive Address	Type	Manufacturer	Speed\ Capacity	Partition Size DOS	NetWare	Mirrored with Controller Drive
0	SCSI	Western Digital	12 ms/20GB	100 MB	19 GB	2

Disk Controller 2

     Type: _SCSI_   Manufacture\model: _Adaptec 2940_

     Interrupt: _11_   I/O Address: _350-353_   DMA channel: _3_

     Memory address:_____ - _____

     Disk Driver name: _AHA2940_

Drive Address	Type	Manufacturer	Speed\ Capacity	Partition Size DOS	NetWare	Mirrored with Controller Drive
0	SCSI	Western Digital	12 ms/20GB	100 MB	19 GB	1

Volume Information

Volume Name	Capacity	Partition (Controller number/Drive)
SYS	2 GB	Controller 1 drive 0
Eng-data	16 GB	Controller 1 drive 0
Free	2 GB	Controller 1 drive 0

Network Card Information

Card Number	Network Type	Manu-id	Driver	LAN Bus	I/O Port	Memory Address	IRQ/DMA
1	100BASET	Microdyne	NE2000	PCI	300	0D000	10/None

Figure B-2   NetWare 5.1 Server Worksheet

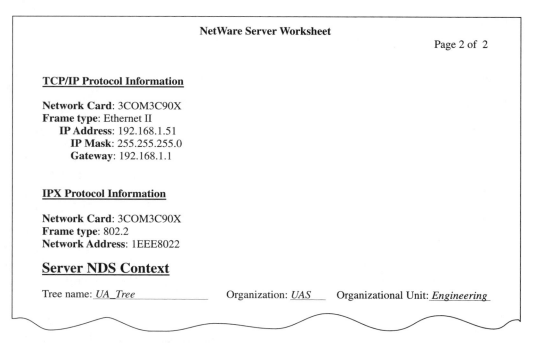

Figure B-2   NetWare 5.1 Server Worksheet (continued)

Determining Server Hardware Requirements

NetWare is a network operating system (NOS) that is designed to perform server functions. Essentially, both NetWare 5.0 and 5.1 consist of an operating system kernel (SERVER.EXE) that provides core NetWare server services to the network along with a software bus that allows other modules containing specialized services and device drivers to be loaded and unloaded, as shown in Figure B-3. In addition to providing file and print services, both NetWare 5.0 and 5.1 servers can run Java-based applications as well as communicate directly using the TCP/IP (Transport Control Protocol/Internet Protocol) protocol.

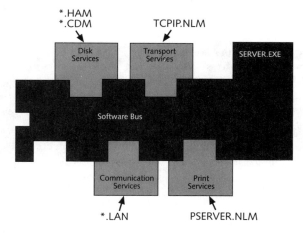

Figure B-3   NetWare software bus

In order to support the Kernel, NLM services, and enhanced Java based console and applications, NetWare 5.1 requires considerably more memory and CPU speed than previous versions. The minimum hardware environment specifications for a NetWare 5.1 server are shown in Table B-1.

Table B-1   NetWare 5.1 minimum hardware requirements

Processor	Pentium 166 MHz or Higher
Disk space	Minimum 50 MB free on DOS partition
	750 MB free space on volume SYS for standard NetWare products and an additional 750 MB for the WebSphere Application Server for NetWare
Memory	128 MB RAM for standard NetWare products and an additional 128 MB (512 MB total recommended) for WebSphere Application Server for NetWare
Network	A NetWare 5.1 compatible Network board
CD drive	A CD drive that can read ISO 9660-formatted CDs
Monitor	VGA or better

The Server Name and Internal Number

Each NetWare server on the network must have a unique name and internal number assigned to it. The internal number is used to create a logical network that is used to send packets of data between modules attached to the software bus. The server name can consist of up to 45 characters, including special characters such as $, &, and *.

The internal network number can consist of up to eight hexadecimal digits, and it can be either a random number assigned by the installation program or a specific number identified by the organization. If your server is to be attached to a wide area network with other servers of which you do not have control, you may wish to register your internal number with Novell to ensure that it is unique. If you do not need a registered number, the best alternative is to allow the NetWare installation program to assign a random number and then record the assigned internal network number on the NetWare Server Worksheet shown in Figure B-2.

Disk Information

Because NetWare 5.1 is a complete operating system that is independent from DOS, it requires its own disk drivers to access the computer's disk system. As a result, one of the first steps you need to perform in preparing for NetWare 5.1 installation is to obtain information regarding the disk controller card and drives used on the server computer. This information is important because during installation you will need to select and configure the correct disk driver for your server's disk hardware. For example, before installing NetWare 5.1 on the new Engineering server, Eric identified the type, make, and model of the disk controller and drives on the NetWare Server Worksheet shown in Figure B-2.

Selecting The Disk Drivers

Most server computers use either IDE (Intelligent Drive Electronics) or SCSI (Small Computer System Interface) disk controller cards. Larger servers that support more storage devices, such as large hard drives, CD-ROMs, and tape back-up systems, often use SCSI controllers because they provide higher speeds and support a wider range of devices than IDE controllers. On the other hand, for the same cost, IDE controllers often provide higher storage capacity at acceptable speeds. Universal Aerospace selected a SCSI disk controller because the corporation is planning to expand its storage devices in the future to support additional disk drives along with a planned optical disk system for archiving engineering designs.

In addition to the type of controller, the make and model are important to select the correct driver during installation. NetWare 5.1 comes with drivers for many popular SCSI disk controllers, such as the Adaptec 2940 being used by Universal Aerospace. In previous versions of NetWare, most disk drivers consisted of a single driver file with the extension .DSK. The .DSK drivers included in previous NetWare versions were used to manage the server's disk controller card along with all storage devices attached to it. To support more sophisticated SCSI controllers with a wider range of storage devices, Novell introduced a new driver system with NetWare 4.11. The new driver system provides for a wider range of storage devices by using Host Bus Adapter (HBA) drivers with the extension .HBA to manage the controller cards and Custom Device Modules (CDM) with the extension .CDM to control the individual storage devices attached to the controller card. Starting with NetWare 5.0, the older DSK modules are no longer supported, and you will need to be sure that the disk controller you select for the server has the necessary HBA and CDM modules available for NetWare 5.1. Disk controllers that do not have HBA and CDM modules included with NetWare will need to have their NetWare drivers loaded from a floppy disk supplied by the manufacturer before they can be used with NetWare. Therefore, to make installation simpler, when selecting a SCSI disk controller for a server, check to see that the disk controller you select is included with NetWare. In most cases, you can best ensure that this is the case by purchasing controller cards that are NetWare 5 certified.

In addition to the SCSI controllers, NetWare includes HBA and CDM modules for IDE controllers that will handle most IDE and Enhanced IDE (EIDE) type controllers with drives ranging from 500 MB to over 2 GB. As with SCSI controllers, it is best to select an IDE controller that has been Novell certified.

Planning Disk Partitions

Once the disk controller has been selected and the driver has been identified, the next step in preparing for server installation is to define the amount of disk storage to be allocated to DOS and NetWare. On a NetWare server, disk storage space is divided into two separate areas called **partitions**—one partition for use by DOS in booting the server computer and the other partition for use by the NetWare operating system. The DOS partition is quite small; usually 50 MB is recommended to start the computer initially and then start the NetWare SERVER.EXE program. The remainder of the disk space on the drive is then reserved for the NetWare partition as shown on the NetWare Server Worksheet in Figure B-2. Once the SERVER program is running, the correct disk driver for the controller card will be loaded to provide access to the NetWare partition.

Another consideration in planning NetWare volumes is disk mirroring or duplexing. **Disk mirroring** is the process of duplicating data on two different NetWare partitions. **Duplexing** occurs when the partitions are on drives attached to different controller cards. To do mirroring or duplexing, the NetWare partitions on the drives to be mirrored must be the same size. The NetWare Server Worksheet shown in Figure B-2 contains a section to identify the NetWare partition size for each disk drive attached to a controller, along with a Mirrored column that may be used to specify any mirrored partitions.

Identifying the NetWare Volume Requirements

After the size of the DOS and NetWare partitions have been defined, the next step is to identify the NetWare volumes to be created. Each NetWare server must have a SYS volume to contain operating system files. At a minimum, the SYS volume for a NetWare 5.1 server should be at least 750 MB, but in most cases you will want an additional 750 MB to contain space for additional services such as the Web server. In the NetWare Server Worksheet shown in Figure B-2, Eric identified two volumes: a 2 GB SYS volume and 16 GB Eng-data volume, leaving at least 2 GB of free space on the NetWare partition. It is a good idea to leave some free space in the NetWare partition. The NetWare partition's free space can later be used to expand an existing volume or to create a new volume.

The Network Environment

To communicate with other devices on the network, a server computer needs at least one network interface card. Additional network interface cards, up to eight, may be installed to allow access to the server from multiple network cable systems. When multiple network cards are installed in a server, the server will act as a router, passing packets of data among network cable systems. Figure B-4 illustrates how a NetWare 5.1 server with multiple network interface cards (NICs) could be used to connect both the Engineering and Business department networks to the Internet. A packet from a workstation in the Business network destined for the Engineering server would first be sent from the workstation to the UAS_HOST server. After receiving the packet, the UAS_HOST server would compare the network address of the receiver to network address assigned to each NIC and then re-transmit the packet on the NIC attached to the engineering network.

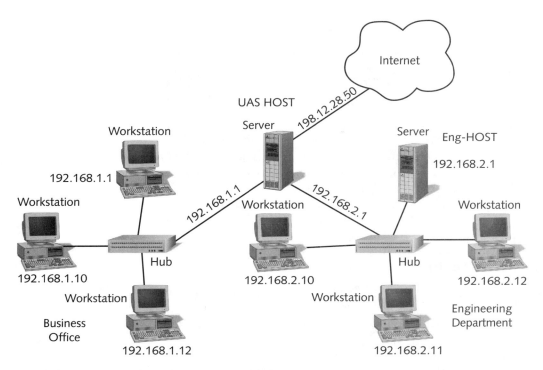

Figure B-4 Universal Aerospace intranet layout

To access network interface cards, NetWare requires a driver to be identified for each NIC during installation. As a result, before installing NetWare 5.1 on the server computer, you will need to identify the make, model, and configuration for each network interface card in your server. To make installation easier, NetWare contains drivers for many popular network interface cards. As with disk controllers, one of the best ways to be sure a driver for your network card is included with NetWare is to purchase a card that has been Novell certified. Along with identifying the make and model of each network card, during installation you will also need to supply the hardware configuration for the card. The card's hardware configuration can consist of an interrupt, Direct Memory Access (DMA) channel, input/output port, and memory address. You can configure the card by using special software or by placing jumpers or setting switches on the card itself. The NetWare Server Worksheet shown in Figure B-2 shows the network card and configuration used with the Universal Aerospace server.

Defining Network Protocol Usage

After you have identified the network interface cards to be installed in the server computer, the other major consideration in configuring the network environment is identifying the network protocol(s) the server will need to support. The network protocol environment consists of network protocols along with the network address and frame type to be used for each network card in the server. In addition to providing the legacy IPX (Internet Packet eXchange) protocol, Novell enables NetWare 5.1 to communicate directly using the TCP/IP protocol. The IPX protocol has the advantage of being simpler to set up as well as providing compatibility with older NetWare servers. Although more complex to implement, the TCP/IP protocol is a more universal protocol and enables you to connect the server to the Internet through an Internet service provider (ISP) or provide services directly to a company intranet. Because of the existing NetWare 3 server and applications, Universal Aerospace has decided initially to install support for both IPX and TCP/IP on the server. After converting all servers, workstations, and applications to TCP/IP, the corporation can remove support for IPX from the NetWare 5.0 and 5.1 servers. In this section, you will learn about the factors that affect the IPX and TCP/IP protocols along with how they apply to the Universal Aerospace server installation.

The IPX Protocol

When installing the IPX protocol, you must assign each network cable system a unique network address and frame type. The frame type specifies the format of the data packets to be sent across the network cable. To communicate, all computers need to use a common frame type. Because the default Ethernet frame type used with IPX packets is 802.2, Eric has entered 802.2 in the frame type field of the NetWare Server Worksheet.

The network address works much like a zip code in that it allows packets to be efficiently delivered to the correct network cable of the recipient. If you are installing the first server on the network cable, you can use any network address consisting of up to eight hexadecimal digits. Additional servers attached to the same network cable will then also need to use the same network address of the existing server. As the NetWare Server Worksheet in Figure B-2 shows, Eric has selected a network address of 1EEE8022 for the 10BaseT network card. He selected this number because it stands for the IEEE 802.2 standard used by the 10BaseT Ethernet card.

The TCP/IP Protocol

As described earlier, in addition to the IPX protocol, NetWare also supports TCP/IP. The TCP/IP protocol column of the NetWare Server Worksheet, shown in Figure B-2, may be used to identify information regarding the TCP/IP protocol that will be configured during installation. To install support for the TCP/IP protocol during installation, you will need to supply the server with an IP address and mask. An IP address consists of a 32-bit (4-byte) number that is divided into a network address and a host or node address. The network part of the address must be the same for all computers on the same network cable segment. The host or node address must be unique for each computer on that network segment. The network mask identifies what bytes in an IP address are part of the network address. The number 255 in the network mask identifies the entire byte as part of the network address. Zeros in the network mask identify bits that are part of the host or node address.

IP addresses are divided into three classes. A Class A address has a default network mask of 255.0.0.0, indicating that only the first byte represents the network address. Class B address has a default network mask of 255.255.0.0, indicating that the first two bytes represent the network portion of the address, and the last two bytes represent the host or node. Class C address has a default mask of 255.255.255.0, indicating that the first three bytes are the network address, and only the last byte may be used to represent the node. Because 0 and 255 are not valid node values, a Class C address provides for up to 254 devices to access the network at the same time. If your company will be attaching its network or server to the Internet, you need to obtain an IP address range for your company to use. You can obtain a registered Internet address by contacting your local Internet Service Provider (ISP). For example, assume that Universal Aerospace is planning to attach its server to the network in the near future, and that Universal Aerospace President David Heise has obtained a class C address of 198.12.28.50 for the Universal Aerospace server. Rather than obtain a unique Internet address for each workstation attached to the Universal Aerospace intranet, David has decided to establish a private address scheme for internal use. The Network Address Translation feature of NetWare 5.1 will be used to attach the Universal Aerospace networks to the Internet using only the class C address as shown previously in Figure B-4. While you could assign computers any IP addresses you want for internal use on a private intranet, Table B-2 lists certain address ranges that have been reserved for this purpose. Because these address ranges are considered non-routable by Internet routers, using the 192.168.1.1 – 192.168.1.254 and 192.168.2.1 – 192.168.2.254 address schemes on the Universal Aerospace internal networks will increase security by preventing Internet computers from sending packets directly to any computers attached to the Universal Aerospace internal networks. The only way for packets to get from the Universal Aerospace internal networks to and from the Internet will be through the Network Address Translation (NAT) feature of the NetWare 5.1 server.

Table B-2   Reserved Private Network Addresses

Class	Reserved network addresses
Class A	One reserved network address: 10.0.0.0
Class B	16 reserved network addresses: 172.16.0.0 through 172.31.0.0
Class C	254 reserved network addresses: 192.168.1.0 through 192.168.254.0

Using the Compatibility Mode Driver

As mentioned earlier, Universal Aerospace is currently using both the TCP/IP and IPX protocols on the network clients. The IPX protocol is used to access the NetWare servers, and IP is used to access the Internet. Using both IPX and IP protocols on your network clients increases network traffic and can cause performance bottlenecks. To provide better network performance in the future, Universal Aerospace wants to convert the clients to use only the TCP/IP protocol to access both the NetWare servers and the Internet. Whereas NetWare 5.1 can use only the TCP/IP protocol to communicate with clients, some application software still requires the IPX protocol stack to access NetWare server. When using only the TCP/IP protocol, NetWare 5.1 servers can still support IPX applications by loading a compatibility mode driver named SCMD on both the client and server. The compatibility mode driver is loaded on the client when you select the **IP with IPX compatibility** option during client installation. The NetWare 5.1 server will automatically load a compatibility driver named SCMD.NLM when you bind only the TCP/IP protocol to the network card. The compatibility mode driver on the client encapsulates an IPX-formatted request from an application into a TCP/IP packet and sends it to the server. The SCMD.NLM software running on the NetWare 5.1 server then removes the IPX-formatted data from the TCP/IP packet and processes the request on the server. In this way, the compatibility mode driver will allow Universal Aerospace to gain network performance while gradually migrating their IPX applications to TCP/IP.

The NDS Context

During NetWare installation, you will have a choice of either placing the new server in an existing tree or creating a new tree. To place the server in an existing tree, you will need to be able to log in as the Admin user of the existing tree and then enter the context of the container where the server will be created. To create a new tree, you will need to determine the name of the tree as well as the context of the container where the new server object and Admin user will be placed. As a result, an important step in preparing for NetWare installation is to identify where the server will be placed in the NDS database.

When you are installing the first server in a new tree structure, the default approach is to place the server within the main Organization container. If necessary, you can later move the server and volumes objects or rename the Organization container as the tree structure is fully developed. In the sample NetWare Server Worksheet shown in Figure B-2, Eric has identified the NDS Context for the new NetWare 5.1 and its SYS volume as being the Engineering Organizational Unit of the UAS Organization within the existing UAS_Tree.

USING DEPLOYMENT MANAGER TO UPGRADE THE EXISTING NETWORK

NetWare 5.1 includes a new utility called Deployment Manager (NWDEPLOY.EXE) that runs from a client computer and is used primarily to prepare your existing network for upgrading to NetWare 5.1. In addition to performing network preparation tasks, Deployment Manager also provides Help information on installation and upgrading options and post-installation tasks. Because Universal Aerospace will be installing the new NetWare 5.1 server into an existing NetWare 5.0 environment, there are two prepara-tion tasks that need to be performed. These tasks are to prepare the existing NetWare 5.0-based NDS tree for the new NetWare 5.1 eDirectory system, and install the new NetWare Licensing Service.

Upgrading the Existing UAS_Tree

To prepare the existing UAS_Tree for the new NetWare 5.1 server installation, Eric performs the follow-ing tasks on the existing UAS_HOST server during a time when no users are attached to the network:

1. Eric makes sure the current server is backed up.

2. After the back-up is complete, Eric makes sure the existing server's volumes are problem free by dismounting the volumes and running the VREPAIR utility.

3. Eric uses the DSREPAIR utility to check the existing NDS tree structure and correct any problems that are encountered.

4. After the volumes and NDS tree are checked out, Eric downloads the latest support pack for NetWare 5.0 from *http://support.novell.com/products/nw5/patches.htm* and installs it.

5. To use the Deployment Manager to update the existing UAS_Tree, Eric goes to a client work-station and logs in to the NetWare 5.0 network as Admin. He then inserts the NetWare 5.1 CD into the client, which automatically starts Deployment Manager.

6. After accepting the license agreement, Eric selects the **Step 3: Prepare for NDS 8** option, and follows the prompts to update the existing NetWare 5.0 tree to the new NDS eDirectory.

7. After the NDS 8 upgrade is complete, Eric selects the **Step 4: Novell Licensing Services** option to install NLS on the existing NetWare 5.0 network.

8. After all upgrades are complete, Eric exits Deployment Manager, logs off, and restarts the NetWare 5.0 server.

INSTALLING NETWARE 5.1

Once the preliminary planning has been done, the existing network has been updated, and the new server's hardware has been installed, Eric is ready to start the installation of NetWare 5.1 on the new server. The installation process consists of two major tasks:

1. Creating the DOS boot partition.

2. Installing the NetWare 5.1 operating system.

In this section, you will learn how to perform these two tasks by following Eric as he installs NetWare 5.1 on the Universal Aerospace server.

Creating the DOS Boot Partition

After completing the installation of the server hardware according to the NetWare Server Worksheet, Eric prepares for installation by first obtaining a copy of a DOS boot disk that contains the FDISK and FOR-MAT programs along with the drivers necessary for DOS to access the CD-ROM drive.

1. To configure a bootable DOS partition initially, Eric starts the server computer with the DOS disk and then enters the FDISK command to obtain the FDISK menu.

2. Next he uses the Create DOS partition option to create a small 100 MB DOS partition.

3. After creating the DOS partition, Eric uses the Set active partition option to make the newly created DOS partition the active partition (the partition from which the computer will start). This is necessary to start from the hard drive after creating a DOS partition that does not use the entire hard disk space.

4. When all the partition changes have been completed, Eric exits the FDISK program and restarts the computer from the DOS diskette. Restarting the computer is necessary in order to access the newly created partition.

5. After the computer restarts, Eric uses the FORMAT C: /S command to format the DOS partition with a copy of the operating system to make it bootable.

6. Once the DOS partition has been formatted, Eric enables the CMOS to boot from the CD-ROM drive.

Installing the NetWare 5.1 Operating System

Now that a formatted DOS partition has been created and the CMOS configured to boot from the CD-ROM, Eric is ready to install NetWare by booting the computer from the NetWare 5.1 CD-ROM. [Note: If the server computer is not able to boot from its CD-ROM drive, you can still install NetWare 5.1 by first installing the necessary CD-ROM drivers in the DOS partition and then running the INSTALL batch file, located on root of the NetWare 5.1 CD-ROM, from the DOS prompt.]

1. To automatically boot the installation program, Eric simply inserts the NetWare 5.1 Operating System CD-ROM and restarts the computer. If your system does not boot from a CD-ROM, you can manually start the installation software by installing the necessary CD-ROM drivers on the DOS partition and then running the INSTALL program from the root of the NetWare 5.1 CD.

2. When the installation program starts it displays the license agreement screen containing options to read the agreement, accept the agreement, or cancel the installation. Eric selects the option to accept the license agreement.

3. After pressing Enter, the installation program checks for a DOS partition and displays the message "Valid boot partition detected, use it or create a new one?" Eric selects the option to use the existing boot partition and then presses Enter to display the Installation Type screen shown in Figure B-5.

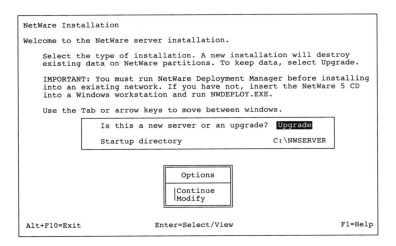

```
NetWare Installation

Welcome to the NetWare server installation.

    Select the type of installation. A new installation will destroy
    existing data on NetWare partitions. To keep data, select Upgrade.

    IMPORTANT: You must run NetWare Deployment Manager before installing
    into an existing network. If you have not, insert the NetWare 5 CD
    into a Windows workstation and run NWDEPLOY.EXE.

    Use the Tab or arrow keys to move between windows.

        Is this a new server or an upgrade?   Upgrade

        Startup directory                     C:\NWSERVER


                    Options
                   Continue
                   Modify


 Alt+F10=Exit            Enter=Select/View              F1=Help
```

Figure B-5   NetWare Installation window

4. To start the installation process, Eric selects the **New server** option along with the default **C:\NWSERVER** directory as the location for the startup files on the DOS partition. He then highlights the **Continue** option and presses **Enter** to display the Server Settings screen.

5. The Server Settings screen contains NDS version, Server Id, and server boot options. NetWare 5.1 needs NDS version 8 to provide the enhanced NDS functionality required by many new Web networking products, such as WebSphere. However, because the Universal Aerospace tree has not already been updated for NDS 8, Eric will need Supervisor rights at the root of the

existing UAS_Tree for the installation program to update that existing tree to NDS version 8. If Eric did not have supervisor rights to the root of the existing tree, he could install NDS version 7 and then the network administrator could update the tree to NDS version 8 at a later time. The Server ID Number contains a randomly generated 8-digit hexadecimal number that must be unique for each NetWare server on the network. The Load Server at Reboot option allows Eric to select whether or not the server will automatically load when the computer is started. As described in the main text, the NetWare 5.1 server reads setup commands from the STARTUP.NCF and AUTOEXEC.NCF file during startup. Some device drivers for network boards and disk storage devices may require customized settings to be made to the server's environment during startup. You can customize many server settings by using the Server SET Parameters option to place commands in the server's STARTUP.NCF file. Information regarding any required SET parameters should be provided in the documentation that comes with the network board or storage device driver. Since no special SET parameters are required for the Engineering server, Eric presses Enter to continue the installation using the randomly supplied Server ID number along with the defaults of NDS 8 and automatic server startup.

6. Eric clicks the **Continue** button on the Regional Settings screen to accept the default Country, Keyboard, and Code page settings.

7. Eric clicks the **Continue** button again to accept the default display and mouse settings.

8. After copying some initial files to the DOS partition, the installation program attempts to detect the disk storage devices and then displays the Device types screen, as shown in Figure B-6. Since the storage adapter type matches the driver identified on the NetWare Server Worksheet shown in Figure B-2, Eric clicks the **Continue** button to accept the detected storage adapter.

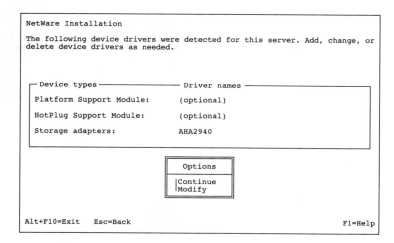

Figure B-6   Device Types window

9. The installation program next attempts to automatically detect the network card driver and displays the updated Device Types window shown in Figure B-7. If the network card was not correctly detected, Eric could use the Modify option to manually select a driver for the network card. After verifying that the detected network driver matches the one specified on the NetWare Server Worksheet, Eric clicks the **Continue** button.

Figures B-7 through B-11 contain sample entries, not those entered by Eric.

B

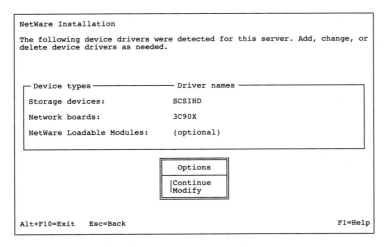

```
NetWare Installation

The following device drivers were detected for this server. Add, change, or
delete device drivers as needed.



 ┌ Device types ─────────── Driver names ──────────────
 │
   Storage devices:         SCSIHD

   Network boards:          3C90X

   NetWare Loadable Modules:  (optional)



            ┌─────────────────────┐
            │     Options         │
            ├─────────────────────┤
            │Continue             │
            │Modify               │
            └─────────────────────┘

Alt+F10=Exit    Esc=Back                              F1=Help
```

Figure B-7   Updated Device Types window

10. The installation program goes out to the disk controller, checks for free space on the boot drive, and then displays the Create a NetWare partition and volume SYS screen as shown in Figure B-8. By default, all free space on the NetWare partition has been assigned to the SYS volume. Because Eric wants to create another volume on this drive, he uses the Modify option to change the size of the SYS volume to match the size specified on the NetWare Server Worksheet and then presses F10 to save his changes.

11. When the NetWare partition and volume sizes match those specified on the NetWare Server Worksheet, Eric highlights **Continue** and presses **Enter** to start copying files to the SYS volume.

12. After the initial file copy is complete, the installation program launches the Java X-Windows environment and displays a Server Properties window similar to the one shown in Figure B-9. Eric enters the name **ENG_HOST** for the server name and then clicks the **Next** button to display a Configure File System window similar to the one shown in Figure B-10.

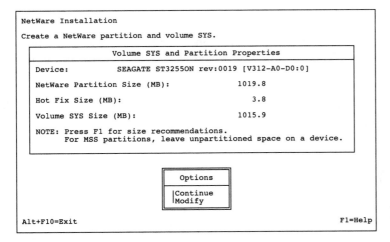

```
NetWare Installation

Create a NetWare partition and volume SYS.
 ┌────────────────────────────────────────────────────────┐
 │        Volume SYS and Partition Properties              │
 ├────────────────────────────────────────────────────────┤
 │ Device:          SEAGATE ST3255ON rev:0019 [V312-A0-D0:0]│
 │                                                          │
 │ NetWare Partition Size (MB):        1019.8               │
 │                                                          │
 │ Hot Fix Size (MB):                     3.8               │
 │                                                          │
 │ Volume SYS Size (MB):               1015.9               │
 │                                                          │
 │ NOTE: Press F1 for size recommendations.                 │
 │       For MSS partitions, leave unpartitioned space on a device. │
 └────────────────────────────────────────────────────────┘


            ┌─────────────────────┐
            │     Options         │
            ├─────────────────────┤
            │Continue             │
            │Modify               │
            └─────────────────────┘

Alt+F10=Exit                                          F1=Help
```

Figure B-8   Create a NetWare partition

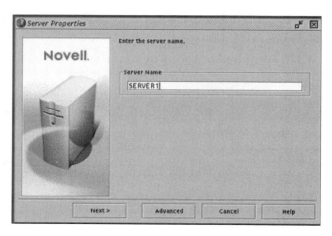

Figure B-9   Server Properties

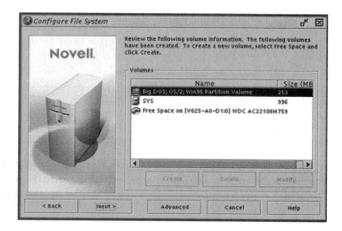

Figure B-10   Configure File System

13. To create a new volume named Eng-data, Eric clicks on the free space and then clicks the **Create** button to display a New Volume window similar to the one shown in Figure B-11.

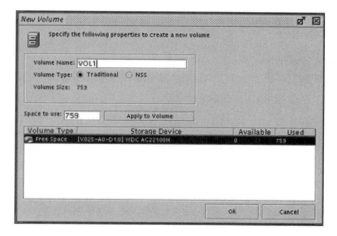

Figure B-11   New Volume window

14. By default, the system assigns all free space to the new volume. To keep space free for future use, Eric next enters the size for the Eng-data volume along with the volume name. He then clicks the **Apply to Volume** and **OK** buttons to return to the Configure File System window.

15. After verifying that the volume information is correct, Eric clicks the **Next** button to save the volume information and display the Mount Volumes window. He then clicks the **No, Mount volumes now** option and clicks the **Next** button to display the Protocols window shown in Figure B-12.

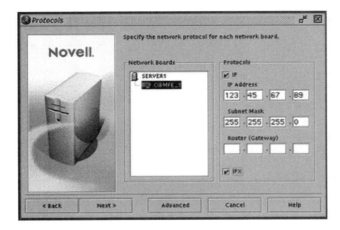

Figure B-12   Protocols

16. Eric highlights the server's network card and checks both the IP and IPX boxes. After clicking the **IP** check box, Eric enters the IP address and Mask values defined on the NetWare Server Worksheet and clicks the **Next** button to display a Domain Name Service window, as shown in Figure B-13.

17. The Domain Name Service window is used to identify the DNS host name and domain of the new server along with the IP address of the DNS server containing this NetWare server's host name and IP address. Since Universal Aerospace does not yet have a DNS server or registered host name, Eric leaves this window blank and clicks Next to continue.

18. When a warning message is displayed indicating that no host name or DNS server has been specified, Eric clicks OK to continue.

19. He next selects the correct time zone for the server and clicks the **Next** button to continue.

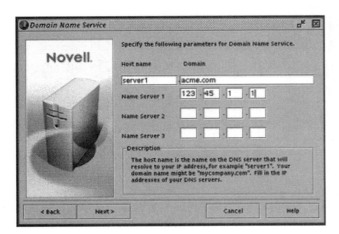

Figure B-13   Domain Name Service

20. When the Install NDS window shown in Figure B-14 is displayed, Eric clicks the Existing NDS Tree option. He is next presented with a window asking him to enter the Tree name and context where the new server will be installed. He enters "UAS_Tree" in the Tree Name field and .OU=Engineering.O=UAS in the Context for Server field. After clicking Next the Login to NDS window is displayed.

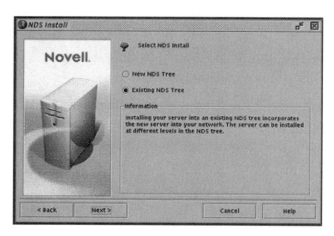

Figure B-14   NDS Install

21. Eric enters the distinguished name and password of the UAS_Tree administrator and then clicks Next to continue.

22. After clicking the **Next** button the server displays an NDS summary window containing the NDS context information. Eric records this information for later reference, and then clicks the Next button to continue.

23. When the license window is displayed, Eric inserts the NetWare 5.1 license diskette into the drive and then uses the Browse button to select the NLF license file contained in the A:\license folder. After the license file(s) are installed, Eric clicks Next to display the Installation Options windows shown in Figure B-15.

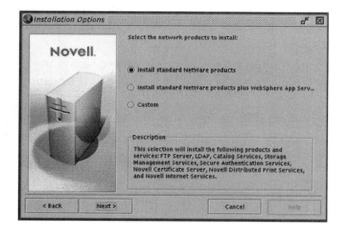

Figure B-15   Installation Options

24. Eric clicks the Custom option and then clicks Next to display the Components window shown in Figure B-16. Eric clicks to remove the check marks from both the NetWare Enterprise Web Server and FTP servers leaving only the Novell Distributed Print Services (NDPS) selected at this time. Eric then clicks Next to continue the NetWare 5.1 installation. [Note: Additional products such as the NetWare Enterprise Web Server and FTP Server can be added later using NetWare 5.1 graphical console.]

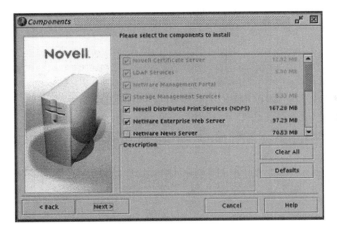

Figure B-16   Components

25. Eric clicks the **Next** button to accept the default components. Because this is the first NetWare 5.1 server in the tree, the installation program next displays the Novell Certificate Server Objects window shown in Figure B-17. The purpose of the Novell Certificate Server is to enable secure data transmissions for Web-enabled products by issuing digital certificates. The *first* NetWare 5.1 server will automatically create and physically store the Security container object and Organizational CA object for the entire NDS tree. Both objects are created at, and must remain at the [Root] of, the NDS tree.

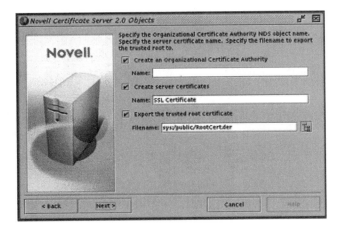

Figure B-17   Certificate Server Objects

26. Eric clicks Next to accept the default certificate settings. He then clicks OK to accept the Certificate warning message. After completing the certificate server installation, a Summary window showing all products along with their space requirements is displayed.

27. After verifying that all components are selected, Eric clicks the **Finish** button to begin the main file copy process.

28. After all files are copied to the server's SYS volume, the completion is displayed. Eric clicks the **Yes** button to complete the installation and reboot the server.

Once the server is up and running, Eric tests the server's operation from a client computer by changing context to the UAS container and logging in as the Admin user. Once the installation of the server is confirmed, the process of setting up the file system for the Eng-data volume can be performed from the NetWare Administrator program.

UPGRADING NETWARE 5.0 TO NETWARE 5.1

Novell provides three major methods that can be used to upgrade an existing server to NetWare 5.1—In-Place Upgrade, Across-the-Wire Upgrade, or Accelerated Upgrade. If the current server meets the NetWare 5.1 upgrade requirements listed below, the simplest method is to use the In-Place upgrade. The In-Place upgrade works much like the new server installation process described previously except that it uses the existing server's configuration and NDS tree information.

- A NetWare 3, NetWare 4, IntraNetWare, or NetWare 5.0 operating system installed on the server
- A 200 MHz Pentium or compatible processor
- A VGA or better resolution display adapter (SVGA recommended)
- At least 35 MB free in the DOS partition
- At least 750 MB free on the SYS volume
- At least 128 MB RAM for standard NetWare products and an additional 128 MB RAM for WebSphere Application Server for NetWare
- A NetWare 5.1-compatible network board
- A NetWare 5.1-compatible disk controller
- A CD drive that can read ISO 9660-formatted CD disks

If you are upgrading an existing NetWare 3.x or NetWare 4.x server that does not meet the NetWare 5.1 requirements, you will need to use the Across-the-Wire method. When using the Across-the-Wire upgrade, you first need to do a new install of NetWare 5.1 on the target server using a temporary tree name and then create NetWare volumes on the target server with the same names as the existing (source) server. The Across-the-Wire upgrade is then run from a workstation logged in to both servers. All NDS tree information, users, and data are then transferred from the source server to the NetWare 5.1 server. An advantage of the Across-the-Wire method is the ability to recover from upgrade problems (such as a power outage in the middle of the upgrade) without losing or damaging data on the original server.

The new NetWare 5.1 Accelerated Upgrade procedure involves copying the NetWare 5.1 files from the Installation CD to an existing NetWare 5.1 server referred to as the Staging server, as shown in Figure B-18.

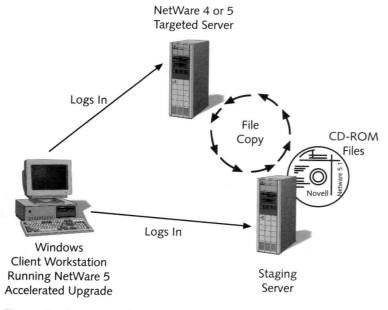

Figure B-18   Using the Accelerated Upgrade Method

The NetWare Accelerated Upgrade program (ACCUPG.EXE), located on the root of the NetWare 5.1 CD-ROM, is run from an existing workstation. When the NetWare Accelerated Upgrade launches, you log in to the target and staging servers using the Admin name and password. After a server-to-server connection is established, the Accelerated Upgrade program compares the existing target server properties with the staging server. Based on the results of the comparison, the upgrade software copies the necessary NetWare 5.1 files from the staging server to the target server. After the files are copied, the target server reboots to complete the upgrade process. Although the NetWare Accelerated Upgrade method is faster than the In-place upgrade when upgrading multiple servers, a disadvantage of this method is that it does not install additional network products, licensing services, or license certificates on the new server.

Because the UAS_HOST server meets the minimum NetWare 5.1 requirements, Eric can upgrade it using either the In-Place Upgrade or the new NetWare Accelerated Upgrade method. Because NetWare 5.1 has been installed on the engineering server, the engineering server could be used as a staging server to perform an Accelerated Upgrade on UAS_HOST. However, given that you only have one server to upgrade, the extra time and trouble it would take to copy all the NetWare 5.1 installation files to the staging server and then install the NetWare 5.1 license certificate after the upgrade do not seem worth the effort when there is only one server to upgrade.

Performing the In-Place Upgrade

Performing an In-Place Upgrade on the UAS_HOST server is similar to doing a new server installation except that the installation process preserves the existing server's data and NDS configuration. Following is an outline of the steps necessary to upgrade the UAS_HOST server from NetWare 5.0 to NetWare 5.1.

1. Back up the existing server and document any hardware settings for network and disk controller cards.

2. Use VREPAIR and DSREPAIR to verify that your volume and NDS tree are in good condition.

3. Be sure all users are logged out until the upgrade is complete.

4. Down the existing server and return it to the DOS prompt.

5. Because the UAS_HOST server can boot off a CD, you can simply insert the NetWare 5.1 CD and use the Ctrl+Alt+Del key combination to restart the computer from the NetWare 5.1 CD. An alternate method is to change the default DOS prompt to the root of the CD drive letter and enter the command **INSTALL**.

6. In the NetWare Installation window, be sure you select the **Upgrade** option and then press **Enter** to continue.

7. You will next be asked to confirm the server settings, including mouse and video drivers. Although at this point you can choose not to install NDS eDirectory, to use all the NetWare 5.1 enhancements, you should be sure **NDS 8** is selected.

8. If needed, modify the automatically detected storage, network, and platform support drivers. Because the UAS_HOST network and disk controller are supported by NetWare 5.1, you should be able to verify the settings and continue.

9. The Installation process will now mount the existing SYS volume and then starts the graphical portion of the upgrade by loading the Java-based virtual machine.

10. Because UAS_HOST will continue to use its IPX and IP protocol settings, you should not need to make any changes to the Protocols window. Verify that the settings match those that you recorded for UAS_HOST and then click the **Next** button to continue.

11. If necessary, select the option to upgrade NDS to version 8 and click the **Next** button to continue.

12. Install the NetWare 5.1 NLF license files from the diskettes provided with your server software. In addition to the NLF license files, your server will also need to install the Novell International Cryptographic Infrastructure (NICI) license. This license is called the encryption foundation key and is contained in a file having a .NFK extension.

13. Given that additional products can be added later, at this time it is easiest to take the default products and complete the upgrade without any customization.

14. After the Installation program has completed copying all files to the server, select the option to reboot the computer.

15. UAS_HOST should now be upgraded to NetWare 5.1

WORKING WITH NETWARE 5.1

NetWare 5.1 provides some new and enhanced utilities to help you manage your network system. Novell's ConsoleOne utility is becoming the cornerstone of NetWare system management. While you will still need to use NetWare Administrator to perform certain network functions, some of the new features of NetWare 5.1, such as the Certificate service and schema extensions, can only be performed using ConsoleOne. In this appendix, you will learn to use ConsoleOne to perform the tasks required by the NetWare 5.1 CNA objectives.

Managing user desktops and providing support for client problems is an important part of a network administrator's job. In this appendix, you will also learn how the Z.E.N.works version 2.0 product can help you provide user support through the use of its Remote Control and Help features.

One of the other new utilities you will learn about in this appendix is the NetWare Management Portal. NetWare Management Portal uses the HTTP protocol to allow you to view and manage NetWare servers and network configurations using a standard Web browser such as Netscape or Internet Explorer.

In order to do the projects in this appendix you will need an environment that simulates the Universal Aerospace network on your server. To keep your work separate from other students, you will be assigned an organization named ##UAS and a directory named ##Corp, where ## represents your assigned student number. During the activities you will occasionally be asked to reference certain network objects such as the UAS_Tree, UAS_HOST server or Corp volume. Since your network's tree, server, and volume names may be different, your instructor will provide you with the names of the objects you will be using. Record the names of the network objects you will be using below:

Tree name: _____

Server name: _____

Physical volume name: _____

Server context: _____

(This is the volume that contains your ##Corp directory.)

USING THE NEW CONSOLEONE

One of the new features included with NetWare 5.1 is the upgraded version of the Java-based ConsoleOne utility. The new ConsoleOne utility included with NetWare 5.1 extends the NDS management capabilities that can be performed from either a workstation or the server console. ConsoleOne can now be used to perform many NDS management tasks such as modifying the NDS schema and object properties, creating and searching for NDS objects, defining user templates, and managing the NetWare file system. Novell is in the process of making ConsoleOne the main Network management utility. Already, certain new NetWare 5.1 features, such as Certificate services, need to be managed from ConsoleOne rather than NetWare Administrator. In addition, if you need to browse huge NDS containers or create and configure LDAP containers and services, you will need to use ConsoleOne because neither NetWare Administrator nor NDS Manager provides these capabilities. Just as snap-ins are used to add capability to NetWare Administrator, ConsoleOne also requires snap-ins to manage certain NetWare products and features.

Novell is in the process of expanding ConsoleOne capabilities and snap-ins. However, until the necessary ConsoleOne snap-ins are available, ConsoleOne is not yet able to perform certain tasks, such as setting up accounting charges on NetWare servers, working with DNS and DHCP services, or managing certain additional Novell products such as Z.E.N.works version 2, GroupWise, BorderManager, and NDS for NT. Future upgrades and releases will add these capabilities as well as allow ConsoleOne to perform NDS partition management tasks, such as checking a server's NDS version, creating partitions and replicas, or deleting server objects. Z.E.N. works version 3 requires the use of ConsoleOne to perform administrative tasks.

In this section, you will learn how to install ConsoleOne on your workstation and then use ConsoleOne from either a workstation or the server console to create NDS objects, extend the NDS schema, and manage the NetWare file system.

ConsoleOne Requirements

To install and run the ConsoleOne on a client computer, the Novell documentation states that you need a Windows 9x or NT workstation using the latest Novell client software with at least a 200 MHz processor and a minimum of 64 MB RAM. In order to run ConsoleOne on the server, the server computer needs to have a display with 800 X 600 screen resolution and at least a 200 MHz processor with 128 MB of RAM and 25 MB free disk space. As is the case with most software, you may experience marginal performance using the minimum hardware requirements. The more memory and processor speed, the better the performance.

Keeping with the theme in Appendix B, Universal Aerospace has again turned to Eric Kenton.(Remember that Eric was hired to upgrade the existing UAS_Host server.)

Although you do not need to use the LDAP capabilities of ConsoleOne at this time, Eric has recommended taking time to get familiar with the product because Novell will be developing more capability and snap-ins for it in the future. In addition, being able to manage the NDS tree and NetWare file system from a server console can save you from running out to a client workstation to perform certain NDS or file system tasks when you are working in the server room.

In this hands-on activity you will create a desktop shortcut to the ConsoleOne utility, and then use ConsoleOne to browse the network tree.

1. Log in to the network using your ##Admin user name.

2. To start ConsoleOne, you need to run the ConsoleOne.exe program from the PUBLIC\MGMT\CONSOLEONE\1.2\BIN folder. To make starting ConsoleOne easier, in this step you will add a shortcut to ConsoleOne on your desktop.

   a. Use My Computer or Windows Explorer to navigate to the F:\PUBLIC\MGMT\ CONSOLEONE\1.2\BIN folder.

b. Drag and drop the **ConsoleOne.exe** program on your desktop and create a shortcut.

c. Close all windows.

3. Double-click **ConsoleOne** and notice how long it takes to start. Does ConsoleOne take longer to start than NetWare Administrator? Why or why not?

4. Expand your tree by clicking the **"+"** icon, as shown in Figure C-1.

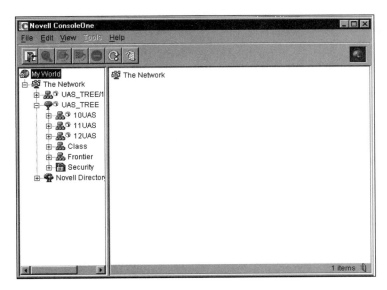

Figure C-1   ConsoleOne tree

5. Expand the Class container by clicking on the "+" icon. Click on the Class container and record the names of any group objects you see in the right-hand results pane.

6. Browse to the container where your server is located and highlight it. Identify the two NetWare 5.1 license container objects.

7. Double-click each of the license objects and, in the space below, record each license container and what objects are in it.

License container: _____

Contents: _____

License container: _____

Contents: _____

8. Double-click the **Students** group object.

9. Click the **Members** tab to display all members of the student group.

10. Click the **NDS Rights** tab and record below the rights assigned to the [Root] object:

11. Click **Cancel** to return to the ConsoleOne window.

12. Exit ConsoleOne.

Assume that as part of the expansion of their engineering and manufacturing facility Universal Aerospace has recently purchased and equipped another building to house engineering and manufacturing staff dedicated to the NASA contracts. Because the users in the new facility have their own network resources that need to be secured from use by other departments, you have decided to create a separate container and disk storage area for the NASA engineering division.

In this hands-on activity, you will learn how to use ConsoleOne to create a new organizational unit that contains a volume object for the new NetWare 5.1 server.

1. If necessary, log in using your assigned Admin account.
2. Double-click the **ConsoleOne** icon on your desktop.
3. Click the "+" icon next to your tree to view all containers.
4. Click the ##UAS organization container object assigned to you.
5. With your organization container highlighted, click **File**, **New**, **Object** and then double-click **Organizational Unit** from the New Object window.
6. In the Name field type **NASA_Eng** and click **OK**.
7. Create a volume object in the new NASA_Eng organizational unit.

   a. If necessary, expand your ##UAS organization by clicking the "+" icon.
   b. Click on your **NASA_Eng** organizational unit to highlight it.
   c. Click **File**, **New**, **Object** and then scroll down and double-click **Volume** in the New Object Class window.
   d. Enter **EngData** in the Name field.
   e. Click the **Browse** button to the right of the Host Server field and then use the up arrow icon to the right of the "Look in" field to navigate to the container holding your server object.
   f. Double-click your server.
   g. In the Physical Volume field, select the volume name assigned to you and then click **OK** to create the volume object.

Once the container and volume objects are created, your next step will be to create a directory structure for the user home directories and shared NASA engineering project data.

In this hands-on activity, you will use ConsoleOne to create the directory structure shown in Figure C-2.

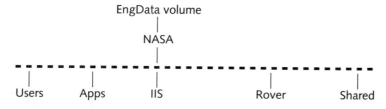

Figure C-2   Universal Aerospace NASA division directory structure

1. If necessary, click the "+" icon to expand the **NASA_Eng** organizational unit object you created.
2. Click the "+" icon next to your EngData volume object to display your assigned directory.
3. Right click your assigned ##Corp directory and then click **New**, **Object** to display the New Object window.
4. Select **Directory** and click **OK** to display the New Directory window.
5. Enter **NASA** in the Name field and then click **OK** to create the NASA directory.

C

6. Right-click the newly created **NASA** directory then click **New**, **Object**, select **Directory**, and click **OK** to display the New Directory window.

7. Enter **Users** in the Name field and click the **Create another Directory** check box.

8. Click **OK** to create the directory and return to the New Directory window.

9. Repeat steps 7 and 8 to create the **Apps**, **IIS**, **Rover**, and **Shared** sub-directories.

10. Click **Cancel** to return to ConsoleOne.

In addition to the two existing engineers assigned to the NASA contract projects, Universal Aerospace has recently hired three additional engineers along with an administrative assistant for the NASA engineering division.

In this hands-on activity, you will use ConsoleOne to create a user account and home directory for Cleo Stowe, the new administrative assistant for the NASA engineering division.

1. If necessary, highlight your **NASA_Eng** organizational unit by clicking on it.

2. Create two groups named **Engineers** and **AdmAsst**.

    a. With your NASA_Eng organizational unit highlighted, click **File**, **New**, **Group**.

    b. In the Name field, enter **Engineers** and then click **Create another Group**.

    c. Click **OK** to create the Engineers group and return to the New Group window.

    d. In the Name field, enter **AdmAsst** and then click to remove the check from the **Create another Group** check box.

    e. Click **OK** to create the AdmAsst group and return to ConsoleOne.

3. With your NASA_Eng organizational unit highlighted, click **File**, **New**, **User**, or click the **New User** button on the toolbar.

4. Enter **Cleo** in the Name/Unique ID property field and enter **Stowe** in the Surname property field.

5. Click the **Create Home Directory** check box.

6. Click the **Browse** button to the right of the Path field and navigate to your **NASA\Users** directory.

7. Click the **Define Additional Properties** check box and then click **OK**.

8. Enter *password* for the password and click **OK** to create the user account for Cleo and display the Properties of Cleo window.

9. Click the **General** tab and enter the following values:

    ■ Given name: **Cleo**

    ■ Title: **Administrative Assistant**

    ■ E-Mail Address: **Cleo@uas.com**

10. Click the **Memberships** tab and then click **Add**.

11. Double-click the **AdmAsst** group to add it to the Group Memberships.

12. Click **OK** to save the changes and return to ConsoleOne.

As you have learned in previous chapters, templates are a great way to standardize and simplify the creation of user accounts. Like NetWare Administrator, ConsoleOne also allows you to create and configure template objects that you can use when creating new users.

In this hands-on activity, you will use ConsoleOne to create a template for the new engineering users that contains the specifications shown in Table C-1.

Table C-1   Engineer template specifications

Template Property	Value
Department	NASA Engineering
Home directory volume	Your assigned volume name (CORP:)
Home directory path	NASA\USERS
Login times	Monday through Saturday 5:00am–11:30pm
Groups	Engineers
Require password	Yes
Password duration	120 days
Require unique passwords	Yes
Grace logins	5

1. If necessary, highlight your **NASA_Eng** container by clicking on it.

2. Click **File**, **New**, **Object**, and then scroll down the Class list box and double-click **Template**.

3. In the name field, enter **_Engineer**. (Starting template names with an underline symbol makes it easier to find templates objects in the container.)

4. Click **Define additional properties** and then click **OK** to create the template object and display the Properties of _Engineer window.

5. Enter **NASA Engineering** in the Department field.

6. Click the **arrow** next to the General table, then click **Environment** from the pull down menu.

7. Click the **Browse** button next to the Home Directory field and navigate to your NASA\Users directory and click **OK**.

8. Click **Memberships**, then click the **Add** button and add the Engineers group.

9. Click the **Restrictions** tab and enter the password restrictions shown in Table C-1.

10. Click the **arrow** next to Restrictions, then click **Time Restrictions** from the pull-down menu.

11. Enter the time restrictions specified in Table B-1.

12. Click **OK** to save your template properties and return to ConsoleOne.

Table C-2 contains the names of the three new engineers recently hired to work in Universal Aerospace's new NASA engineering facility.

Table C-2   Engineering users for NASA division

User Name	Login Name	Group Membership	Template
Travis Scott	TScott	Engineers	_Engineer
Lucas Teague	LTeague	Engineers	_Engineer
Lindsey Barton	LBarton	Engineers	_Engineer

In this hands-on activity, you will use your new engineering template to create the three engineering users.

1. If necessary, highlight your **NASA_Eng** container by clicking on it.

2. Click the **New User** button on the toolbar.

3. Create a user account for Travis Scott.

   a. Enter **TScott** in the Name property and **Scott** in the Surname property.

   b. Click **Use Template** and then use the **Browse** button next to the Use template box to double-click your **_Engineer** template.

   c. Click **Create Another User** and then click **OK**.

   d. Enter an initial password of **password** and then click **OK** to create the first engineering user account.

4. Create a user account for Lucas Teague.

   a. Enter **Lteague** in the Name property and **Teague** in the Surname property.

   b. Click **Use Template** and then use the **Browse** button next to the Use template box to double-click your **_Engineer** template.

   c. Click **OK**.

   d. Enter an initial password of **password** and then click **OK** to create the second engineering user account.

5. Create a user account for Lindsey Barton.

   a. Enter **LBarton** in the Name property and **Barton** in the Surname property.

   b. Click **Use Template** and then use the **Browse** button next to the Use template box to double-click your **_Engineer template**.

   c. Click to remove the check from the **Create Another User** check box and click **OK**.

   d. Enter an initial password of **password** and then click **OK** to create the third engineering user account and return to ConsoleOne.

6. Enter an initial password of *password* and then click **OK**.

7. Enter the name and Surname of the second engineer, use the **Browse** button to select the _Engineer template, and click **OK**.

8. Enter an initial password of *password* and then click **OK**.

9. Enter the name and Surname of the third engineer, click to remove the check from **Create another User**, use the **Browse** button to select the _Engineer template, and click **OK**.

10. Enter an initial password of *password* and then click **OK** to create the third user and return to ConsoleOne

To work with the file system, the new engineering users will need rights to the system.

In this hands-on activity, you will use ConsoleOne to assign the rights specified in Table C-3.

Table C-3   File system rights

Path	AdmAsst	Engineering	All UAS Users
NASA\Shared	RWCEMF	RWCEMF	RF
NASA\IIS	RF	RWCEMF	None
NASA\Rover	RF	RWCEMF	None
NASA\Users	RF	None	None

1. If necessary, expand your EngData volume object to display all folders in the NASA directory.

2. Grant the rights specified in Table C-3 for the Shared folder.

   a. Right-click the **Shared** folder and click Properties, then click the **Trustees** tab.

   b. Click the **Add Trustee** button and then click the up arrow to display all objects in your NASA_Eng container.

   c. Double-click **AdmAsst** group and then click the **Write**, **Create**, **Erase**, and **Modify** rights.

   d. Click the **Add Trustee** button and click the up arrow to display all objects in your NASA_Eng container.

   e. Double-click the **Engineers** group and then click the **Write**, **Create**, **Erase**, and **Modify** rights.

   f. Click the **Add Trustee** button and then click the up arrow three times.

   g. To give all your UAS users Read and File Scan rights, click your **##UAS** container and then click **OK**.

   h. Click **OK** to return to ConsoleOne.

3. Grant the rights specified in Table C-3 for the Rover folder.

   a. Right-click the **Rover** folder and click Properties, then click the **Trustees** tab.

   b. Click the **Add Trustee** button and then click the up arrow to display all objects in your NASA_Eng container.

   c. Double-click **AdmAsst** group to assign the default Read and File Scan rights.

   d. Click the **Add Trustee** button and click the up arrow to display all objects in your NASA_Eng container.

   e. Double-click the **Engineers** group and then click the **Write**, **Create**, **Erase**, and **Modify** rights.

   f. Click **OK** to return to ConsoleOne.

4. Grant the rights specified in Table C-3 for the IIS folder.

   a. Right-click the **IIS** folder and click Properties, then click the **Trustees** tab.

   b. Click the **Add Trustee** button and then click the up arrow to display all objects in your NASA_Eng container.

   c. Double-click **AdmAsst** group to assign the default Read and File Scan rights.

   d. Click the **Add Trustee** button and click the up-arrow to display all objects in your NASA_Eng container.

   e. Double-click the **Engineers** group and then click the **Write**, **Create**, **Erase**, and **Modify** rights.

   f. Click **OK** to return to ConsoleOne.

5. Grant the rights specified in Table C-3 for the Users folder. Because of inheritance, providing the AdmAsst organizational role object with Read and File Scan rights to the Users folder will allow the administrative assistant user to retrieve files from individual user's home folders when they are away from the office.

   a. Right-click the **Users** folder and click Properties, then click the **Trustees** tab.

   b. Click the **Add Trustee** button and then click the up arrow to display all objects in your NASA_Eng container.

      c. Double-click **AdmAsst** group to assign the default Read and File Scan rights.

      d. Click **OK** to return to ConsoleOne.

  6. Exit ConsoleOne

After setting up the users and file system for the NASA Engineering department, the last activity you should perform is to test the user accounts and access rights by performing the following steps for each user:

1. Log in as Travis Scott.

2. Use Network Neighborhood to map the N: drive letter to your NASA folder.

3. Launch Wordpad.

4. Create a document containing the user's name and title.

5. Save the document in the user's home directory with the name Test.doc.

6. Save the document in the shared directory using the user's name as the document name.

7. Save the document in the NASA/IIS folder and then exit Wordpad.

8. Use My Computer or Windows Explorer to browse the N: drive and view the files in each directory.

9. Log out.

10. Log in as Cleo, the administrative assistant, and repeat steps 2–8. Are you able to save the document in the NASA\IIS folder? _____

    Can you see files in Travis Scott's home folder? _____

Using Z.E.N.works Version 2

The Z.E.N.works starter pack is included with NetWare 5.0 and 5.1. However, to use certain Z.E.N.works features, such as workstation inventory, remote control, and Help information, you will need to purchase the full version of Z.E.N.works from Novell. To install Z.E.N.works, you will need a minimum of NetWare 4.11 with Support pack 6 (NetWare 5.0 or 5.1 recommended), NDS version 6.x or higher, and 175 MB of additional disk space if client software is copied to the server. In this section, you will learn how to upgrade the Starter pack to Z.E.N.works version 2 and then use Z.E.N.works to set up the Help requester and implement remote control of a workstation.

Assume that Universal Aerospace management has approved the request you made to purchase the full version of Novell's Z.E.N.works through Computer Technology Services. In this section, you will follow Eric Kenton as he upgrades the Z.E.N.works starter pack installed on the UAS server to the full version.

1. Before installing Z.E.N.works, Eric selects the UAS_HOST server to act as the main Z.E.N.works host and prepares the UAS_HOST by exiting the graphical console and unloading the JAVA module.

2. To install Z.E.N.works, Eric needs to log in to the network as an administrator with Supervisor rights to the root of the tree. After logging in as the system administrator, Eric inserts the new Z.E.N.Works 2 CD into the workstation, which automatically launches the Z.E.N.works installation wizard.

3. He clicks **English**, **ZENworks**, **Install ZENworks**, and then clicks **Next** to display the license screen.

4. After clicking **Yes** to accept the license agreement, Eric clicks the **Custom** option and then clicks **Next** to display the product options.

5. In addition to the Application Management, Remote Management, Workstation Management, and NWAdmin32 options, Eric clicks the **Copy Clients to Network** option and then clicks **Next** to display the Part Selection window.

6. Eric clicks **Next** to select the default Files, Schema extensions, Application Objects, and Workstation Registry components.

7. The installation needs to identify the Tree on which Z.E.N.works will be installed. Eric selects the **UAS_Tree** and clicks **Next**.

8. In addition to the Tree, the installation program also needs to know the names of the server or servers to contain the Z.E.N.works software. He selects **UAS_Host** and clicks **Next**.

9. Z.E.N.works needs a volume in which to store the workstation inventory information. If using the SYS volume, you need to be sure there is sufficient space reserved to prevent filling up the SYS volume and halting the server. When the installation displays the Inventory Database Server Selection window, Eric clicks **Next** to select the default UAS_Host server. He then selects the SYS volume from the Inventory Database Volume Selection windows and clicks **Next**. A warning message is displayed indicating that the inventory database may use large amounts of disk space and that placing it on the SYS volume is not recommended. Since Eric has verified that approximately .5 MB of space is reserved on the UAS_Host server's SYS volume for each workstation, he clicks **OK** to acknowledge the warning message.

10. Eric then clicks **OK** again to acknowledge the message informing him that some components will be automatically loaded on the server running the inventory database.

11. The installation program next displays the language. Eric confirms that **English** is selected and clicks **Next**.

12. Finally, he verifies the summary list of installation options and then clicks **Next** to begin the installation. During installation the files are copied to the server and then the NDS tree's schema is extended to include the new Z.E.N.works NDS objects.

13. Z.E.N.works 2 requires workstations to be registered before they can be imported into the NDS tree. Workstation registration is usually done automatically by Z.E.N.works when a user first logs in. To provide users with the rights necessary to register their workstations in the tree, the installation program next displays a dialog box prompting Eric to enter the context in which to grant users auto-registration rights. To provide users the auto-registration rights throughout the entire tree, Eric clicks **OK** to select the default [root] container and all subcontainers. When a message box appears stating that workstation auto-registration rights were successfully set up, Eric clicks **OK** to continue.

14. When the Setup Complete dialog box is displayed, giving Eric options to Launch Read Me and Setup Log files. Eric clicks to remove the check from the Launch Read Me check box and then clicks **Finish** to read the Setup Log using Notepad. After verifying that that there are no errors in the setup log Eric prints the log and exits Notepad. A Congratulations on installing Z.E.N.works message is displayed suggesting that you distribute and install the new client software on all workstations. Eric exits the Congratulations message and then logs out.

15. To complete the installation, Eric issues the RESTART SERVER command on the server console to reload NetWare 5.1. Z.E.N.works is now ready to configure and use.

In addition to installing the Z.E.N.works components, implementing Z.E.N.works requires creating objects for users, applications, workstations, and policies within the NDS tree structure. Because proper placement of these objects affects setting up and managing Z.E.N.works capabilities, there are several NDS design considerations you should be aware of when setting up and managing Z.E.N.works. Table C-4 lists some of the NDS objects and how Novell recommends implementing them in your NDS tree structure.

Table C-4   NDS objects

NDS Object	Implementation
Application objects	Placing application objects in the same container as the majority of users that run the application reduces search times when Application Launcher starts, as well as makes it easier to associate users with the application object.
Application folders	Application folder objects are a method of grouping application objects for administrative purposes. Information in each application folder object is linked to any applications that are associated with it. Linking information from application folder objects to applications reduces NDS traffic and provides for centralized administration. Because application folder objects are used by administrators and do not need to be accessed by the users, you should consider placing all application folder objects in a container that is convenient for you. For example, you may wish to place application folder objects in the same container as your Admin user name.
Group objects	To reduce the number of user associations you need to make, whenever possible you should associate applications objects with group objects and then make the users that need to use the application members of the associated group. When creating groups, try to place group objects in the same container as the application and avoid having members in the group that are separated by a WAN.
Workstation objects	To use workstation policies, inventories, or the new remote control feature, you will need to register and import workstations into the NDS tree. When workstation objects are imported into the tree, they are created in the container you specify in a user policy package. If workstations are normally used by a specific user, you should set the import policy to create the workstation object in the same container as the user object. Because workstation objects can double the number of objects in a container, be careful that the number of objects in any one partition does not exceed 1500.
Policy packages	Container policy packages govern how the policies in the container and its subcontainers are managed. Novell recommends placing container policy packages at the beginning of a location or site container to control the search policy for that location. For example, in the Universal Aerospace structure, a container policy package could be created for the NASA organizational unit because it is located in a different building. When workstations are used by multiple users located in different containers, consider creating a separate container for the workstations and placing the corresponding workstation objects in that container. User policy packages should be created in the same container as the user accounts.

Establishing Remote Control of a Workstation

Because the new engineering users will be located in a different building, you would like to implement the new Z.E.N.works remote control feature to help engineering users who have technical problems accessing the network resources. In the past, Universal Aerospace has been reluctant to implement other third party remote control software because of the possibility of unauthorized access to the systems. The Z.E.N.works remote control feature provides security by allowing you to use NDS to authorize which users can remotely control a system as well as providing the user with notification when remote control is being used. The management at Universal Aerospace would like you to configure security for the remote control feature by limiting remote control to only the Admin user and requesting the user to authorize the remote control session.

Before you can use the remote control feature of Z.E.N.works, you need to perform four preparatory steps, each of which is detailed in the following sections. First you need to import the workstations into the NDS tree. Once the workstation objects are imported into the tree, you need to create a workstation policy package and configure it for remote control of the workstations associated with the package. Then use Application Launcher to run the Z.E.N.works Remote Management utility on each workstation that could be remotely controlled. The final step is to test the remote control feature to ensure it is configured correctly.

In the following hands-on activities, you will implement remote control by performing the preparatory steps and then testing remote control by working with a lab partner to remotely control their workstation. As mentioned previously, one of the remote control preparatory activities involves importing your workstation into a container of the NDS tree. If your workstation already exists in another NDS tree or container, you can either perform the optional activity to remove it from that location or skip to activity 2 and enable the remote control policy on the workstation in its current location.

To practice importing your workstation for remote control purposes, you may wish to perform the optional step in this hands-on activity and remove your workstation from the tree. If your workstation has not been imported into a tree, you can skip the optional step and continue with importing your workstation in step 1.

Optional Activity: Removing Your Workstation from the Tree

The process of removing a workstation from a tree involves two steps. First you will need to delete the workstation object from the tree using either NetWare Administrator or ConsoleOne. After the workstation's object is deleted, you next need to modify the workstation's client so that it will re-register itself in a different tree or container. The most reliable method to reset the workstation's client is to un-install and then re-install the client software. An alternate method is to manually modify the workstation's registry and then delete the remote id files.

Follow these steps to remove the workstation from the tree by uninstalling and reinstalling the Novell client.

1. If necessary, log in as your Admin account and start NetWare Administrator

2. Browse to the container where you workstation object is located, click on your workstation object to highlight it, and then use the Delete key to delete your workstation object.

3. Exit NetWare Administrator and log out.

4. Insert the Novell Z.E.N.works Client CD-ROM.

5. If the autostart launches the install wizard, click the **Exit** button to exit the wizard.

6. Click **Start**, **Run**, then click the **Browse** button and navigate to the Products\Win95\ibm_enu\Admin folder of the Z.E.N.works Client CD-ROM.

7. Double-click the **Unc32.exe** program and click **Continue** to start the uninstall process.

8. Reboot your computer.

9. Install the Novell Z.E.N.works client by inserting the CD-ROM and following the installation guidelines presented in the textbook.

The alternate method of removing the workstation from the tree and resetting the client by modifying the workstation's registry is described in the following steps.

1. If necessary, log in as Admin and start NetWare Administrator.

2. Browse to the container where your workstation object is located, click on your workstation object to highlight it, and then use the Delete key to delete your workstation object.

3. Exit NetWare Administrator and start RegEdit.

4. Highlight **HKEY_LOCAL_MACHINE** and then click **Edit**, **Find**, enter **Workstation Object**, then click **Find Next**.

5. Delete the following values in the Identification key: **Registered In**, **Registration Object**, **Tree**, **Workstation Object**.

6. Exit RegEdit.

7. Delete the following files from the root of the C: drive: **Wsreg32.log**, **Wsremote.id**.

8. Restart your workstation.

Activity 1: Importing Your Workstation into the NDS Tree

Assume that you have decided to test the Z.E.N.works remote control feature on Cleo's computer. To import Cleo's workstation into the NASA_Eng container, you first need to create a User Policy package in that container and enable the workstation import policy by performing the following steps:

1. If necessary, log in as the Admin user and launch NetWare Administrator.

2. Highlight your **NASA_Eng** container and click the **Create a new object** button.

3. Double-click the **Policy Package** object type, then double-click the **Win95-98 User Package** option.

4. Click **Next** to accept the default name and location.

5. Click to place a check mark in the **Workstation Import Policy** option and click **Next**.

6. Click **Next** to associate the policy with all objects in the NASA_Eng container.

7. Verify your results in the selections windows, then click **Finish** to create the policy package.

8. To configure the workstation import policy, double-click the newly created policy package, click **Workstation Import Policy** and then click **Details**.

9. Verify that the workstation objects will be created in the User Container, then click the **Workstation Naming** tab.

10. Notice that by default a workstation name will consist of Computer name and network address. To use the IP address of the workstation, click **Network Address** and then use the scroll down arrow next to the Preferred network address to select **IP Address**.

11. Click the **Add** button under the Add name fields pane and record the possible name fields below:

    _____

12. Click **Cancel** and then click **OK** to use the default name fields.

13. Click **Cancel** to return to NetWare Administrator.

14. Exit NetWare Administrator and log out.

15. Log in to the NASA_Eng container as Cleo. (Logging in registers the workstation in that container.) Use My Computer to open a window to the root of your C: drive and then use Notepad to open the **Wsreg32.log**. Did the workstation successfully register? _____ If not, perform the **Remove workstation from the tree** procedure and try again.

 If the message in the Wsreg32.log indicates that users do not have rights to register workstations in the NASA_Eng container, perform the following process:
Log in using your ##Admin username and start NetWare Administrator. Highlight your ##UAS container and then click **Tools**, **Workstation utilities**, **Prepare workstation registration**. Click the **Include subcontainers** check box and then click **OK**. After workstation registration rights are granted, close NetWare Administrator and repeat step 15.

16. Log out, then log back in as the Admin user.

17. Start NetWare Administrator.

18. Right-click the **NASA_Eng** container and click **Details**.

19. Click **Workstation Registration**. Your workstation should appear in the Workstations that are registered to be imported pane.

20. Click your workstation, then click **Import** to import your workstation into the NASA_Eng container.

21. Click **Close**, then click **OK** to return to the NetWare Administrator window.

22. Expand your NASA_Eng container and verify that your workstation object is not listed in the container.

23. Exit NetWare Administrator and log off.

Activity 2: Creating and Configuring the Remote Control Policy

In order to be remotely controlled, a workstation must have its remote control property enabled. This can be done by enabling the remote control property on each workstation object individually, or by associating the workstation object, a group it belongs to, or its parent container, with a policy that has remote control enabled. When multiple workstations in a container need to the same remote control settings, you should associate the workstations' parent container with a policy that has the remote control policy settings you want. In this activity you will create a workstation policy object with remote control enabled and then associate that object with the container that your workstation object is located in.

1. Log in as the Admin user and start NetWare Administrator.

2. Highlight the **NASA_Eng** container and click **Create a new object** button.

3. Double-click **Policy Package**, click **Win95-98 Workstation Package**, then click **Next**.

4. Click **Next** to accept the default name and location.

5. Click to place a check in the **Remote Management Policy** check box and then click **Next** twice to display the summary window.

6. Click **Finish** to create the workstation policy package.

7. Double-click the newly created **Win95-98 Workstation Package**.

8. Click to highlight the **Remote Management Policy** and then click **Details**.

9. Click the **Control** tab and verify that **Enable Remote Control** is selected along with **Prompt user for permission to remote control**.

10. Click the **View** tab and verify that the settings are the same as in step 9.

11. Click the **Execute** tab and remove the check from the **Enable Remote Execute** check box.

12. Click **OK** to return to the Policy Package.

13. Click the **Associations** button and record the associations below:

_____

14. Click **Cancel** to return to NetWare Administrator.

15. Exit NetWare Administrator.

Activity 3: Running the Remote Management Software

In order to control a remote workstation, the workstation needs to run the Z.E.N.works remote control software named "zenrc32.exe". This program is located in the SYS:PUBLIC\ZENWORKS directory and can be run manually, placed in a login script, or added to the Novell Desktop Management scheduler. In this activity you will run the zenrec32 program manually to test your remote control setup.

1. Click Start, Run, and then browse to your SYS:PUBLIC\ZENWORKS directory.

2. Double-click the zenrc32.exe program and then click **OK**.

After the remote control program is loaded, a small remote management computer icon will appear in your system tray.

Activity 4: Testing the Remote Control of the Workstation

Now you will test the remote control of your workstation by working with a lab partner. Wait until your lab partner has completed Activities 1–3 and then take turns performing the steps below with one person playing the role of Cleo while the other plays the role of the Administrator.

1. The Cleo user should log into their NASA_Eng container as Cleo.

2. Double-click the **Remote Management** icon located in the lower-right task bar of Windows to display the Remote Management window.

3. To remote control Cleo's station, the person playing the Admin user should perform the following steps:

   a. Log in as the ##Admin user for Cleo's ##UAS organization.

   b. Start NetWare Administrator and **Browse** to Cleo's workstation and highlight it.

   c. Click **Tools, Workstation Remote Management, Remote Control**.

4. On Cleo's workstation click **Yes** to allow the remote control of the workstation.

5. Perform the following steps from the Admin's workstation:

   a. The upper right of the remote computer's windows contains control icons that perform the functions listed below. Place your cursor on each of the icons and sequence the following functions from left to right:

   _____ **System Key Passthrough**. This icon allows control keys such as Alt+Esc to pass through to the remote computer.

   _____ **App Switcher**. This icon allows you to rotate the remote computer's screen between currently running applications.

   _____ **Start**. This icon can be used to open the Start menu on the remote computer.

   _____ **Navigate**. The complete screen of the target computer may not fit in the window on the controlling workstation. You can use this icon to view other areas of the controlled computer's screen.

   _____ **Reboot**. This icon allows you to reboot the remote computer.

   b. Use the **Start** button to start **NotePad**, **Paint**, and **Calculator** on the remote computer.

   c. Use the **App Switcher** to switch between the applications.

   d. Close all applications.

   e. Use the **Navigate** button to view other areas of the remote computer's screen.

   f. Click the **System Key Passthrough** button. Table C-5 contains a list of hot-key sequences.

   g. Try various hot-key sequences so that you become familiar with their function.

   h. Click the **System Key Passthrough** button and then use the appropriate hot-key sequence to release control of the target workstation.

6. Log out both the Admin and Cleo users.

Table C-5   Remote control hot-key sequences

Option	Hot Key Sequence	Description
Full screen toggle	Ctrl+Alt+M	Sizes the viewing window to use the full screen
Refresh screen	Ctrl+Alt+R	Refreshes the target workstation's screen
Restart viewer	Ctrl+Alt+T	Reconnects your workstation to the target and refreshes the viewing window
System key routing toggle	Ctrl+Alt+S	Switches between passing Windows-reserved keystrokes to the target workstation and using them locally
Hot key enable	Ctlr+Alt+H	Enables the Control Options hot keys on the target workstation
Accelerated mode	Ctrl+Alt+A	Increases screen refresh rate of the viewing window without changing the refresh rate on the target workstations's monitor
Stop viewing	Left-Shift+Esc	Releases control of the target workstation

Configuring the Help Requester

To help users with problems or questions, Z.E.N.works includes a Help Desk feature that can be configured to allow users to send messages to an administrator or obtain the phone number and e-mail address of their assigned support person. A Help Desk message when combined with remote control can sometimes allow you to quickly solve certain types of problems by accessing the user's desktop and then working through the problem.

To help speed up the user support at Universal Aerospace, in this hands-on activity you will configure the Help Desk feature to include a desktop icon that users in the Engineering Department can use to send you a message briefly describing their problem or question.

1. Log in as the Admin user and start NetWare Administrator.

2. Double-click the **Win95–98 User Package** in your NASA_Eng container.

3. Click to place a check mark in the **Help Desk Policy** check box.

4. With the Help Desk Policy highlighted, click **Details**.

5. Enter the Contact name, E-mail address, and Telephone number that you want displayed to the user in the Help Requester application.

6. Click the **Help Requester** button.

7. Click to place a check mark in the **Allow user to launch the Help Requester** check box.

8. To allow users to e-mail trouble tickets, click to place a check mark in the **Allow user to send trouble tickets from the Help Requester** check box and then select the delivery mode. Since Universal Aerospace is not yet using Novell's Groupwise system, click **MAPI** to enable delivery of trouble tickets using a standard Internet e-mail format.

9. Click the ellipsis button to the right of the Trouble ticket subject lines text box and use the **Add** button to add the following subjects:

   ■ Network problem

   ■ Workstation problem

   ■ Application problem

10. Click **OK** to return to the Help Desk Policy window.

11. Click the **Trouble Tickets** tab and select the following items to be sent with each trouble ticket: **User Context**, **User Location**, and **Workstation ID**.

12. Click **OK** to save your Help Desk Policy configuration.

13. Click **Associations** and verify that all users in the NASA_Eng container will be able to use the Help Requester.

14. Click **OK** to save the Help Requester configuration.

15. Create a Help Requester application in the NASA_Eng container.

    a. Highlight your **NASA_Eng** container and click the **Create a new object** button.

    b. Double-click **Application** and click **Next** to accept the default of creating a simple Application object.

    c. In the Object name text box type **Help**.

    d. Click the **Browse** button to the right of the Path field to navigate to the Z:\Public folder.

    e. Double-click the **Hlpreq32.exe** program and click **Open**.

    f. Click **Finish** to create the Help application object.

    g. Double-click the **Help** application and verify the settings in the System Requirement and Environment tabs.

    h. Click the **Associations** tab and use the **Add** button to select the **NASA_Eng** container as shown in Figure C-3. When the "Add Container Association" dialog box appears, verify that the "Users within this container" option is selected and then click **OK** to continue.

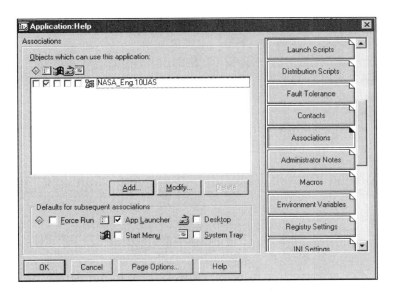

Figure C-3 Associations tab for Help Application

    i. Click the **System Tray** and **Desktop** check boxes to have the Help icon easily available.

    j. Click **OK** to save your Help configuration.

16. Exit NetWare Administrator and log out.

17. Test the Help Requester by performing the following steps:

    a. Log in to your NASA_Eng container as Cleo.

    b. Click **Start**, **Run**, enter **NALEXPD**, and press **Enter** to place the help application icon on the desktop and system tray.

    c. Double-click the **Help** icon from the desktop or system tray.

    d. Click the **Mail** tab, select **Workstation problem** for the subject and enter a message.

e. Click the **User** and **Workstation** tabs to determine user name, context, and workstation Id.

f. If you have e-mail software such as Outlook Express on your computer, click **Send**. Your computer e-mail software should be started. Exit the e-mail software and return to the Help Requester.

g. Click the **Call** tab to display the help number you configured. Notice that the user's context, tree, and workstation information is available.

h. Exit the Help Requester and log off.

Using the NetWare Management Portal

NetWare 5.1 includes a new feature called NetWare Management Portal. NetWare Management Portal provides for remote management of server and network environments using a browser such as Netscape Navigator or Internet Explorer. NetWare Management Portal allows many management tasks to be performed without additional software needed on either the server or workstation. To implement NetWare Management Portal, all you need is TCP/IP installed on your server and a 32-bit Windows client running either Netscape version 4.5 or later, or Internet Explorer version 4 or later. The TCP/IP protocol uses port numbers to route packets to applications. For example, the standard port number used by web servers is port number 80. When you install NetWare 5.1, as described in Appendix B, port number 8009 is reserved for NetWare Management Portal use. When accessing the NetWare Management Portal, you need to supply the IP address or URL of the server followed by a colon and the port number as shown in Figure C-4.

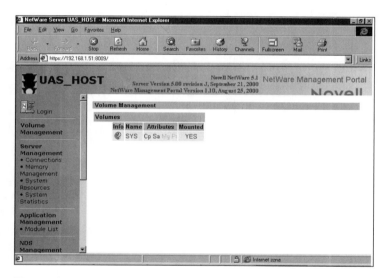

Figure C-4   NetWare Management Portal

Notice that the NetWare Management Portal window contains a stop and go light for showing the server's health, along with management options for volumes, servers, applications, NDS, remote access services, hardware, and health.

Part 1: Accessing NetWare Management Portal

In this hands-on activity, you are to assume that you are attending the Comdex convention in Las Vegas and, being bored one evening, you decide to check on the status of the Universal Aerospace server using your hotel room's Internet connection.

1. If you are currently logged in to the server, log out.

2. Click **Cancel** to exit the Login window.

3. From your Windows desktop, start either Netscape or Internet Explorer.

4. In the Address or Location field, enter **http://IPaddress:8009** (where **IPaddress** is the IP address of your server) and press **Enter**.

5. If necessary, click **OK** to view information over a secure connection.

6. The NetWare Management Portal main window should be displayed.

Part 2: Server Health

The traffic light indicator that appears on the main NetWare Management Portal window allows you to quickly view the server's health. A green light means that all server components are in good health, yellow indicates a potential problem with at least one of the components, and red indicates the failure of a component or service. You can view the status of an individual component by clicking on the traffic light indicator or clicking the Health Monitor tab and then selecting the component you want to view.

In this part of the activity, you will use the Health Monitor tab to check the status of several components on your server.

1. Click **Login** and then enter the distinguished name of your admin user (.##admin.##UAS). Enter your password and click **OK**.

2. Click on the **traffic light** icon to display the Server Health Monitor window similar to the one shown in Figure C-5.

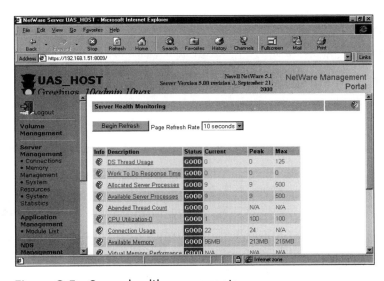

Figure C-5 Server health components

3. The check marks in the check boxes under the User and Admin columns are used to control which users can view these fields. To prevent users other than Admin from accessing one of the server components, remove the check mark from that monitor's User box.

4. Scroll through your server's health monitors and check their status. Is the status of all your health monitors good? _____

5. Looking at the server health monitors shown in Figure C-5, what two health monitors should we be most concerned about? _____ _____

6. Click the **Info** icon next to the CPU utilization and record the criteria for Green, Yellow, and Red below:

   Green:

   Yellow:

   Red:

7. Click the browser's "Back" button to return to the Volume Management window.

8. In the left-hand pane, scroll up and click **Logout**. If necessary, click **Yes** to close the browser window.

In order to perform server management tasks you will need to log in as an administrator who has supervisor rights to the server. If you do not have access to a user that has supervisor rights to the server object, skip this part of the activity.

Part 3: Server Management

Server management includes the ability to manage user connections, view and set parameters, view system statistics, manage memory, and access current console screens. Being able to access the server console screens remotely is a powerful management feature when troubleshooting or repairing NetWare server problems.

In this activity, you will access your server's console and check the status of virtual memory.

1. If necessary, use your browser to connect to the NetWare Management Portal. Click **Login** and then enter the distinguished name of the admin user that has supervisor rights to the server object. Enter the password and click **OK**.

2. Scroll down the left-hand pane and view the options under Server Management.

3. To display the current console screens, click on the **Screens** option.

4. Click **System_Console** to display a replica of the server console screen.

5. Enter **Swap** in the command line box located at the bottom of the window.

6. Click **Execute Command Line** button or press **Enter** to display the Swap information screen.

7. After viewing the virtual memory settings, close the system console screen by clicking the **Close** button.

8. In the left-hand pane, scroll down and view the options under Application Management.

9. To view the NLMs currently loaded on the server, click **Module List**.

10. To view the modules in descending order by allocated memory, click the **Alloc Memory** button. Record below the two modules that use the most Alloc memory: _____,
_____

11. To sort modules by name, click the **Name** button.

12. Click **Home** from the NetWare Management Portal web page to return to the main menu.

13. In the left-hand pane, scroll up and click **Logout**. If necessary, click **Yes** to close the browser window.

Part 4: Volume Management

In addition to working with server information, NetWare Management Portal allows you to view volume information, mount or dismount volumes, and perform many file management tasks, such as uploading, downloading, and renaming or deleting files. Assume that while at Comdex you discover that you need to replace a .DLL file for one of the engineering applications.

C

In this activity, you will use NetWare Management Portal to simulate accessing volume information and then uploading and renaming a file.

1. If necessary, use your browser to connect to the NetWare Management Portal. Click **Login** and then enter the distinguished name of your admin user (.##admin.##UAS). Enter your password and click **OK**.

2. In the left-hand pane, if necessary, scroll up and click the **Volume Management** option.

3. Click the **Info** button next to the **SYS** volume and record the volume statistics requested below:

    Name: _____
    % Free: _____
    Sub-Allocation size: _____
    Salvageable blocks: _____

    Name: _____
    % Free: _____
    Sub-Allocation size: _____
    Salvageable blocks: _____

4. Click on the name of the volume object containing your NASA directory structure.

5. Navigate down to your NASA\Apps folder.

6. Click the **Upload** button.

7. Use the **Browse** button to navigate to the Windows directory on your local workstation.

8. Select a .DLL file by double-clicking it.

9. Click the **Upload** button. The file will be copied to your NASA\Apps folder.

10. Click the **Home** button to return to the NetWare Management Portal main window.

In order to perform NDS tasks you will need to log in as an administrator that has supervisor rights to the root of the tree. If you do not have access to a user that has supervisor rights to the root of the tree, skip this part of the activity.

Part 5: NDS Management

NetWare Management Portal also provides the administrator with the ability to view and delete NDS objects.

In this activity, you will use NetWare Management Portal to walk the tree and view your NDS objects.

1. If necessary, use your browser to connect to the NetWare Management Portal. Click **Login** and then enter the distinguished name of the admin user that has supervisor rights to the root of the tree. Enter the password and click **OK**.

2. In the left-hand pane, if necessary, scroll down to view the NDS Management options.

3. Click on the **Tree Walker** option and then browse your ##UAS organization and view the details on each user. Notice that the only NDS function you can perform is to delete an NDS object, so be careful.

4. Click on the **NDS Partitions** option and record the number of partitions in your tree: _____.

5. In the left-hand pane, scroll up and click **Logout**. If necessary, click **Yes** to close the browser window.

Part 6: Hardware Management

The hardware management option allows you to view the current hardware configuration settings. This information can be useful in helping you to diagnose problems or plan for new equipment. For example, assume that while at Comdex you find a 1GB network card that you would like to install in the engineering server.

In this activity, you will use NetWare Management Portal to determine the feasibility of installing the new network adapter by viewing the slots and interrupts currently available on your server.

1. If necessary, use your browser to connect to the NetWare Management Portal. Click **Login** and then enter the distinguished name of your admin user (.##admin.##UAS). Enter your password and click **OK**.

2. In the left-hand pane, scroll down to view the Hardware Management options.

3. From the Hardware Management pane, click the **Hardware Resources** option.

4. Click the **Interrupts** option and record the interrupt assigned to your server's network adapter:_____

5. List two available interrupts:_____ , _____

6. Click the **Back to Hardware Resources** option.

7. Click on **Slots**.

8. List any Non–ISA slots and modules used by your server: _____

9. Click the **Back to Hardware Resources** option.

10. View information for the Ports, DMA, and Shared Memory resources.

11. In the left-hand pane click on the **Processor Information** option and record the following processor statistics:
Speed: _____ Family: _____ Model: _____

12. In the left-hand pane, scroll up and click the **Logout**. If necessary, click **Yes** to close the browser window.

D

FORMS AND WORKSHEETS

The amount of planning involved in administering a network can seem endless. As a network administrator, it is your task to not only plan, design, and implement the network, but also to keep all the information involved in some kind of accessible order. Many networking professionals have found that having a standardized set of organizational tools can be beneficial.

To help you plan and implement your network, the following Forms and Worksheets are included in this Appendix:

- Storage Requirements Form
- Volume Design Form
- Directory Design Form
- User Template Planning Form
- User Planning Form
- Group Planning Form
- Directory Trustee Worksheet
- Directory Attributes Planning Form
- File System Usage Planning Form
- NDS Security Worksheet
- NDPS Definition Form
- Container Login Script Form
- Profile Login Script Form
- User Profile Worksheet

Storage Requirements Form

Created by:

Date:

Organization:

Workgroups:

Workgroup Name	Members

Directories:

Directory Description	Type	Users	Capacity

D

Volume Design Form

Designer:

Date:

Volume Name:

Maximum Capacity:

Block Size:	4 KB	8 KB	16 KB	32 KB

Directory Design Form

Designer:

Date:

Volume Name:

Directory Name:

Estimated Size:

User Template Planning Form

Designer:

Date:

Template name	
Context	
Home directory path	
Minimum password length	
Require unique passwords	
Days before password changes	
Grace logins	
Valid login times	
Maximum connections	
Groups	
Users	

Template name	
Context	
Home directory path	
Minimum password length	
Require unique passwords	
Days before password changes	
Grace logins	
Valid login times	
Maximum connections	
Groups	
Users	

Template name	
Context	
Home directory path	
Minimum password length	
Require unique passwords	
Days before password changes	
Grace logins	
Valid login times	
Maximum connections	
Groups	
Users	

D

User Planning Form

Company:

Date:

Created by:

User Name	Login Name	Context	Template Name	Home Directory	Groups	Additional Properties

Group Planning Form

Designer:

Date:

Group Name	Members	Context	Description

D

Directory Trustee Worksheet

DIRECTORY TRUSTEE WORKSHEET for:

Page ___ of ___

Directory Path	IRF														

Directory Attributes Planning Form

Created by:

Date:

Directory	Attributes

D

File System Usage Planning Form	
Created by:	
Date:	
Organization or Organizational Unit Name:	
User/Department	**File System Usage**

NDS Security Worksheet

Created by:

Date:

Organization or Organizational Unit Name:

Object		Trustee			Property		
Name	Type	Trustee Name/Type	Object Rights	IRF	Property Name	Rights	IRF

Notes:

NDPS Definition Form

Created by:	
Date:	
NDPS Manager:	
NDS Context:	
Server:	
Database Volume:	
Managers:		

Printer Name	Make/Model	Port and Interrupt	Location	Users	Print Queue Name/Volume	NDS Context	Operators

Notes:

Container Login Script Form (Page 1 of 2)

Designer:

Date:

Container Context:

REM Preliminary Commands

NO_DEFAULT
MAP DISPLAY OFF
MAP INS S1:=UAS_HOST_SYS:PUBLIC
CLS
WRITE "Good%GREETING_TIME, %LOGIN_NAME"
PAUSE

REM DOS Setup

REM Common Application

REM Mapping for_____Workgroup

REM Mapping for_____Workgroup

REM Mapping for_____Workgroup

REM End of Login Script Commands

D

Container Login Script Form (Page 2 of 2)

Container Context:

REM Preliminary Commands

REM Mapping for_____Workgroup

REM Mapping for_____Workgroup

REM Mapping for_____Workgroup

REM End of Login Script Commands

D

Profile Login Script Form

Created by:

Date:

Container Context:

Profile Object Name:

Users:		

Profile Object Name:

Users:		

User Profile Worksheet

Company/Department:

Date:

Created by:

Profile Name	Context	Associations	Wallpaper	Screen Saver	Desktop Scheme

Index